D1607931

ETHICS

in the

SHADOW

of the

HOLOCAUST

Christian and Jewish
Perspectives

THE BERNARDIN CENTER SERIES
GENERAL EDITOR: ROBERT J. SCHREITER, C.PP.S.

The Bernardin Center Series presents works of scholarly and general interest that grow out of activities at the Joseph Cardinal Bernardin Center for Theology and Ministry at Catholic Theological Union.

Areas of activity and interest of the Bernardin Center include the ongoing interpretation and implementation of the Second Vatican Council, church leadership, the consistent ethic of life, Catholic health care, the Catholic Common Ground Initiative, interreligious dialogue, and religion in American public life.

ETHICS

in the

SHADOW

of the

HOLOCAUST

Christian and Jewish
Perspectives

Edited with an introduction by
JUDITH H. BANKI
and
JOHN T. PAWLIKOWSKI, O.S.M.

SHEED & WARD

Franklin, Wisconsin

Chicago

As an apostolate of the Priests of the Sacred Heart, a Catholic religious congregation, the mission of Sheed & Ward is to publish books of contemporary impact and enduring merit in Catholic Christian thought and action. The books published, however, reflect the opinions of their authors and are not meant to represent the official position of the Priests of the Sacred Heart.

2001

Sheed & Ward
7373 South Lovers Lane Road
Franklin, Wisconsin 53132
1-800-266-5564

Judith H. Banki's piece, "Vatican II Revisited" is a slightly enlarged version of "Catholics and Jews: Vatican Holocaust Statement Will Help" which was published in *Commonweal,* April 4, 1998©1998 Commonweal Foundation, reprinted with permission. For Subscriptions, call toll-free 1-888-495-6755.

John T. Pawlikowski's piece, "The Vatican and the Holocaust: Putting *We Remember* in Context," first appeared in *Dimensions*, Vol. 12, No. 2, October 1998. It is reprinted with permission of the Anti-Defamation League.

Printed in the United States of America

Cover and interior design by Robin Booth
Cover drawing "Brother Joseph" by Robin Booth
    Copyright ©1997 Catholic Theological Union

Library of Congress Cataloging-in-Publication Data

Ethics in the shadow of the Holocaust: Christian and Jewish perspectives / edited with introduction by Judith H. Banki and John T. Pawlikowski.
John T. Pawlikowski and Hayim Goren Perelmuter.
        p. cm. — (The Bernardin Center series)
    Conference papers presented at Catholic Theological Union in Chicago during 1999.
    ISBN 1-58051-109-0
            1. Holocaust, Jewish (1939-1945)—Influence—Congresses. 2. Catholic Church—Relations—Judaism—Congresses. 3. Judaism—Relations—Catholic Church—Congresses. 4. Catholic Church. Commission for Religious Relations with the Jews. We Remember. 5. Holocaust, Jewish (1939-1945)—Moral and ethical aspects—Congresses. 6. Christianity and anti-Semitism—Congresses. I. Banki, Judith Hershcopf. II. Pawlikowski, John. III. Series.
D804.3 .E895 2001
940.53'18—dc21   2001054209

1 2 3 4 5 04 03 02 01

TABLE OF CONTENTS

CHAPTER FIFTEEN
Conscience, Knowledge, and "Secondary Ethics":
German Corporate Ethics from "Aryanization"
to the Holocaust:
A Response to Peter Hayes
DONALD J. DIETRICH
337

349

INDEX
353

INTRODUCTION

JOHN T. PAWLIKOWSKI

This volume brings together the papers from two remarkable conferences held at Catholic Theological Union in Chicago during 1999. The first, in March of that year, assembled more than thirty Catholic and Jewish scholars and interfaith leaders for an in-depth discussion of the Vatican document *We Remember: A Reflection on the "Shoah,"* issued by the Holy See's Commission for Religious Relations with the Jews in March 1998. Cardinal Edward Idris Cassidy, the President of the Holy See's Commission and principal architect of the document, was present for the entire consultation, offering initial perspectives as well as concluding observations. The consultation was co-sponsored by the Tanenbaum Center for Interreligious Understanding in New York and Catholic Theological Union's Joseph Cardinal Bernardin Center for Theology and Ministry.

The consultation focused on four areas that had elicited considerable critical discussion in the year since the appearance of the Vatican document. These were: 1) anti-Semitism and the Christian tradition; 2) *We Remember*'s understanding of the Church in light of Vatican II; 3) the relationship between classical Christian anti-Semitism and Nazi ideology; and 4) the role of Pius XII during World War II. Cardinal Cassidy delivered a public lecture during the consultation, reflecting on the intent of the Vatican document and its reception. The remainder of the two-and-a-half-day consultation consisted of intensive discussion of papers on the above issues by one Christian and one Jewish scholar in each session. Cardinal Cassidy and Peter Steinfels, of Georgetown University and the *New York Times*, respectively, concluded the consultation with summaries of the principal points raised in the discussion.

The consultation was dedicated to two great leaders in the fostering of Catholic-Jewish relations: Rabbi Marc H. Tanenbaum, whose memory and ideas the Tanenbaum Center preserves and promotes through its varied pro-gramming; and Cardinal Joseph L. Bernardin of Chicago, who expressly requested that Catholic Theological Union establish a center to keep alive the spirit and values of the Second Vatican Council which were so central to his ministry in Chicago and throughout the world. One of the central aspects of Cardinal Bernardin's ministry was his fostering of the Catholic-Jewish dialogue.

Included in this section are reprints of earlier commentaries on *We Remember* by the co-covenors of the consultation, Judith H. Banki and John T. Pawlikowski. Also included is an original study on the Vatican and the Final Solution by Professor Kevin Madigan. Professor Madigan was a partic-ipant in the consultation.

The second set of papers comes from the annual conference of the Catholic-Jewish Studies program of the Bernardin Center. Held in May 1999, in partnership with the Church Relations Committee of the United States Holocaust Memorial Museum, the conference examined contemporary ethi-cal issues in light of the Holocaust experience. Overviews of the moral chal-lenge of the Holocaust for contemporary humanity were presented by Rabbi Michael Berenbaum, who played a central role in the development of the museum in Washington; and John T. Pawlikowski, of the CTU faculty, who has served on the United States Holocaust Memorial Council by presidential appointment since the council's creation by the United States Congress in 1980. Subsequent papers focused on economic ethics and medical ethics. Personal stories from the Holocaust era were presented by Gerda Klein, a noted author and Holocaust survivor; and the late Rabbi Hayim G. Perelmuter, professor of Jewish Studies and co-director of the Catholic-Jewish Studies program in the Bernardin Center. These personal testimonies are not included in this volume. The Bernardin Center would like to express its gratitude to Margaret Obrecht, director of church relations at the United States Holocaust Memorial Museum, for her support and active participation in the conference.

In conclusion, a word of tribute is due to a powerful presence now absent from Catholic Theological Union and its Bernardin Center. Doctor Hayim Perelmuter, an original member of the school's faculty and the co-director of the Catholic-Jewish Studies program since the inception of the Bernardin Center, died in January 2001 as this volume was being prepared for publication. Rabbi Perelmuter played a central role in the creation of programs and courses in Jewish studies, which eventually became incorporated into the Bernardin Center. He was deeply involved in planning both the March consultation and the May conference, and actively participated in each of them. We shall miss his presence and his wit at the Bernardin Center. We dedicate this volume to him as well. May his cherished memory live on among us.

A word of appreciation is also in order for the work of Cardinal Edward Cassidy. The Tanenbaum and Bernardin centers are both grateful for his active participation in our co-sponsored consultation on *We Remember*. His willingness both to listen attentively and to engage the scholars helped to make this consultation the meaningful experience it proved to be for all participants. We are also grateful for his many years of service as president of the Holy See's Commission for Religious Relations with the Jews. In that capacity, he has helped implement Pope John Paul II's new constructive vision of the Catholic-Jewish relationship with tireless energy. We wish him well in his retirement.

RABBI MARC H. TANENBAUM REMEMBERED

JUDITH H. BANKI

R abbi Marc H. Tanenbaum's voice and influence are still felt in the field he helped create and led for more than three decades: the field of inter-religious affairs.

In his ten years as director of the Synagogue Council of America and twenty-five years at the American Jewish Committee, he opened up relations with Christian leaders and vigorously pursued the goals of mutual understanding and honest dialogue. A writer and radio personality whose weekly comments reached hundreds of thousands of readers and listeners for more than a quarter of a century, he was designated in a national poll as "one of the ten most influential and respected religious leaders in America," and by *New York* magazine as "one of the foremost Jewish ecumenical leaders in the world today." Rabbi Tanenbaum played a key role in organizing White House conferences on foreign aid and energy conservation, and was a trailblazer and activist on behalf of the human rights of immigrants and refugees. His counsel was sought by presidents—including Jimmy Carter and George Bush—and religious leaders of many faiths. A genuine humanitarian, he was concerned for the human plight and religious liberty of all people, but always rose first and foremost in defense of his own people. His universal concerns remained firmly rooted in a very particularist Jewish base.

However, many people remember Rabbi Tanenbaum vividly from his radio broadcasts. Beginning in 1965, he broadcasted a weekly religious commentary on WINS-Westinghouse Broadcasting, a news radio station in New York. Brief, pungent, and timely, his commentaries were enormously popular. He also wrote guest editorials on a regular basis for the Religious News Service, the Jewish Telegraphic Agency, and the Worldwide News Service.

Marc Tanenbaum died of heart failure on July 3, 1992, at the age of sixty-six, leaving a legacy of intellectual achievement and interreligious activism. He also left a devoted, accomplished, and pregnant wife, Dr. Georgette Bennett. Their son, Joshua-Marc Tanenbaum, was born seven weeks after his father's death. To perpetuate his work and his memory, Dr. Bennett established the Tanenbaum Center for Interreligious Understanding, which is honored to co-host this important and very timely symposium.

In the almost quarter of a century that I worked with Marc Tanenbaum, what I remember most vividly was his passionate conviction that Jews needed to get involved in the Christian-Jewish dialogue, both for their own sake—to help Christians confront and correct anti-Judaism and anti-Semitism in their own tradition—and for the sake of America, which he believed would be enriched by a Jewish contribution to the discussion of public issues. "We constitute less than three percent of the American people," he would say, "but we can contribute one third of the religious presence in America." He fought resistance, suspicion, and negativism among his own coreligionists, and I believe he convinced most of them that the goal was worth the effort. He never gave up.

Although involved in every aspect of interreligious dialogue, Rabbi Tanenbaum was particularly drawn to the area of Jewish-Catholic relations, in the course of which he befriended much of the Roman Catholic hierarchy in many parts of the world. He had a special regard, esteem, and affection for Cardinal Bernardin. It is entirely appropriate that this meeting should honor the memory of both of these remarkable men.

CARDINAL JOSEPH L. BERNARDIN REMEMBERED

The late Cardinal Joseph Bernardin came to his ministry in the archdiocese of Chicago well committed to the vision of Catholic-Jewish relations laid out in chapter four of the Second Vatican Council's document on the Church and non-Christian religions, *Nostra Aetate*. In his work as General Secretary of the National Conference of Catholic Bishops, as well as his tenure as archbishop of Cincinnati, he showed himself to be an ardent supporter of the conciliar vision of Catholic-Jewish relations. Soon after his arrival in Chicago, Cardinal Bernardin invited Monsignor John J. Egan to become the director of the archdiocesean Office for Human Relations and Ecumenism.

Under the leadership of Monsignor Egan, with the full support of Cardinal Bernardin, the archdiocese launched a varied set of activities to promote Catholic-Jewish relations. At Mundelein College (now integrated into Loyola University), Cardinal Bernardin presided over a convocation of Jewish and Catholic leaders to mark the twentieth anniversary of *Nostra Aetate*. In that event, Cardinal Bernardin prayed that the commemoration would signal a new phase in the history of Catholic-Jewish relations in Chicago. Rabbi Louis Jacobs, professor of Talmud from Leo Baeck College in London, gave the main address and joined in Cardinal Bernardin's prayer.

Cardinal Bernardin's prayer at Mundelein College did not go unanswered. Local parish-synagogue dialogues were begun in collaboration with the American Jewish Committee, and the archdiocese began an annual series of retreats for Jewish and Christian clergy. When Sister Joan Maguire, O.P., took over the Office of Ecumenism and Interreligious Affairs, she began a Scholars' Dialogue with the support of the Chicago Board of Rabbis and the

Jewish Community Relations Council. A women's dialogue, as well as programs dealing with interfaith marriage, also began with the support of Cardinal Bernardin. In 1995 Cardinal Bernardin led a joint Catholic-Jewish delegation to Israel and the Palestine Authority. The highlight of that visit was a scholarly lecture he delivered at the Hebrew University in Jerusalem, which received widespread coverage in the press. This lecture is now commemorated by an annual Bernardin Jerusalem lecture given by noted Christian and Jewish scholars and cosponsored by the archdiocese and various Jewish institutions and organizations.

Cardinal Bernardin's many talks and lectures on Catholic-Jewish relations have been collected in a volume entitled *A Blessing to Each Other: Cardinal Joseph Bernardin and Jewish-Catholic Dialogue* (Chicago: Liturgy Training Publications, 1996). During the cardinal's wake, when this book was released, Jewish leaders from Chicago who had joined him on the trip to Israel and Palestine conducted a service in his honor at Holy Name Cathedral. Truly, Cardinal Bernardin regarded Jews and Catholics as a blessing to each other. The Cardinal Bernardin Center at Catholic Theological Union is proud to have the mandate from the cardinal to carry on his work in Catholic-Jewish relations.

PART I

CONSULTATION ON

WE REMEMBER

Cosponsored by the Tanenbaum Center for Interreligious Understanding, New York,
and the Joseph Cardinal Bernardin Center for Theology and Ministry
at Catholic Theological Union, Chicago

MARCH 28–30, 1999

WELCOMING REMARKS

JUDITH H. BANKI

This conference is about a document—but it is also about a way of approaching questions raised by that document and not yet fully answered, a way of addressing issues not yet resolved. It is the way of providing a forum for communication, of building trust on the basis of scholarship, on a careful examination of the historical and theological questions that underlie some of our different responses to the document.

When *We Remember* was issued one year ago, it received mixed reviews from the Jewish community (also, incidentally, from the Catholic community). At that time, Cardinal Cassidy noted that the document was not the final word, and he invited further study. This conference is partly a response to that invitation. We are delighted that Cardinal Cassidy has come from the Vatican to share our deliberations.

I remind you that when *Nostra Aetate* was promulgated in 1965, it also drew mixed reviews . . . and much of the criticism was expressed in similar language: too little, too late, too weak, etc. But it nevertheless proved to be the foundation stone of a new relationship between the Church and the Jewish people, between Catholics and Jews. It, too, was not the final word. It was followed by official Vatican *Guidelines* (1974) and *Catechetical Notes* (1985) intended to bring the positive message of *Nostra Aetate* into Catholic parishes and classrooms.

We hope to advance a similar process here over the next two-and-a-half days. One of the ground rules of dialogue is to assume the goodwill of the other party. That is not hard to do. Another is to accept the other's self-definition. That is harder than it sounds. It has not been easy for Catholics to accept—even to understand—the self-definition of Jews as a people whose mission has a national as well as a spiritual dimension. But they have made that effort. It is not easy for Jews to accept the concept of a sinless Church, or any sinless institution. But as long as the concept provides the grounds for self-criticism and self-correction, we can build on it.

We may disagree, even disagree passionately, but we will not trade punches in the headlines. We hope that our exchange will be candid and forthright, but also civil and respectful. We believe that is the best way to honor the memory of the six million, of all the innocent victims whom we are pledged to remember.

In that spirit, the Tanenbaum Center for Interreligious Understanding is pleased to join the previous speakers in warmly welcoming you to this consultation. May the force be with us!

1

The Vatican Document on the Holocaust: Reflections toward a New Millennium

CARDINAL EDWARD IDRIS CASSIDY

The document *We Remember: A Reflection on the Shoah*, which was published on March 16, 1998, must be seen, in my opinion, as a further positive milestone in the building up of a new relationship between Jews and Catholics. This process began, as I am sure you all know, with the almost unanimous decision of the Second Vatican Council to approve the council decree *Nostra Aetate*, in which a radical change occurs in the attitude of the Catholic Church toward the Jewish people.

A considerable amount of effort has gone into developing this new relationship, with the generous participation of Jewish organizations and leaders. As a result, I do not hesitate to affirm that Catholic-Jewish relations today are the best that they have ever been.

Still much remains to be done. On the Jewish side, there are deep wounds caused by memories of the past that are not yet healed. On the Catholic side, not all the members of our Church have, by any means, come to terms with this new mentality. It is simply not possible, in a period of only thirty-five years, to change deeply rooted anti-Jewish attitudes in each and every member of a Church of one billion people spread throughout the world. For this reason, more information and further education continue to be primary tasks for both communities.

Nor is it possible for the Catholic Church—or indeed for Christians in general—simply to close the book, as it were, on the past two thousand years of anti-Jewish teaching without seeking to understand more fully this strange anti-gospel phenomenon and being aware of its tragic consequences for the Jewish people.

A particularly propitious moment has come for such a reflection in the form of the celebration next year of the end of the second Christian millennium and the beginning of a new period in Christian history. In the apostolic letter *Tertio Millenio Adveniente*, with which Pope John Paul II called upon the Catholic Church to prepare for and celebrate the Great Jubilee of the year 2000, we read:

> It is appropriate that, as the Second Millennium of Christianity draws to a close, the Church should become more fully conscious of the sinfulness of her children, recalling all those times in history when they departed from the spirit of Christ and his Gospel and, instead of offering to the world the witness of a life inspired by the values of faith, indulged in ways of thinking and acting which were truly *forms of counter-witness and scandal.* Although she is holy because of her incorporation into Christ, the Church does not tire of doing penance: before God and man *she always acknowledges as her own her sinful sons and daughters.* As *Lumen Gentium* affirms: "The Church, embracing sinners to her bosom, is at the same time holy and always in need of being purified, and incessantly pursues the path of penance and renewal."[1]

I have quoted this extract from the Holy Father's apostolic letter since it has much bearing on our reflections here. It is particularly in this context that we must consider the Vatican document on the *Shoah.* We remember the past and seek to understand why such a great tragedy took place "in Europe, that is, in countries of long-standing Christian civilization"[2] and we ask ourselves what influence the long Christian teaching of contempt had on that terrible event of the twentieth century. As a consequence of this reflection, we who are members of the Church at the close of this twentieth century realize that we are called to repentance (*Teshuvah*), even while we look forward with confidence to the future.

Already in 1987, the decision was taken by the Vatican Commission for Religious Relations with the Jews to prepare an official Catholic statement on the Church and the *Shoah*. This was in response to a request from our Jewish partners in dialogue, and received the immediate approval of Pope John Paul II. At that time it seemed possible for us to prepare a common statement with several Episcopal conferences of Europe, but it soon became obvious that the situations from one European nation to another were so different that a common statement appeared very problematic.

In fact, a number of Episcopal conferences went ahead and made their own statements: Hungarian, German, Polish, Dutch, Swiss, and French. These have recently been published, together with other similar documents issued by the bishops of the United States of America and with the Vatican documents, in a booklet entitled *Catholics Remember the Holocaust*.[3]

Thus it was left to the Holy See to speak to and in the name of the Catholic Church throughout the world, looking beyond the particular circumstances of one or other nation, and seeking to involve the whole Catholic community in a reflection on the *Shoah*.

This was no easy task. As I have already indicated, much effort is still needed before the mentality of the Catholic community throughout the world becomes fully attuned to the new Jewish-Catholic relationship developed since the Second Vatican Council. There is still a certain uneasiness in many circles to the idea of a *mea culpa*, such as that proposed by the Holy Father. There are, moreover, new local churches in Africa, Asia, and elsewhere that have not had any experience of past Catholic-Jewish relations and that did not even know of the *Shoah* until well after it happened. These were sensitivities that had to be kept in mind.

On the other hand, our Jewish partners were expecting from the Vatican a document that would not only fully endorse what the European bishops' conferences had stated, but would hopefully go even further and clearly declare a direct link of cause and effect between the anti-Judaism of the Church and the tragedy of the *Shoah*.

Repentance

What, then, are the principal acquisitions of the Vatican document? At the heart of the document *We Remember: A Reflection on the Shoah* is a statement that has not always been understood, yet has a profound significance in this context. I quote from Section V of that document:

> At the end of this Millennium the Catholic Church desires to express her deep sorrow for the failures of her sons and daughters in every age. This is an act of repentance (*Teshuvah*), *since as members of the Church, we are linked to the sins as well as to the merits of all her children* (emphasis added).

The Catholic Church makes here an act of repentance (using the Hebrew word so dear to our Jewish brothers and sisters, *Teshuvah*). This is much more than an "apology," which would be much easier to make, but would also, in fact, be far less significant. The members of the Church today cannot be considered responsible individually for what happened in past centuries. But neither can they ignore what happened, as if it had no meaning for them. What is being stated solemnly in our document is that the sons and daughters of the Catholic Church, at the end of this millennium, are linked to the sins as well as to the merits of all the children of the Church who have gone before. This means that there is, in fact, a kind of collective responsibility, which Jews should be able to understand and appreciate, for both Judaism and Catholicism are "coventual." Jewish and Catholic prayers frequently begin with the plural and include members of the congregation that may not be present at the time the prayers are being said. David Novak finds in this relationship an explanation for the Church's act of *Teshuvah* in relation to the *Shoah* that seems to me perfectly logical:

> In a coventual community, even though one is not *morally* responsible for the sins of fellow members of

the community, there still is an *existential* sense of collective sorrow and shame when other members of the community [. . .] commit sins, especially sins having great
public consequences.[4]

Anti-Judaism and Anti-Semitism

The question, of course, still remains: What about the responsibility for
the *Shoah* of those "sons and daughters of the Church," many of them in positions of authority in the Church or even renowned teachers of faith, who fostered the long-standing sentiments of mistrust and hostility that the Vatican
document refers to as *anti-Judaism*? The document itself poses the question:

[. . .] it may be asked whether the Nazi persecution of
the Jews was not made easier by the anti-Jewish prejudices imbedded in some Christian minds and hearts. Did
anti-Jewish sentiment among Christians make them less
sensitive, or even indifferent, to the persecutions
launched against the Jews by National Socialism when it
reached power?[5]

The answer given in the document is:

[A]ny response to this question must take into account that
we are dealing with the history of people's attitudes and
ways of thinking, subject to multiple influences [...]. A
response would have to be given case by case. To do this,
however, it is necessary to know what precisely motivated people in a particular situation."[6]

At the same time, the Vatican statement states clearly that many Christians
failed to give every possible assistance to those being persecuted.

If, as I have suggested, we take this document together with the statements issued by the Church in those nations particularly affected by the Nazi

presence, then there can be no doubt that the anti-Judaism of the Church down through the centuries was responsible for the attitude of a great number of members of the Church in this century who failed to give the witness that might have been expected of them as Christ's followers, and that this teaching made it easier for the Nazis to carry out their diabolic intentions of removing the Jewish people from Europe by massacre.

The document *We Remember*, however, makes a clear, and in my opinion, perfectly valid distinction between the *anti-Judaism* of the Church and the *anti-Semitism* of the Nazis. This has given rise to quite a lot of discussion and controversy, and so merits our attention as we speak about reconciliation toward a new millennium. To some it seemed that the Vatican statement was seeking to absolve the Catholic Church of all responsibility for the *Shoah*. As I have indicated, that was certainly not the case. There is a relationship between these two evils, but not one of cause and effect.

For their part, the Nazis made use of the anti-Judaism of the Church and its effects in the hearts and minds of Christians in their attacks on the Jewish people, adopting symbols and recalling events of the past to justify their deadly campaign. But to make a jump from the anti-Judaism of the Church to the anti-Semitism of the Nazis is to misread completely the nature of the Nazi persecution. As the Vatican statement points out, "the *Shoah* was the work of a thoroughly modern neo-pagan regime. Its anti-Semitism had its roots outside of Christianity and in pursuing its aims, it did not hesitate to oppose the Church and persecute her members."[7] It is our firm conviction that there is no *intrinsic link* between the anti-Judaism of the Christian Church and the anti-Semitism of National Socialism, or *direct* responsibility of the Church for the Nazi persecution.

The French bishops, in their *Drancy Statement on the Shoah*, had already made this quite clear, as is obvious from the following conclusion:

> To the extent that the pastors and those in authority in the
> Church let such teaching of disdain develop so long, and
> that they maintained among Christian communities an

underlying basic religious culture which shaped and
deformed peoples' attitudes, they bear a heavy responsibility […]. This is not to say (however) that a direct cause
and effect link can be drawn between these commonly-
held anti-Jewish feelings and the Shoah, because the Nazi
plan to annihilate the Jewish people had it sources elsewhere (*Drancy Statement*).[8]

It might be worthwhile to take a moment to recall precisely the nature of
the Nazi persecution of the Jewish people. This was not a question of reacting
to a people who had rejected Christ. Rather, it was a consequence of so-called
racial superiority. There was no place in Nazi ideology for the Jewish people,
because of their race. To a lesser extent, other peoples—many or even most
of whom were themselves Christian—were similarly the objects of their contempt. This was no Christian anti-Judaism. Even the Christian Church itself
was considered an enemy of the Nazi regime. As my predecessor Cardinal
Johannes Willebrands observed in London in 1988, Aaron Steinberg clearly
saw as early as 1934 that "the deeper motive of Nazi anti-Semitism is its
anti-Christian, politico-cultural Pan-Germanism."[9]

Rabbi Abraham Heschel, who exercised such vital influence on the
decision of Pope John XXIII to include Catholic-Jewish relations on the
agenda of the Second Vatican Council and made such an important contribution to bringing about the present Jewish-Catholic relationship, reflects
deeply on this very point and provides us with the following insight:

Nazism in its very roots was a rebellion against the Bible,
against the God of Abraham. Realizing that it was
Christianity that implanted attachment to the God of
Abraham and involvement with the Hebrew Bible in the
hearts of Western man, Nazism resolved that it must exterminate the Jews and eliminate Christianity, and bring
about instead a revival of Teutonic paganism.[10]

Still we must not seek to play down or neglect the evil of *anti-Judaism*. Reflection within the Catholic Church over recent years has raised the question as to how this *anti-Judaism* entered into Christian thought and resulted in the centuries-long Christian teaching of contempt for the Jewish people. Fundamental to the gospel of Jesus Christ is the commandment of love, based on the Law of Moses (cf. Deuteronomy 6:5). The followers of Jesus were told: "Love your enemies, do good to those who abuse you" (see Luke 6:27–28). As Christ died on the cross, he prayed for the Roman soldiers and for his Jewish brothers who were involved in his own crucifixion: "Father, forgive them; they do not know what they are doing" (see Luke 23:34).

Yet, the Christian Church, down through the centuries, certainly did not teach its members to show to the Jewish people that love which its founder, Jesus Christ, made the fundamental principle of his teaching. Rather, an anti-Jewish tradition stamped its mark in differing ways on Christian doctrine and teaching.

Already in the second century, Melito of Sardis, in a sermon on Good Friday, accuses the Jewish people of being guilty of deicide. This was a time of bitter polemics between the Jewish community and the young Christian community, yet one cannot speak of anti-Judaism. Many of the members of the early church had come from a Jewish background. But the seed was already being sown and there can be no denial of the fact that from the time of Emperor Constantine on, Jews were isolated and discriminated against in the Christian world. There were expulsions and forced conversions, and Christian theology taught supersessionism. The "old Law" was ended and the Church had superseded Judaism as the chosen People of God. The Jews were doomed to homeless wandering because of the part of some of their ancestors in the crucifixion of Jesus. Literature propagated stereotypes; the ghetto, which came into being in 1555 with a papal bull, became in Nazi Germany the antechamber of the extermination. Jews naturally reacted to this with distaste, distrust, and a polemic of their own. Over the centuries economic, political, sociological, and the above-mentioned theological factors resulted in two communities that all too often have defined themselves in opposition to each other.

There is much need for reflection and repentance in this history, and it is our hope that *We Remember*, despite the shortcomings that many have seen in its contents, will encourage such reflection. In this sense, the Vatican statement is not to be seen as the final word on this delicate and complicated question, but rather as an official contribution to the process of reconciliation between Catholic and Jews as we prepare to enter a new Christian millennium.

I have mentioned that our document was seen by many as disappointing. More had been expected. I have referred already to one of the reasons for this negative reception, namely the distinction that we make between anti-Judaism and anti-Semitism.

The Church and the Christian World

Another difficulty, especially for our Jewish partners, centered on the distinction made between the *Church as such* and the *Christian world*. This was unfortunately seen as a way of placing all blame for the failures of the past on members of the Church not having any particular authority or responsibility for the Church's teaching. But as the earlier quote from *Tertio Millennio Adveniente* (no. 33) points out: "Although she is holy because of her incorporation into Christ, the Church does not tire of doing penance—before God and man *she always acknowledges as her own her sinful sons and daughters.*" And who are those "sinful sons and daughters"? They can include any member of the Church, from the pope of the day to the cardinals, bishops, priests, religious, and laity, and the guilt is greater according to the responsibility exercised. There was no intention here of limiting those responsible for the practice of *anti-Judaism* to what we might term "ordinary" Christians. Nor is this a new distinction created for the document *We Remember*, but one that is beautifully explained in the Second Vatican Council's Dogmatic Constitution *Lumen Gentium*.[11] The unfortunate thing about this particular point is that misunderstandings over the distinction made in a statement by Pope John Paul II have taken attention away from the rest of an important affirmation by his Holiness, which is quoted in the document *We Remember*:

In the Christian world—and I do not say on the part of the Church as such—erroneous and unjust interpretations of the New Testament regarding the Jewish people and their alleged culpability have circulated for too long, engendering feelings of hostility towards this people.[12]

Pope Pius XII

A third negative comment on the Vatican document *We Remember* refers to the positive evaluation given there regarding Pope Pius XII's efforts to save the threatened Jewish people of Europe during the Second World War. In our document we do not discuss at any length this question, but simply state that "during and after the war, Jewish communities and Jewish leaders expressed their thanks for all that had been done for them, including what Pope Pius XII did personally or through his representatives to save hundreds of thousands of Jewish lives." In a footnote, we mention some of those Jewish leaders who spontaneously came after the war to personally thank Pope Pius XII for what he had done to help them or the Jewish people throughout Europe during the war.

I think it is obvious from what I have just stated that we were not seeking to close the historical discussion on the role of Pope Pius XII during the Second World War. We did intend, however, to keep the question open for further study, in the face of a growing tendency on the part of Jewish organizations to condemn Pius XII on emotional judgments with no historical foundation.

I am pleased that our references to Pius XII have contributed to renewed interest on the part of historians in this pope, who is much revered within the Catholic Church. In very recent history, we have witnessed in Rome two events that have confirmed to some degree our positive evaluation. In January 1998, the Israeli Ambassador to Italy presented the Medal of the Just to the Sisters of Sion in Rome. This sign of appreciation and gratitude on the part of the State of Israel was given because two members of that congregation protected 167 Italian Jews from persecution during the Second World War.

On March 12, 1998, I took part in the presentation of the Italian translation of Sister Margherita Marchione's book *Theirs Is a Precious Witness*, which tells of other religious houses who took in the Jewish residents of Rome and protected them from 1943 to 1945. None of this would have been possible without the active support of the Vatican under Pope Pius XII. These religious houses were given a special document from the Vatican to exempt them from German inspection. It would have been impossible, moreover, for the sisters to find food for their "guests" had this not been delivered to them from the Vatican, often at night and with the personal assistance of Sister Pasquilina, who was directly in the service of Pope Pius XII.

The Future: Working Together

The final section of the document *We Remember: A Reflection on the Shoah* is entitled "Looking Together to a Common Future." It appeals once again to Catholics "to renew the awareness of the Hebrew roots of their faith," and expresses the hope that our sorrow for the tragedy that the Jewish people suffered in our century will lead to a new relationship between Catholics and Jews. In his letter accompanying the Vatican document, Pope John Paul II expresses the fervent hope that *We Remember: A Reflection on the Shoah* will help heal the wounds of the past and "enable memory to play its necessary part in the process of shaping a future in which the unspeakable iniquity of the Shoah will never again be possible."[13]

It is a great joy for me to be able to state that over the past thirty-five years, Jews and Catholics have gradually built such a new relationship. It has been a difficult process, calling for deep self-reflection on the part of Catholics and generous acceptance of the outstretched hand on the part of the Jews. Much has been achieved, and the way is open now for us to move ahead into a new Christian millennium that will be free from the *anti-Judaism* of the past and based on "a shared mutual respect, as befits those who adore the one Creator and Lord and have a common father in faith, Abraham."[14] The approaching Jubilee 2000 offers us the possibility of using this "graced time" for reconciliation between our two faith communities.

The president of the International Council of Christians and Jews, Orthodox Rabbi David Rosen, has described this process "as one of the greatest revolutions in human history." For him, the Church is no longer to be seen as being part of the problem for Jews, but rather as "part of the solution."[15]

Speaking recently to members of the United Jewish Appeal Federations of North America, His Holiness recalled the "very close bonds of spiritual kinship which Christians share with the great religious tradition of Judaism stretching back through Moses to Abraham," and went on to state:

> For the good of the human family, it is crucial at this time that all believers work together to build structures of genuine peace. This is not just because of some political necessity which will pass, but because of God's command which endures forever (cf. Ps. 33:11). In our different ways, Jews and Christians follow the religious path of ethical monotheism. We worship one, true God: but this worship demands obedience to the ethic declared by the prophets: "Cease to do evil, learn to do good; correct oppression; defend the fatherless; plead for the widow" (Is. 1:17).[16]

Rabbi Abraham Heschel, to whom I have already made reference, once wrote:

> Nazism has suffered a defeat, but the process of eliminating the Bible from the consciousness of the western world goes on. It is on the issue of saving the radiance of the Hebrew bible in the minds of man that Jews and Christians are called upon to work together. None of us can do it alone. Both of us must realize that in our age anti-Semitism is anti-Christianity and anti-Christianity is anti-Semitism.[17]

This, I believe, is the challenge that faces us, Jews and Christians, in view of growing secularism, religious apathy, and moral confusion, in which there is little room for God. As we leave behind this tragic century, we are no longer called simply to reconciliation, but to genuine partnership. Rabbi Rosen, in the interview already quoted, puts it like this: "I think we have to try to have a deeper communion, while respecting those very fundamental differences. I see us as partners in divine destiny with two different models of the message."[18]

We are called to speak a prophetic word to the world in which we live. We do not live for ourselves alone but to be "a light to the nations" (see Isaiah 49:6; Acts 13:47). For this we need to deepen our understanding, each of the other, and while maintaining our distinct identities, witness together a new consciousness and a new conscience based on the common core of belief that is embodied in the Hebrew Bible and the Christian Bible. As we have stated so often, there is need for a much greater effort in the work of formation, so that this new spirit replace the former spirit of "suspicion, resentment and distrust."[19]

The possibilities for common witness and cooperation are immense. Is there any reason why we cannot work together for a better, more just society? Or fight together against every form of evil in our societies, and especially every manifestation of racism and *anti-Semitism*? It is not enough for us to deplore or even denounce the social evils of the present age. For example, it is not enough for us to be against *anti-Semitism*. In a recent address, Cardinal Carlo Martini, archbishop of Milan, reflecting on the challenge of "remembering today for the future," stated:

> To be "anti-anti" runs the risk of finishing up in denunciations of little effect. More is needed. It is not enough to be against someone who is against; rather one must be *for* someone and this in a consistent way. It is necessary therefore to be *for* the Jewish people, for their culture, for their values, for their human and spiritual riches, for

their history, for their extraordinary religious witness. It is
necessary to be for those values that enrich all humanity.[20]

Are we not called by our common heritage to promote together the care
and conservation of the environment, respect for life, the defense of the weak
and oppressed? The International Liaison Committee of the Commission for
Religious Relations with the Jews and the International Jewish Committee for
Interreligious Consultation (IJCIC) has been able to make common statements
on the family in Jerusalem (1994), and on the environment, in Rome (1998).

Could we not, for example say something together to a world in which
millions lack the basic necessities of human existence, while nations spend
billions of dollars on armaments and weapons of mass destruction? At a time
in history when ethnicity continues to divide nations and cause untold suffering to millions of innocent people, surely we Jews and Christians have something that we can say together to a troubled world through the example of our
own profound reconciliation.

Then there are challenges for us in the field of human rights, for the
protection of the rights of religion, for dialogue with the other great religions
of the world—with a special place in this context for dialogue with the believing followers of Islam—and for the collaboration in the realm of culture. For
both our communities, there is need to pay special attention to the youth, by
offering them programs of formation on the great themes of peace and justice,
and helping them to know our respective histories and traditions. I welcome
most warmly the work already being done here in the United States, through
the Catholic-Jewish Educational Enrichment Program, to bring authentic
views and information to young people in Jewish and Catholic schools. New
centers of Catholic-Jewish studies at university level have been established in
recent years. Chicago has been to the forefront in implementing the new program of healing the wounds of the past for a new future of mutual trust and
cooperation between Jews and Catholics. I thank you for that most cordially.

For those of us who have the possibility and the responsibility of building up this partnership, there is a further agenda that has still to be explored.
As two *faith communities* with common roots, we must now move beyond the

agenda of the past thirty-five years and begin to examine more closely the spiritual bonds that unite us, while at the same time seeking to deepen our understanding of the various teachings of our faiths that constitute our separate identities. We must throw off all fear in this regard. What is there to be afraid of if we approach this dialogue with sincerity and with respect for each other's identity? Will not a dialogue that goes beyond a discussion about problems and concentrates rather on what can bring us to a deeper understanding of one another be valuable also in helping us to proceed further and more securely along the path of common action?

Speaking just a few weeks ago in Boca Raton, Florida, the president of the University of Notre Dame asked his audience: "How can one be a Christian person without also being a Jew? How can one understand the God of Jesus without also understanding the God of Moses?" And he went on to state that "Catholics and Jews should be able to look into each other's faces and see the face of God." Cardinal Martini, in a pastoral letter for 1998–1999, writes of the continuous mysterious presence of the face of God in the history of the Jewish people and of the love of God for the children of the covenant that has never been revoked, and then calls on the Catholic people of Milan "to contemplate in this Father of Israel the Father of Jesus, the Father of all humanity, the One who wants us to be sons in the Son." Another eminent leader of the Catholic Church in Europe, Cardinal Christoph Schönborn, archbishop of Vienna, in a lecture on "The Name of God" in the Lateran Basilica, toward the end of January 1998, reflects on the fact that "only in our century—and especially as a consequence of the horrors of the *Shoah*—do we begin to become conscious of the fact that the uniqueness of Jesus, in whom we Catholics believe, is inseparably linked to the uniqueness of Israel, since Jesus is 'a light to enlighten the pagans and the glory of your people Israel' (Luke 2:32)."[21]

There are many similar fields of study open to us, and I am glad to state that we are at last moving in that direction. This, I believe, is a sign of the maturity of our new relationship. We hope in the coming year to begin to discuss freely and without coercion questions like that just indicated and others connected with the relationship between the two covenants. It is here, in particular, that the Commission for Religious Relations with the Jews intends to concentrate in the years ahead. We are people of religion and we wish to dialogue with people of religion about religion.

For the Catholic Church, the program of study and action that I have set out is one to which we are deeply committed. I believe that the great majority of our members support these efforts, if not by positive involvement, at least by silent approval. I would just emphasize once again two basic principles that have been valuable in bringing us this far.

The first is, of course, *sincere dialogue*. We must have a clear idea of where we wish to go, and then be consistent in our actions and words by making sure that they do not contradict that goal. We cannot say one thing today and the opposite tomorrow, if we wish to be faithful to our dialogue.

Then we must have *genuine respect*, one for the other. I believe that on the Catholic side, we have, with Pope John Paul II, gone beyond respect and made our Catholic-Jewish relationship a *work of love*. We will continue to see it as such, but we expect and hope that the Jewish partner will extend to us at least respect.

This is not something new that I am proposing. In Prague in 1990, the International Liaison Commission of IJCIC and the Commission for Religious Relations with the Jews set before us an agenda, much of which we have succeeded in fulfilling. That agenda called for "cooperation, mutual respect, and understanding, goodwill and common goals."[22] As we prepare to cross the threshold of the new Christian millennium, Jews and Christians need still to respond sincerely and enthusiastically to that same challenge. We cannot and should not forget the past—but we must not remain chained to the past. A new and wonderful opportunity has opened up before us. Let us not miss it! All that is required of us is to learn to listen to each other, to seek to understand the other as the other understands himself or herself, to be open to and respect the other, to work together without compromising faith or distinct identity, to be seen as children of the one and only God who know that God loves them and wants all men and women to know and experience that love, to be together a "light to the nations."

Notes

1. Pope John Paul II, *Tertio Millennio Adveniente*, no. 33.
2. Holy See's Commission for Religious Relations with the Jews, *We Remember: A Reflection on the Shoah* (Vatican City: Editrice Vaticana, 1998), p. 9
3. *Catholics Remember the Holocaust*, a publication of the Secretariat for Ecumenical and Interreligious Affairs of the National Conference of Catholic Bishops of the United States, Washington D.C., 1998.
4. David Novak, "Jews and Catholics beyond Apologies," *First Things*, (January 1999), 20ff.
5. Holy See's Commission for Religious Relations with the Jews, *We Remember*, IV.
6. Ibid.
7. Ibid.
8. *Catholics Remember the Holocaust*, a publication of the Secretariat for Ecumenical and Interreligious Affairs of the National Conference of Catholic Bishops of the United States, Washington D.C., 1998, p. 34.
9. J. Willebrands, "The Church Facing Modern Anti-Semitism," *Christian Jewish Relations* 22/1 (1989), pp. 5–17.
10. A. J. Heschel, "No Religion Is an Island," *Union Theological Seminary Quarterly* 21 (January 1966), p. 118.
11. Second Vatican Council Dogmatic Constitution *Lumen Gentium*, no. 8, which distinguishes "the society furnished with hierarchical agencies and the Mystical Body of Christ" and states that they are not to be considered as two realities. "Rather they form one interlocked reality which is composed of a divine and a human element"—a reality that is compared by the council to the mystery of the Incarnate Word. In the same council document, the fathers describe the Church as "that Jerusalem which is above," "the spotless spouse of the spotless lamb," for whom "Christ delivered himself up so that he might sanctify her" (no. 6).

12. Holy See's Commission for Religious Relations with the Jews, *We Remember*, III. Cf. John Paul II, Speech to Symposium on the Roots of Anti-Judaism, 31 October 1997, in *L'Osservatore Romano* (1 November 1997), p. 6.

13. Letter of Pope John Paul II to Cardinal Edward Idris Cassidy in Holy See's Commission for Religious Relations with the Jews, *We Remember*.

14. Holy See's Commission for Religious Relations with the Jews, *We Remember*, V.

15. Ecumenical News Service of the World Council of Churches, 17 September 1998.

16. *L'Osservatore Romano*, 4 September 1998.

17. A. J. Heschel, "No Religion Is an Island," *Union Theological Seminary Quarterly* 21 (January 1966), p. 118.

18. Ecumenical News International of the World Council of Churches, 17 September 1988.

19. Information Service of the Pontifical Council for Promoting Christian Unity, 75/IV (1990), p. 176.

20. C. M. Martini, *Ricordare oggi per il futuro*, Milano, 18 November 1998 (private copy).

21. *L'Osservatore Romano*, 28 January 1998, p. 11.

22. Information Service of the Pontifical Council for Promoting Christian Unity, 74/IV (1990), p. 176.

2

Christian Tradition,
Anti-Judaism, and Anti-Semitism

GERARD S. SLOYAN

It is painful to explore, but even more, to recount the mutual antipathy between Jews and Christians, Christians and Jews, over the centuries. Examining its roots is extremely important because they provide the clue to much that followed.

At the beginnings of this doleful history there was a mutual antipathy between Jews and Jews based on a religious difference, much as in modern Israel. The question then as now was: "Who is a true Jew?" Josephus the historian leaves the only chronicle of happenings in that land, and it is highly incomplete, especially on the early first century of the Common Era. His chief concern is the political and military events that led up to the revolt against Rome. He deals with the religious situation only cursorily. In his history called the *Jewish Archaeology,* popularly known as the *Antiquities of the Jews,* he devotes more than half of its twenty books to a paraphrase of the Bible. Coming on to the Common Era, he mentions three schools of religious thought which he calls *philosophies* for his pagan readership: the Pharisees, the Sadducees and the Essenes.[1] He characterizes each of the three briefly. Later in the same book, he tells of the antipathy that arose between the first two during the reign of the Hasmonean high priest John Hyrcanus, who deserted the Pharisees to give his allegiance to the Sadducees.[2] This mutual opposition of the aristocratic temple priests and elders, the Sadducees, and the teachers of the ordinary religiously instructed populace, the Pharisees, would continue into the New Testament period. Josephus describes the Pharisee position and influence at some length in the book later known as *The Jewish War.*[3]

Josephus further reports in detail on the imprisonment and execution of "John, surnamed the Baptist," as the victim of Herod Antipas's fear of John's growing influence with the crowds[4]; on a certain "wise man" named Jesus, whom Pilate condemned to be crucified after hearing him accused "by men of the highest standing among us"[5]; of the stoning death of "a man named James, the brother of Jesus" at the order of the high priest Ananus, at which "the fair-minded" Jerusalemites "who were strict in observance of the law" took umbrage and had King Agrippa depose him.[6] Josephus recounts all three deaths in a flat, disinterested tone, but he is interested in events in his homeland as viewed from his residence in the emperor's court of Rome. He would still have been in Galilee as a man of twenty-five at the time of James's death. Jesus and John were both executed before his birth, but he could have gotten the information on both from Roman Jews, native to Palestine like himself, whether believers in Jesus or not. His report on the latter, Jesus, is the shorter, credible version testified to in the tenth-century Arabic text of the Bishop Agapius published by Professor Shlomo Pines, not the longer version in the Slavonic Tradition, which was clearly amplified by a Christian hand.[7]

To complete the account of recorded deaths in the Jesus community, there is the story in the Acts of the Apostles of death by the sword of another James who figures in the gospel narratives. He is the brother of John and they are sons of Zebedee, a Galilean fisherman. Having been followers of John the Baptist, they became disciples of Jesus. Luke's second volume, the book later called the Acts of the Apostles, attributes this killing—it would have happened around the year 44—to Agrippa's desire to curry favor with the populace. It should be noted that, while all three of the last named deaths had religious overtones, chiefly Pharisee-Sadducee—that of the Baptist did not—they were primarily exercises of political power and not religious aggression.[8]

The gospel narratives are another matter. They tell us more about first-century Jewish life than any other source, including the Mishnah, the legal arguments of which would have been recorded between 85 and 200. Mark was in the style of Hellenistic biography in some diaspora city, perhaps Rome. His audience seems to have been made up largely of gentile new believers who did not have any Aramaic; Mark himself did not know the geography of Palestine well. Matthew is thoroughly knowledgeable in things

Jewish, incorporates more than ninety percent of Mark's material into his narrative, and means chiefly to claim the superiority of Jesus' interpretation of the religion of Israel to that of the Rabbis, which put the oral law of their recent forebears' devising on a par with the written law. Matthew, who may have written around the year 85, retrojected the arguments between the Jesus Jews and the Pharisee Jews of his day to Jesus' brief public career. He chronicles the sharp and bitter exchanges he was familiar with as if they had happened fifty years before. Surely Jesus was challenged on, and argued, religious questions, but the *gerousia* or academy of Iavneh had not yet been formed. The disputes could not have taken the precise form recorded in the Gospels, nor would it have occurred to learned Jews to wish to eliminate Jesus even if he had prevailed in argument. We can be sure that a rabbinical account of these fifty-year-old exchanges would have had him vanquished in dispute every time. What is important about Matthew's mode of argument is that he has Jesus teaching a way of fidelity to the Torah that contains no discernible elements of *halakah*. That fact, and his putting forward a Jew executed by the gentiles on a criminal charge as the hoped-for deliverer in David's mold, ensured resistance to his message.

Luke wrote the most polished Greek of the four and wrote for gentiles. He softened the hard edges of Mark's writing style and took a line other than the judgmental one on God's behalf adopted by Matthew. In his account of Jesus' last days and hours, however, he resembled the other two by featuring the desire of the temple priests to remove Jesus from the scene, pressing on Pilate a civil charge for his condemnation, when their position as custodians of the temple revenues and as fiscal agents for the empire would have been their reason for wanting him gone.

The Jewish believers in Jesus represented by John's Gospel were as bitterly opposed by the larger community in that diaspora city as in Matthew. On the evidence of that writing, the chief bones of contention were the claim that he was the Messiah and was being presented as Son of God in a sense of that term unique to Jewish ears, namely as one equal to God. The Jesus community, moreover, was accepting Samaritans as full members, which alone would have qualified it as apostate Judaism. Its designation for its majority opposition was the sarcastic "the Jews," namely those who thought themselves to be the only Jews. It was not unlike the claim of the *haredim* who, in their minds, are the only authentic Jews in Israel. Secular Jews, Conservative, Reform, and Reconstructionist Jews do not qualify. The *Notsrim,* the Jesus sect, was evidently viewed in much the same way in a community made up exclusively of ethnic Jews.

Two things occurred that were to have far more tragic consequences than anything I have mentioned so far. Throughout the 50s, the Jew Saul/Paul, who would have had both names from birth in the province of Cilicia, wrote seven letters, and his disciples another two, that were saved. Paul became a proselytizer for the Jesus believers much as he had been in his young manhood as a Pharisee. He appeared to be unable to see another side in his zeal for his cause—proclaiming a Galilean Jew as having been raised up from the dead and experienced by him. Paul divided Jewish and pagan audiences everywhere he went. In one letter, written in white heat, he excoriated some new gentile believers in the province of the Galatia for accepting the line of a "truth squad" that was following him. These were more likely to have been gentile converts to Christ than observant Jews. We gather that they were not embracing the full yoke of the Law but only Philo's "special laws," the distinguishing marks of Jewishness.[9]

Paul wrote that God had given Israel the Law for two reasons only: as a means to identify sin, and as a stopgap until God sent Abraham's "seed," the heir to the promise. The proof that Jews had the faith of Abraham was to accept that seed or offspring, Jesus, as the Christ. Paul wrote a follow-up letter to the mixed community of Jews and gentiles in Rome, where he had never been. He suspected that the Jews and gentiles there were living in an uneasy religious community, each uncertain of the full membership of the other in the new faith. Consequently, he sent them a carefully worked-out rationale showing that faith alone in God's deed in Christ was necessary. The "works of the law," as he termed the special laws, were nonobligatory for gentiles and had become neutral, an indifferent matter, for Jews. The only sin for both would be to think these observances necessary as a complement to their faith in Christ.[10] It is obvious that anywhere in the diaspora Jews heard of the content of these letters—and the anti-law language in them is very strong—they would consider him an apostate Jew. That probably included segments of the Jesus-believing Jews in Jerusalem and Galilee. Christians and Jews alike have mistakenly credited Paul with achieving this settlement single-handedly. But, while his written rhetoric and argument were uniquely his, they must have described the common practice in Edessa, Alexandria, Rome, and the many other cities to which he bad not brought the gospel. Otherwise, his teaching would not have been received so calmly in those churches. There is little record of resistance to it as something new, namely in Jerusalem only.

The Acts of the Apostles probably did something much worse than Paul's vigorous argumentation to affect the relations of Christians and Jews over the ages. In three speeches attributed to Peter and one to Stephen, Luke accuses all the Jews of Jerusalem as being responsible for Jesus' death. These are reconstructions. They are arguments framed over many decades for the proclamation and defense of Jesus as the world's savior by his death and resurrection. But they are presented as authentic accounts of the absolutely earliest history of events: "This man . . . you crucified and killed by the hands of those outside the law."[11] "You killed the prince of [new] life whom God raised from the dead."[12] "Which of the prophets did your ancestors not persecute? They killed those who foretold the coming of the Righteous One, and now you have become his betrayers and murderers."[13] In another place, Luke groups Herod and Pilate with the gentiles and the peoples of Israel as having carried out their predestined plan,[14] but the Christians of later centuries remembered little of broad-based responsibility for the death, only the direct charge against the Jews.

Toward the year 110, a Greek-speaking gentile bishop of Syria, Ignatius of Antioch, warned the Christians of a certain city in the province of Asia: "It is better to hear about Christianism from one of the circumcision than Judaism from a gentile."[15] He wishes to hear talk only about Jesus Christ. This passage suggests two things: the slow emergence of one religion from the other, and the fact that the ancient world knew no interreligious dialogue or even peaceful coexistence. The religion of the other was, by definition, false.

A learned pagan who had become a Christian by the name of Justin wrote a fictitious dialogue with an equally learned Jew, in which be respectfully but quite naively expected him to be convinced of the message about Jesus simply by examining passages in the Scriptures Justin thought to have prophesied him. At one point he wrote: "[a] later covenant voids an older."[16] This is the first expression we have, after phrases in Hebrews (8:7, 13) and Ephesians (2:15), of what came to be called *supersessionism*. He writes a little later in the same treatise: "You dishonor and curse in your synagogues all who believe in Christ . . . [a]s often as you could you employed force against us."[17] What data he had to back up this charge we do not know. Justin, too, has the charge that Trypho's Jewish people "crucified the only just and sinless man," plus the absurd notion that God gave Israel circumcision so that, after Hadrian's troops sacked Jerusalem (in 135), Jewish males would be recognizable and thus refused reentry to Jerusalem.[18] His first *Apology*, written earlier, contains similar sentiments. The tissue of accusation had been well launched. At the time Justin wrote, the Jesus-people were a tiny minority in the empire and diaspora Jews a sizeable population. The latter could brush off these charges as the work of religious cranks. But in the course of the next one hundred years, the Christian population grew rapidly. Not long after that, the majority-minority ratio was reversed with tragic consequences for the Jews, even though the pagan majority outnumbered the two combined.

We find Irenaeus of Lugdunum in Gaul—Lyon nowadays—writing in his five books *Against Gnosis Falsely So-Called,* some time around 180, even as Judah the Patriarch was compiling the Mishnah, that Peter and John had a heavy task in Acts. Irenaeus is arguing against the Christian gnostics who did not believe that the body of Jesus was real but a figment created by the Demiurge. The two apostles had to present Jesus, "whom the Jews had seen as a man and fastened to the cross, . . . as Christ the Son of God. . . . They told them to their face that they were the slayers of the Lord."[19] He repeats the charge twice more in his next section, but, overall, there is not as much animus in this lengthy treatise as in Justin.

The Latin-speaking Tertultian's anti-Judaism is pervasive in his voluminous writings. His target is the Jews of the Bible, for he does not seem to have had contact with many actual Jews. Arguing against the heretic Marcion, who taught that it was "the Christ of the other god [the creature Demiurge] who was brought to the cross," he maintained that the Mosaic Law—which Marcion thought base and interior—was the work of the true God. He conceded to the heretic that the Church had abandoned the law and replaced it by a new law, but he then had to explain what could account for this. His answer was that, since God's law and cult could not be owing to any inferiority on God's part, the cause had to be the inferiority of the people with whom God was working at the time. "Thus the God of the Hebrew Bible was 'salvaged' for Christians by means of the anti-Judaic myth."[20] Tertullian managed as a result to speak ill of the Jews at every turn.

Origen of Alexandria and later of Caesarea in Palestine could not have known many Jews in his native city; it was largely devoid of them after Rome put down the Jewish uprising of 115–117. He speaks frequently, however, of "my Hebrew teacher," and of another whom he consulted, the Patriarch Ioullos. Writing against the anti-Christian polemicist Celsus, who had researched Christianity thoroughly for his "True Discourse," (*Alēthēs Logos*), Origen attacks him for saying the Jews were never of any reputation or account. They had enjoyed God's protection for many centuries, he writes, but while God had abandoned them many times for longer or shorter periods, God's final and complete desertion came when they committed their greatest sin in killing Jesus. "For this they were entirely abandoned."[21] This accusation is firmly fixed in all the patristic writings. Joined to it is the charge that Rome's destructions of Jerusalem in 70 and 135 were God's punishments for their not having believed in Jesus.

The poetic sermon of Melito, bishop of Sardis, "On the Pasch," was a tissue of the fulfillment of many types or figures in Israel's history in the sufferings that that people inflicted on Jesus. It is a sort of "Daiyenu" in cruel reverse and, indeed, resembles a Passover *aggadah*. Its beauty of language regrettably commended it to Christians all the more. It and a passage in the prophet Micah are the basis for the "Good Friday reproaches."[22]

Eusebius's, Augustine's, and Ambrose's writings all contain bitter diatribes against the Jews.[23] In each case, the biblical Jews are their targets. They shared an incomprehension that the people of Israel had not received their great one in his day or in the intervening years. John Chrysostom stands out from the rest in the ugliness of his invective which all Jews are familiar with and most Christians have never heard of. Directly after his ordination as a priest of Antioch, aged thirty-seven (386), he launched a series of sermons against the Arians but interrupted it as the Jewish holy days came on. His Catholic congregation included some who were participating in Jewish feasts, admiring the holiness of some Jews, and saying that an oath taken in a synagogue was especially sacred. He responded with some choice obloquy brought on by their actions, asking: "Is it not folly for those who worship the crucified to celebrate the festivals of those who crucified him?"[24] and "Do anything to rescue [your brother] from the devil's snare and deliver him from the fellowship of the *Christoktonōn* [the Christ-killers]."[25] Five years after these sermons, but unrelated, Emperor Theodosius I issued a code declaring the faith of Catholic Christians the faith of the empire.

Gregory I, bishop of Rome (590–604), was in effect the organizer of the city of Rome, which he had served as prefect in his 30s—owing to the breakdown of civil government. Shlomo Simonsohn credits him with "laying the foundations of papal Jewry policy in the Middle Ages" for his "practical treatment of problems connected with the presence of Jews in Christian society."[26] Yet, as a theological writer and not an administrator, he could employ when speaking of them such terms as superstition, vomit, perdition, perfidia, and refer to Jews as the enemies of Christ.

What effect did all this writing in Greek and Latin have on the Catholic, a part of which later became the Orthodox, world? Surely it was repeated in sermons and catechisms for centuries. It must have made Christians despisers of Jews. To read through Simonsohn's six volumes of letters from the papal archives from 492 to 1555, however, one gets this picture: as bishops, nobles, civil officials, and Jews brought cases to the popes for adjudication, you find them to be chiefly disputes over things like property seizure (synagogues), harassment during Jewish festivals, forcible circumcision, and reduced taxes for Jews who accepted baptism. Poring over these letters, one deduces that the popes were by and large the protectors of the Jews, that many bishops were but some were not, and that no one could restrain certain of the lower clergy and the people from the cruel conduct toward Jews that sometimes erupted in mob action: looting and burning, and in periods of calm, lesser harassments and social sanctions. All alike were victims of the myth of demonizing this people for its disobedience to God which their forebears in faith had concocted. Some readers of these lines know the history of periods of persecution of Jews by Christians much better than I: the legend called "the blood libel"; the pillaging of the Jewish quarters of cities by the Crusaders; Little Hugh of Lincoln and Simon of Trent who died from entirely different causes than the ones falsely alleged; the specious hunt for heresy among the *conversos* of Spain when Jewish heritage would do as a charge; nineteenth- and twentieth-century anti-Semitism, a new and different phenomenon from religious anti-Judaism, with its horrible outcome, the *shoah*.

Were any of these motivated by the commitment of Christians to their Christian faith? Permit me to doubt it. We are talking here about sins of Christians in every case that had the myth of Jewish failure to believe in Jesus as the Christ as its subtext. These were the sins of the learned for not troubling to probe the deeper meaning of their own Scriptures; the sin of wilful disobedience to the command to be one's brother's keeper, to love one's neighbor as oneself, the sin of superstition which is a sin against faith and the sin of slander which is false accusation without evidence; and the meanest sin of all, resentment at the gifts of others, coveting the possessions of others, and the monomania—not xenophobia—that lies behind it all: the positive madness at the thought that others living side by side with a gentile population would presume to be different in religion and custom, and act as if it were their right to do so.

We have explored the roots of Christian opposition to Jews on the basis of a total misconception of the religious situation. That misconception has led to the post-Enlightenment phenomenon known as anti-Semitism, which has its basis in the ethnic, economic, and political orders. It has retained only a well-remembered anti-Judaic rhetoric from the days of religious obloquy. The churches cannot successfully cope with anti-Semitism on those grounds, but they can deal with anti-Judaism on religious grounds. They can purge their pulpits and classrooms of any scrap of sentiment that the Jews of Jerusalem were responsible for Jesus' death that was extrapolated to all Jews everywhere. They can do something equally important; namely, teach that whereas their faith is that the gospel succeeded to the Torah, it did not supplant it. In other words, Christians must teach and be taught that the entire Mosaic deliverance remains in place, and that the Jewish people, as believers in it, are faithful to a living, vigorous religious tradition that God has in no sense repudiated, but continued to foster and cherish.

Christians have begun to make some small progress in the first matter. They have not yet seen the absolute necessity of the second.

NOTES

1. *Ant. XIII*, 171–173.
2. *Ant. XIII*, 288–298.
3. *Bell. Iud*, 110–14; II, 162–164.
4. *Ant.* XVIII, 116–119.
5. *Ant.* XVIII, 63–64.
6. *Ant.* XX, 200.
7. Shlomo Pines, *An Arabic Version of the Testimonium Flavianum and Its Implications* (Jerusalem: Israel Academy of Sciences and Humanities, 1971).
8. Acts 12:2.
9. Galatians 1:6–9; 3:1–29.
10. Romans 2:17–4:25.
11. Acts 2:24. Cf. v. 36.
12. Acts 3:15.
13. Acts 7:52.
14. See Acts 4:27–28.
15. *Philadelphians* 6.1.
16. *Dialogue with Trypho*, 1.
17. Ibid., 16.
18. Ibid.
19. *Adv. Haer.* III, 12, 6.
20. David P. Efroymson, "The Patristic Connection" in *Antisemitism and the Foundations of Christianity*, ed. Alan Davies (New York: Paulist Press, 1971), p. 101.
21. *Against Celsus,* IV, 2; on his Hebrew teachers, *Prologue to Commentary on the Psalms* (PG 12, 1056).
22. See Eric Werner, "Melito of Sardis: The First Poet of Deicide," *Hebrew Union College Annual* 37 (1966): 191–210.

23. See Gerard S. Sloyan, *The Crucifixion of Jesus: History, Myth, Faith* (Minneapolis: Fortress Press, 1995), pp. 90–95; see Efroymson, "Whose Jews? Augustine's *Tractatus* on John," forthcoming in Professor Robert Kraft *Festschrift*.

24. John Chrysostom, "Against the Jews," *Homily 5* (PG 48.850).

25. Ibid., *Homily 4* (849).

26. Shlomo Simonsohn, *The Apostolic See and the Jews: History, Studies, and Texts* (Toronto: Pontifical Institute of Medieval Studies, 1991), p. 10.

3

The Jewish-Christian Schism:
Reflections on the Vatican Document We Remember
CLAUDIA J. SETZER

> Be not like some, heaping up your sins and saying that the
> covenant is both theirs and ours. It is ours: but in this way
> they finally lost it when Moses had just received it, for the
> Scripture says, "And Moses was in the mount fasting forty
> days and forty nights, and he received the covenant from
> the Lord, tables of stone written with the finger of the hand
> of the Lord (Ex 34:28). But they turned to idols and lost it.
>
> *The Epistle of Barnabas* 4, 6–8

These severe remarks from the late first-early second century Christian work, *The Epistle of Barnabas* are revealing. They show *Barnabas* struggling with some of the problems posed by the continued existence of the Jews. His solution to these problems is via an anti-Jewish exegesis of Scripture, a route also taken by a number of later Christian exegetes. But notice something else. *Someone* is proposing another solution, "The covenant is both ours and theirs." Even nineteen hundred years ago, someone thought Jews and Christians need not exclude each other in their theologies. These anonymous opponents that *Barnabas* complains about could be our spiritual ancestors, people proposing a dual covenant.

I would like to respond to the Holy See's document *We Remember* and its remarks about the early period by expanding on it. Its treatment of the earliest phase of Jewish-Christian relations, the parting of the ways, is careful and balanced, and few New Testament scholars would quibble with it. First, it says "At the dawn of Christianity, after the crucifixion of Jesus, there arose disputes between the early church and the Jewish leaders and people who, in their devotion to the Law, on occasion violently opposed the preachers of the gospel and the first Christians." Did they? Why? What is the evidence?

We hear Paul in these words and his self-description of his former life in Judaism. He alludes to his zealousness for the traditions of his fathers and violent opposition to the church in Galatians 1, and in Philippians 3:6 he tells us he was "as to zeal a persecutor of the church, as to righteousness under the Law blameless." He also claims to have suffered the synagogue discipline of flogging five times (see 2 Corinthians 11:24). Mark and Matthew transmit the saying "They will beat (or flog) you in their synagogues" (see Mark 13:9; Matthew 10:17). Also in the New Testament appears the stoning of Stephen in Acts 7, which most scholars consider more of a lynch mob than a judicial proceeding, the spontaneous opposition to Paul's preaching in Thessalonica reported in Acts, and the ambiguous claim in John 16:2 that expulsion from the synagogue will be followed by religiously motivated killing: ". . . they will put you out of the synagogues. Indeed the hour is coming when whoever kills you will think he is offering service to God." Josephus reports that the high priest Ananus takes advantage of a power vacuum and kills off James, the leader of the Jerusalem church, but the more respectable Jewish citizens protest to the Romans and have him removed. These are the sum total of examples of violent Jewish opposition to Christians. This does not amount to a great deal. The Vatican document is therefore careful to say that violent Jewish opposition happened "on occasion."

The number of references to Jews acting directly against Christians is limited, but real. More important to note is that they are all intra-communal, either synagogue discipline or Jews spontaneously acting against other Jews. Although Jews are frequently accused of *wanting* to kill or persecute Christians, the number of references where they do so directly is very limited. And they almost all come before the year 100 (Bar Kochba is an exception). Justin Martyr, for example, writing in 150, complains about Jewish opposition, but he also betrays Jewish powerlessness. He says, "You curse Christians in the synagogues, and other nations carry out the curse, putting to death those who simply confess themselves to be Christians" (*Dialogue with Trypho,* 96.2). The vast majority of negative Jewish reactions to Christians seem to be in the verbal sphere, and may range from disagreeing with them, to slandering them to the Romans to removing the umbrella of protection offered by the Jewish community.

Why did Jews oppose Christians? There were three parts to it, a triangle of reasons: practice, theology, and politics.

Practice

The first area in which believers in Jesus and other Jews parted company is related to practice. Some scholars of ancient Judaism think that is the only thing that separated groups, which I think is an oversimplification.[1]

When we talk about Jewish law and practice, now and in the ancient world, we are talking about two things. First, the Written Law, or the Torah, and the first five books of the Bible, Genesis through Deuteronomy. That contains all sorts of laws: what you can and cannot eat, whom you may have sex with, how you may transact business, how you assess damages in cases of personal injury. There is no doubt that Jesus and his first followers and virtually all other self-identified Jewish groups bought into these rules. The Torah was God's revelation, and its laws had the force of divine command. But there was less agreement about another set of laws, later called the *Oral Torah*, that were "read into" or derived from the Written Torah, that were given the same authority even though not explicitly found in the Written Torah. Oral Torah as a term comes later, but a forerunner of it is what Mark calls "the tradition of the elders" (see 7:35). For example, the Written Torah says simply to observe the Sabbath day and do no manner of work, while the rabbis come along with their Oral Torah and define exactly what *work* is, delineating thirty-nine activities as work forbidden on the Sabbath. They also make a bold claim: This Oral Torah is just as binding on you Jews as the Written Torah. In fact, God gave this law, too, at Mount Sinai to Moses, but it was not written down.

The potential for fireworks is obvious. Other Jews could come along and say "Who says? How do you know what God meant when he forbade work on the Sabbath? You rabbis are making up these rules and claiming they are God's law, when in fact they are merely your own." That is precisely what seems to be hinted at in disputes over fasting and harvesting on the Sabbath in Mark 2 (and parallels), and disputes over ritual hand-washing in Mark 7 (and parallels). Only the opponents are not yet called *rabbis*; rather, they are called *Pharisees*, and it is not yet called the *Oral Law*, but the *tradition of the elders*.

Belief in Jesus and his authority allowed his early followers to understand and interpret the Torah differently. And, indeed, they criticize these rules as mere human invention: "You leave the commandment of God and hold fast to the tradition of men" (see Mark 7:8). Christian interpretation drives a wedge between the written Torah and some Pharisaic/rabbinic interpretations of it. This period of the gospels' composition is around the 70s to the 90s of the first century, although they contain earlier material. By the time Justin is writing, between 155 and 160, the issue has changed. The Jew Trypho in Justin's *Dialogue with Trypho* is puzzled because Christians, now overwhelmingly gentile, do not seem to observe even the Written Torah at all, neither circumcision, nor the food laws, nor Sabbath on the seventh day, much less any oral law. With the gentilization of the church, disputes over how the Torah should be observed turned into disputes over whether some parts of it need be observed at all.

Theology

There were also theological reasons why Christians were not always welcome in larger Jewish groups. Quite simply, some claims Christians made about Jesus were impossible for Jews to tolerate. First, that someone who was crucified and died this gruesome death was actually the Messiah: most Jews would have treated this as a very bizarre notion. They shared the general repugnance of the Greco-Roman world at crucifixion. It was a punishment not for any garden-variety criminal, but reserved for slaves, foreigners, and those guilty of *maiestas*, treason. Furthermore, they read or heard the Bible, and Deuteronomy 21:23 says explicitly "He who hangs on a tree is cursed by God." How could someone God curses be the Messiah? It certainly fails to fit with the Hebrew Bible's Messiah, literally "the anointed one," that is the king chosen by God and anointed to rule as a prince over his people in Israel, to restore Israel to peace and security. Many Jews expected a Messiah to be something like a new King David. Christians, through a certain amount of reflection and interpretation, were able to put together the traditional idea of a Messiah with the crucified Jesus, but we can easily see how Jews who did not go that route would be puzzled and offended by the claim. And indeed, there is evidence that they were. Paul tells us "Christ crucified is a scandal to the Jews" (see 1 Corinthians 1:23)—literally a stumbling block, something they could not get past. In the mid-second century, Justin is still worrying about this verse. In his *Dialogue with Trypho*, he says in five different places that Jews cite Deuteronomy 21:23, arguing that he who is crucified is cursed by God. He devotes the largest amount of space on a single issue to proving the crucifixion is really predicted by Scripture. What this implies is that even by 150–160, in a gentile context, the crucified Messiah is still a live point of debate.

The other issue that seemed to trouble Jews, not surprisingly, is the Resurrection. If Jews, in their traditional view of the Messiah, did not expect him to die an ignominious death, they hardly expected him to rise from the dead. The earliest explicit hint that this was a problem is in the Gospel of Matthew, where there are two odd vignettes on either side of the story of Jesus' Resurrection, sandwiching the resurrection story. One is Matthew 27:62–65, where Jewish leaders go to the Roman procurator on the Sabbath of Passover, worried ahead of time that the disciples will steal the body and claim Jesus' Resurrection. I doubt very much that this is historical, but let us look at it another way. Let us say that after the fact, Jews are going around saying, "Look the disciples stole the body. That's why the tomb is empty. And now they're saying he's risen from the dead!" If Jews are saying this, is not Matthew giving the perfect refutation here? They (the Jews) suspected of fraud and even got soldiers to guard the tomb, so they know the Resurrection is genuine.

Next, Matthew narrates the story of finding the empty tomb and proclaiming Jesus' Resurrection, but on the other side of it is the second part of the sandwich, Matthew 28:11–15, the story of Jewish leaders bribing a soldier to say he fell asleep and the disciples stole the body. Again, this is probably not historical. The idea of a soldier starting a rumor of his own negligence is unlikely, and would earn him serious punishment. But it does link the Jews with the rumor that the body was stolen. What is really telling is v. 15: ". . . this story has been spread among the Jews to this day." In this aside, Matthew steps out of the narrative, saying that, in his time, Jews are arguing against the Resurrection, calling it a fraud and saying that the reason the tomb was empty was that the disciples stole Jesus' body. Matthew offers a refutation of their argument (the Resurrection) and an explanation of how it got started (they bribed the soldier to start a false rumor).

Some decades later, an apocryphal work called the *Gospel of Peter* elaborates considerably on the theme of Jews and the issue of the Resurrection. All the details contrive to show that the Resurrection happened, that the Jews saw it, and that they intentionally suppress reports of it. One scholar calls this *fail-safe apologetic*.[2]

Justin, too, cites the story of Jews claiming the body was stolen and the Resurrection being faked by the disciples. He may simply be repeating Matthew, but he also brings a large number of quotations from Scripture to prove the Resurrection, implying that it is still a live point of debate with Jews such as his opponent Trypho. This is quite imaginable. If one group claims its leader rose from the dead and the tomb was empty, and the other group does not believe it, a logical claim would be "someone moved the body."

Politics

The Holy See's document continues: "In the pagan Roman Empire, Jews were legally protected by the privileges granted by the emperor, and the authorities at first made no distinction between Jewish and Christian communities." The document reminds us that relations between believers in Jesus and Jews did not take place in a vacuum. Neither side had much power. Rather, events played themselves out within a triangle: Jews, Romans, and the local (often gentile) populace. People who belonged to the Greco-Roman religions (or pagans) were generally ambivalent about Jews. The Romans especially were quite proper and conservative, and had a strong sense of "family values." Jews, they thought, were superstitious, had odd customs, were lazy for abstaining from work once a week, worshipped an ass's head, were a motley band of slaves, xenophobic, lecherous, and had too many children.³ Readers will recognize how many of these slurs remain part of the language of racism and anti-Semitism to this day.

The Roman historian Tacitus says of Jews: ". . . they scorn the gods, cast off their native country" (*Hist.* 5.1–13). They are unpatriotic. The Romans distrusted anyone who did not worship the gods of the Roman pantheon (sometimes including the deified emperor) and regularly made offerings to the gods and the "genius" (spirit) of the emperor. Neither Jews nor Christians could do this, because it is a form of idolatry. But from the Roman point of view, it was unpatriotic, equivalent to someone today who refuses to say the pledge of allegiance or sing the "Star-Spangled Banner." Jews are accused of atheism by some writers because they do not acknowledge the divinity of the emperor and the Roman gods. In a society where religion and the state are joined, this is equivalent to treason. Later, people will accuse Christians of the same crimes. But Jews had two advantages that Christians did not:

1) They had the defense of antiquity, as even Tacitus admits. Pagans respected things that were old, that were traditional. So, although Jews had odd customs, they were *ancient* odd customs and they had learned them from their ancestors.

2) Jews had a semi-legal status. From the time of Julius Caesar, they were exempt from worship and sacrifice for the gods, and from military service. They had the right of assembly. They were the only group in the empire with these privileges. Jews were also allowed to meet for worship.

So Jews had certain privileges from the Roman government that they wanted to hang on to. These were *ad hoc* privileges that could be rescinded at any time, however—and, in fact, were. Jews experienced several expulsions from Rome, e.g., in 139 B.C.E., and in 19 C.E. under Tiberius, who later ceded the running of the empire to the military leader Sejanus. Sejanus is credited with an anti-Semitic policy aimed at no less than the complete extermination of the Jews. Twenty years later (39–40), the mad emperor Gaius Caligula, who declared both himself and his horse divine, became annoyed with the Jews and ordered the Jerusalem Temple to be turned into a shrine to the imperial cult, with a statue of himself as Jupiter positioned in the Holy of Holies. The orders were never carried out, thanks to intervention by the provincial governor, but it was a close call. Within a decade, the emperor Claudius did expel the Jews from Rome.

So, although they had privileges, the Jews could not take those privileges for granted. Because many Jews no doubt were anxious to preserve the peace and keep a low profile, they would have dissociated themselves from politically dangerous, upstart movements, such as the Zealots, the anti-Roman revolutionaries, or another questionable group that revered their dead leader—a man who preached a different kingdom, a man crucified by the Romans as a political threat. Some Jews may have been anxious to distance themselves, thus making clear that they had nothing to do with those trouble-makers, the Christians.

One of the ways to deal with problems of anti-Judaism in early Christianity has been to "blame the Romans"—for everything. Some imply it was merely the oppressive situation created by the Roman presence that drove everyone to act out of fear and self-preservation. Its corollary has been to "blame the pagans" for anti-Judaism, to argue that gentile Christians carried on a legacy of anti-Judaism that they inherited from their pagan past. Theology was used to whitewash and justify an already present antagonism. John Meagher wrote an article along these lines in the Davies volume *Anti-Semitism and the Foundations of Christianity*.[4] The question of the relative admiration or dislike of Jews by the Greco-Roman world is still under discussion. Louis Feldman wrote a book a few years ago suggesting Jews were, relatively speaking, more admired than hated by pagans.[5] But it is doubtful that anyone, including these scholars, thinks this will solve the problem of Christian anti-Judaism.

Now, to consider the last quote from the Holy See's document on early Jewish-Christian relations, from John Paul II himself: "In the Christian world—I do not say on the part of the Church itself—erroneous and unjust interpretations of the New Testament regarding the Jewish people and their alleged culpability have circulated for too long, engendering feelings of hostility towards this people."

Here is the rub, really. Hostile statements against certain groups of Jews engendered by communities in the painful process of pulling apart are first frozen in time and cut off from their historical moorings, and are then elevated to the status of Scripture. A common scholarly solution has been to focus on the intention of the author and explain his perspective and context. Luke Johnson wrote a very influential article in the *Journal of Biblical Literature* a decade ago, where he shows that, relative to the polemic of other Jewish groups talking about each other in the first century, the anti-Jewish parts of the New Testament are fairly mild.[6] Similarly, the volume by Evans and Hagner, *Anti-Semitism and Early Christianity* (Minneapolis: Fortress, 1993), focuses on the context and intentions of the authors of the New Testament. Looking only at intention, it is fairly easy to exonerate the New Testament writers of the charge of anti-Semitism or anti-Judaism. Looking at the passage in John 8, for example, where Jesus tells the Jews that they are of their father, the devil, few notice that he is talking to Jews who believed in him. So these are not Jewish outsiders, but people who believe in Jesus, although their faith is inadequate in John's eyes. We can usually contextualize any of these passages to explain away apparent anti-Judaism. But the problem is not the intention of the author; rather, the problem is the effect of the words. They took on a life of their own once they became Scripture. In this way, they become not expressions of hostility against particular Jews, but bearers of generalized anti-Semitism.

At the root of anti-Semitism, racism, and homophobia is the ability to see a group of people as other, as a despised profile, as people who do not possess the same feelings. When we hear about the death by dragging in Jasper, Texas, or the gay student beaten and left to die in Wyoming (and a whole host of similar incidents, chronicled in a recent editorial by Bob Herbert in the *New York Times*), it is hard to fathom how anyone could so ignore the humanity of their victims, see them as so unlike themselves. When we consider how Jews were demonized, we see that certain words, phrases, and disembodied

ideas about them have been kept alive in the culture, in part because they have
the seeming authority of being part of Scripture. The two most pernicious
ideas are: first, those of Jews as Christ-killers, generalized from the part
played by the high priest and the authorities in Jesus' arrest and the Jewish
trial in the gospels (and much ink has flowed evaluating the relative historical value of this material) and the crowd's self-curse, "His blood be upon us
and our children" in Matthew 27:25; and second, the picture of the Jews as
children of the devil in John 8:44. How limited these references are, and how
easy to explain in their historical context.

Four Issues

But the images endured, because as the gap between believers in Jesus
and Jews widened, hostility between the groups grew, fueled by four subtler
issues. The hostility calcified because of these issues, these problems that
would not go away as long as Jews and Christians lived in proximity, and they
set the stage for late antiquity and the Middle Ages.

First, there is the problem of Israel's "no" to Jesus, or to the Christian
understanding of him. This Jesus, predicted by the Scriptures as the fulfillment of God's promises to Israel, is not recognized as such by Jews. Did God
not know this would happen? Did God make a mistake? Why did Israel not
accept Jesus? As early as the 50s, Paul sees that the mission to the Jews is a
failure, and he struggles with the problem in Romans 9–11. Interestingly, he
finds a way out of the problem that is not anti-Jewish, which is why it is so
congenial to groups like ours. It is part of God's plan. Gentiles are the wild
branches grafted on to the root Israel: "Remember it is not you that supports
the root, but the root that supports you" (see Romans 11:18). Acts struggles
with the problem of Israel's "no" in a less pleasing way, and three times Luke
has Paul "give up" on the Jews and twice cite Isaiah against them and their
hard-heartedness (see Acts 13:46–47; 18:5–6; 28:25–27). Our friend
Barnabas is typical—Jews had the covenant but lost it, or they were influenced by the devil, or they were never meant to have it. He says all three. As
long as Jews are around, their existence is an unspoken, living critique of
Christian interpretation of history and the Hebrew Scriptures. Jews possess

the same Scripture and claim to be the continuation of biblical Israel, but do not accept the Christian reading of history. Often the way out of this dilemma is an anti-Jewish reading of Scripture and events, such as in *Barnabas*. Jews are under the sway of the devil, they are blind, hard-hearted, lying, and their subsequent sufferings, from 70 on, are punishment for their refusal of Jesus.

Second looms the problem of "Whose book is it?" Who rightly inherits and understands Israel's Scriptures, the Hebrew Bible or Old Testament? Who benefits from its promises? Who can use its symbols and heroes—the Exodus, the Passover sacrifice, the Akedah, Abraham, Moses? What about its many commandments? Are circumcision and food laws still in force? Is the Church's gentile constituency responsible for them? While in the New Testament there are disputes between Jesus and Pharisees over *how to* interpret and observe the commandments, by the middle of the second century, the Jew Trypho chides Justin Martyr: "Why are you ignoring the commandments?" If you are the true Israel, why are you not performing God's commands to Israel—circumcision and Sabbath on the seventh day and dietary laws? Often these challenges were explained away with allegory and symbolic language, such as "God meant circumcision of the heart." Paul provided a way out. But another way out was to see these commandments in a negative way, as God's punishment of the Jews. Christians could not simply get rid of the Hebrew Scriptures (although some like Marcion tried). They needed to hang on to them, because a) the belief that Jesus is predicted by Scripture is at the heart of Christian faith (his life and death fulfill the Torah and the Prophets), and b) they needed to prove themselves an ancient religion. They needed the antiquity of Scripture, especially when dealing with the Romans, and they had to plug into that ancient tradition for its respectability. Fairly early, of course, some Christians claim, "We are the true Israel" (Justin is the first, but the claim is implicit in Paul and Matthew). So, Christians claimed, the Old Testament, with its covenant, history, heroes, and symbols, is now really ours. Jews, for their part, however, were not done using it. They had their own understanding of its symbols, heroes, and events, which did not include Jesus. So by their existence, Jews are an annoying reminder that there is another way to interpret this book.

Third, Christians had to contend with the relative respectability, antiquity, and numbers of the Jews. Estimates vary, but S. Baron and R. Wilken put the numbers of Jews in the Mediterranean world in the first two centuries at four to six million of the sixty million, or one in ten. The number of Christians was much smaller, and even harder to calculate; Stephen Wilson estimates about 110,000 to 250,000.[7] In any case, they would be a small minority. As for the Jews, for all that some Greco-Roman writers thought them peculiar, the pagans respected things that were old, and the Jews were an ancient people. The pagan Celsus, for example, thought Jews and Christians both inferior to those who espoused the timeless truths of Plato. But Jews, he says, at least have the merit of being traditional. Their peculiar customs are at least ones learned from their ancestors. He chides Christians for departing from the traditional ways of the Jews, while claiming to be their inheritors (*Against Celsus* 2.1–4; 5.33). Thanks to their good relations with Julius Caesar, Jews enjoyed some privileges in the empire—the right of assembly, exemption from military service, exemption from sacrifice to the emperor. In Acts, Luke seems to want to borrow the respectability and antiquity of the Jews and claim it for Christians as the authentic inheritors of biblical Israel. Jews, having experienced expulsions and local violence in some places, probably recognized how quickly such favors could evaporate and would not want a suspicious group like the Christians upsetting the social situation.

Last, the attractiveness of Judaism and Judaizing was an ever-present irritant. Synagogues were not secret societies. It is clear from the presence of "God-fearers" in synagogue inscriptions and references in Acts that gentiles could go to them and feel at home, and even contribute money to them. Gentile Christians were attracted to Jewish ritual, holidays, and customs as early as Paul's time. He has to talk the Galatians out of circumcising themselves. At the turn of the second century, Ignatius complains about those who preach Jesus Christ and practice Judaism at the same time (*Epistle to the Smyrnaeans* 5.1; *Epistle to the Magnesians* 8.1, 9.1, 10.3; *Epistle to the Philadelphians* 6.1, 8.2). Tertullian warns against practicing ritual immersion like the Jews, saying Christians are baptized once, but Jews have to immerse every day because they are every day defiled (*On Baptism* 15.3; CCSL 1.29).

The most dramatic is John Chrysostom in fourth-century Antioch, who complains about gullible women lured into the synagogue and his congregants celebrating Sabbath and holidays and how vile it all is. Most scholars agree with W. Meeks and R. Wilken, however,[8] that his congregants were attracted to synagogue worship and Jewish practices. A good deal of anti-Jewish material springs from a need to discourage Christians from taking on Jewish practices and congregating around the synagogues. People are particularly edgy when the boundaries are blurred between Judaism and Christianity, even in our own day.

These issues stayed in place, no doubt even when the tide turned for Christians with Constantine in 312. The turnabout was quite sudden. Diocletian had signed an edict outlawing Christianity in 303, which was followed by a severe persecution of Christians. As late as 311–312, Eusebius reports being an eyewitness as Christians are martyred in Egypt. Then in 312, Constantine signed the edict of toleration, and Christians found themselves in the unaccustomed position of power. Christians must have had the same feelings and problems with Jews. What then, to do with these Jews?

There are several routes that might be taken. One, suggested by Ambrose, bishop of Milan, is to extend to Jews the same treatment as to heretics. He chides the emperor for ordering the local bishop to rebuild a synagogue in Asia destroyed by anti-Jewish riots (in 388), because the synagogue is "a place of unbelief, a home of insanity, which God himself has condemned" (*Epistles* 40–41). And he says, although he himself has not yet burned down the synagogue in Milan, it would not be a bad idea.

It was Augustine who argued that the problem of continued Jewish existence was not a problem. He turns these four issues of Jewish presence and alternative history inside out. For one thing, Jews are continuing witnesses to the antiquity and authenticity of the Hebrew Scriptures, therefore to the antiquity and respectability of Christianity, which claims those Scriptures as its own. In arguments with pagans that Christianity is an upstart, an innovation, Christians can use the Jews as witness to their antiquity. They can trade on the antiquity and respectability of the Jews. Even after Constantine, Greco-Roman religion was alive and well. Augustine's own father was a pagan. Christians were still looking over their shoulders at the Greco-Roman world.

Second, Augustine says that Jews are living proof of what happens to a people who refuse Jesus. Their suffering and exile from their land is proof that they do not enjoy God's favor. He compares them to the biblical Cain, who, on the one hand, was permanently cursed, but on the other had, was under God's protection. The mark of Cain is circumcision, and these Jews, who killed their brother, Jesus, were to wander as fugitives on the earth, but like Cain, they were not to be killed.[9] This is hardly acceptable theology to us today, but you can see how Augustine is responding to these same four issues: the shared Scripture, the antiquity of the Jews, the problem of Israel's "no," and perhaps even the attractiveness of Judaism. For his theology to work, Jews must remain suffering and subordinate, but they must remain.

The principle behind all of this is that the problems between Jews and Christians stemmed from the fact that we two communities are too alike—and we are too different. That is where the pain and hostility come in. We share a Scripture, symbols, heroes, and ideas of God acting in history, but what we do with them is so different. Christians articulated a very sophisticated understanding of Israel's history and appropriated her Scripture, but Jews felt a certain, "wait a minute, we're still using it," and besides, "we were here first."[10]

I end with a question. Here with this consultation and with the readers of this volume, I am speaking to the already converted. I expect we are all the descendants of those anonymous people in *Barnabas* who argue for the dual covenant. But how does this work in the congregations and classrooms? Not everyone has the privilege or inclination to spend years studying these texts. How do we take advantage of the "teachable moments" in our worship and classes to articulate this ancient idea, "the covenant is both ours and theirs"?

NOTES

1. See my article, "You Invent a Christ!: Christological Claims as Points of Jewish/Christian Dispute," *Union Seminary Quarterly Review* 44 (1991), 315–328.
2. W. L. Craig, "The Guard at the Tomb," *New Testament Studies* 30 (1984), 273–281.
3. For a useful gathering of Greco-Roman writers' attitudes towards Jews and Judaism, see M. Whittaker, *Jews and Christians: Graeco-Roman Views* (Cambridge: Cambridge University, 1984) or M. Stern, *Greek and Latin Authors on Jews and Judaism,* 2 vols (Jerusalem: Israel Academy of Sciences and Humanities, 1974, 1980).
4. *Anti-Semitism and the Foundations of Christianity*, ed. A. Davies (New York: Paulist, 1979), 1–26.
5. L. Feldman, *Jew and Gentile in the Ancient World* (Princeton: Princeton University, 1992).
6. L. Johnson, "The New Testament Anti-Jewish Slander and the Conventions of Ancient Polemic," *Journal of Biblical Literature* 108 (1989), 419–441.
7. These estimates appear in S. Wilson, *Related Strangers* (Minneapolis: Fortress, 1995), 21.
8. W. Meeks and R. Wilken, *Jews and Christians in Antioch in the First Four Centuries of the Common Era,* SBLSBS 13 (Missoula: Scholars Press, 1978).
9. See the excellent discussion of Augustine in M. Saperstein, *Moments of Crisis in Jewish-Christian Relations* (Philadelphia: Trinity, 1989), 9–11.
10. Islam, by contrast, did not create the same problems. There is much debate about this, too, but many argue that Jews fared much better under Muslim rulers in Spain than in medieval Christian Europe. Mark Cohen's book *Under Crescent and Cross* (Princeton: Princeton University, 1994) talks about many reasons for this: the founder of Islam dies a natural death leaving no one to blame; there was no iconographic tradition in Islam to carry negative images of the Jews as in the Christian

world; there was no hostile Roman enemy to placate; it was not a creedal religion, so there was no refusal to explain. Islam did not claim to be the new Israel, did not borrow the idea of a Messiah, and did not tamper with the idea of God's divinity. Although it incorporated Israel's Scripture, heroes, and history into its theology, it did not try to replace Israel. So it did not attempt to outwit the Jews at their own theology. Hence, there was less friction, although Cohen counsels us not to think of Jews under Islam as a utopia.

4

The Church as Sacrament and as Institution:
Responsibility and Apology in Ecclesial Documents
ROBERT J. SCHREITER

One of the neuralgic points for many in the *We Remember* document has been the distinction that was drawn between the Church as institution and the membership of the Church regarding guilt for actions taken in the past or attitudes held, whether in the past or in the present. By making this kind of distinction between the institution and its members, the impression can be given that only individuals were responsible for past actions, and that it was not institutional policy that prompted the actions or failure to act. Here are a number of the citations from the document where this issue arises:

> . . . in the Christian world—I do not say on the part of the church as such—erroneous and unjust inter-pretations of the New Testament regarding the Jewish people and their alleged culpability have cir-culated for too long, engendering feelings of hostility toward this people.

> We deeply regret the errors and failures of those sons and daughters of the church. We make our own what is said in the Second Vatican Council's declaration *Nostra Aetate*, which unequivocally affirms: "The church . . . mindful of her common patrimony with the Jews and motivated by the Gospel's spiritual love and by no political considerations, deplores the hatred, persecutions and displays of anti-Semitism directed against the Jews at any time and from any source."

The Catholic Church therefore repudiates every persecution against a people or human group anywhere.

Looking to the future of relations between Jews and Christians, in the first place we appeal to our Catholic brothers and sisters to renew the awareness of the Hebrew roots of their faith.

At the end of this millennium the Catholic Church desires to express her deep sorrow for the failures of her sons and daughters in every age. This is an act of repentance (*teshuva*), since as members of the church we are linked to the sins as well as the merits of all her children. The church approaches with deep respect and great compassion the experience of extermination, the *Shoah*, suffered by the Jewish people during World War II. It is not a matter of mere words, but indeed of binding commitment.

We Remember has been criticized in some quarters for what appears to be an oscillation between speaking on behalf of the entire Catholic Church, on the one hand, in accepting guilt and pledging repentance for things done and not done during the *Shoah*, and making a distinction, on the other hand, between the Church itself and the acts of its membership (typically referring to its "sons and daughters"), thereby seemingly distancing itself from responsibility. What is involved here is a thicket of issues—representing historical, theological, and cultural matters—that requires a sorting out. The purpose of this sorting out is not to defend or exonerate any position as much as it is to try to get at the various elements that crosshatch here within the document. Without some understanding of these, it becomes impossible to address them in such a way that will be constructive for discussions now about this document, and any future directions we might hope to suggest.

Let me treat each of these elements in turn: historical, theological, and cultural. These cannot be separated entirely one from another, but for the sake of analysis and argument, it is important to see what each of these elements contributes to the larger picture.

Historical Elements

Understandings of the Church have never developed in a vacuum. The self-understandings of the Church, expressed in full-blown theologies of the Church, date from the sixteenth century, from the time of the split within the Western Church between Catholics and Protestants. They first appear, therefore, in a polemical context. The debate at that time was about who represented the true Church of Christ as handed down from the apostles. In that dispute, Robert Bellarmine, the first head of the department which in our times is known as the Congregation of the Doctrine of the Faith, developed a polemical understanding of the Church as the *societas perfecta*, the Church as the perfect society that mirrored the realization of the reign of God in heaven.[1] It was first directed at the proliferation of ecclesial bodies in the Reformation, maintaining that the true Church of Christ was one and perfect, not the creation of human beings. Later, it was also directed at the emerging absolute monarchies and later the nation-states of post-Westphalian Europe. The states of Europe, after the Reformation, no longer accepted the tutelage of the Church, and were acting more independently. By emphasizing that the Church represented the perfect society, the Church hoped to maintain some preeminence over the political powers. Its hierarchical structure stood as a countersign to the formations of political entities in Europe—from absolute monarchies, through nation-states, to various forms of (or aspirations to) republicanism in the nineteenth century, and finally to the democratic nations of the early twentieth century.

The emphasis on the *perfect* society made it next to impossible to admit any change in the order of the Church as it was presented. Moreover, it necessarily required a distinction between the Church itself and the foibles and vicissitudes in the behavior of its membership.

At another level, the description of the Church as a perfect society legitimated a certain isolation from the world, which was imperfect and changing. Such a distancing from the world made possible detachment from political events and social movements that might be seen as contaminating the purity of the Church.

Reform movements within the Church in the twentieth century sought alternative understandings of the Church in order to allow a more direct engagement with the world. In order to do so, the impasse created by the image of the Church as the perfect society had to be broken through. The image that was able to effect this was that of the Church as the Body of Christ.

Before looking at the image of the Church as the Body of Christ, we can reflect on how this historical inheritance would have contributed to the inertia that kept the Church from taking action on behalf of the Jews during the Second World War, and why it can make the distinction between the Church as institution and the Church in its membership. If the Church as perfect society saw itself set against the world, then what happens in the world is not seen as its immediate concern. Nonetheless, as an institution in the world, the Church must have some way of expressing its engagement in the world. The distinction between the Church in itself and the Church's membership provides a way of doing that. One must remember also that the Catholic Church (as does the Orthodox Church) does not see itself as a human institution, but as something divinely instituted. The Church, therefore, is always more than the sum of its membership. To understand this more clearly, we now move to the theological elements that enter into this discussion.

Theological Elements

The theological understanding of the Church always takes precedent over a sociological or historical understanding of it, at least for Catholics and Orthodox. Protestants would come out at a variety of different places on this topic. Catholics believe that the Church was not an accidental outgrowth of the movement which grew up around Jesus of Nazareth. It is something directly willed by Christ, and related to Christ in a special way. This relation of Christ and the Church already in the New Testament is imagined in a variety of ways. Exegetes have noted a host of images that were presented in those documents—some ninety-six such images in all.

An especially strong one is that of the Body of Christ, as found especially in the writings of Paul and addressed to communities that had not known Christ when he was alive on earth (see especially 1 Corinthians 12). The members of the Church are seen as constituting the Body of Christ on earth, with Christ as the head of the body.

Christians believe that, although Jesus Christ is no longer physically present among believers, he nonetheless exercises a presence among them in a variety of ways. For example, already in the formative period of the first century C.E., the pneumatic presence of Christ in the believing community exercised a special role. Exegetes believe that many of the *ego eimi* or "I am" sayings found in the Gospel represent spirit-filled testimonies of early believers that were indeed the words of Christ himself expressed through the words of believers.

The Body of Christ was, therefore, the entire Church as Christ's visible presence on earth. It was also to be found in the eucharistic elements of bread and wine, which Christ had designated as his body and his blood. The symbol of the Body of Christ, the *corpus Christi*, is therefore polyvalent for Christians.

As this was developed in subsequent history, the *corpus Christi* took on additional forms. The eucharistic elements of bread and wine also bespoke a presence of Christ in the believing community. In early figures such as Ambrose, those elements represented the *corpus mysticum* of Christ, while the assembled community was the *corpus verum* or *corpus reale* of Christ.

In the European Middle Ages, the referent of this distinction between *corpus mysticum* and *corpus reale* or *corpus verum* was reversed: the Eucharist became the *corpus reale* and the Church became the *corpus mysticum*. Two factors figured into this. One was the controversies about the nature of the presence of Christ in the eucharistic elements. To emphasize his genuine presence, *corpus reale* seemed more appropriate than the less specific *corpus mysticum*. The other was the emerging of the political order as separate from the ecclesiastical order—the body politic, if you will. The assembled people became the *corpus mysticum*, and the eucharistic elements became the *corpus verum* or *reale*.

The image of the Church as the mystical body was revived in the nineteenth century by German theologian Johann Adam Möhler (1796–1838), who sought to develop a theology of the Church more dynamic than that of the perfect society. Möhler's theology connoted an organic rather than a structured image of the Church. The image of the Church as the mystical body of Christ became increasingly influential among theologians in the twentieth century (see especially the work of Henri de Lubac), and in the emerging Catholic Action movements in France and Belgium, and later in Latin America of that period. The image received official sanction in Pope Pius XII's encyclical *Mystici Corporis* in 1943, and had direct influence on the theology of the Church developed during the Second Vatican Council.

The great advantage of the image of the mystical body was its dynamism over the more static view of the perfect society. The difficulty of the image was that it was a *mystical* body. In the work of such persons as the French philosopher Jacques Maritain, it came to represent a Church that hovered above the messy give and take of politics. In a recent study, William Cavanaugh has shown how a theology of the Church as the mystical body actually impeded the Church in places like Chile from responding to the crimes committed under the Pinochet dictatorship.[2]

I note especially the theology of the Church as the mystical body, because it dominated progressive understandings of the Church through the 1930s and 1940s, culminating in the 1943 encyclical of Pius XII by that name. While it was intended to correct the more static notion of the Church as a perfect society, it also helped create an image of the Church as beyond the immediate immersion in what we call the political realm. It is no longer the predominant image of the Church among Roman Catholics today, but it was formative for many who now exercise leadership.

The Second Vatican Council put forward another set of images, again addressing the nature of the presence of Christ within the Church. These were based on the notion of *sacrament*, that is to say, the analogical presence of Christ amid the believers. The Church acts on Christ's behalf, and can serve as a mediator of God's grace to the world. It has therefore a profound identi-fication with Christ, yet is separate from him. Most striking in the dogmatic constitution of the Church *Lumen Gentium* was that of the Church as *sacramentum mundi*, sacrament of and to the world, that is to say, a special presence of Christ to the world. This is expressed in a special way in the Church as the sacrament of the unity of humankind—the unity within the Church is the foretaste of the unity intended for all humankind. The significance of the use of sacrament is that it underscores the holiness of the Church because of the presence of its Lord, yet leaves room for the Church's engagement in the concrete world and its affairs.

Like the image of the Church as mystical body, the Church as sacrament has both positive and negative dimensions. Positively, it allows Christians to speak of how Christ continues to be truly present among his followers. Negatively, the mediation of the Church of Christ's presence can lead to conflating Christ and the Church. The sinlessness of Christ becomes the sinlessness of the Church, since it must be an adequate and appropriate medium for Christ's presence. This leads to the oscillation between the Church as such, and the Church in its membership that we find reflected in *We Remember*.[3]

What we find in *We Remember* is a combination of a theology of the Church as mystical body and as sacrament, with the positive and negative elements of these two theologies. This allows for a distinction between the Church itself, as the mystical and sacramental presence of Christ on earth, itself a holy and sinless reality, and the Church's membership of men and women, who are sinful and fail in significant ways—in this instance, with regard to the Holocaust. While this may make theological sense to those within the Church, and protect the sinless mediation of Christ's presence from the sinful acts of members of the Church, it is not immediately apparent to others who hear pronouncements made from this perspective. One could argue that such lines of thinking are inappropriate in documents intended for or directed to audiences outside the Church community, precisely because of the likelihood of this misunderstanding. At the very least, some commentary would need to be given.

Cultural Elements

Along with the historical and theological elements just mentioned, one should note some cultural elements that figure into a document such as *We Remember*. While the Catholic Church claims a certain universality throughout the world, its center is in the Mediterranean. Local cultural elements perhaps should not be immediately evident in the documents it produces, but they are nonetheless there. English, French, or Spanish may be the major languages among Catholics, but Italian is spoken in the Vatican. And language has its anchor in culture.

Mediterranean culture has remained a strongly collectivist culture, even under the pressure of modernization. This means that the group has priority over the individual, and the honor and "face" of the group is something every individual is bound to maintain. Individuals may err, but the collective "face" of the group has to be upheld at all costs. In contemporary Italian society, one still speaks of the *bella figura*, collective face which needs to be maintained in spite of individual failings.

The Roman Curia has been internationalized in its membership, but the cultural context is still strongly Italian. The distinction between the sinless Church and the sins of its members is understandable within such a cultural context. Others have noted, too, the frequent use of passive or reflexive verbs in the text. This is a common feature in Italian (and all Romance languages, for that matter). That this usage shows up in English translations may simply represent a too literal rendering of Italian grammatical forms.

This cultural element, again, does not excuse or exonerate the position *We Remember* takes regarding the Church's responsibility for its actions and inaction during the Holocaust. It only explains why such a position might be possible.

Conclusion

The historical, theological, and cultural elements discussed here help us see some of the dynamics that may have gone into the formulation of key points in the *We Remember* document. The explanation does not excuse or condone these usages. In view of the intended audiences of this document—and especially the reception of the document—the question can be raised whether these points about the Church's responsibility should have been formulated in this fashion. It is only hoped that what has been presented here will at least help clarify some of the circumstances under which the document was written, and help in the continuing dialogue about what the document hoped to say.

Notes

1. For a brief overview of this concept, see Avery Dulles, *Models of the Church* (New York: Doubleday, 1974).
2. William T. Cavanaugh, *Torture and Eucharist* (Oxford: Basil Blackwell, 1998).
3. A further development of these theological ideas may be found in an essay that appeared after this presentation: Bradford E. Hinze, "Ecclesial Repentance and the Demands of Dialogue," *Theological Studies* 61 (2000), 207–238.

5

The Church as Sacrament and as Institution:
Jewish Reflections
RABBI IRVING GREENBERG

I personally am "Exhibit A" of the impact of the Holocaust on religious thinking. In 1962, I came back from Jerusalem, after my first year of total immersion in the topic of the Holocaust, not only shattered religiously but also outraged and full of anger and fear. I was angry at Christianity for having set up my family, myself, and my children for such persecution.

On my mother's side, my siblings and I are four out of a family of thirty-plus cousins. There are six cousins alive, the four of us and two descendants of my mother's brother who went to Mexico before the Holocaust. The families of my mother's four brothers who stayed in Poland were wiped out. Reading the record of the *Shoah*, I personally felt extremely threatened and imagined similar outrages inflicted on my children and grandchildren in the future. These emotions drove me to the Jewish-Christian dialogue.

I came with a demand to Christians to stop purveying the negative images that created this ring of hatred around Jews. Then came one of the lucky breaks of my life: I met people like Roy and Alice Eckardt, John Pawlikowski, Eva Fleischner, Franklin Littell, and others. Not only were they ready to listen to my concerns, but their integrity and their ability to self-criticize and confront the problem were greater than mine.

After the first rush of anger came pouring out and I was finished with it, it dawned upon me that these Christians were religiously extraordinary; as our connection deepened, their ethics and liturgical life won my admiration. Furthermore, they were truly listening. Far from rejecting my rebukes, they did much more than turn the other cheek (a Christian idea that I had made fun of in my earlier days). They outdistanced me in the profundity of their self-examination. Eventually, I grasped that only an incredible religion could generate such prophetic self-critique. To paraphrase the famous Oliver Goldsmith line, I came to scold and stayed to praise. Ultimately, I came to realize that Christianity really was a gospel of love; unfortunately, the Jews had no way of knowing this because Christians had not acted toward them with love. Rather, they treated Jews with hatred and contempt. Still, to the billions of humans who received the Christian teaching of God's love, the experience was tremendously moving. As Christianity moved away from its past position of purveying dismissal and hostility toward Jews, I was able to see it in greater perspective as a source of love for the world.

I also came to see how cunningly the contempt for Jews legitimated unchristian behavior in Christians. This summoned up a Hasidic story, which the founder of the movement the Ba'al Shem Tov was reputed to have told. When Hasidism started, it was a tremendous source of religious vitality and redemption. Naturally, Satan fought Hasidism bitterly because he foresaw that this movement would bring redemption and good religious values to many. After a while, when Satan realized that he could not stop the movement by opposing it, he joined Hasidism and became a Hasid; then he was able to undermine its message from within. I believe that, at first, the Satan of hatred fought Christianity but was losing the battle. Then he wised up and simply crept inside the gospel, where he could hide in this privileged sanctuary of hatred and from there lash out against the Jews and others.

But it is essential for Christianity's future, as a religion of redemption, that the hatred be removed. That is what *We Remember* is struggling to do. Jews have a stake in the Christian struggle to redeem Christianity and its message of love from the corrupting elements of bitter enmity. However, since the hatred has been subtle enough to penetrate the center of Christianity, removing it is no easy task. Some of the most contemptible images of Judaism are in the Gospels themselves. Challenging the Gospels is a heroic task, and the challenge will hardly be undertaken unless Christians are driven by an urgent sense of failure and yearning for repentance. To truly repent, however, involves confronting great figures of past history and coming to grips with vile behaviors by saints, popes, etc. The person of faith hesitates to face these issues head on—partly because they are painful, partly because believers fear they will undermine respect for the Christian tradition.

On the other hand, Christians who are sensitized to this issue know that the very future and credibility of Christianity is at stake. They also understand that Christianity will fail if it is not reborn. In the interim, they realize that Jesus and his family are Jews who could be (and are) victimized by the persecution of Jews. And Jews realize that if this moral purging does not succeed, Jews will be victimized again and again in the future. So, here is our common interest; just as you would like to get Jesus off the cross, I would like to get my grandchildren off the cross, or off the potential cross.

In this spirit, I approach the document *We Remember*, which profoundly reflects a remarkable Christian desire to confront the record by confession and repentance and overcome past sins. The strengths of *We Remember* are clear: its description of the *Shoah* and affirmation that this event demands new behavior from Christians; its acknowledgment of past Christian persecution of Jews; its raising the question of Christian responsibility for the *Shoah*; its condemnation of anti-Semitism and racism. *We Remember* also makes clear that the Catholic Church wants a new relationship with Jews and Judaism, and makes a serious commitment to pursue this goal.

At the same time, the declaration mirrors the deep ambivalence of Catholic leadership about such admissions, and the fear of unintentionally undermining Christianity's authority in the course of this self-examination. Surely this accounts for the evasions and euphemisms in the text. Thus the document stresses the distinction between anti-Judaism (which it implies is defensible or at least not reprehensible) and anti-Semitism (which it finds sinful). The contrast it makes is far too sharp because the two behaviors overlap repeatedly in history. Moreover, the text attributes the negative effects to erroneous interpretations of the New Testament; it cannot come to grips with the problem posed by the gospel Scriptures themselves. *We Remember* repeatedly portrays Pope Pius XII in a favorable light, embellishing his pro-Jewish efforts and softening, if not covering, his failures to take full responsibility to oppose the heinous murder campaign of the Nazis. Above all, the apologetic fear of undermining Christianity's authority drives the distinction the document seeks to make between sinful Christians and the transcending eternal, pure Church as a sacramental institution which can never be stained by any hatred or evil behavior, however sinful.

We Remember speaks with great integrity when it asks "whether the Nazi persecution of the Jews was not made easier by the anti-Jewish prejudices embedded in some Christian minds and hearts." (N.B. This is a very Jewish document; its questions are much better than its answers all the way through.) At the end, however, when it states that the Catholic Church desires to express her deep concerns for the failures of her sons and daughters in every age, many Jews reacted with criticism and suspicion. The phraseology seemed to exonerate the Church (or Christianity corporately) from failure or guilt and hence, of any responsibility for creating the penumbra of hatred for Jews within which more evil and virulent forms of anti-Semitism could root and grow. Jewish concern was deepened by the citation of Pope John Paul II's earlier speech: "In the Christian world, I do not say on the part of the Church as such, erroneous and unjust interpretations of the New Testament regarding the Jewish people and their alleged culpability have circulated for too long engendering feelings of hostility towards these people."[1] Again, many Jews asked: Is this an exculpation of the Church for its role, an attempt to whitewash the Scriptures and the Magisterium of their all-too-real responsibility for spreading such a hateful image of Jews and of their religion?

Actually, Cardinal Cassidy himself gave an important and helpful clarification of *We Remember* in his talk to the American Jewish Committee on May 15, 1998. There he said that the term *members of the Church* "can include according to circumstances, popes, cardinals, bishops, priests and the laity." This explanation is clearly intended to assure Jews that the document holds serious, important leaders of the Church responsible for Catholic Christian mistreatment of the Jews. On the other hand, Jews continue to worry that the placing of the Church above the fray and the guilt of history may result in weakening the urge to correct deeply enough to prevent future misbehavior. Cardinal Cassidy was unyielding on this point and told the American Jewish Committee that "for Catholics, the church is not just the members that belong to it, it is looked upon as the bride of Christ, the heavenly Jerusalem, holy and sinless." Regarding "the distinction between sinful members and a sinless church," Cardinal Cassidy said that "you may find it hard to understand but it is one which is essential to our understanding of the Church." It should be noted that not only Jews but Catholic commentators including Philip Cunningham in the Trinity College Center for the Study of Religion in Public Life panel discussion and Father John Pawlikowski's article "We Remember: Looking Back, Looking Ahead" (*The Month*, 33 (2000), 387) also expressed disappointment with this distinction.

One of the fundamental rules of dialogue is to understand the partner in his or her own terms, language, and concepts rather than fitting them into one's own categories, which all too often turn out to include stereotypes and negative concepts of the other faith, fueled by a hermeneutic of suspicion. Upon reflection, I conclude that the continuing criticisms that the Church is seeking to avoid admitting the truth i.e., by dismissing the distinction between admitting individual leaders' misbehavior and upholding the innocence of the sacramental Church, are too harsh. The cardinal's clarification is designed to place responsibility for the past on the shoulders of the leadership of the Church. Furthermore, the distinction between sinful individuals and leaders and pure community/people of God is found in Jewish sources as well. In particular, there is a significant Jewish analog to this distinction especially developed in the work of Rabbi Joseph D. Soloveitchik, the greatest theologian of modern Orthodoxy in twentieth-century America.

Knesset Yisrael

Soloveitchik writes extensively of *Knesset Yisrael*. I would translate the phrase *Knesset Yisrael* loosely as the Community or the Assembly of Israel. Literally, *Knesset Yisrael* means "the Gathering of Israel," which includes all the Jews who were, are, or will be members of the covenant of Israel. "This community," Soloveitchik writes, "is not a functional utilitarian one but an ontological one." "*Knesset Yisrael* is really a metaphysical entity, an individuality. I would say a living whole" (that is, above and beyond the individuals who make it up). "In particular," says Soloveitchik, "Judaism has stressed the wholeness and the unity of *Knesset Yisrael*, the Jewish community." (N.B.

Wholeness and unity is a Jewish way of saying that Judaism is transgenerational but also unmarked by human divisiveness. In other words, this mystical community, *Knesset Yisrael*, has no moral flaws; as a religion it is not tainted by human sins. Soloveitchik states, "It [*Knesset Yisrael*] is an autonomous entity endowed with a life of its own." He is annoyed by the implied reader who objects to this philosophical uplifting of Jewry into a timeless metaphysical entity. He remarks, "However strange such a concept may appear to the empirical sociologists, it is not at all a strange experience for the Halachist and the mystic for whom Knesset Yisrael is a living, loving and suffering mother."[2]

In a later essay, Soloveitchik writes that God "himself becomes a partner in this [mystical/covenantal] community. God is never outside of the covenantal community. He joins man and shares in his covenantal existence . . . they bind themselves together and participate in a unitive existence."[3] It would appear that both religions developed similar concepts, at least in part, to insulate their traditions from the stains of history. However, there is a cost for this theological transmogrification. I would like to explore the needs that this concept serves, as well as its spiritual and ethical costs. We can then consider whether the loss outweighs the gain.

The mystical community functions as a person, as a transgenerational individual who can accept and carry on the covenant of redemption. Liberals and others like myself are uneasy with this Mystical Body that is out of history. However, this concept validates precisely a multigenerational approach that deeply respects the human, because it removes the temptation to force redemption in one generation. Such a concept paves the way to accept the human rhythm of change. Humans do not quickly or easily give up familiar patterns and ways of living. One alternative, exhibited repeatedly in the twentieth century, is to declare all-out war on the *status quo* and on human recalcitrance, and to use violent pressure to force radical change at once. The alternative is to allow room for slower human change, to accept that it will take generations to improve the *status quo*. This very respect for the needs and expectations of humans means that the covenant goals will not be achieved in one generation. However, the passage of time generates the crisis of who will be responsible for the covenant in the next generation. Moreover, the multigenerational transmission raises the likelihood that, over time, there will arise laity and spiritual leaders who will engage in sinful behavior in a particular generation. This danger motivates church and synagogue to conceptualize such ideas as *Knesset Yisrael* and the *Mystical Body of the Church*—i.e. metaphysical entities that assume some responsibility for the covenant over the generations. The goal is that such "transcending" bodies assure standing and respect for the tradition even though its practitioners have been implicated in sin, crime, and persecution.

The existence of a metaphysical entity validates that the covenant is binding on future participants in real time. Otherwise, why would acceptance at Sinai (or the analogous experience of Jesus in the disciples' lifetime) bind or even meaningfully address later generations? *Knesset Yisrael*, the analog to the Mystical Body, assures that the binding force of the covenant does not die with the death of individual human beings. Furthermore, the concept also upholds the principle that no moral or spiritual failure by any generation, however catastrophic, will forfeit the covenant.

Remember this question of forfeiting the covenant, due to misbehavior, haunted Jews. The prophets and later religious leaders return again and again to the question of whether the sins of any one generation might have led to a withdrawal of the covenant altogether. Furthermore, this forfeiture of the covenant was the very claim that Christians made against Jewry. Of course the prophets' biting critique of particular (i.e. their) generations was the source of the very imagery that was so cruelly used against Jews in Christian polemics to undermine Jewry's religious legitimacy. So the *Knesset Yisrael* image protected against the supersessionist interpretation; it assured that no matter what the failures of the living, God's permanent relationship with Israel would not be broken. Such a conception may well be the mystical basis of Paul's affirmation (from his perspective) that the promises of Israel are never forfeited despite its rejection of a new revelation.

The paradigm of *Knesset Yisrael* also expresses the presence of a transcendental sign and meaning in the midst of revelation's incarnation in the very human body of community. The category allows the Word to become flesh or, in Jewish language: "that the covenant [is] sealed [i.e. 'carved'] in our flesh" without losing its sense of transcendent connection. Finally, the idea of *Knesset Yisrael* (or Mystical Body) reminds us of the divine dimension of religion which, however intermixed in the human, never loses its divine connection and its eternal character and ultimate authority.

Dealing with these crosscurrents of history are legitimate religious objectives for any religion. Religious liberals, of course, have it easier because they can repudiate the past record of misbehavior and/or failure more comfortably. Those, such as Orthodox Jews or Catholics, who are more bound by the authority of the past (which in no way is meant to imply that the past is absolute) have more difficulty struggling with this tension; hence, the legitimate and significant role of such models as *Knesset Yisrael*/Mystical Body. It is no accident, therefore, that there are strong religious parallels and articulations in our two traditions, albeit the Jewish paradigm is balanced differently, given the specifics of Jewish theology.

The application of the principle of understanding the dialogue partner in his or her own terms means that *We Remember* deserves the benefit of the doubt. The distinction between sinful individuals and pristine Church is legitimate—as long as it does not dull the Church's conscience or weaken its effort to correct the past misbehavior. Jews who assume the worst—or summon up past church attitudes to explain *We Remember* as if these teachings were not in the course of being seriously revised—are guilty of stereotyping and of "mocking the poor," i.e., putting down those who are trying to correct themselves. This is a grave sin in Jewish tradition. Jews should make clear to the Catholic Church that they appreciate the steps taken in *We Remember,* and that they will work with the Church to clear up the points of controversy (e.g., the evaluation of Pius XII's role and stature) that still remain.

Consequences

Having spoken so positively of the mystical concept of the Church and the synagogue, however, we must confront the cost of such an articulation. Any time one seeks to attain infinite truths and live them in finite lives (or encapsulate them in human institutions), there is always a trade-off. Whatever is included, something else is always left out—for finite humans are dealing with the infinite. The trade-off in this case is that the timeless model leads to less response in the here and now—and less responsiveness to the real world, in turn, translates into less ability to admit error or to articulate the justification/need for change. Finally, there is the danger of dualism, of splitting the world and the spirit—a behavior that all too often creeps into religions under the cover of such language. (Another variant of the spirit/world division is the human practitioners/mystical community dichotomy).

We Remember as a document wrestles with this persistent tension, a tension that exhibits itself in Judaic responses to history as well as Christian ones. In both cases, often unspoken, the driving force of this theological ambivalence is the deep fear that human practitioners of the faith will inevitably sin and fail. Indeed, there is recognition that they have already sinned and failed. In the very attempt to whitewash, there is a profound sense of unease with the painting over and the recognition of the deeper truth of the failures. Still, there is a profound, gripping fear that such admissions by the authorities, now living, will lead to the conclusion that the entire faith, religion, or community is implicated and responsible; therefore, this admission might invalidate the Magisterium (or, in Jewish terms, the authority of the Torah). There is a natural trepidation in taking responsibility for a covenant that is now multigenerational and whose future, until the Messiah finally comes, is in one's hands. In admitting past failures, contemporary authorities fear that they might break the authority that has guided the community along the way. Then they will have been guilty of wiping out all that is good; the sacrifices and achievements of all before this generation will be undermined by good intentions. So, in an act of love and reverence intended to shield the tradition, one blames those who have practiced the faith, thereby to glorify God and the Torah (or in Christian terms, the Magisterium). This can be compared to Rebecca's outburst in Genesis 27:13. She knows that Jacob deserves and should get the blessing, yet he is afraid to lie to his father lest he be detected. Out of an overwhelming sense of motherly love, Rebecca tells her son to steal the blessing: "My son, [I promise that] your curse [and punishment] will be on me."

One can only have reverence for a people who plead guilty to draw fire on themselves and away from God and the Torah (or the Magisterium). However, the price is (likely) failure to plumb the depths of the previous wrongdoing. It is hard to clear out an infection (especially of hatred) if there is not a total confession and purging. The softening of the problem, implicit in separating the institution from the guilt, encourages taking a path of least resistance in further efforts to purify the tradition. In the end, leaders are tempted to cling to the image of the perfect tradition; this weakens the capacity and the will to identify sin and error to overcome it.

An Alternate Model

Let us, then, explore an alternate model of dealing with the tension of admitting failure and upholding authority. The perfect model of authority is based ultimately on a Hellenistic ontology. (It is always good to blame someone who is not alive anymore as the bad source. It is an old Jewish trick against Christianity.) This model is based on an Aristotelian or a medieval conception that the definition of perfection is that which is unchanging. In this approach, God is the Unmoved Mover. Eternity, not temporality, is the criterion of the absolute. Today, the subtext of our culture is the opposite. In our scientific conception, the universe is long-lived, if not eternal, ceaselessly changing. There is a process continuity in everything; dynamism rather than being above time is the source of stability. The only permanence is change. The capacity for growth—rather than an untouched, undifferentiated perfection—is the definition of excellence and eternity. In every moment we are seeing the partial, the unfinished, the broken representation of the Divine. That flawed piece—as it were, broken off from infinity—is the presence of the Divine. To become fully incorporated in a human life as God wants it to be, the Torah must be incarnated in the living human community. In so doing, it must become flesh. Flesh by definition is subject to flaws and brokenness. Yet God loves humans, and, perforce, also the inevitable flaws and brokenness of the mortal. Humans should imitate God and embrace the sacredness of the broken and flawed.

Rabbi Israel Salanter, a nineteenth-century Jewish moralist and theologian, interprets the classical verse that "the Torah is not in heaven" (see Deuteronomy 30:12), widely cited in rabbinic literature, to mean that the Torah is given over by God to humans whose flaws and misjudgments will inevitably become part of the Torah by that very act of giving over. But this handing down is the will of God. Accepting these human intermixtures is the essence and spirit of the generous and unselfish love with which God gives revelation. When one gives something one loves to someone one loves, one does not hold the gift frozen in one's own image. Rather, one gives the precious gift to the other in categories and forms in which the beloved can absorb it. A Torah, still heavenly perfect, would be unlivable. Hence, the famous statement in Leviticus that the high priest purifies the Tent of Meeting on Yom Kippur. "Thus shall he do to the Tent of Meeting which *dwells with them in the midst of their impurities*" ([rabbinic emphasis], Leviticus 16:16). This is exactly the parallel insight that Christianity has sought to articulate in its incarnational theology. But if Christ is fully human as well as fully divine, then his Mystical Body must also be broken. Indeed, this is the truth that is signaled in the central symbol of Christian religion—of Jesus' broken body hanging on the cross.

As a Jew, I pause and apologize for projecting Christian theology. I realize that I may have run afoul of Rabbi Joseph D. Soloveitchik's warning that when one dialogue partner articulates theological categories for the other, the partner may interfere in or disrupt the private unique language of the other. Nevertheless, I permit myself to do so because I do not demand that Christians accept my interpretation. Also I repeat that I—that is to say all Jews—have a fundamental stake in Christianity. I believe in covenantal pluralism. God cannot achieve God's goals—and Jews cannot achieve Jewish goals—without Christianity's role in the mission, and vice versa. So we are partners in *Tikkun Olam* (world order). Partners have the right to make comments about each other's basic values. Furthermore, if God has called Christianity into existence, Jews want to help it cope with history because it is our desire, too, that God's will be done on earth as it is in heaven. We want

Christianity neither to be smashed by its past failures nor to continue with its misdeeds toward Jews.

Tzimtzum

In this spirit, I offer another classic Jewish model to guide judgment on reconciling sinfulness and authority: the classic Kabbalistic idea of *Tzimtzum*—of divine self-limitation. According to Lurianic Kabbalah, since the Divine Infinite is so overwhelming, it leaves no room for any other existence, let alone human existence. Therefore, the Infinite One seeks to shrink itself to make room for cosmic existence and, thereafter, for human existence. However, it is impossible to pour, i.e., to shrink the Divine Infinite into the limited, finite vessels of the universe and of human existence. This leads to the cosmic catastrophe that Lurianic Kabbalah calls *Shvirat HaKelim:* the breaking of the vessels. The finite vessels of the world cannot contain the infinite force of the Divine and love. Therefore they blow apart, scattering matter and scrambling divine sparks, physical matter, holiness, and impurity everywhere. This vision means that all finite existence is inescapably broken. Thus, evil and good are intertwined; they must be separated (and the good strengthened) and the original wholeness restored in human religious activity. It follows that even revelation—and eternity, as it is present in the human world—is broken. The paradox is that the brokenness makes revelation more adequate to serve God's purpose; it's more suited and more able to sustain the human way that is also inevitably both finite and broken.

It follows that the goal of true perfection requires the brokenness of the Divine Torah (or in Christian terms, the Magisterium), otherwise the tradition is "unfit", i.e. too perfect and, therefore, unavailable in the human context. Believers with idolatrous tendencies will tend to deny any failures or errors in the system for fear that the confession connotes an admission of limitations. Our task is *tikkun*, to heal and correct this brokenness.

The first step toward healing is to acknowledge the presence of wounds and failure. Thus, in affirming the limits and partial nature of our categories in truth, we are bringing them into harmony with the cosmic forces, as they are now constituted. This is, in itself, an act of identifying with the Divine, and moves us away from idolatrous behavior. Idolatrous behavior typically involves taking our partial truths and making them absolute. Understanding this paves the way to assert even true beliefs and revealed values in ways that are more modest and respectful of others and their claims. Such a mindset reduces the chances that the propositions and values we admire are asserted in runaway fashion (for the sake of good) and thereby lead us into evil.

After all, *We Remember* is a reflection on the *Shoah*. Nothing could be more appropriate than to recognize our personal brokenness and our faith's (be it our Torah's or our Magisterium's) brokenness in the light of the *Shoah*. It follows that the attempts in *We Remember* to soften guilt are unnecessary and undesirable. The deeper the recognition of failure, the safer and the more effective will be the future performance of the Church.

The *Shoah* itself was made possible by the lack of limits, by unbroken, triumphant categories and modes of behavior. If the beginning of the techno-logical revolution had brought much blessing, then modem culture was con-vinced that fuller realization of technology could only bring an overflowing of blessings. In actual fact, the technology had outstripped the moral growth needed to control its use, thus enabling the extraordinary dimensions of the Nazi genocide. Bureaucracy is a source of order, productivity, equal treat-ment, and dependable processes in modern life. By acting without significant check in the destruction process and without the limits that inner or externally asserted values might have applied, bureaucrats carried out the mass murder successfully. Many other good qualities were perverted by their exponential extension. Thus, only a utopianist ideology without limit in its promises and claims could have driven such a radically evil policy to overcome the human revulsion and natural obstacles that would have normally blocked carrying out such monstrous evil.

The final solution and its machinery was the outcome of a *Gleichschaltung* policy that brought all elements of society—political, eco-nomic, institutional, and cultural—together in a focused way behind some core authority and value system. None of the principals involved had a sense of their own limits and of the principles' brokenness; nor, since power was centralized, could those ruling forces be challenged. Let us put this in classic theological terms. In establishing authority without limits, and in issuing the absolute commands that governed the war against the Jews, Nazism became idolatry. The definition of *idolatry* is that a partial (in many cases, a good, partial religion/system/faith) assumes the guise of being whole and unlimited—and thereby becomes unlimitedly evil. Thus we learn from the *Shoah* that all absolutes intertwined with humans—even divine ones, even good ones—must be reduced, must be made partial. One way of doing this is to break them; paradoxically, this breakup will make them sources of life and not death.

I would point out also that the key to resistance to the *Shoah* lay in the ability to set limits. The Nazis exploited people's hope to stay alive to co-opt people into the work of death. The capacity for resistance, both armed and spiritual—as people as varied as Abba Kover and Victor Frankl have argued—lay in the ability to put limits around the world the Nazis created. If the denizens of *l'univers concentrationnère* were able to link in their mind or in daily process to another universe, to see the limit of the Nazi world and its brokenness, they could identify and locate themselves in another universe of values. This could be a source of alternate judgment and, therefore, lead to resistance.

In another treatment of *We Remember*, Ronald Modras has referred to the principle "no statement, theological or otherwise, should be made that would not be credible in the presence of the burning children."[4] Whenever I think in those terms, when I see those children, I am broken. My theology is broken. My faith is broken. But that is the authentic response. The impact of the *Shoah* is to establish the brokenness of all religious worldviews and value systems. Internalizing the implications of the Holocaust inexorably leads to the recognition of the inescapable fragmentariness and essential limits of religious and ethical categories and explanatory paradigms. The one thing we know for sure is that a satisfactory or even a full resolution of the tormenting questions raised by the *Shoah*, in any direction, is wrong. It is almost certainly achieved by not taking some aspect of this surd sufficiently seriously. After the Holocaust, there should be no final solutions, not even theological. If one accepts that brokenness, the broken system recognizes that it is partial. Perhaps it sees itself as broken off from a larger whole and, for that reason, necessarily incomplete; or the brokenness may stem from flaws in the system/truth paradigm. Recognition of the failings is an important source of modesty and openness to others.

The concrete application of this recognition that all categories of meaning are broken after the Holocaust is obvious. It is less a matter of deciding whether the theist or atheist response is right. Rather, whatever one's position, one admits its limitations. It is only credible some of the time or with some people, and its truth does not refute the truth of polar positions. Under these circumstances, one willingly self-limits in recognition of the others—perceived not as the enemy necessarily, but as holding a complementary position, or as a corrective movement, or as a challenge that tests and purifies one's own position. The recognition that one's system is partial and flawed frees up the capacity to self-criticize in order to deal with these flaws. Having yielded the claims of absolute perfection, one is free to admit errors and correct them. One is free to be ashamed of one's own errors and sins, and to admire and learn from the strengths and values of others. There is, in fact, less fear of erring by learning from the other, or being labeled as the *other*, when the *other* is on the same continuum.

At a rabbinical convention, I once argued that none of the denominations had the insight to anticipate, prevent, or deal in some superior way with the ongoing *Shoah*, let alone respond adequately afterward. This argument was challenged by a colleague. In light of my analysis of the *Shoah*, should one be Orthodox, Conservative, or Reform (since they were all equally incompetent to deal with the *Shoah*)? My reply was that after the Holocaust, it is not so important if you are Orthodox, Conservative, or Reform, as long as you are ashamed of it. That shame is the recognition of brokenness.

If I can write a codicil to that comment today, I would suggest that after the Holocaust, it is not so important if you are speaking/acting/witnessing as a Christian or Jew, as long as you are ashamed of it. Let me stress, I am proud to be ashamed of certain aspects of our overall great religion. Thus, shame should not be confused with distancing. My "shame principle" was challenged (I was, after all, an Orthodox rabbi speaking at an Orthodox rabbinic convention) when a colleague arose and yelled, "If all denominations are

equally incompetent and should be ashamed, then why are you Orthodox?" I
replied, "Because Orthodox is the group that I am most ashamed off." This
answer is more than paradox. I truly identify with that of which I am most
ashamed. As a Jew, I am not all that ashamed of Christianity's failures; nor
am I all that ashamed of Buddhist's failures. Jewish failures profoundly trouble me because that is the religion to which I am deeply committed. Judaism
is the faith whose life I live; it is the one whose record of failure eats at me.
The record challenges me. In what sense am I responsible for continuing it?

Personally, I am willing to feel limited shame for Christians in order to
help them out, but one focuses on one's own to the maximum possible. I am
much more ashamed of the Orthodox than of the Reform, although I am
ready to help the Reform and Conservative movements discover their
shame too, so that they may deal with it. In all cases, *shame*—i.e., affirmation of brokenness—should not be confused with *distancing*. One has to
love a system at its best enough to be free to notice its flaws. One has to
really love a faith enough to be sufficiently ashamed to work to correct it.
This very love/shame operates to prevent outbreaks of potential evil as well
as move the system toward its own *Tikkun*. For this reason, I believe that the
authorities of the Catholic Church would do well to move beyond the temporizing and cosmetic elements of *We Remember* to an even more fundamental confession and self-critique, thus enabling the Church to purify itself and
its message even more deeply. Its spiritual stature would grow, and its
capacity for religious transformation of itself and of its believers would be
immeasurably strengthened.

In conclusion, the most powerful and effective method of preventing
pathological absolutism from rearing its head, even in divinely given systems,
is to create the conditions of pluralism. There are worldwide movements,
some of which are perceived as threats to tradition, yet in many ways I would
argue that they are trying to break up cultural hegemony. Such a breakup is
constructive for the ultimate authority of the systems being challenged.
Deconstructionism and feminism—whatever their moral problematics, and
they have serious problematics—are significant attempts to break up ethical
and cultural centralization. Moral decentralization is essential to prevent

concentrations of power, for power centers, when backed by a conviction of correctness, can lead to tyranny and imperialism. Diversification of voices is also insurance against creation of scapegoats, and of outsiders so isolated that they can be victimized. This is not to agree with the allied attempt to utilize deconstructionism and other such isms to deny that there are any standards other than arbitrary, imposed, or self-referential norms. Such a claim confuses relativism with the needed pluralism.

The valid, deepest insight is the recognition that all humanly processed truths, even divinely revealed systems, are, perforce, limited. Pluralism is an alternative to relativism. Pluralism does not mean giving up one's own commitments and deep convictions. Rather, pluralism includes serious commitment; pluralism encompasses absolutism—but an absolutism that knows its own limits and accepts its own limitations. A pluralist Christianity affirms that Christ is an ultimate religious revelation, but that God did not necessarily intend this revelation for everybody else in the world. Other humans have their equal or equivalent experiences. The same principle holds true for Judaism; its adequacy also depends on its willingness to admit that others have had religious experiences that Jews have not had. This in no way undermines the truth or the personal experience of the validity of Jews' own encounter with the absolute.

The alternative is a group/faith/culture/religion that feels fully adequate, but thereby does not know its own limitations and carries the seeds of totalitarianism, idolatry, etc; it is a potential threat to others. By contrast, that group/faith/religion/culture/system that recognizes its inadequacy thereby becomes adequate to function constructively in human society. It becomes more likely to make room for the dignity and values of others.

The application of this principle to the Jewish-Christian dialogue is obvious. We have lived a miracle in the sharp reduction of the claims that led to hatred (and mutual contempt) between us. The problem with the Church Fathers as sources of hatred for Jews (as the problem with the Gospels) is not a claim that those generations lacked religious and divine inspiration and presence; rather, it is that they did not know their own limitations. They could not imagine the breadth of God's love. God having given them such a powerful religious signal, they could not imagine that God had not with-drawn the equivalent Jewish experience. Their divine encounter was so real, how could there be room for anybody else's? That is where the confusion lies. One's own finite encounter with Infinity is limited. The claim that it is without limit brings with it a danger—potential idolatry. Idolatry expresses itself in hatred and in death dealing.

This fortress of mutual hatred has been disassembled in one generation by many forces. The driving force is the impact of the *Shoah*. The horror at the monstrous evil was intensified by the recognition that the Gospel of Love was a primary (if not *the*) source of hatred. This led to the determination that the Gospels could not be allowed to continue as a source of hatred, because it contradicted Christianity's commitment to perfect the world through love. Those Christians broken by the *Shoah* quickly identified Christian supersessionism, the claim that it has authority without limit, as the key motivating force for the rest of the degradation of the Jews—so they repudiated that claim. This led to the affirmation of the Jewishness of Jesus, etc., which resulted in an incredible series of church statements yielding imperialist claims, affirming Jewish validity, and accepting moral guilt for past failures.

The process, of course, is far from complete, but it is remarkably advanced. Nevertheless, resistance to the admissions shows up and expresses itself in certain passages and phrases of *We Remember* as it does in certain Protestant fundamentalist circles. They grasp at the straw that, after all, it was Catholicism that committed all those terrible acts vis-à-vis Jews in the Middle Ages—not Protestantism. By this claim, fundamentalists show their own lack of brokenness and their own lack of knowledge of history. In seeking to uphold Protestant Christianity's unlimited authority, they keep alive the source of hatred and the threat of a renewed imperialist Christianity.

In the end, one must apply this principle of brokenness to the Jews as well. Jews feel no guilt for the Holocaust, so they have not spent quite as much time meditating on Judaism's brokenness vis-à-vis the world and vis-à-vis Christianity. Yet the Jewish tradition is full of hostile and degrading images of Christians and Christianity. Fortunately, Jews in the past were too weak to act on these images. (To be fair to liberal Jews, many simply sweep away these text and images.) Because there is not enough sense of brokenness, there has been very little work on challenging these denials of Gentile's humanity, and even less pressure on Judaism to articulate a positive vision of Christianity as the independent dignified religion of a billion people alive today—not to mention the millions and billions who have lived it in the past. Filling this void is a central moral agenda for Jewry today.

Do not misunderstand these words about brokenness. Brokenness is not a shortage, a sign of decline, but a source of profound growth and insight. Consider the biblical account of Jacob. To become Israel, he first had to struggle and be broken. Only when he was wounded, e.g. broken, did Jacob become Israel—the one who struggles with God and humanity, and overcomes. Jews and Christians alike must be ready to be broken by wrestling with the Magisterium as with the Torah until the traditions become forces of love and *Tikkun Olam*, rather than sources of hatred and division.

NOTES

1. Pope John Paul II, Speech to a symposium on anti-Judaism, October 31, 1997. Published in *L'Osservatore Romano,* November 1, 1997, p. 6.
2. Joseph Dov Soloveitchik, "Community," *Tradition* 17 (Spring 1978), 9–11.
3. Idem, *The Lonely Man of Faith* (New York: Doubleday, 1992), 28.
4. In "Cloud of Smoke; Pillar of Fire: Judaism, Christianity and Modernity after the Holocaust," Eva Fleischner, ed., *Auschwitz: Beginning of a New Era* (New York: KTAV, 1977), 22.

6

Jewish Citizenship in Emerging Nation States: Christian Anti-Semitism, Nationalism, and Nazi Ideology
RONALD MODRAS

Hinnay ma tov umanaiim shevet achim gam yahad (Psalm 133:1). How does one translate that verse from the psalms? "Behold how good and pleasant it is for—brothers? brothers and sisters? siblings?—to dwell together as one." And whom do we include in that concept? All people or just our co-religionists? This conference is an exercise in hermeneutics, in the interpretation of texts and events. And interpretation can never be a purely objective enterprise. In this post-modern age, we have come to recognize that there is no such thing as complete objectivity. All knowledge is perspectival and therefore personal. We bring personal horizon and history to our texts, a history of memories, anecdotes, and relationships.

In the late eighteenth century, German philosopher Moses Mendelssohn and German critic and dramatist Gotthilf Ephraim Lessing met over a chessboard—and began a conversation and a relationship that changed both of them and then the world, or, at least much of the Western world. Mendelssohn became the first modern Orthodox Jew, the Father of Haskalah, and Lessing's historic drama, *Nathan the Wise*,—its lead character inspired by Mendelssohn—is still being performed as well as read, with its message of tolerance and respect despite religious differences.

We have gone beyond Mendelssohn and Lessing, of course, but only because of the conversations that have taken place and the relationships that have been formed over the last thirty years among us here. I would suggest that we, too, like Lessing and Mendelssohn, have helped change the world. A sea change has taken place in Christian-Jewish relations over the last thirty years. Rabbi David Rosen has called it "one of the greatest revolutions in human history." It took place because of the Second Vatican Council, its decree *Nostra Aetate*, and us—Jews and Christians who have been determined to build on the council and who have entered into conversations and relationships that have changed us and, in doing so, have helped to change the world.

My task here is to analyze and interpret some of the texts and events determinative of Catholic-Jewish relations from the early modern period up to the *Shoah*. The topic is fraught with controversy, sometimes passion, and I do not pretend to an objectivity I believe is unattainable. But I do claim a certain sympathy for both the Jewish and the Catholic readings of those texts and events. Allow me to attempt to justify that claim by sharing with you some of the experiences that have affected me with respect to Catholic-Jewish relations—conversations and relationships that have touched and transformed me and, thereby, color my perspective and judgment.

Experiences That Color Perspective

In my late twenties, I began studying German under Rabbi Max Kapustin, the Hillel director at Wayne State University. Rabbi Kapustin was unfailingly observant of traditional Talmudic prescriptions, but he was also a man very much a participant in the life of a modern secular university, very much, therefore, a modern Orthodox Jew. Max was born in Germany and had studied at Heidelberg. The love of his life was his wife, Brunhilde. (It tells you something about Jews and German culture to know that Orthodox Jewish families in 1920s Germany named their daughters Brunhilde!) Max and Brunhilde fled Germany in 1938. Max tutored me first in German, then Hebrew, but he taught me so much more. I sat at his seder table for Pesah and under his sukkah during the season of Sukkoth. Max taught me Halachah and Yiddishkeit.

I remember Max's son coming home from college at the University of Toronto and Max asking, "What are you studying these days?" Saint Augustine, came the answer. "Good," came Max's response, "he was quite a guy." I had never till then thought of St. Augustine as "quite a guy." I learned a new respect for Augustine that day and for Max, an Orthodox rabbi who could respect my Christian heritage and tradition.

Max told me stories about his youth, how one winter vacation he went to Paris and attended Christmas Midnight Mass at the cathedral of Notre Dame. "Ron," Max confessed, "I had to walk out. I was having a religious experience." When, years later, I invited Max to one of my classes, he told my students how, when he read Exodus, he sometimes was so moved that it was as if he were there at the foot of Sinai with his people Israel. And I knew that Max had experienced the *Shechinah*, the presence of God.

Max had his faults. Once we were discussing Halacha, and Brunhilde said something like, "The one mitzva I cannot understand is the one about Momzerim (the prohibition for Orthodox Jews to marry Jews who are born outside a lawful marriage)." It was perhaps the only time I saw Max bristle. "I don't want to discuss it," he said. "The Law is law." Max also had the failing of so many intellectuals—a certain attitude of disdain for the *am haaretz*, the culturally limited, Jewish and otherwise.

Max and I had not seen each other for over a year, when, one evening in December, in the late 1970s, I was writing Christmas cards and came to "K." I didn't have any Chanukah cards, so I decided to phone him instead. "Is Rabbi Kapustin in?" I asked. "Who is this?" came the response. "Dr. Ronald Modras, a former student of his. I called to wish him a happy Chanukah."

"Rabbi Kapustin died this morning."

I attended the funeral, where I learned "he was often criticized by his *schul* for spending so much time with the Goyim." I was one guy who was glad that he did. He lives on in my classroom.

Aleiho shalom. Peace be upon him.

Not all Jews are like Max Kapustin. There is more than a grain of truth to the story about two Jews and three opinions. The Jewish community is no more monolithic than any other.

* I have experienced Friday afternoon in Mea Shaarim, where the children looked at me curiously; but for their Chassidic parents, I was invisible. I did not exist. I have no doubt but that Reform and perhaps even some modern Orthodox Jews would be treated the same way.

- I remember an Israeli tour guide, an officer in the army. He also had no use for Chassidim. But he demonstrated other problematic attitudes when he asked, How many Arabs does it take to change a light bulb?
- I also remember the early days of the Auschwitz Convent controversy, when a certain rabbi from Brooklyn made international news by going to Poland and breaking into the Carmelite convent near Auschwitz. When he scaled the fence and began shouting and pounding on the door, a workman poured a bucket of water on him. I do not regard that particular rabbi as in any way typical of American Jewry, so he did not disturb me. What disturbed me was another rabbi, a colleague of mine at the time, who shook his head and said, "There go those anti-Semitic Poles again." Was my colleague untypical?

These are some of the experiences that affect my reading of the texts and events we are considering here, along with several years of dialogue not only on Catholic-Jewish relations but also more specifically on Polish-Jewish relations. Three of my grandparents came from Poland, described once by a Jewish-American journalist as the land of priests and peasants—and for the last twenty years, a Polish pope. I remember when Karol Wojtyla was elected. Concerns were raised at the time in the Jewish community about the impact a Polish pope would have on Catholic-Jewish relations. The assumption was, if he's from Poland, he must be biased against Jews. After all, as Prime Minister Yitzhak Shamir once put it, "Poles imbibe anti-Semitism with their mother's milk." Which is to say, it's in the culture, their traditional Catholic culture.

For the last twenty years, I have been involved in a dialogue that has become the Polish-American Jewish American Council, sponsored by the American Jewish Committee. It was involvement in this dialogue that led me to do research on the Catholic periodical literature produced in the 1930s in Poland, and the attitudes expressed there about Jews and Judaism, attitudes not at all idiosyncratic.[1] My intentions here are to summarize some of my findings and to put them into the larger context of Roman Catholic thinking at the time.

But there is one last anecdote I should share. Eight years ago, at a similar Holocaust conference at Oxford University, I spoke on the Catholic anti-Semitism in 1930s Poland. A Jewish gentleman, a survivor, came to me after my presentation and assured me with an attitude I could only describe as smug: "Believe me, the contempt was mutual."

Poland and Jews before the Interwar Period

Poland in the late Middle Ages became what first Babylonia and Spain had been earlier: the spiritual center of world Jewry.[2] Rabbi Isserles of Krakow, one of the most influential sages in Jewish history, interpreted the Hebrew word of Poland (*Polin*) to mean "here" (*poh*) there is "rest" (*lin*). Expelled from Western Europe, harassed in Germany and Bohemia, Jews came to Poland as a land of refuge. And there, with the so-called Council of Four Lands (Vaad Arba Artzot), they achieved more autonomy than anywhere else in the history of the Diaspora.

Jews traditionally extended their loyalties not to nations but to monarchs. So when Poland was partitioned off the map of Europe by its more powerful neighbors (1773, 1793, 1795), the Jews of Poland attached their fortunes to the new rulers. So oppressive was life under the czars, however, that Jews joined Poles in two failed uprisings (1830–31 and 1863–64) against Russia. For 123 years Poland was no more than an idea; but it was an idea that would not go away—kept alive by the Polish language and an identification of Poland with Roman Catholicism. Poland, for its expatriate romantic poets, was the Christ among nations, crucified between thieves and endowed with a divinely ordained messianic mission similar to that of Israel.

When against all odds, Poland reemerged as a nation at the end of World War I, it was not by chance that even secular Poles called that reemergence a *resurrection*. The resurrection was not glorious, however, as the fighting continued for another three years between Poles, Ukrainians, and Soviet Russia over boundary disputes. With no vested interest in the victory of one side or another, Jews were accused of disloyalty by all sides. During the fighting over the Polish-Soviet border, thousands of Jews perished, stereotyped as Bolsheviks, most at the hands of Ukrainian nationalists. But the western press focused on the Poles. Jewish-American newspapers questioned whether the Poles deserved independence. For Roman Dmowski, the head of the *Endecja* (National Democrats), Jews were an international force to be reckoned with, powerful and, he was sure, endemically anti-Polish.

Interwar Poland

When the Polish-Soviet frontier was finally settled, Poland was once again a national state.[3] But like modern-day Israel, it had a serious minority problem: over one-third of its population was non-Polish. Ukrainians formed the largest minority, concentrated in the east; Jews numbered some three and a half million, or eleven percent of the total population, mostly in towns and cities, the largest concentration of Jews in all of Europe. Warsaw alone had over 350,000 Jews, thirty percent of its population: more than all the Jews of England or France, and more than seven times all the Jews in Italy.

The Catholic press in interwar Poland was fond of providing statistics to prove the peculiarity of its social situation.[4] According to the 1931 government census, in Warsaw and its environs, Jews made up thirty-two percent of the lawyers and over sixty-six percent of the medical doctors. In southern Poland, barely one lawyer in ten was not Jewish.

The Polish constitution of 1921 guaranteed equal rights to all religions; Poland was a democratic republic, modeled after France. Marshall Joseph Pilsudski, the leader of interwar Poland for most of its twenty-one years, envisioned a Poland founded on the multiethnic, federalist traditions of the old Polish commonwealth. The National Democrats under Roman Dmowski rejected Pilsudski's vision out of hand and insisted that Poles alone should be masters in their own house. The National Democrats called for excluding all national minorities from political power, polonizing the Slavic minorities, and expatriating the Germans and the Jews as being incapable of assimilation.

It bears noting that, although they set the agenda, especially after 1935 and the death of Pilsudski, the National Democrats never grasped the reins of power. That was not for lack of support from the Roman Catholic clergy and hierarchy. Dmowski identified Poland and Polish culture with Catholicism, much the way Eduard Drumont had identified Catholicism with France and

French culture. Forty years earlier, in turn-of-the-century France, the so-called "Jewish question" figured prominently in the clash between Catholic conservatives and liberal republicans. The point at issue was no less than defining what it meant to be French. In interwar Poland, the question was the same: defining what it meant to be Polish. In both instances, the upshot was a culture war, not altogether unlike that going on in Israel today, over what constitutes a Jewish state.

The 1998 Vatican document, *We Remember: A Reflection on the Shoah*, describes the nineteenth century as characterized by "a false and exacerbated nationalism": "Thus there began to spread in varying degrees throughout most of Europe an anti-Judaism that was essentially more sociological and political than religious." That statement, I believe, requires qualification; if the anti-Judaism was more sociological and political, it was also very much religious.

Masons, Jews, and Secularity

Catholics in 1930s Poland thought very much like Catholics in the rest of Europe. In a very revealing phrase, a German Catholic historian writing in the 1930s found it striking that Providence seemed to unleash Satan at two hundred year intervals; first in 1517, then 1717, and most recently 1917. Those of you with a sense of history will recognize 1517 as the onset of the Protestant Reformation and 1917 as the year of the Bolshevik Revolution. But what happened in 1717? Most reflection on the 1930s ignores or gives short shrift to the founding of the Grand Lodge in London in 1717, the organization of modern freemasonry. But for some Catholic thinkers in the 1930s, the advent of freemasons ranked with the revolutions of Luther and Lenin. In the last months before the invasion of Poland by Nazi Germany, the editor of a scholarly Jesuit journal (*Przeglad Powszechny*) wrote that Poland would fight Germany and its neo-pagan racism. But, he continued, joining the democracies of the West did not mean identifying with them. Poland, he assured his readers, would continue to distance itself from their "secularity and masonry."[5]

In 1797, Abbé Augustin Barruel published a four-volume work blaming masons for the French Revolution and the disestablishment of the

Catholic Church in France (*Mémoires pour servir d'histoire au Jacobinisme*). The book was translated into English, Italian, Spanish, and Russian, one of the first books in publishing history to become a bestseller because of its conspiracy theory. Masons were plotting to overthrow Christian civilization and culture.

Modern scholarship recognizes that freemasonry neither provoked nor facilitated the French Revolution. But by the latter part of the nineteenth century, the myth of masonic responsibility had become a commonplace, accepted by France's freemasons themselves. By that time, they were anti-clerical Republicans happy to take credit for the revolution even as their monarchist Catholic adversaries reviled them for it. Pope Leo XIII (1884) accused freemasons of attempting to overthrow the religious and political order produced by Christian teaching. The kind of secular society envisioned by masonry, the pope continued, could only result in socialism and communism. Masons had become the arch enemies of Christian culture and of the Catholic Church.

But what did Jews have to do with any of this? Only after the revolution did masonry become open to French Jews. In Germany Eduard Emil Eckert in his book, *Der Freimauer-Orden in seiner wahren Bedeutung* (*The True Meaning of Freemasonry*), argued that masonry was under the influence of Jews, and that both groups were in an alliance to undermine traditional society. In Germany, Eckert's book was dismissed even by Germans who were in principle anti-masonic. But when Eckert's book appeared in French translation (1854), his ideas found more fertile ground. Jews were well represented in French masonic leadership. Adolph Cremieux, the most prominent Jewish freemason in France, eventually became the head of the Scottish rite.

With some justification, French Catholics saw their church as the most important institutional victim of the French Revolution. And they blamed masons, the self-appointed protagonists of the revolution, and Jews, certainly among its foremost beneficiaries. At the turn of the century, during the Dreyfus Affair, no less than three separate periodicals were taken up with masons and Jews, each sponsored by an anti-masonic organization.

The word *liberalism* has acquired a variety of meanings over its long career, depending on its context. When Pope Pius IX condemned liberalism in 1864 (*Syllabus of Errors*), he defined it an "absurd principle" that the state should treat all religions alike without distinction.[6] The Vatican rejected the idea of the modern secular state in theory right up to the Second Vatican Council (1962–1965). What we here in the United States called Jeffersonian democracy, in Europe was regarded by conservative Catholics as "masonic democracy."

At issue was not only separation of church and state, however, but culture. When any aspects of modernity clashed with what was viewed as traditional Catholic culture, the cry that went out was "Judaization." The word rings clumsy and foreign in the English language. But as early as 1869, it was used in France to describe the changes taking place in European society. That was the same year that composer Richard Wagner wrote of the *Verjüdung* of modern art. Ten years later, in 1879, Wilhelm Marr, an anti-Christian journalist, coined another German neologism—one that translated more easily—*Antisemitismus*.

Before Hitler came to power in 1933, the German Catholic Church came into repeated conflict with the growing Nazi movement—for its racialism, however, not its anti-Semitism. Jewish historian Moshe Zimmermann points out that the word *anti-Semitism* had a much more ambiguous, far less pejorative meaning before the holocaust than it did after, comparable to the early usage at least of the word *anti-Zionism*.[7] Wilhelm Marr coined the word anti-Semitism because he wanted a word other than anti-Judaism, with its religious connotations. Jews for Marr were a racial unit, religious or not, baptized or otherwise. Despite his intentions, Christians in Germany took over Marr's word in their concern to preserve a Christian Germany. Like the word *anti-Zionism*, the word was given a political connotation.

In the 1930 edition of the prestigious *Lexikon für Theologie und Kirche*, in his article on anti-Semitism, Catholic theologian Gustav Gundlach made the following distinctions: racist anti-Semitism was unchristian because it contradicted Christian love of neighbor. But political anti-Semitism was permitted, so long as it used morally admissible means to counteract what

Gundlach called the "exaggerated and harmful influence" of Jews over the economy, politics, the press, science, and the arts. In the 1930s, anti-Semitism was still a synonym for anti-liberalism. And for Polish Catholics, anti-liberalism meant struggling to preserve a Catholic Poland.

The Struggle for a Catholic Poland

Mainly because of a glaring need for radical agrarian reform, the effects of the world depression lasted in Poland until 1936, far longer than in most countries. Hardest hit were people in the countryside, who headed for the cities for jobs that were scarce or nonexistent. The Catholic press and clergy thought to alleviate their plight by supporting the boycott of Jewish merchants. Father Maximilian Kolbe, however, discouraged the use of the negative term *boycott* in favor of a more positive term: *fostering Polish enterprise.* Today, I'm sure he would have used the term *affirmative action.* No matter what one called it, however, the boycott failed miserably. "It was not easy to convince Poles to abstain from patronizing Jewish enterprises."[8] Jewish merchants sold cheaper.

The issues were more than economic, however. One does not have to be a Marxist to acknowledge the impact that economics has on culture. People living at a subsistence level of income do not patronize the arts. Poland's upper- and middle-class Jews not only had the means to patronize cultural productions but the capital and skills to create them: books, newspapers, motion pictures, theater. Jews in 1930s Poland were already having a marked influence on Polish culture. But even more troubling to Catholic nationalists was the fact that many had the means to facilitate their children's higher education—and that could only mean an increase of Jewish influence toward the secularizing of Catholic culture. Masonic-Jewish efforts to secularize Polish culture had to be resisted, the Catholic press and leadership insisted, *but* in a manner that was ethical and moral. Not all Catholics heard the "but."

The rise of Nazism to power in Germany had its impact on Poland. It encouraged younger nationalists in 1934 to split off from the *Endecja* and form the National Radical Camp (ONR), based on the Nazi model. As elsewhere in East Central Europe, universities became centers of anti-Jewish riots, much of it in imitation of the Nazis. After only a few months, the Polish government disbanded the ONR because of its violent anti-Semitic agitation, but its former members continued their efforts under guise of different youth organizations. Not satisfied with merely calling for the boycott of Jewish merchants, more radical nationalists devised methods to enforce it, especially in the countryside. Incidents erupted into full-scale riots with the police often looking the other way. For the radical right, any means that encouraged Jews to leave Poland was justified.

The years 1936 to 1939 were among the darkest in modern Polish history. No racial laws were passed; no Jewish newspapers or cultural institutions were suppressed; none of the thousands of Jews who held political positions was driven from office. Official state violence was never used against Jews in Poland, as it was in Germany or earlier in Russia. There were no Polish pogroms. But the government did not act forcefully in combating the unofficial but organized violence instigated by the radical nationalists. University authorities claimed to be powerless to quell the organized attacks that Endek youths were making against Jewish students. Claiming it was for the sake of peace, university rectors acquiesced to Endek demands for segregated seating for Jews and created the so-called ghetto benches.

Interwar Poland was a pluralistic society, and Jews were not without ethnic Polish allies. The Polish Socialist Party marched in opposition to anti-Semitism. Individual Polish students and Odrodzenie, a Catholic student organization, joined in solidarity with their Jewish classmates and were attacked by the radical right as crypto-communists and masons. The response of the Catholic press and leadership to the "ghetto benches" at universities was silence. Their reaction to anti-Jewish agitation and violence at universities or in the countryside was to condemn the violence, but then try to explain it, which is to say, justify it.

According to the Catholic press, the sporadic violence that erupted around the ghetto benches and the economic boycott was an unfortunate but inevitable by-product of a necessary struggle. Victims of anti-Semitic violence were unlucky but not altogether innocent casualties of a just war. And in a just war, self-defense was justified. Nationalist Poles had a long and justified tradition of describing themselves as victims. Now, however, not the partitioning powers but Jews were described as the alien and hostile force. Jews were at best "guests" who had outstayed their welcome or worse, "the fourth partition." They were either outsiders or enemies. Traditional Polish tolerance was a virtue Poland could no longer afford. And if Christians were to love even their enemies, they were nonetheless allowed to love their family and neighbor first.

The most celebrated Catholic response to anti-Semitic violence in Poland came from Cardinal August Hlond in a pastoral letter he issued in 1936 on Catholic moral principles.[9] In that letter he spoke out against the influence of Nazism in Poland and condemned anti-Semitic violence: "I warn against that moral stance, imported from abroad, that is basically and ruthlessly anti-Jewish. It is contrary to Catholic ethics. . . . Beware of those who are inciting anti-Jewish violence."

The context for his condemnation, however, was ambiguous, to say the least: "It is a fact that Jews are waging war against the Catholic Church, that they are steeped in free-thinking, and constitute the vanguard of atheist, the Bolshevik movement, and revolutionary activity." After describing other moral failures to be found in the Jewish community, like pornography, the cardinal went on: "But let us be fair. Not all Jews are this way. There are very many Jews who are believers, honest, just, kind, and philanthropic. There is a healthy, edifying sense of family in very many Jewish homes. We know Jews who are ethically outstanding, noble, and upright."

The cardinal both condemned violence and supported the boycott: "It is good to prefer your own when shopping" but it is forbidden to damage Jewish stores, homes, or property. "It is forbidden to assault, beat up, maim, or slander Jews. One should honor and love Jews as human beings and neighbors . . . " But it is not this excerpt with its description of Jews as neighbors that has caught the attention of historians. The line most quoted from the cardinal's pastoral letter reads: "One may love one's own nation more, but one may not hate anyone. Not even Jews." "Not even Jews" implied "not even enemies." The cardinal was not consistent. Were Jews to be loved as neighbors or enemies?

Would the cardinal's 1936 statement have been different if he had issued it after Pope Pius XI made his celebrated remarks to representatives of a Belgian pilgrimage to Rome in 1939, when the pope described Christians as "spiritual Semites"? Not necessarily, if one considers the entire quotation. As it was reported, the pope stated: "No, it is not possible for Christians to participate in anti-Semitism. We acknowledge everyone's right to self-defense, to take the means to protect themselves against any threat to their legitimate interests. But anti-Semitism is inadmissible. Spiritually we are Semites." The middle sentence did not receive the same press attention as the last. "We acknowledge everyone's right to self-defense, to take the means to protect themselves against any threat to their legitimate interests." That is what the Polish Catholic bishops, clergy, and press saw themselves as doing. That is what the boycott and the struggle for a Catholic Poland was all about: protecting the "legitimate interests" of the Polish people and church.[10]

Interpreting the Past

The only reason for this review of Polish Catholic history is the fact of the *Shoah*. Nazi Germany perpetrated most of its genocide of Jews on occupied Polish soil. We do not look at the facts and events themselves but view them through the prism of Auschwitz, Treblinka, and Majdanek. Among the six million Jews murdered in those camps were three million Polish Jews. Along with those three million Polish Jews, three million ethnic Polish civilians were murdered as well. Poles and Jews who, for the most part, lived side by side as strangers, were murdered, burned, and buried together by the Nazis—the Poles as *Untermenschen* (subhuman), Slavs worthy only to be slaves; the Jews as *Ungeziefer* (vermin), and thereby a danger to the "master race."

The Israeli Holocaust scholar, Yehuda Bauer, has described National Socialism as "the most radical revolution that had ever taken place": a revolt against Judeo-Christian morality, the Enlightenment, against all that was thought of as humane. The "master race," according to the Nazi ideology, had not only the right but the duty to enslave or murder all those it considered different from itself. The Jews of Europe were the first and foremost victims of this radical revolution. The ethnic Poles came second. To quote Bauer: "If we adopt the United Nations' definition of genocide, then what happened to the Polish nation . . . was indeed genocide. The Polish nation as such was to have disappeared . . ."[11]

For as long as the Holocaust will be remembered, Jews and Poles will be encountering one another at Auschwitz, as at a cemetery. Thus far, those encounters have not always been attended by mutual understanding and respect. Extremists in both communities have used Auschwitz for their own personal and political purposes. Both a Carmelite convent and the cross have become sources of confrontation and hostile agitation from the right wings of both the Jewish and the Catholic nationalist communities. Cemeteries deserve more respect, and the Polish government has taken and is taking legal measures to ensure that respect.

In 1990 the Polish bishops issued a pastoral letter on Jewish-Catholic relations quite different from that of Cardinal Hlond's. In it the bishops stated categorically, "Not by our wish, and not by our hands . . . Murderers did this on our land." The bishops noted the heroic example of Poles who risked their lives to rescue Jews, and the culpability of Polish Catholics who cooperated with the final solution or were indifferent to it. The bishops asked for forgiveness if only one Polish Christian caused a death or could have helped and did not.

It bears remembering here that in occupied Poland helping Jews was exceedingly more difficult and dangerous. (Note that the Dutch family that harbored Anne Frank and her family were not sent to their deaths for doing so.) Unlike the situation in the West, the death penalty for helping Jews was automatic in Poland, and the German occupiers made sure there was no doubt about the seriousness of their resolve. Entire families were killed and their property burned when it was discovered that they had hidden Jews.

Visiting Yad Vashem in Jerusalem or the United States Holocaust Memorial Museum in Washington, D.C., one encounters thousands of Polish names among those "Righteous among the Nations" who helped save Jewish lives—with the exception of Holland, more than any other nation by far. No one person could save a Jew in hiding; it took several. So I believe it is altogether remarkable that so many thousands, arguably tens of thousands, of

Poles risked their lives to save people whom their Church's and nation's moral leaders for years had marked as alien and hostile to Polish interests.

Since 1987, a number of prominent Polish writers (Jan Blonski, Jerzy Turowicz, et al.) have begun to address the neuralgic issue of the Polish response to the mass murder the Third Reich carried out on Polish soil. Although Poles could have done more, they admit, they could not have done much. But these authorities still acknowledge that they feel a certain guilt and shame—not that the Poles participated in the murder or withheld reasonable assistance, but that they were widely indifferent to the crime perpetrated before their eyes. Despite the long cherished Polish tradition of resistance to tyranny, the Poles, they say, did not rise up en masse and resist what the Nazis were doing. They thus condemned the Jews to lonelier and solitary deaths than they would have suffered otherwise.[12]

The daughter of Polish Jewish Holocaust survivors, Eva Hoffman, writes the following about ethnic Polish behavior during the *Shoah*:

> Before the war, most Poles and Jews did not include each other within the sphere of mutual and natural obligations. A Pole who decided to risk his or her house, life, and family for a Jewish person was stretching his compassion beyond the bounds of absolute responsibility. And there are Jewish survivors honest enough to say that if the roles had been reversed, they cannot vouch for how they would have acted toward people whom they still call "the goyim."[13]

Hoffman goes on to ask: Were there more Poles who helped or more who harmed? She points out:

> In the impossible calculus of that time, it took at least several people to save a Jewish life; it took only one person to cause the deaths of many. Moreover, the presence of a few who were willing to betray a Jewish presence was

enough to paralyze many others. The fear of informers
must have been as strong for the helpers as for those who
were hidden.

Hoffman relates interviewing a woman who, in her account of survival,
told of many instances of help from Poles but the activity of informers as
well, concluding with, "Now you see why we hate the Polacks." Hoffman
notes that there was no word about hating the Germans. She states: "It is possible that the Nazis were beyond hate, transferred to the realm of psychological trauma, of numbing and wordlessness."[14] I believe, however, that there
may be a less Freudian explanation.

I have long puzzled at the sensitivity of authors on the Holocaust,
Jewish and non-Jewish alike, who will write about the Nazi, not German,
invasion of Poland (as if the Democrats declared war on Japan after Pearl
Harbor), and then will link together in one sweeping phrase the anti-Semitism
of Nazis and Catholic Poles. (The analogy is obscene, of course; just as
obscene as the comparisons sometimes made between Nazi Germany and
Israel.) Why are Poles more apt to be labeled as anti-Semitic than Germans,
Austrians, or the French for that matter? The predictable answer to that question is that anti-Semitism was endemic in Polish Catholic history and culture
but was exceptional in Germany. After all, Germany is the land of Bach,
Goethe, the *Aufklärung*. Poland is the "land of priests and peasants."

Why are American Jews in particular more likely to condemn or label
Catholic Poles rather than Germans as anti-Semites? One very plausible
answer is simply because there were more Jews in Poland and there are more
American Jews with roots in Poland. Therefore, there are more experiences to
be handed down in familial oral tradition.

But Israel Shahak offers another explanation.[15] A survivor himself of
Bergen Belsen and an Israeli citizen born in Poland, Shahak blames Talmudic
tradition. He writes of classical Jewish contempt for gentiles in general and
the *am haaretz*, the peasants, in particular. He writes of Jews in Israel identifying peasants, whether Palestinians or Poles, with the Ukrainian peasants
who rose up against Jews and Poles in the 1648 Chmielnicki massacres.

(Need I point out that there are also Jews in this country, with less than stellar knowledge of history, who believe that the Chmielnicki massacres were perpetrated by Catholic Poles and serves as an example of endemic Polish anti-Semitism.)

Shahak is a retired professor of chemistry, not a Talmudist. He claims that the basic Talmudic principle is that "gentiles are not to be lifted out [of the well] nor hauled down [into it]." And he cites Maimonides: for a gentile "is not thy fellow."[16] Shahak finds it a reason for reproach that the Talmud teaches: "It is forbidden to deceive anyone, not even Gentiles" (Hullin 94a). I personally do not find that a reason to reproach Talmudic tradition but simply to acknowledge its historical context. But, by all appearances, Cardinal Hlond is not alone with his "we may not hate anyone, not even Jews." The cardinal, like the Talmud, deserves to be understood within the same historical context.

The Talmudic tradition toward gentiles is complex, as the late Israeli historian Jacob Katz has demonstrated. Talmudic teaching on the Noachide laws for gentiles is much more humane than Christian teaching about no salvation outside the Church, and in the twelfth century Maimonides explicitly taught that "the righteous of all peoples have a part in the world to come."[17] Rabbi Menachem Ha-Me'iri, at the beginning of the fourteenth century in southern France, explicitly excluded Christians from the category of pagans and idolaters from whom Jews had to segregate themselves. But his opinion remained largely unknown for centuries.[18] And, on the Internet at least, one can find Jews who contest it.

Let me be very clear. I am not making a case for a moral equivalency between what Jules Isaac called the Christian *teaching of contempt* for Jews and the Talmudic view of gentiles, including Christians. In Jewish-Christian discussions over the so-called papal cross at Auschwitz, it is important to acknowledge that for many Jews, the cross is not only an alien religious symbol but also an emblem that is at once offensive and hateful.

Ever since the Second Vatican Council, Catholic leaders have attempted to correct the "teaching of contempt." The Vatican and U.S. bishops have called upon Catholic educators to learn about and present Judaism positively, to instill respect for Jewish tradition and values, and above all, to condemn and resist all manifestations of anti-Semitism. And sociological studies indicate that their efforts have been successful. I confess that I know of no similar efforts being made to educate Jews about Christianity or Catholicism. I know of no similar efforts to counteract anti-Catholicism in the Jewish community. I do not claim that most Jews are anti-Catholic, but there is a vocal and not insignificant minority who are. And the silence of the majority may lead one to presume consent. Moreover, anyone apologist, Jew or Christian, who would attempt to explain Jewish anti-Catholicism, falls into the same pit that the Catholic press in Poland did when they tried to explain Polish anti-Semitism. To explain is to justify.

I do not expect Jewish leaders to control the anti-Catholic speech or actions of other Jews. But I do think that Catholics have a right to expect Jewish leadership to speak out against Jewish anti-Catholicism the way Jews have a right to expect Catholic leaders to speak out against anti-Semitism. I believe we have to look at our textual traditions and acknowledge that there are problematic areas in both traditions that need addressing. John Chrysostom and Maimonides both need to be read and criticized in their respective historical contexts. Again, without making any claims for equivalency, there were attitudes of prejudice, contempt, and ignorance in both communities, and a radical fringe in both communities continues to maintain those attitudes. The silent majority in both communities has a right to expect its leaders to speak out against those attitudes.

Remembering the *Shoah* means remembering a radical revolution that despised both of our traditions and attempted to destroy the values of what we call Judeo-Christian morality. The word *Judeo-Christian* is a neologism, created by self-described "enlightened" thinkers hostile and contemptuous of both our traditions. Both Jews and Christians once drew circles that excluded the other from their respective "universe of obligation" (Helen Fein). That most of our peoples no longer do so is why Christian-Jewish relations represent "one of the greatest revolutions in human history." That most of us Catholics and Jews no longer do so is the result of a thirty-year-old conversation and the relationships it has engendered.

Hinnay ma tov umanaiim shevet achim gam yahad. "Behold how good and pleasant it is for brothers and sisters to dwell together as one." May the day come soon when Jews and Christians explicitly include the other when we pray those words. *Va yimru kol Yisrael Amen.* And let all Israel—and let the Church—say Amen.

Notes

1. See Ronald Modras, *The Catholic Church and Antisemitism: Poland, 1933–1939* (Chur, Switzerland: Harwood Academic Publishers, 1994).

2. The bibliography on the millennial history of Jews in Poland is not unexpectedly immense. An overview is provided by Gershon David Hundert and Gershon C. Bacon, *The Jews in Poland and Russia: Bibliographical Essays* (Bloomington, Ind.: Indiana University, 1984).

3. For the interwar period see M. K. Dziewanowski, *Poland in the Twentieth Century* (New York: Columbia University, 1977); Antony Polonsky, *Politics in Independent Poland, 1921–1939: The Crisis of Constitutional Government* (Oxford: Clarendon, 1972); Ezra Mendelsohn, *The Jews of East Central Europe between the World Wars* (Bloomington, Ind.: Indiana University, 1983).

4. Modras, *The Catholic Church and Antisemitism*, 244.

5. Modras, *The Catholic Church and Antisemitism*, 43.

6. Claudia Carlen, I.H.M., *The Papal Encyclicals, 1740–1981.* 5 vols. (1981; reprint, Ann Arbor, Mich.: Pierien Press, 1990), 1:381–385.

7. Moshe Zimmermann, *Wilhelm Marr: The Patriarch of Anti-Semitism*, (New York: Oxford University, 1986). Anti-Zionism, of course, is a quite pejorative term in certain (especially Arab) circles and in many instances has become a cover for blatant anti-Semitism.

8. Celia Heller, *On the Edge of Destruction: Jews of Poland between the Two World Wars* (New York: Schocken, 1980), 115–116.

9. For a complete English translation of Hlond's statement, see Modras, *The Catholic Church and Antisemitism*, 346–347.

10. For a full description of the origin of the term *spiritual Semites* by Pope Pius XI, see Modras, *The Catholic Church and Antisemitism*, 354–356.

11. An address to the German Bundestag, reprinted in SICSA, the fall 1998 Annual Report of the Sasoon Center for the Study of Antisemitism (Hebrew University, Jerusalem), 3.

12. See Antony Polonsky, ed., *My Brother's Keeper: Recent Polish Debates on the Holocaust* (London: Routledge, 1990).

13. Eva Hoffman, *Shtetl: The Life and Death of a Small Town and the World of Polish Jews* (Boston/New York: Houghton Mifflin), 247.

14. Hoffman, *Shtetl*, 244–245.

15. Israel Shahak, *Jewish History, Jewish Religion, the Weight of Three Thousand Years* (London/ Boulder, Co.: Pluto, 1994), 72–73.

16. Shahak, *Jewish History*, 80.

17. Jacob Katz, *Exclusiveness and Tolerance: Studies in Jewish-Gentiles Relations in Medieval and Modern Times* (London: Oxford University, 1961), 174.

18. Katz, *Exclusiveness*, 114–123, 164.

7

Some Reflections on Nationalism, Romanticism, Anti-Semitism, and the Holocaust
STEVEN T. KATZ

It is a great pleasure to be here. The reason why I accepted this invitation, to fill in for someone who was unable to come at the last minute, is not only because it came from John Pawlikowski and involved such a distinguished group of participants but also because I realized that this week, the time just before Easter, has historically been a terrible week for Jews. It was often a time of pogroms and violence. Jews and Christians did not sit together as we are doing. The cross represented real and manifest evil for Jews. So, whatever I might say today and whatever might be said here this week, I think we should understand the historic context of this meeting and its long prehistory. Then, too, we must appreciate that we, i.e., the Jewish and Christian communities, have recently made enormous progress in talking to one another. The fact that we come together this week, which is Holy Week and Passover, is a remarkable accomplishment. For all the hiccups and bumps in the road, I am confident that we will continue to make progress in building a better relationship, and thus we should take a certain optimism from this auspicious moment. I have been asked to talk about the connection between the medieval and the modern periods in Jewish history, with a special focus on anti-Semitism.

The Medieval Period

Let me say first of all that I didn't hear Professor Sloyan's talk, or those of several other speakers. Moreover, for me to analyze the history of the Church in this setting would be akin to bringing coals to Newcastle. Therefore, I will make only the fundamental point that, despite the wrongs that the medieval Church committed vis-à-vis the Jewish people, the medieval Church did have its own deep moral center vis-à-vis the "Israel of the Flesh." This was incarnated and reflected in the Pauline-Augustinian position regarding the "mystery of Israel." Even though the Jews were guilty of a deicidal crime—they were like the biblical Cain who killed his brother Abel—the Catholic Church, the Catholic community, had a responsibility not to murder them. That is, just as God warns the people of the generation of the biblical Cain who, for his grave sin must forever carry a special mark, a distinctive stigma, and wander the earth but must not be murdered, so, too, the Jews have lost their homeland and must wander the earth, but they must not be murdered. And that position was essentially adhered to by the Catholic hierarchy. That is to say, if one looks at the history of the Catholic Church and its relations with the Jewish people from the early period of its ascension to worldly power, one sees that the papacy generally adhered to what one might call a mediated, if severe and assuredly highly prejudiced, policy toward the Jews.

Catholic society as a whole was, of course, more variegated, more complicated in its attitude toward the Jews in its midst but, when necessary—and it was often necessary—the church hierarchy came to the defense of Jews. So, for example, we know that the papacy continuously exonerated the Jews of the "blood libel." It sent out commissions to investigate this charge very carefully, and, as late as the twentieth century, the reports came back that the Jews were innocent of this terrible accusation. Popes and cardinals also provided other sorts of protection during the time of the Crusades. Here the tale of Bernard of Clairveaux's protective acts in Provence at the start of the Second Crusade is especially worth recalling. It should also be remembered that it was to the local bishops that the Jews ran during the Crusades. Now, why did they go to them? Because the Jews knew that the Catholic bishops were committed to save them. In practice, they could not always save them, but as a rule they did try.

Then, too, the Church did a remarkable thing after the Crusades. On some occasions it allowed Jews who had been baptized by force to return to their Jewish faith, even though such an action was against official Catholic doctrine. All this, and much more, constitutes what I call the Eleventh

Christian Commandment: "Thou shalt not murder Jews." The fact that the Jewish people survived approximately fifteen hundred years under Christian domination, from Constantine to the French Revolution, is hard evidence in support of the claim that the Church was true to this theological-ethical position in its generality, never forgetting all the real, terrible, often deadly violence that did occur over the centuries.

Here I also need to note one further odd historic fact. At the same time that the papacy and the Church exonerated Jews from charges of the "blood libel," it often canonized the victims of such libels. Thus, while it judged that the Jews didn't murder the Christians involved in such libels, the Church still often made such victims martyrs. One thinks here, for example, of the famous case of Hugh of Lincoln, who became St. Hugh. So there was at least some significant ambiguity relative to Jewish matters even in official Catholic circles.

Moreover, at the lower levels of Catholic society, you have a social order where the diabolization of the Jew—an image that begins very early on with the characterization of the Jew as "the spawn of the devil" in John 8—first becomes fixed and widely disseminated through the *Adversus Judaeos* tradition, and then is translated into practical, political, and social categories in the lived reality of late Roman and then medieval Christian law and life. For example, Jews could not go into the medieval marketplace until late in the day when the good fruit had already been picked out, and even then they couldn't touch the remaining fruit because once they had touched it they would have polluted it. Again, there was a widespread myth in the Middle Ages that Jewish men menstruated and that all Jews gave off a special foul odor that could only be overcome through baptism. There was also the widespread caricature of Jews as beings with horns and tails and cloven, pig-like feet (characteristics also attributed to the devil).

Therefore, to summarize, the medieval period represents a multilayered reality relative to Jewish-Christian relations. While the church hierarchy acted with considerable social and political "correctness," the overall social environment represented by the middle and lower classes of society was much more hostile. Here the diabolization of the Jew became, for many Christians, something like an authentic representation, a real understanding, of the "otherness" of the Jew.

The Modern Period

Now, it is against this medieval background that we have to begin to consider the defining features of the modern period. To begin my own reflections on the modern era, I note that this afternoon's session is structured in a tripartite form: Christian anti-Semitism, the Nation, and the *Shoah*. I'm not sure that I would have accented the Nation to such a marked degree because the Nation (and nationalism) is only one factor in a very diverse circumstance. What happened historically, just to remind ourselves, is that with the coming of Jewish emancipation in the late eighteenth and early nineteenth centuries, you also have the arrival of a new phenomenon called the *Judenfrage*. There is no *Judenfrage* before emancipation because both Christians and Jews knew who and what the Jews were. Both agreed that the Jews were a nation in exile as a result of sin or sins. For the Church, the sin was that of deicide, the rejection and crucifixion of Jesus. For the Jews themselves, the sins were the violations of the Halacha (Jewish Law) and the disregard of their covenantal obligations for which God had punished them. Thus, both Jews and Christians knew that the Jews were in exile because God was punishing them, and that in some future time he would redeem them from exile, from the *Galut*, and return them to the land of Israel.

With the arrival of emancipation, however, the situation became more complicated because emancipation was predicated on the liberal sociopolitical assumption that you could eliminate Jewish nationalism and peoplehood and, at the same time, separate Jews from Judaism. I would say that this was, in fact, the fundamental thesis behind emancipation. One sees it present, for example, in the famous repercussive remark of Clermont Tonnere to the French Assembly: "To the Jews as a people, nothing; to the Jews as individuals, everything." A comment to which he appended the dictum: "We cannot have a nation within a nation."

Here we have, clearly stated, the idea that Jews have to relinquish their national identity and become essentially a religious sect, or even better, lose their "Jewish" identity altogether and merge—given the fact that they now have the opportunity to merge—into the larger nation-state. Now, such merging would have been a benign solution to the *Judenfrage* in the sense that it would not have included violence—assuming that the non-Jewish society actually meant this offer to be taken seriously and that the Jews had accepted this arrangement. But, of course, most Jews were not prepared to give up their Jewishness without further ado. Instead, there was within the Jewish community a wide variety of views on what should happen. These ranged from suggestions that recommended conversion to Christianity on the one hand, all the way to Zionism (by the end of the nineteenth century), which rejected all the other solutions as making an undignified, unacceptable, and unrealistic compromise of one sort or another with Europe. Compromises that were, in any case, impossible, because Europe could never ingest its Jewish community in a reasonable way.

On the Christian side, there was also a variety of opinions ranging from liberal to hostile, and the most hostile, of course, would be the late arrival of racial anti-Semitism. Remember what racial anti-Semitism is. In Hitler's version, it is the *Endlösung der Judenfrage*, the "Final Solution" to the Jewish problem. In other words, for the racial anti-Semite, all the other solutions that had been tried—whether Jewish solutions like assimilation, Reform Judaism, the *Wissenschaft des Judentums*, and neo-Orthodoxy, or Christian solutions, whether liberal or conservative—were all chimerical. The only possibility of successfully dealing with the *Judenfrage* was by confronting its root, which is a racial root, while at the same time realizing that Jews cannot change their genetic inheritance and therefore, as an honorable Aryan, one must be willing to participate in the annihilation of the Jewish people.

Thus, the entire context of our conversation is grounded in the post-emancipation reality of the *Judenfrage*, of what it means to be a Jew and for there to be a Jewish community in Europe after the French (and subsequent) Revolution. Of course, this situation was, as I have already noted, polymorphous. But there is one essential fact that I would like to emphasize: even the liberal Christians, i.e., those who espoused liberal solutions to the *Judenfrage*, were anti-Jewish. I specifically do not use the word *anti-Semitic* but *anti-Jewish*, by which I mean that even the liberals wanted to separate Jews from their Judaism because they held that, while Jewish men and women might be made over into acceptable men and women, Judaism as such was a negative phenomenon that needed to be disregarded.

I do not think that you will find any sympathetic portrayal of Judaism in European literature, philosophy, or theology, written by a non-Jew, before World War II—with one exception: George Eliot's *Daniel Deronda*. Moreover, even here there are certain difficult questions to answer regarding Eliot's views of Jews and Judaism that I cannot pursue in this context.

In effect, following emancipation, on the non-Jewish side you have no friends of Judaism and only a few friends of the established and ongoing Jewish community. You have friends of Jews, for example, Lessing, but remember at the high point of Lessing's *Nathan the Wise,* he says about Mendelssohn: "My God, you are a Christian, you are a Christian." That is, Mendelssohn is wonderful because he acts like a Christian not a Jew. So the fact is, even here, Judaism as an ism, as a positive way of life, is denigrated.

One has to understand that the enormous weight of the historical tradition of anti-Judaism did not disappear just because the French Revolution came and gave the Jews citizenship. It did not disappear because Napoleon's armies brought down the ghetto walls in Germany and northern Italy. It did not disappear because in 1858 Britain allowed the Jews to vote and to hold seats in Parliament. Despite the political progress that did occur, there remained a residual, highly influential, phenomenon at work within European society: the "mythic" image of the Jew. And it is precisely here that the Church bears some responsibility for what happened to the Jewish people in the modern world, for it was the Church above all other actors and factors—as already briefly described above—that created, from the New Testament and patristic periods onwards, the "otherness" of the Jew. And this "otherness" does not dissipate, does not disappear completely in the modern era: it is present all the time in the stereotype—whether the liberal stereotype or the right-wing stereotype—of "the Jew." Moreover, this continuing belief in Jewish "otherness" permits all kinds of contradictory elements to be attributed to "the Jew" and "the Jews." If you are a socialist, for example, "the

Jew" is a capitalist. If you are a capitalist, "the Jew" is a socialist. If you are a rural person, "the Jew" is a city person. If you are a nationalist, the Jews are international cosmopolitans. If you are a cosmopolitan internationalist, the Jews are narrow-minded, self-interested nationalists. Whatever you don't like, that is "the Jew." It is in this sense that "the Jew" and "the Jews" are "mythic" creatures.

Nationalism and the "Jewish Question"

Let me now turn to the challenging issue of nationalism and the "Jewish question." Certainly the idea of the Nation and the concept of nationalism are important in the modern period, and I would note immediately that nationalism is not, as is sometimes thought, always a bad thing for Jews. Nationalism is, as a historical actuality, a polyvalent thing.

When the first nation-state in Europe was created in Spain at the end of the fifteenth century, it was bad for Jews because the Spanish state needed a new cement to hold it together, and this cement, not surprisingly, turned out to be Catholicism. In consequence, Spain's Jews (and Muslims) had either to be converted or expelled. Alternatively, in other places, nationalism was a good thing for Jews because it helped break down the extant Catholic culture and the existing politics of medieval Europe, and thereby helped to create new sociopolitical opportunities for Jews, like those that came into being in Protestant England and Holland. Already in 1795, Holland was willing to grant Jews freedom, and even before that, during the period of the Dutch Republic in the seventeenth century, Holland showed a very liberal face toward Jews and Judaism. So it's not nationalism *per se* that is a problem.

Also, I would argue that nationalism is overemphasized in the contemporary analysis of the *Judenfrage* and modern anti-Semitism. I think, for example, of Arno Mayer's highly misleading book on the Holocaust, *Why Did the Heavens Not Darken?* that misunderstands the issue in a very serious way. The fact that an Austrian who became the führer of Germany sets out to murder the Jews of Rhodes and Salonika in Poland is not a phenomenon explained by "nationalism." In fact, it has almost nothing to do with nationalism. If one considers all the diverse geographical locations and all the diverse populations involved in the *Shoah,* one comes quickly to understand that what is at issue is not a matter of nationalism. Rather, it is something else. Thus, nationalism is too narrow a category to explain what happens in the Holocaust.

Instead, I would call your attention to romanticism, which I think is a crucial factor in this matrix. What happens after the emancipation is that Europe quickly turns from Enlightenment rationality to romanticism. The romantics argue that what defines the nature of society and the nature of human identity is not reason but passion, instinct, inborn sensitivities, and the like. Remember, Enlightenment "reason" was the basis on which Europe had moved forward toward Jewish emancipation and liberation. According to the dogmas of the Enlightenment, you could liberate Jews as well as separate a Jew from his Judaism because all people, including Jews, were rational. Therefore, the fact that the Jew smelled of garlic or wore special clothes and spoke Yiddish was epiphenomena. You could eliminate these social practices and get to the real man or woman who shared the common intellectual faculties possessed by all human beings. Romanticism now denied this elemental premise.

Very soon, by the beginning of the nineteenth century, romanticism had taken hold, and it has continued for the past two hundred years to be one of the foundational forces of modernity. In a sense, Hitler is a romantic, and Freud is a romantic, and Nietzsche is a romantic. By *romantic* I mean someone who emphasizes that the fundamental, defining feature or features of the human personality (and the social order) is not reason, not intellect, but something else.

Now, what else is it? The romantics had a theory, as I began to note above, that the individual is defined by passions and by "natural" associations, and that these passions and associations are deeper, more abiding, and ultimately far more consequential than reason. The depth of these phenomena entails, among other things, that the nature of meaningful life, as well as the meaning of life, including one's moral and spiritual well-being, is "caused" by these nonrational factors as well as by the kind of group one "naturally," and therefore necessarily, belongs to.

Importantly, whatever such ideas meant in Herder when he talked about the *Volksgeist*, they soon became a basis for a process of differentiation that came to be used against Jews. The way in which this idea becomes historically embodied is very interesting. Scholars and others begin to look for evidence of national distinctiveness in various places, most especially in those cultural sources that are truly the product of the national spirit putatively uncorrupted by modernity and its allies. So, for example, the Brothers Grimm began to study folktales. Why? Because the real German spirit is still to be found alive in folktales. It's not in Kant and it's not in Hegel. Likewise, Wagner goes back to pre-Christian Nordic myths, because the real German is the Ur-German, the pre-Christian Aryan Superman, not the contemporary Mendelssohn-Bartholdy who is writing bad music. Wagner, I note, hated Mendelssohn-Bartholdy and wrote an essay on the "Jewification" of music although, in fact, he nearly always had Jewish conductors; indeed, he seems only to have trusted Jewish conductors. In addition, one has the creation of national dictionaries, because in the national language you have the essence of a people. And you have Schlegel's poetry and the (hateful) work of Father Jahn and the (anti-Semitic) philosophizing of Fichte and later of Schopenhauer.

The Jews have their romantics, too. Buber's Hasidic tales, for example, are a form of Jewish romanticism. Buber re-edits the original Hasidic tales in his own distinctive way, and then tells his audience that these represent authentic Judaism. They do so because they are folk religion. They are not *Halacha;* they are not high religion; they are not the work of learned rabbis; they are not the metaphysical treatises of Maimonides. They are the work of the simple person, but that's really where you find the authentic Jewish spirit.

Now, the sociopolitical significance of this sort of doctrine, reinforced by this sort of material, is that it leads to the conclusion that Jews cannot be citizens. Why? Because being a member of a nation is not a matter of a social or legal contract. The idea of contract, which is at the basis of the modern state, is, for the romantics, a mistake. You cannot create the state in this "artificial" way. Rather, the state is best and most properly understood as a *Volksgemeinschaft* and, as such, must exclude the Jew who belongs to a different folk and a different national community. It is on the basis of this kind of political theory that you get the anti-Semitic calls for Jewish exclusion. Accordingly, romanticism becomes a fundamental force not only for romantic theory in the arts and culture but also for anti-Semitic social and political theories and certain forms of nationalism.

I need to add, in fairness, that for some anti-Semitic romantic political thinkers there was a legitimate way out for the Jews. They could convert and thus become members of the Christian state because they would now be Christian. In consequence, romantic anti-Semitism need not, and in practice did not, propose a genocidal solution to the *Judenfrage*. The main goal of romantic anti-Semitism is exclusion, not extermination. It is in this fundamental aspect that it differs from, and is far less radical than, racial anti-Semitism, which denies any and all possibility of conversion.

What the Jews are accused of in such romantic sociopolitical theorizing is particularly interesting. Jews are accused in these folkish ideologies of what one may call *folkicide*, as compared to the earlier Christian accusation of deicide. In other words, the earlier myth of the Jew as the religious enemy, the "unassimilableness" of the Jew, his otherness, is now translated into political and cultural terms marked by the unassimilability of the Jew as anti-folkish. He doesn't belong to the state, and he cannot really use the national language. So, for example, Jews don't really speak German; they speak Yiddish, and when they do speak German, they do so badly. If you read German literature of the turn of the century, you see how the authors always make fun of the way Jews speak German because they are not really German. You also see how they make fun of other kinds of Jewish behavior because, once again, Jews are not really German.

We find this notion of Jewish "otherness" everywhere in nineteenth- and early twentieth-century European politics and culture. For example, we see it in the literature of all the countries of Europe, whether it is high literature or pseudo-high literature, like that produced by Houston Stewart Chamberlain, or the literature of the streets that we would buy on train station platforms. In this literature, we always find a radical dualism between Jews and non-Jews and a disparagement of Jews and Judaism. For example, the folk live on the land while the Jews live in the city. The folk is a peasant; the Jews are sophisticated city dwellers. The folk, of course, are Catholic or Protestant, depending on which national community is producing this literature, while the Jews are Jews, that is, religious aliens. The folk are honest; the Jews are dishonest. The folk are sexually constrained; the Jews are salacious and sexually deviant. The folk are patriotic; the Jews are loyal only to themselves and their people. The folk are physically strong and healthy; the Jews are effete and sickly. The folk always share a common ancient language; the Jews don't share that language.

This theorizing was also felt in the political arena in complex ways that drew on the older legacy of Catholic anti-Judaism that excluded the Jew from the mainstreams of political life. In this sense, i.e., recognizing both the continuity and the novelty of modern anti-Jewish politics after 1789, we are not surprised to find that, after the Napoleonic Wars and the restoration in France, Catholics were the ones who led the right-wing effort to once again disemancipate the Jews. Or that the disemancipation of the Jews was encouraged by Catholic circles in France right up to and including Vichy. Again, it is not an accident that the anti-Dreyfus forces were heavily Catholic and connected to the Catholic hierarchy. And there is no doubt that Drumont drew on deep roots in the Catholic community and that the *Action Francaise* drew on a wide array of Catholic associations. Now I don't say this to be anti-Catholic. Rather, I want to call attention to the fact that when one tries to examine this historical and theological record, one cannot make a simple distinction between the official policy of the Church and the historical experience of the Church, of the Catholic community, as a living reality.

I understand the difference between the Church and its followers. In this context, I recall a line in a play I saw many years ago entitled *Hadrian VII*. One of the characters in the play made a distinction between the faith and the faithful, and I think this is a very important distinction. The faith has its pure ideal, and the faithful are human beings who are subject to all kinds of pressures and manifest all sorts of weaknesses. But that is the reality of Catholic-Jewish relations. The Jewish people do not deal with the faith;

they deal with—and have dealt with—the faithful, and that is an issue that one has to face.

Also, in the modern period, one has in the United States the phenomenon of Father Coughlin and the American Catholic right, while in England one has Chesterton and the whole Catholic intellectual community, almost all of whom were anti-Semitic. It was in this circle that the famous ditty, "How odd of God to choose the Jews," was coined. In addition, Catholics constituted powerful anti-Semitic forces in Slovakia, Croatia, Poland, Vienna, and the Austrian Empire. I remind you that Karl Lueger, the mayor of Vienna in the 1890s, was one of the first politicians in the late nineteenth century to run successfully on an official anti-Semitic program. Lueger became the mayor of Vienna as an official anti-Semite. It is true that he did not fully act out this anti-Semitism in the actual governing of Vienna, and that the Jews of Vienna experienced a golden age under Lueger. It is an odd paradox. But the fact that he was elected as a declared anti-Semite in Catholic Vienna was not serendipitous.

It's not accidental that Hitler was Catholic. It's not accidental that the leadership of the SS was Catholic. Now I don't lay the SS at the foot of the Church; indeed, I insist on distinguishing, on separating, the two very clearly. But I do say that one has to look at the deep and profound roots of the historicized human personality, at the specific context of people's lives.

Alternatively—and this is one of the key reasons why I insist on separating Christian anti-Semitism and Nazism—in the modern era the Church, in fact, loses much of its authority and therefore, even if it wished to impose certain views, it lacked the authority to do so. At the same time, the secular state came to the fore and replaced the Church. What then followed is at the core of the issue we are analyzing today. On the one hand, the old anti-Jewish image fostered by the Church passed as a common inheritance into the modern world. On the other hand, the constraints on anti-Jewish violence that the Church had imposed, that it linked to its anti-Judaism, were discarded by the modern, autonomous, all-powerful, semi-secular, or secular state. As a result, what is left of the Christian tradition of anti-Judaism is the vile baggage of anti-Judaism without the restraining, transcendental, moral center of "Thou shalt not."

The modern state is an immanent state. It sees itself as being required to solve its problems here and now. Thus, whereas the Catholic Church held a metaphysical doctrine that entailed a willingness to put things off, including the "final solution to the Jewish problem," to the eschaton, i.e., to a time when God himself would resolve the issue, the modern state has an immanent, historical scale of values and therefore requires a solution to its problematic now. Hence, one cannot avoid the challenges that existence presents, or transfer them into symbols and metaphors as occurs, for example, in passion plays. Instead, one has to do something here and now. For a racial anti-Semite of Hitler's breed, this means, relative to the "Jewish problem," building death camps.

Conclusion

Let me conclude by repeating and extending a point made earlier.[1] It must be clearly stated so as not to be misunderstood that Nazism is the radicalization of all prior anti-Semitism *plus* something new. Nazism is a *novum*. The idea that you have to physically exterminate every Jewish man, woman, and child, that the ultimate enemy is a Jewish fetus—a fetus—that is a n-o-v-u-m. There is no historical precedent for such an idea or such a practice in Christian theology. Christian theology always allowed, indeed encouraged, the conversion of the Jews—and indeed there has been large scale Jewish conversion in many places throughout history. Likewise, the Nazi doctrine of annihilation and its translation into practice differs from the anti-Semitic doctrine and practice of the nineteenth century. That is to say, Nazism is not merely the recycling of earlier Christian polemics or, again, the extension of modern anti-Semitic theories. It is, rather, a novel, radical amalgam of social Darwinism, modern Manicheanism, a specific form of racial theory that is based on a model that interprets racial conflict in aggressive parasitological forms, and the negative metaphysicalizing of the Jew. Here, in the Third Reich, we find something without precedent, although sadly not something wholly *sui generis*.

NOTES

1. As this paper was going to press the Vatican, under the direction of Cardinal Ratzinger, issued a very troubling document entitled *Dominus Iesus*. This document, despite all the progress since Vatican II, appears to reaffirm the more traditional teaching that "outside the [Catholic] Church, there is no salvation," and to recycle the traditional notions of supersessionism—and even to drive for conversion—vis-à-vis Jews and Judaism. The optimism about the future of Jewish-Catholic relations expressed when this paper was first delivered in March 1999 has, I am afraid, to be reconsidered in light of this recent development.

8

We Remember:
The Vatican and the Holocaust in Historical Context
MICHAEL R. MARRUS

More than a decade in preparation, *We Remember: A Reflection on the Shoah,* issued in March 1998 by the Vatican's Commission for Religious Relations with the Jews, speaks sympathetically to Jews who believe that the Church abandoned them during the Second World War and who trace this abandonment to centuries of Christian hostility toward the Jewish people. "At the end of this millennium the Catholic Church desires to express her deep sorrow for the failures of her sons and daughters in every age," it says. Declaring its sorrow for what happened, and using the Hebrew word for repentance, *teshuvah,* the document "approaches with deep respect and great compassion the experience of extermination, the *Shoah,* suffered by the Jewish people during World War II." Looking to the future, *We Remember* draws from this reflection a "binding commitment" to better relations between the two communities, and to prevent such catastrophes from ever happening again. "The victims from their graves, and the survivors, through the vivid testimony of what they have suffered, have become a loud voice calling the attention of all humanity," the document concludes. "To remember this terrible experience is to become fully conscious of the salutary warning it entails: the spoiled seeds of anti-Semitism and anti-Judaism must never again be allowed to take root in any human heart."[1]

We Remember locates the murder of European Jews in historical time, but the accent is in the title, on *remembrance,* rather than historical analysis. "Before this horrible genocide," the document states, "no one can remain indifferent"; its inhumanity "is beyond the capacity of words to convey"; "the *Shoah* was certainly the worst suffering of all." That is why there is a "duty of remembrance." *We Remember* "calls upon all Christians, and indeed invites all men and women, to seek to discern in the passage of history the signs of divine Providence at work," but, as that language suggests, the categories for this discernment are overwhelmingly moral—based upon empathy, responsibility, and obligation—and not those of the historian, understanding events in the context of particular times.[2] As the document insists, the murder of European Jews "cannot be fully measured by the ordinary criteria of historical research alone." Indeed it cannot. But historical reflection can certainly assist the process of greater understanding.

We Remember presents its historical overview as a way of pointing to the consequences of misreading sacred texts, and of assigning responsibility, rather than as a detailed investigation. The history of relations between Jews and Christians has been "a tormented one," it says, in which the balance over two millennia "has been quite negative." Hostility toward the Jews flowed from "erroneous and unjust interpretations of the New Testament regarding the Jewish people and their alleged culpability" for the death of Jesus. At the end of the eighteenth century and the beginning of the nineteenth century, "a false and exacerbated nationalism took hold," promoting "an anti-Judaism that was essentially more sociological and political than religious." Occasionally, the Church denounced the accompanying racism, underscoring:

> . . . the difference which exists between anti-Semitism, based on theories contrary to the constant teaching of the Church on the unity of the human race and on the equal dignity of all races and all peoples, and the long-standing sentiments of mistrust and hostility that we call anti-Judaism, of which, unfortunately, Christians have also been guilty.

Nazism represented a culmination of this nationalist and racist ideology—assaulting the very core of religious commitment. Nazi ideology "refused to acknowledge any transcendent reality as the source of life and the criterion of moral good"; and some Nazis went even further, giving "proof of a definite hatred directed at God himself." This was the driving force behind

the murder of European Jews. "The *Shoah* was the work of a thoroughly modern neo-pagan regime. Its anti-Semitism had its roots outside of Christianity
and, in pursuing its aims, it did not hesitate to oppose the Church and persecute
her members also." To be sure, the document concedes, the Nazis persecution
of the Jews was "made easier by anti-Jewish prejudices imbedded in some
Christian minds and hearts." The "governments of some Western countries of
Christian tradition . . . were more than hesitant to open their borders to persecuted Jews." Some Christians did less than they might have done to assist the
persecuted, especially Jews. Quoting John Paul II, *We Remember* points out that
along with the outstanding instances of rescue efforts by some, "the spiritual
resistance and concrete action of other Christians was not that which might
have been expected from Christ's followers." Hence, a "heavy burden of conscience" and "a call to penitence" are required for Christians today.

Controversially, *We Remember* introduces the wartime pope, Pius XII,
in a passage referring to "those who did help to save Jewish lives and did as
much as was in their power, even to the point of placing their own lives in
danger." Jewish testimony is introduced to drive the point home: "During and
after the war, Jewish communities and Jewish leaders expressed their thanks
for all that had been done for them, including what Pope Pius XII did personally or through his representatives to save hundreds of thousands of
Jewish lives." A lengthy footnote, at this point, expatiates on "the wisdom of
Pope Pius XII's diplomacy" and testifies to his rescue efforts, citing the
appreciation of such personalities as Leon Kubowitzki, secretary general of
the World Jewish Congress, and the Israeli foreign minister Golda Meir.

We Remember understands Pius XII, together with others who assisted
Jews, within a framework of fidelity to the teachings of Christianity, acknowledging those who had the courage to challenge pagan doctrines of racism, the
supremacy of the state, and a hatred of God. For historians, this approach is
not wrong, but rather inadequate. Whatever their personal beliefs or commitments, historians ponder the conditions within which men and women make
decisions and look at the interaction between the two; and they examine how
outlooks were shaped by preceding circumstances and how visions of the
world changed in the kaleidoscope of events. While not abjuring judgments,

as historians they tend to see the world in shades of gray, rather than black and white, recognizing that most historical actors are neither entirely faithful to their ideals, nor blown off course by "errors and failures," but rather spend most of their time somewhere in between—tugged this way and that by historical forces to which we are all subject. This is the framework, I believe, in which one can profitably examine the role of Pope Pius XII, drawing upon the limited evidence we now have at our disposal.

Whatever else can be said about *We Remember,* it seems obvious that this was not a statement written by historians. The document offers little sense of the time-bound ways in which the men and women who faced the murder of European Jews saw the world, understood it, and acted in a manner conditioned at least in part by the environment in which they lived. To "build upon" *We Remember* and to promote the fuller understanding, called for in its pages, of what Pope John Paul II describes as "an indelible stain on the history of [this past] century," I believe that such historical thinking can be useful.[3] What follows, without weighing the substance of the question of the Vatican's role, suggests how historical context might assist us in examining that question.

Three Background Conditions

Among the background conditions helpful to explain the role of the pope during the Holocaust, three seem essential: Pius XII's personal diplomatic style, the traditional neutrality of the Holy See, and the concrete circumstances of the Vatican in the Second World War. Together, these shaped the historical context for the pope's actions, defining both what he felt were the appropriate objectives of diplomacy and the catastrophes that loomed if things went awry. Commentators often spoke of the anguish of the wartime pope, his struggles with himself, and his difficulties in charting his course.[4] I believe that such observations were not merely complimentary appreciation of the seriousness with which the pope took the demands of his office, but rather accurate reflections of how the pope contemplated his options during the Second World War.

Elected pope in March 1939, Eugenio Pacelli assumed office as Europe moved ominously toward war. Historians have drawn attention to how steeped the new pontiff was in the outlook and habits of mind of Vatican diplomacy. Known as ascetic, solitary, and a man of great personal dignity and reserve, Pacelli had served as papal nuncio in Munich and then Berlin 1917 to 1929, and for a decade thereafter as cardinal secretary of state. Although he had supported his predecessor ably during the 1930s, when Pope Pius XI came into increasing confrontation with the fascist dictators, Pacelli was also known to favor a more moderate policy—one that sought accommodation rather than conflict on several fronts at once, and appeasement, rather than confrontation in an increasingly dangerous international scene. "Cardinal Pacelli constantly strives to pacify and to exert a moderating influence on the Pope," wrote the astute and perceptive Diego von Bergen, the German ambassador to the Holy See in 1936, reflecting on his own experience to that point.[5] If anything, the differences between Pius XI and Pacelli widened in the last three years of the former's reign, so that the contrast between the two became pointed. Pius XI was outspoken and quick tempered, observes historian George Kent. "Pius XII was reticent and cautious. While the former was known for his impulsiveness and stubbornness, his successor was known as the 'diplomatic' Pope."[6]

To Pius XII, a world war was the great calamity, particularly dangerous for the Catholic Church. Remembering no doubt the First World War with its accompanying social upheaval, the Bolshevik Revolution, and the collapse of the Catholic bastion of the Hapsburg Empire, Pacelli strove mightily to prevent the outbreak of fighting, and once it began, to limit its extent and to bring the parties to a peaceful resolution. At all costs he wanted to avoid the dilemmas of his predecessor, Benedict XV (pope from 1914–1922), who found his authority draining away as Catholics fought each other to the death for four years over the ruins of once-stable, church-supporting societies. Hence the risks Pacelli took in launching several peace initiatives, in acting as a conduit for German opponents of Hitler, and hence his reluctance to upset the diplomatic equilibrium by protesting both the persecution of the Church in Germany and Germany's flagrant victimization of Catholic Poland, the latter in the face of sometime poignant appeals by Polish clerics who pleaded for a more outspoken condemnation from the Holy See.

The Vatican's neutrality, in these circumstances, was not only required for a noncombatant with certain well-defined humanitarian responsibilities that depended upon engagement with both sides, but it was genuinely felt to be the pope's duty as the leader of the Church in a world torn apart by war. As each side proclaimed the rightness of its cause, Pius sought to preserve the influence and the standing of the Holy See as the voice of truth extending everywhere. As the world divided into two camps, each seeking the submergence of the other, the pope struggled to prevent the shattering of the Church and to maintain the allegiance of Catholics on both sides. And as violence and destruction spread, Pacelli also believed it his responsibility to preserve the monuments, the structures, and the institutions of Catholicism, particularly in its Italian heartland, for the existing and future generations. The pope, declared Pius XII in his first encyclical, *Summi Pontificatus,* issued in October 1939, had to stand "above the storm of error and passion." As God's representative on earth, it was his job to look to the future—a future committed to "the spread of the Kingdom of Christ." "Once the bitterness and cruel strifes [sic] of the present have ceased," he proclaimed, "the new order of the world, of national and international life, must rest no longer on the quicksands of changeable and ephemeral standards that depend only on selfish interests of groups and individuals. No, they must rest on the unshakable foundation, on the sold rock of natural law and of Divine Revelation." "The accomplishment of this task of regeneration," the pope declared, " . . . is an essential and maternal office of the Church."[7]

Neutrality, in the Vatican's calculations, also held out some promise—an element that commended it as a policy and discouraged deviations, even for humanitarian purposes. Fortified by belief in his own supranational capacity, Pius XII nourished the hope that the Holy See could play a constructive and even a triumphant role in the global upheaval—limiting the conflict, bringing an early end to the hostilities through negotiations among the belligerents, and emerging at the end of the war invigorated, having confounded the forces of irreligion, anticlericalism, and anti-Catholicism. What an achievement, at one point mused Pius' lieutenant, Monsignor Giovanni Montini, the future

Pope Paul VI, "if everyone could see yet again, and now more than in any other instance, that the Holy See saves Italy."[8]

"How many divisions has the pope?" Napoleon is supposed to have asked in a derisory way, underscoring the weakness of the Vatican—without military force, without a secure territorial base, and without even the means to speak to the outside world if whoever was in charge of its Roman precincts decided otherwise. In war, the Vatican was especially vulnerable, in the middle of Rome, the capital of one of the Axis powers, and unable to ensure its own food, water, gas, and electricity, except with the willingness of the Italian (and after September 1943, German) authorities. To this day, historians debate as to whether, at various points, the Germans intended to break into Vatican City, brush aside the quaintly dressed Swiss guards with their pikes, and kidnap the pope. Whatever the führer's intentions—and the balance of opinion seems to tell against the notion that this was an idea sustained seriously, or for very long—there seems little doubt that the pope and his entourage genuinely worried about this prospect. In 1943, officials in the Vatican certainly activated contingency plans and prepared for the worst, a reminder of just how vulnerable was the Holy See, and how fraught with dangers were any moves outside the framework of neutrality and established diplomatic rituals.

Physically vulnerable, the Vatican was also culturally walled off from the rest of Rome, not to mention the rest of Italian society and the wider world. Present-day readers are struck by the archaic, abstract language in which the pope expressed himself in his formal communications—but the barriers to interaction with the outside were not just built of words.

Historians David Alvarez and Robert Graham comment on the intense "ecclesiastical flavour" of "Vatican City," seeing this as one reason that German espionage failed, despite considerable efforts, to penetrate the Vatican and succeed in its campaign against the Holy See. They write:

> Aside from laborers, gardeners, guards, a few technicians in the museums and library, and a scattering of junior clerks in a few departments, all posts in the Vatican were filled by priests or members of religious orders . . . This

> community of priests, nuns, and brothers represented a
> largely closed society which consciously recognized
> boundaries between itself and secular society, and which
> encouraged only limited interaction across those bound-
> aries. Distinguished by dress, education, lifestyle, and dis-
> cipline from their counterparts in the secular world, the
> ecclesiastical citizens of the Vatican were also products of
> an administrative tradition and allegiance to the Church
> and its Pontiff.[9]

These were not circumstances that bred a close and empathetic interaction
with victim groups, and particularly, as we shall see, a group of victims so
outside the sphere of traditional Church outreach as the Jews.

"We can be sure that Pacelli did not particularly care for Jews," writes
István Déak in a recent review.[10] Déak's point is the very opposite of John
Cornwell's sensationalist arguments in *Hitler's Pope,* and indeed is offered in
refutation of the idea, in that book, that Pope Pius XII harbored a special
animus against Jewish people or had any particular reason to refuse to help
them.[11] What seems far more likely is that Pacelli simply participated unre-
flectingly in the widespread and nearly universal disparagement of Jews so
common in the Catholic Church before the revolutionary transformations of
the Second Vatican Council in the mid-1960s. "Priests saw the Jews as Christ-
killers, or at least as the Chosen People who had proven deaf and blind to the
teachings of Jesus of Nazareth." Nearly as bad, Jews were seen to be at the
forefront of so many of the currents of modernity that had assailed the standing of the Church, had eroded its authority, and had contributed to what the
pope called, in *Summi Pontificatus,* "the spiritual and moral bankruptcy of
the present day." "The clergy tended to feel that Jews were behind the
Enlightenment, Freemasonry, rationalism, the French Revolution, liberalism,
capitalism, democracy, socialism, communism, anarchism, radicalism, anticlericalism, secularism, materialism, evolutionary theory, and urban
immorality: all mortal enemies of the Church and of Catholic teachings."[12]
Such views did not prevent some of those who held them from treating Jews

with courtesy, and in some cases from courageously helping them during the war. But the very commonplace character of these ideas means we cannot avoid them as part of the historical context within which the Vatican acted during the persecution and murder of Jews during the war.

Traditional anti-Judaism of this sort undoubtedly played a role in the reaction of the Holy See to anti-Jewish persecutions leading up to the implementation of the "Final Solution," constituting an essential precondition for the European-wide campaign to round up, deport, and murder the Jewish population of Europe. The evidence suggests, for example, that the Vatican had no quarrel with the collaborationist government of Vichy's anti-Jewish persecutions in France in the first two years of the German occupation. Sounded out by the French head of state, Philippe Pétain in the summer of 1941, the French ambassador to the Holy See, Léon Bérard, reported that the Vatican harbored no fundamental objection to the confiscation of the Jews, property, seizing of their livelihood, and marginalizing of them in French society—so long as such measures did not entrench upon important church prerogatives in the field of marriage, and so long as these policies were administered with "justice and charity."[13] Similarly, the Vatican did not call to account the Slovak, Croatian, Hungarian, or Rumanian governments when they instituted similar policies that ultimately facilitated more extreme measures during the Holocaust. To be sure, whether for legalistic reasons or out of a commitment to its own, the Vatican embraced the cause of converted Jews, often referred to as "non-Aryan Christians"—arguing that the persecution of these individuals violated the terms of prewar concordats, treaties negotiated with the Holy See that assigned to the Church matters concerning the religious classification. It is important, in any overall assessment of the role of the Vatican during the Holocaust, to keep in mind the distinction that the Church made, perhaps with some justification, between Jewish converts to Christianity and Jews who remained Jewish—sometimes referred to as *Mosaic Jews*. Church officials regularly supported the rights of the former, with the blessing of the Vatican. So far as the latter were concerned, the record is much more mixed.

What all this suggests is simply that most churchmen, and the Vatican as well, took as a point of departure the anti-Jewish assumptions common in the pre-*Nostra Aetate* Church, and that such ideas should simply be understood as part of the ideological landscape of the times. Students of Vatican policy and its diplomatic corps, the papal nuncios, find traces of such attitudes in questions having to do with conversion, emigration, anti-Jewish legislation, religious education, the confiscation of property, Palestine, and many other matters that became associated with what we understand as "the Holocaust." Such assumptions, commonplace in the 1930s, almost certainly dulled responses to the Nazis' campaign against the Jews when this turned in a genocidal direction—beginning in a massive scale with the Germans attack on the Soviet Union in June 1941, and extending across Europe in mid 1942, to include West European countries as well.

However, we should take care not to pounce on occasional remarks or expressions, coming from a world quite different from our own, as evidence of an anti-Jewish agenda. There is no evidence that anti-Semitism lurked within the Vatican itself, or even that Jewish issues were importantly on the minds of the leaders of the Church during the murderous phase of the Nazis' campaign. Like other heads of state during the war, Pope Pius XII contended with many humanitarian appeals—from Catholics and non-Catholics, individuals, groups, and entire societies. Innately cautious and ill disposed to risk taking, Pius maintained his focus on the safeguarding and the promotion of the institutions, integrity, and the apostolic mission of the Church in a turbulent world. Overall, the truth seems to be that Jews simply did not figure very high on the priorities of the pope or his principal advisors. And as historians of the Holocaust can certainly attest, in that he was hardly alone.

Chronology

Historical context cannot help but involve chronology, the historian's essential tool. This means that historians must be attentive to the way in which attitudes and circumstances changed over the course of the war, and they must take these changes into account in their evaluation of the policies of the Holy See. It is clear, for example, that the fate of European Jews was simply not much of an issue for the Vatican in the early period of the war. While it was true that Jews suffered mightily from the persecution inflicted upon them by Nazi Germany and collaborationist regimes, these policies, as we have seen, did not radically depart from what the Church had countenanced when pursued by the conservative and authoritarian regimes it favored. Sensing the Catholic Church's preferences in these relationships, it hardly occurred to Jews to approach the Holy See at all as persecution mounted. Reflecting on his wartime experience as the representative of the World Jewish Congress in Geneva, Gerhart Riegner explained that he and his colleagues never thought of appealing to the Catholic Church at any level. "It was only in 1942, when the whole tragedy began to unfold, that the World Jewish Congress turned to the Vatican for help and tried to mobilize the great moral authority of the head of the Catholic Church."[14]

Matters changed radically that year. From the middle of 1942 information on the grisly fate of Jews in Eastern Europe became common in the Western press. Diplomatic channels, including those of the Vatican, buzzed with rumors, and then hard facts, about killings of Jews deported from west to east. Pressures mounted everywhere as never before. What seemed appropriate in 1939, 1940, or 1941, therefore—general appeals to humane conduct, unspecific urgings to alleviate the suffering of innocents—no longer seemed enough, at least to some. "Why . . . does [the pope] not denounce the German atrocities against the populations of the occupied countries?" asked Francis d'Arcy Osborne, the British representative to the Vatican, in his diary at the end of July 1942.[15] Months passed, and still the Vatican did not speak. On December 13, Osborne referred specifically to Jews, and his tone was shrill: "The more I think of it, the more I am revolted by Hitler's massacre of the Jewish race on the one hand, and, on the other hand, the Vatican's apparently exclusive preoccupation with the effects of the war on Italy and the possibilities of the bombardment of Rome. The whole outfit seems to have become Italian."[16]

Following the German surrender at Stalingrad a few months later, matters changed importantly for the Vatican, as the pope's anxieties increased about the possibilities of the advance of Communism westward, carried forward by the Red Army—with all that that entailed for the submergence and possibly extinction of the Church under Marxist rule. Preoccupations with Communism were thereafter never far from the thinking of the Holy See, although it is difficult to judge precisely how these concerns intersected with other appeals to other actions, some of them having to do with the fate of the Jews. The juxtaposition, sometimes, is suggestive. Thus on October 19, 1943, the very day after the deportation of a thousand Roman Jews to Auschwitz, Pius actually called for the *augmentation* of the German police presence in the Italian capital, fearing a Communist uprising there. On the other hand, fears of Communism did not always work against appeals on behalf of Jews. In the summer of 1944, as the Russians entered Rumania on their way to Hungary, the Holy See responded positively to urgent appeals on behalf of Hungarian Jews, abandoning previous hesitations and appealing to the beleaguered Admiral Miklós Horthy to stop the deportation of Hungarian Jews to their deaths.

Finally, reference to historical context involves another consideration that should be mentioned here—the need to place the Vatican's response to the murder of European Jews alongside other events in which there were comparable demands that the pope "speak out," or comparable charges that he ought to have done so. Certainly, historians have no difficulty generating a list of roughly comparable circumstances—and can point to comparable instances of "silence." For example, the Vatican did not denounce the aggression against Abyssinia in 1935, or the use of poison gas in that campaign. The pope did not explicitly condemn the Nazi regime for its campaigns of forcible sterilization and then euthanasia, and this despite the fact that these policies assaulted fundamental aspects of church doctrine. The Vatican did not condemn Nazi Germany directly for the imprisonment of hundreds of priests in Dachau, Mauthausen, Sachsenhausen, and elsewhere; and it refrained from criticizing the Germans by name for their genocidal policies in Poland, with the attendant murder of some twenty percent of the Catholic clergy there. The Holy See did not condemn the slaughter of Orthodox Serbs by the pro-Nazi regime in Croatia, a murderous campaign carried out at least to some extent with the support and involvement of local clergy. And the pope received Ante Pavelic, the Catholic dictator of that country, within days of a spectacular massacre of Serbian men, women, and children that almost certainly the pope learned about. In each of these, there was a mix of circumstances at work, but caution constantly told against "speaking out" or abandoning the posture of impartiality.

As with so many bystanders to great wrongs who had weighty and conflicting responsibilities, there is evidence in the documentary record of the Vatican in these years of a dulling of awareness of particular atrocities in the face of a great ocean of human suffering during the war. Often, as well, there were rational calculations that negative consequences would ensue if particular protests were issued. (Sometimes, before doing so, Vatican officials warned that they *might* be obliged to protest—a threat, real or feigned, intended to accomplish some result.) And lastly, we should not ignore the presence, even within the Holy See, of a garden-variety timidity, sluggishness, bureaucratic thinking, lack of imagination or spirit, or simply a disinclination to face the possibility of harsh consequences even if these were unlikely to ensue.

To understand and assess such responses, we need to enter into the minds of churchmen who were unchallenged in their apostolic leadership, and unhesitating in the priorities for which they claimed divine authority. There is little evidence that Jews tugged at the consciences of Vatican officials. The truth is that the Catholic leadership of the day placed far more importance on the protection and promotion of its mission in the world—saving souls and preparing for the world to come—than it did upon issuing specific denunciations of atrocities against Jews, or Christians for that matter. Such an emphasis was a product of the Church's past, environment, and culture—in short, its historical context. "Mainly on the defensive against the state, nationalism, and socialism," as Leonidas Hill notes, "always preoccupied with the preservation of its remaining rights, little could be expected from the Church in the age of genocide."[17]

It is perhaps no accident that some of the most strenuous criticisms of the role of the Vatican during the Holocaust have come from Catholic writers, whose harsh evaluations spring from high humanitarian expectations based, as some are quick to point out, on the Church's own pronouncements about its role in the world, or on the critics' own religious commitments, frustrations, or disappointments. As a non-Catholic, without such religious points of departure, I approach the "failures" I detect with more equanimity. Reflecting on this theme, one might well draw the conclusion that our view of "speaking out" has itself been conditioned by time, in this case by the Holocaust. My own contention is that the contemplation of so many of bystanders who did not respond adequately to the murder of European Jews has promoted a set of expectations, now deeply engrained in our culture, that denunciations of great wrongs in wartime are morally required *for their own sake* and this irrespective of whether they might have any meliorative effect in the short or longer term, and sometimes even irrespective of the harm that might ensue.

This leads me to one final observation about historical context. The events of the Holocaust have changed history itself and the way in which we understand the world we inhabit. Horrified, and justifiably so, by what we have learned humanity is capable of, and shamed and angered by the abandonment of the victims, we now value "speaking out" as a measure of historical rectitude. We seem to assume that we can do better than our predecessors. We shall see. But we should take care lest we understand the latter from our own perspective, rather than theirs. To some degree, I believe, we seek vicarious involvement in the events of the Holocaust, for which most of us were not present and upon which we had no impact, by condemning those who did not live up to *what we would like to think we would have done.* Is this a way to write or understand history? You will appreciate that I have my doubts.

NOTES

1. Commission for Religious Relations with the Jews, *We Remember: Reflection on the Shoah*, March 1998.
2. Ibid.
3. Pope John Paul II, letter to Cardinal Edward Idris Cassidy, March 12, 1998, Commission for Religious Relations with the Jews, *We Remember: Reflections on the Shoah,* March 1998, pp. 1–2.
4. "I was convinced then and am still convinced today," wrote Albrecht von Kessel, one of the aides of the German ambassador Ernst von Weizsäcker, after the war, "that he almost broke down under the conflicts of conscience. I know that day by day, week by week, month by month he struggled to find the right answer. No one could relieve him of the responsibility for this answer." Quoted in Meir Michaelis, *Mussolini and the Jews: German Italian Relations and the Jewish Question in Italy 1922–1945* (New York: Oxford University Press, 1978), 377.
5. Quoted in George O. Kent, "Pope Pius XII and Germany: Some Aspects of German-Vatican Relations, 1933–1943," *American Historical Review* LXX (1964–65), 62. An observer of Vatican diplomacy since 1906, when he first joined the staff of the German legation to the Holy See, von Bergen first met Pacelli during the First World War, when the latter was papal nuncio in Germany.
6. Ibid., 64.
7. *Summi Ponfiticatus, Encyclical on the Unity of Human Society*, October 20, 1939.
8. *Actes et documents du Saint Siège relatifs a la Seconde Guerre Mondiale,* 11 vols. (Vatican City: 1965: 81), VII, 319.
9. David Alvarez and Robert Graham, *Nothing Sacred: Nazi Espionage against the Vatican 1939–1945* (London: Frank Cass, 1997), 176.
10. István Déak,"The Pope, the Nazis and the Jews," *New York Review of Books* (March 23, 2000), 46.
11. John Cornwell, *Hitler's Pope: The Secret History of Pope Pius XII* (New York: Viking, 1999).

12. Ibid.

13. *Actes et documents*, op. cit., VIII, 295–297, 334. See also Michael R. Marrus and Robert O. Paxton, *Vichy France and the Jews* (New York: Basic Books, 1981), 200–202.

14. Gerhart Riegner, "A Warning to the World," *The Stephen S. Wise Lecture*, November 17, 1983, 5.

15. Owen Chadwick, *Britain and the Vatican during the Second World War* (Cambridge: Cambridge University Press, 1986), 211.

16. Ibid.

17. Leonidas B. Hill, "History and Rolf Hochhuth's *The Deputy*," in R. G. Collins, ed., *From an Ancient to a Modern Theatre* (Winnipeg: University of Manitoba Press, 1972), 149.

9

Pope Pius XII in Historical Context

JOHN F. MORLEY

Medieval painters often used triptychs to depict religious scenes from the Bible and from the life of Christ and the saints. The central panel was the most important and would contain the image of the person or mystery being portrayed. I think of this because as we begin to try to understand Pope Pius XII in historical context, we are forced to do so within a certain contemporary framework, not unlike the triptych. The pope, of course, would be in the central panel, framed, I suspect, by Rolf Hochhuth and *The Deputy*[1] on one side, and, on the other, the document issued by the Commission for Religious Relations with the Jews a year ago, *We Remember: A Reflection on the Shoah.*[2]

These two points of reference, I fear, extreme as they may be, provide not only a framework but also have an impact on any consideration of this pope in historical context. *Mutatis mutandis,* I suspect that each of us, to some degree, is influenced by one or other of these points of view.

It is not only Hochhuth's dramatization of Pius XII—which, in any case, might be arguable as an exercise in literary license—that is so extreme but also his so-called *Sidelights on History.* Consider the following statement:

> The Pope must surely have realized that a protest against
> Hitler . . . would have elevated the church to a position
> that it has not held since the Middle Ages. He would have
> had to realize it, had he given the matter thought . . . The
> Pope cannot have been so anguished by the manhunt for
> defenseless people that went on in Europe for years. His

speeches alone—he left a legacy of twenty-two volumes
of discourses—show what trivialities occupied him during this period.

He was not a "criminal for reasons of state;" he was a
fencesitter, an overambitious careerist, who, having
attained his goal, wasted his time on inconsequential tri-
fles, while the tormented world . . . waited in vain for a
word of spiritual leadership from him.[3]

Words from *We Remember* constitute the other side of our framework:

During and after the war, Jewish communities and Jewish
leaders expressed their thanks for all that had been done
for them [by Catholics], including what Pope Pius XII did
personally or through his representatives to save hundreds
of thousands of lives.[4]

There is a Latin adage, *in medio stat virtus.* Let us also seek the truth
which must lie between these two extreme points of view and let it be the
underpinning of our efforts to establish the historical context of Pius XII.

The facts of Eugenio Pacelli's life are well known, particularly his service as nuncio to Bavaria and later to Germany, and as secretary of state to
Pope Pius XI. What is frequently ignored, however, is any effort to understand
the *Sitz im Leben,* the historical context in which he conducted his papacy. The
emotions attached to the interpretation of his role as pope has blinded many
to this fundamental effort to ascertain the historical and contextual aspects to
which he was subject, which he had to interpret and to which he had to react.
The end result of this is the tendency to project back into the past, therefore,
into Pius XII's life of several decades ago, the values, ideals, perspectives,
goals, etc., of contemporary society. Allied to this is the benefit that we have
of hindsight, of knowing how history unfolded, which for some becomes the
criterion for judging the actions of the past.

There are three areas of study that would be necessary and valuable in order to come to a better understanding of Pope Pius XII in his historical context: the Church, the war, and the Holocaust. My purpose is not to give an exhaustive analysis of each of these, but to propose certain points within each that contribute to our knowledge of Pius XII in his historical context. It should be acknowledged, too, that these three points cannot be strictly and unilaterally delineated because they overlap with each other. Ecclesiastical policies, for example, were evident in the Vatican's response to various military exigencies, while the military situation itself influenced the policies. This is also true for the events of the Holocaust and the Vatican's response.[5]

The Church

One cannot begin to understand Pius XII without examining his perception, his theological understanding, of the Church of which he was the head. This appears to be a logical and necessary first step, often overlooked or downplayed. I would suggest that the ecclesiology of Pius, his view of the Roman Catholic Church and his role within it, had a tremendous impact on him, of course, and influenced all his actions and decisions on ecclesiastical matters. One could presume that this view would be a causative factor in his reaction to the events of his time. How he saw the Church, its spirituality and ideals, its prerogatives, its goals, both terrestrial as well as heavenly, were necessarily essential to him as he fulfilled his role as the Vicar of Christ in every dimension of that task.

Let us say in passing that Pius XII might be considered the last of the pope-kings.[6] Every aspect of Vatican protocol contributed to his status as a monarch. He was surrounded by—indeed, he was enveloped in—acts of obeisance typical of medieval kings, and carried out with a special Vatican panache. People genuflected to him, bowed before him, and walked out of a room backwards so as not to turn their backs to him.

Officials of the Holy See, after conferring with the pope on certain issues, would write a notation on their record of the meeting, *ex audientia sanctissimi.* His appellation and treatment as "the most holy one," would certainly contribute to his regal and unapproachable status.

The ecclesiology of Pius XII was basically exclusivist. Protestants were heretics who denied certain tenets of Church teaching. Jews were outside the Church and their conversion to Christianity was a desideratum since God had repudiated his covenant with them when they rejected and killed Christ, the Son of God. Christians have become the new people of God, superseding the Jews.

Evidence of such supersessionist theology may be found in the encyclical *Mystici Corporis Christi,* issued by the pope on June 29, 1943. It is not a major part of the pope's theological study of the Church as the mystical Body of Christ but, nonetheless, represents the attitude of church officials at that time. It demonstrates, therefore, one aspect of Pius's thinking on the Jews as he dealt with the theme "On the Cross the Old Law gave place to the New":

> With the death of the Redeemer the Old Law was abolished and the New Testament took its place; it was then that the Law of Christ, with its mysteries, its laws, institutions and sacred rites, was ratified for the whole world by the blood of Jesus Christ. So long as the Divine Savior was preaching in a restricted territory (for He had been sent only to the lost sheep of the house of Israel) both the Law and the Gospel were in force together; but by His death on the Cross he made void the Law with its decrees and fastened the handwriting of the Old Testament on the Cross, establishing the New Testament in His blood which he shed for the whole human race . . . On the Cross, then, the Old Law died—soon to be buried and to become lethal—and was succeeded by the New Testament . . .[7]

It is of some interest to note that the so-called "lost" or "hidden" encyclical of Pope Pius XI, *Humani Generis Unitas,* reveals the same supersessionist attitude. No matter what its provenance or intended purpose, or the reaction of Pius XI or Pius XII to it, the document indicates the thinking of the highest church officials of the time. It should be no surprise that Pius's later document reflects similar thinking.[8]

The corollary of this theological position is that the Jews would have had no place in the ecclesiastical vision of Pius XII. This is not the view of the Roman Catholic Church since Vatican Council II's 1965 declaration, *Nostra Aetate,* which has led to an unprecedented appreciation of Jews and Judaism in the Church. Pope John Paul II has taught very clearly that Jews are the elder brothers of Christians, that Christianity has a unique relationship to Judaism, unlike what it has with any other religion, and that God's choice of the Jews as his people, and his covenant with them, remains valid, vibrant, and fruitful.[9] As much as contemporary Catholic liturgy with its use of the vernacular, an altar facing the congregation, and a variety of altar ministers, both male and female, would have amazed and shocked Pius XII, so would the contemporary Church's relations and attitude toward the Jews.

Jews and Judaism, therefore, had no particular importance for Pius XII. This is not to be interpreted as disdain for them, but as a realistic evaluation of their role in his ecclesial worldview. This would in no way imply that the pope would have been indifferent to the sufferings and fate of the Jews.

In looking at the historical context of Pius XII, there are other aspects that must be briefly considered. The Holy See believes that it has the right to send accredited diplomatic representatives to various nations. These emissaries are ordinarily apostolic nuncios who have the rank of an ambassador, and usually are archbishops. They represent the pope to the government and Church of the country to which they are posted, and report back to the Vatican on the status of the Church in these various nations.[10]

An important historical aspect of this diplomacy as exercised by the Holy See is its belief that its conduct of diplomacy is unique and performed at a higher level of religious and human values than that of other states. Consider, for example, what Archbishop Valerio Valeri, nuncio to France and to Vichy during the war years, said about a decade after the end of the war:

> . . . It is clear that the activity of the Holy See is not limited, and cannot be limited, to purely diplomatic efforts, in the strict sense of that word, inasmuch as it indicates juridic relations between the states. The Roman Pontiff is

identified with the Church . . . [which] has a universal
mission that distinguishes it from every other earthly society and it basically tends to continue through the centuries
the salvific work of its Divine Founder. With such a mission the Church has entered into history and it has the
highest awareness of this.

The development in time and according to circumstances of this mission can also be called diplomacy, if one
wishes, but only in an elevated sense, above the purely
natural and secular order. From this point of view, the
supreme law of the Church, and indeed, of the Holy See,
is the salvation of souls. All of its activity is directed to
this end . . . even when the Church, because of historical
circumstances, has to concern itself with its temporal
interests.[11]

The Holy See had representatives in sixty-one countries throughout the
world, of whom thirty-eight were nuncios. It is of interest to note that during
the war years, Vatican diplomats were assigned to France, Germany, Hungary,
Italy, Portugal, Romania, Spain, and Switzerland. The nuncios in Belgium,
Holland, and Poland were expelled by the Germans; those in Estonia, Latvia,
and Lithuania, by the Soviets. Both Slovakia and Croatia, newly created
states, also had a Vatican presence, although of different types. In addition,
there were apostolic delegates, representatives without diplomatic status, in
Albania, Bulgaria, Great Britain, Turkey, and the United States. Frequently,
the apostolic delegates, even though of purely ecclesiastical status, acted as,
or were treated as, diplomats.[12]

An analysis of the Vatican's foreign policy, published in early 1944,
gave a positive evaluation of it:

The diplomacy of the Church is normally directed toward
securing its own position in the various nations, whenever possible by means of . . . concordats. Its objectives are

always to obtain freedom to practice the Catholic religion
and to propagate it, to gain recognition of Catholic marriages, and to maintain in Catholic hands the right of edu-
cating Catholic children. The Church does not seek
beyond this to intervene in political questions and the kind
of government does not matter. It makes no distinctions,
and expresses no preference for one political system as
against another. Basically, of course, the Church is neither
democratic nor totalitarian in philosophy, despite its
authoritarian structure. It teaches that God, not man, is the
best judge of man's needs and the source of his ideals and
further, that God created the Church on earth as a visible
and permanent institution to interpret His will to man and
to instruct men in matters of moral right. Therefore, the
Church denies the ultimate sovereignty of the individual
or collection of individuals.[13]

The Vatican official responsible for this diplomatic network was
Cardinal Luigi Maglione, who was appointed by the newly elected Pius XII
as his secretary of state. He had been nuncio in France from 1926 to 1935.
Under Pius XI, Pacelli had enjoyed great prominence and exercised great
authority as Secretary of State. It appears, however, that Maglione's power
was more limited because of Pius XII's desire and ability to conduct his
own foreign policy. An indication of this may be seen in the fact that after
Maglione's death in August 1944, the pope never appointed anyone else to
the position.

The minister representing Great Britain at the Vatican, Francis d'Arcy
Osborne, gave his impression of this when, on two occasions, he reflected on
his relationship with the deceased cardinal:

... he was always a loyal executor of the Pope's policy, but
I often had the impression that, had he been in a situation to
inspire that policy, he would have taken a different and

stronger line. If I am right, he must have suffered on occasion under his loyalty and self-imposed restraint.

I am convinced that his sentiments were with us all through and that, had it rested with him, the Vatican would have taken a much stronger line.[14]

The Church over which Pope Pius XII reigned had over one third of a billion members, with two hundred million of these in Europe, and another forty million in the United States. These Catholics were entrusted to the jurisdiction and pastoral care of twelve hundred bishops in dioceses all over the world, ranging from Aberdeen in Scotland to Zulia in Venezuela.[15]

Hochhuth may have dismissed the writings and speeches of Pius XII as "trivialities," but in the context of the Roman Catholic Church, they were far from that. For example, his encyclicals on the Church as the mystical Body of Christ,[16] on promoting biblical studies,[17] on the sacred liturgy,[18] on "False Opinions Threatening to Undermine the Foundation of Catholic Doctrine,"[19] and on sacred music[20] remain pertinent to the contemporary Church.

These documents authored by Pius XII not only demonstrate his theological acumen but also reveal the progressiveness of many of his ideas on the Church of his day. Moreover, Vatican Council II used a number of his teachings in these encyclicals and in other statements as points of reference for its discussions and in its documents. There was nothing "trivial" about his contributions in the area of theology.[21]

Additionally and quite remarkably, the number of addresses given by the pope over the two decades of his pontificate has been tallied. These thirteen hundred speeches were given in a variety of languages: Latin, Italian, French, English, Spanish, German, and Portuguese. Some of these, no doubt, were pious homilies but others dealt with topics that were practical and meaningful to his listeners: the upbringing of children, the relationship of the Church to labor, physical culture and sport, farmers and rural life, women, television, teaching sisters, the lay apostolate, midwives, art, morality, science, medical research, the morality of pain prevention, the contemplative life, and the spirituality of the lay person.[22]

There are two other facts to consider about the papacy during this period. The first involves the neutrality of the Vatican city state. Italy entered the war on June 10, 1940, as an ally of Germany. The newly created military situation required the British, French, and later, the American representatives to seek housing within the confines of Vatican City itself. The British government also demanded that Italians representing the Holy See in any British territory be removed.

The status of Vatican City itself also became precarious in that electricity, water, and sewer facilities were all supplied by the Roman authorities and the Italian government. These utilities were guaranteed by the Lateran Treaty, but Vatican officials also realized how easy it would have been for an angry or vengeful Mussolini to shut them down. Moreover, Italy at war with Great Britain and France exposed Rome to the threat of bombing.

The status of Vatican City became more complex when German troops occupied the city and northern Italy in September 1943. This was a tragic time for the Jews of Rome when a thousand of them were deported to Auschwitz. It was only with the arrival of allied forces in early June 1944 that Rome was liberated, and that Vatican City achieved a greater level of freedom. This change in the military situation required diplomats from Germany and their allies to leave Rome and find residence in Vatican City, thereby reversing the process of four years earlier.

The other factor that must be taken into account must be a realistic appraisal of the Holy See's power and prestige at this point. Earlier in the century, Pope Benedict XV and his seven-point peace plan had been ignored in the peace negotiations at the end of the war.

England, of course, for centuries had been alienated from the papacy and the Roman Catholic Church. The secularization of the French government had become so extreme that its hostility to the Church became endemic. Father Robert Graham, S.J., the English-speaking editor of the Vatican documents, pointed out the ramifications of this in very frank terms:

> The traditional papal policy had to undergo severe challenges on many occasions during World War II. The

British and the French could not understand why the Pope
had not excommunicated their enemies. In the crisis of
war both of these countries forgot their long years of "No
popery," or anticlericalism, to revert to medieval concep-
tions, certainly anachronistic, of a Boniface VIII launching the curse of Rome on malefactors. The Vatican was
not impressed by this belated deference to the moral
authority of the head of the Catholic Church. Its essentially political motivation and its limited terms were too obvious. They were probably not even meant seriously but
served as an excellent propaganda platform. The invitation to the Pope to condemn Nazi crimes in the name of
his religious authority did not include a like invitation to
stigmatize crimes outside of the narrow terms set unilaterally by the petitioners.[23]

Before concluding this section on the ecclesiastical aspects inherent in
the historical situation of Pius XII, we must go back to the triptych and take
note of the statement in *We Remember* that the pope saved hundreds of thousands of Jewish lives. It is most likely a reference to the work of an Israeli
journalist and diplomat:

. . . the Catholic Church, under the pontificate of Pius
XII, was instrumental in saving at least 700,000, but
probably as many as 860,000 Jews from certain death at
Nazi hands.[24]

There were thousands of Jews who were saved because of Vatican
efforts on their behalf, but these figures appear excessive. Those who support
the role of Pius XII during the war are ready to accept them not only because
they tend to demonstrate how proactive he was on behalf of the Jews but also
because their source is someone who is not a member of the Church and whose
objectivity would be more easily accepted. We are familiar with *ad hominem*

arguments; it seems to me that this is an *ad hominem* defense, accepting facts because of who the person is giving them.

In looking at this panel of the triptych, however, there is also in the background the growing effort to canonize Pius XII. The Reverend Peter Gumpel, the priest responsible for this task, stated recently in words that allow for no contrasting views that:

> The cause of the beatification and canonization of Pope Pius XII, who is rightly venerated by millions of Catholics, will not be stopped or delayed by the unjustifiable and calumnious attacks against this great and saintly man. . . . We welcome any information and documented criticism. But those who launch these gratuitous attacks should realize that they are trampling on the sensibilities of Catholics and in doing so they hinder efforts to build better relations between the Catholic Church and the Jews. This is most regrettable. May truth, justice and fairness finally prevail with regard to Pius XII, to whom so many Jews and their descendants owe their lives.[25]

This is a statement that is presumptuous and self-righteous to such an extent that it would prevent any criticism of Pius XII. For those of us who have been Catholics all our lives, it is offensive in a way that is unprecedented. It is also detrimental to Jewish-Catholic relations, not for the reason he says, but because of its implied assumption that all "unjustifiable and calumnious attacks" against the pope come from Jewish sources.

In a remark that is as prescient as it is critical, although without any factual or historical proof, Hochhuth dealt with the canonization of Pius XII, noting that the pope felt that " . . . he had a great chance to be canonized, provided he himself helped the process along."[26]

It would be appropriate to conclude this section with the words of a historian from the Catholic University of Lublin, a priest personally touched by the war in Poland:

Pacelli never lost his sympathy toward Germany. Nazism,
World War II, and the defeat of Germany tempted Pacelli
very much, especially in regard to his neutrality, of which
he was very proud. But the neutrality of a moral authority
like the Pope was not univocal. The fundamental question—whether in the face of such evil a moral authority
like the Pope can remain neutral—is a problem which still
plagues Church historians. Pius' neutrality, however, was
based not only on his sympathy towards the Germans but
also resulted from the kind of diplomatic training Pius had
inherited from Benedict XV. It was a kind of diplomacy
with deep roots in the 19th century, but one totally unable
to confront the situations posed by the totalitarian era.[27]

The War

The European war dominated the first six years of Pius's papacy. Three
days after his coronation as pope on March 12, 1939, German troops occupied Prague, establishing the provinces of Bohemia and Moravia as a German
protectorate and granting independence to Slovakia, which would then serve
as a willing German satellite.

The pope was personally opposed to this German action, and, indeed,
considered writing an encyclical on peace to deal with it. The burdens of his
new position, however, the daily audiences, and the matters left untouched
during the interregnum dissuaded him from doing anything.[28]

Three days later, the nuncio in Warsaw telegraphed the secretariat of
state about the growing tensions between Germany and Poland.[29] For all
intents and purposes, Pius XII, from the earliest days of his papacy, was
plunged into the growing militarism and bellicose spirit that was spreading
across Europe. Experienced as he may have been from his years as secretary of state, he now had to confront unprecedented situations involving
most of the nations of Europe and millions of Catholics. The dismember-
ment of Czechoslovakia also had the result of solidifying Britain and France

in their resolve that Germany had to be prevented from any further territorial aggrandizement.

The pope responded to the growing tensions by suggesting early in May that a peace conference of the major European powers—France, Britain, Germany, Italy, and Poland—be convened to discuss the problems that were leading to conflict. For a variety of reasons and motivations, the conference did not take place.[30]

As the war became imminent, the pope made last minute efforts to prevent it by meeting with the ambassadors of the five European powers on August 31 and expressing this hope:

> The Holy Father does not want to give up hope that negotiations currently underway may lead to a just and peaceful solution [of the German-Polish conflict], something that the entire world wishes.
>
> His Holiness prays, as a result, in the name of God, that the governments of Germany and Poland will do all possible to avoid any incident, and to refrain from taking any measures capable of aggravating the present situation. He also asks the governments of England, France and Italy to support his request.[31]

At the same time, the pope was encouraging Poland to exercise a greater sense of moderation in response to Germany's demands. On August 30, the pope telegraphed the nuncio in Warsaw to ask the Polish government to admit the principle of international intervention to protect the rights of the German minority in Poland.[32]

All these efforts of Pius XII failed, and by September 3—after the invasion of Poland—Great Britain, France, and Poland were at war with Germany. Nonetheless, Pius continued his efforts on behalf of peace. Disappointed that there was no Christmas truce, he used his first Christmas message to list five conditions for a just peace.[33]

The pope's activities during these early months of the war have been summarized in this way:

> That was all the Pope could achieve in 1939. Undoubtedly, he had tried to incline Poland to give in to Hitler's demands. He knew, however, that the threat of force automatically excluded chances for avoiding war. Poland would not make concessions that threatened her very existence. The Pope had even expressed a wish to fly to Berlin and Warsaw on August 31 to press the cause of peace. He ultimately settled for a diplomatic note . . . begging for the avoidance of war. He did not believe, however, that his words would stop the conflict.[34]

The Vatican continued its efforts in 1939 and the first half of 1940 to maintain Italian neutrality. The pope personally appealed to Mussolini in late April. The *Duce* replied on April 30 that he understood the pope's desire to keep Italy out of the war, and that was the situation at the present, but he could not guarantee that this would long continue.[35]

Hitler's invasion of France, Belgium, Holland, and Luxembourg on May 10, 1940, and its spectacular success was enough to persuade Mussolini to enter the war on the side of Germany on June 10. The Italian leader feared that the war would end without Italian participation and, as a result, without any right to participate in the territorial spoils.

The pope used his annual Christmas messages to outline and delineate his proposals and suggestions for peace. The titles of these messages show his determination in this regard:

1940:   Conditions for a New World Order
1941:   Christianity and the World Crisis
1942:   The Internal Order of States and People
1943:   Peace and the Function of Force
1944:   True and False Democracy
1945:   Conditions for a True and Lasting Peace[36]

As much as the pope might have feared Communism, he certainly did not see Germany as any kind of bulwark against it,[37] particularly not before June 22, 1941, and the German invasion of the Soviet Union. He did fear repression in the occupied countries. His commitment to neutrality was based on several factors, the chief of which was his belief that a neutral Vatican might have a role to play in the eventual peace negotiations and bring to them a greater sense of justice than might otherwise be present. This approach was credible and might have succeeded, except that this war had no precedent, and exposed an ideology of anti-Semitism and annihilation so out of control that no human logic, no rational principles, could deal with it.

A major preoccupation of the pope during the war was for the safety of Rome. He continually made demands of Britain and the United States that they refrain from bombing the city. The fears of Vatican officials were heightened after massive bombing raids by the British Air Force inflicted great damage on Genoa, Turin, and Milan in November 1942. The Vatican was not particularly pleased with the British response to its pleas for the safety of Rome, which reminded these church officials that Mussolini himself had asked Hitler to permit Italy to participate in the bombing of London. This was also the period when there were growing demands in the English press and Parliament calling for the bombing of Rome.[38]

This concern for the security of Rome is an amazing aspect of Vatican reaction to the war, one that is understandable at one level but appears selfish and chauvinistic at another. In the absence of any earlier protests from the Vatican over the bombing of Warsaw and London, the continual threat emanating from the Holy See that the pope would speak out openly in protest if Rome were bombed appears most insensitive and was interpreted in that way by British and American authorities.[39]

Rome was bombed on July 19, 1943, with the destruction of a residential area, a basilica, and the loss of fifteen hundred lives. An hour after the bombing ceased, Pius XII visited the devastated area and remained for several hours. It was a dramatic gesture unlike anything else done by him, and was followed the next day by a telegram from Maglione to nuncios all over the world informing them of the raid and protesting it.[40]

The Vatican's anxiety over the fate of Rome was exacerbated by the confidential information given to Maglione that Mussolini and the fascist leadership did not intend to leave Rome because they wanted the city to have the honor of being bombed as other Italian cities had been.[41]

The British attitude toward these complaints was summarized in a cable sent to Osborne from the Foreign Office on May 7, 1944:

> We feel strongly, however, that a distinction must be drawn between intervention by, or on behalf of, the Pope as a neutral or head of the Catholic Church and intervention in matters of purely local Italian concern, however much the Pope and the bulk of Vatican officials may, as Italians, be concerned by the loss of Italian lives and damage to Italian property.
>
> It is, of course, most regrettable that civilian lives should be lost owing to military actions but this is unfortunately occurring constantly in all countries involved in the war. Many thousands of lives have been lost in this country by enemy action and when Vatican officials complain about such incidents in Italy, it is pertinent to inquire whether the Vatican has made, and is continuing to make, representations about loss of civilian lives in Allied countries and, in particular, in this country.[42]

One of the great dilemmas facing Pius XII, at least as he envisioned his responsibilities, was discussed in his address to the College of Cardinals on June 2, 1943. He spoke of those who were appealing to him because they were destined for extermination, not for any fault of their own but only because of their nationality or race. As clear as this and other allusions may have been (e.g., the Christmas address of 1942), they were not the explicit condemnations that many wanted the pope to issue. The pope explained the ongoing problem:

> Every single word in Our statements to the competent
> authorities, and every one of Our public utterances, has
> had to be weighed and pondered by Us with deep gravity,
> in the very interest of those who are suffering, so as not to
> render their position even more difficult and unbearable
> than before, be it unwittingly and unintentionally.[43]

On two other earlier occasions, in private correspondence with German bishops, the pope made similar comments. In February 1941, he wrote:

> There where the Pope would like to speak out loudly and
> clearly, it is unfortunately waiting and silence that are
> often imposed upon him; there where he would like to
> act and to assist, it is patience and delay that is imposed
> upon him.[44]

He repeated this theme in March 1944:

> Frequently, it is painful and difficult to decide how to react
> to a situation: a reserve and prudent silence, or on the con-
> trary, a strong word and vigorous action.[45]

One of the clearest indications of the pope's attitude in this regard was revealed by him in a letter of April 30, 1943 to the bishop of Berlin. He explained his conviction that local bishops were in a better position than Vatican officials to decide on the advisability of protests because they could weigh the possibility of reprisals or other punishments that might result from their protests. Moreover, he added, that to avoid a greater evil, sometimes an attitude of reserve should be retained.[46]

An informative summary of the pope's actions during the war was provided by Osborne in his report to the Foreign Office for 1945. He wrote:

The year that saw the final ignominious defeat of
Germany and Japan. The inglorious deaths of Hitler and
Mussolini, the passing of President Roosevelt and the
electoral defeat of Winston Churchill also witnessed the
emergence of Pius XII from the nullity and neutrality of
the war years. It has been said that the Pope had at his disposal against Hitler and the satanism of Nazism the two
strongest weapons in the world—excommunication and
martyrdom—and that he failed to use them. It is easy to
accuse him of jettisoning the moral leadership bequeathed
him by Pius XI by failing to specify Nazi criminality in his
condemnation of the crimes and cruelties of war. But it
should first of all be remembered that he always hoped, by
preserving a meticulous neutrality, to shorten the war by
offering himself as a mediator acceptable to all the belligerents. In the second place he genuinely believed that
he had sufficiently, although admittedly generically, condemned German misdeeds, while it was his unshakable
conviction that a more specific condemnation of the Nazi
regime . . . and of Nazi war crimes would in no way have
deterred Hitler, would have exposed German Catholics
to severe reprisals and would have imposed upon these
same German Catholics the cruel dilemma of choosing
between their conflicting loyalties to their country and
their religion.[47]

The Holocaust

There is no event in modern history that arouses emotion as much as
the Holocaust. Dispassionate study and analysis appear to be absent from the
representatives of both panels of my imaginary triptych. Yet, it is here that a
knowledge of the historical context in which Pope Pius XII and the Vatican
acted and reacted is essential. There are those who support the pope and who
make generalizations claiming that he did everything he possibly could.

Likewise, there are those who come to conclusions favorable to the pope, but which, however, are logically deficient because they are based on one or two facts and are then extended to encompass other places or time periods during the Holocaust. Such points of view obviously ignore the historical context. On the other hand, there are those who, equally lacking a sense of the historical context, make statements, often, indeed, accusations, that impute to Pius XII a responsibility and malevolence that have no basis in historical fact.

Let us look at three situations in which there was Vatican activity and intervention, in Italy, in Slovakia, and in Hungary. These examples are cited because of their importance, but also because they are used as arguments in defense of Pius XII.[48]

As was noted above, the German occupation of Rome in September 1943 radically altered the situation of the Jews. This was tragically made clear when, on the morning of Saturday, October 16, 1943, beginning around 5:30, an SS force suddenly surrounded the area known as the Roman ghetto and began rounding up the Jews living there. Within the next several hours, over twelve hundred people were arrested. They were taken to the *Collegio Militare,* where most of those of mixed descent or involved in mixed marriages were later released. Two days later, however, 1,007 of them began their journey to Auschwitz.

The pope was personally informed of this early that same morning and later directed Maglione to meet with Ernst von Weizsäcker, the German ambassador to the Holy See, to lodge a protest. The cardinal secretary of state and the ambassador met later that morning, and Maglione's own notes of the meeting are published in the Vatican documents. What should have been a protest in defense of the Jews and is often depicted as such cannot be interpreted that way when one reads the actual content of the conversation of these two officials. There was neither confrontation nor criticism nor a plea for justice. The cardinal recorded the following:

> Having learned that this morning the Germans made a raid
> on the Jews, I asked the German Ambassador to come to
> me and I asked him to try to intervene on behalf of these

unfortunates. I talked to him as well as I could in the name of humanity, in Christian charity.

The Ambassador, who already knew of the arrests, but doubted whether it dealt specifically with the Jews, said to me in a sincere and moved voice: "I am always expecting to be asked: 'Why do you remain in your position?'" I said: "No, Ambassador, I do not ask and will not ask such a question. I say to you simply: Your Excellency, who has a tender and good heart, see if you can save so many innocent people. It is sad for the Holy See, sad beyond telling, that right in Rome, under the eyes of the Common Father [pope], so many people have been made to suffer only because they belong to a particular race."

The Ambassador, after several moments of reflection, asked me: "What will the Holy See do if events continue?"

I replied: "The Holy See would not want to be put into the necessity of uttering a word of disapproval."

The Ambassador observed: "For more than four years I have followed and admired the attitude of the Holy See. It has succeeded in steering the ship in the midst of rocks of every kind and size without colliding and, even if it has greater confidence in the Allies, it has known how to maintain a perfect balance. I ask myself if, at the very time that the ship is reaching port, it is fitting to put everything in danger. I am thinking about the consequences which such a step of the Holy See would provoke . . . The order came from the highest source. . . .

"Your Eminence will leave me free not to report this official conversation?"

I remarked that I had asked him to intervene appealing to his sentiments of humanity. I left it to his judgment to make or not make mention of our conversation which was so amicable.

I wanted to remind him that the Holy See, as he himself has perceived, has been very prudent so as not to give
to the German people the impression that it has done or
wished to do the least thing against Germany, during this
terrible war.

But I also had to tell him that the Holy See should not
be put into the necessity of protesting: if ever the Holy See
is obligated to do so, it will rely upon divine Providence
for the consequences.

In the meantime, I repeat: "Your Excellency has told
me that you will attempt to do something for the unfortunate Jews. I thank you for that. As for the rest, I leave it to
your judgment. If you think it more opportune not to mention our conversation, so be it."[49]

The point here is not a discussion of how successful Vatican authorities
and religious institutions all over Rome were in saving the lives of eight thousand other Jews in Rome during this same period. My contention is that this
encounter of Maglione and von Weizsäcker cannot be legitimately described
as a protest when the ambassador candidly admitted that he would not forward any information about the meeting to Berlin, and the cardinal agreed. It
is not within the prerogative of any ambassador to withhold information from
his government, particularly when it comes from the highest level of the state
to which he is posted. Maglione would certainly not have expected or
accepted such independent judgment form any of the nuncios.

This was the meeting of two diplomatic colleagues, each of whom had
respect for the other. The historical context is ignored when it is presented as
an immediate and forceful intervention by the Vatican in the face of this
tragedy unfolding against the Jews.

One might argue that von Weizsäcker's decision may have had some
positive results. It is interesting to note that later that day, Monsignor Alois
Hudal, the rector of the German College in Rome, wrote to General Rainer
Stahel, the German military commander of Rome, encouraging him to suspend

the ongoing arrests of the Jews because it might lead to a public protest from the pope. This message was transmitted to Himmler himself and the deportation process was suspended.[50]

This may be an overly simplistic view of the events of those days, but, nonetheless, the round-up process was ended, not to be repeated. It is evident, however, that von Weizsäcker's apparent fear of the consequences of bringing the cardinal's appeal to the attention of his superiors was unfounded since a similar intervention coming from Hudal apparently had immediate results.

In all of this, let us not forget that, indeed, the deportations were suspended and eight thousand Roman Jews were saved, but, unfortunately, another one thousand Jews languished for two days at a site within minutes of the Vatican with no direct intervention on their behalf. It is not historically tenable to accept credit for efforts, heroic as they may have been, on behalf of these Jews, while ignoring the absence of similar activity to help the Jews who were arrested and soon afterward killed.

The situation in Slovakia in the fall of 1944 is another example of the need for historical accuracy and background. The secretariat of state was informed in a telegram from Monsignor Giuseppe Burzio, *chargé d'affaires* at Bratislava, on September 15, that the recently arrived German occupation troops in Slovakia were arresting large numbers of Jews. Burzio suggested that the Holy See intervene with the government to save the Jews who were in great peril.[51]

Several days later, on September 20, the Secretariat of State sent a note to the Slovak legation at the Holy See. It was forceful:

> From various sources the Holy See has been petitioned to become involved in the fate of those belonging to the Hebrew race, residing in the Slovak republic, against whom grave measures are actually taking place. It is claimed . . . that many of them have already been arrested.
>
> The Holy See, moved by those sentiments of humanity and Christian charity which have always inspired its activity on behalf of those who suffer, without distinction

of parties, nationality or race, cannot remain indifferent to such appeals.[52]

This was, indeed, a forceful intervention by the Holy See on behalf of Slovakian Jews, although I suspect that any student of this period will find these diplomatic words self-serving and not consistent with previous practice. The earlier deportations from Slovakia had occurred between March and June 1942 and resulted in over fifty thosand Jews being removed from the country. There were several interventions by the Holy See but, nonetheless, almost two-thirds of the Slovak Jews were deported. Of those remaining, several thousand had escaped to Hungary; of the other twenty thousand, about half had been baptized.

One could suspect that the Vatican intervention of 1944, as that of 1942, was on behalf of the Jews, but, at the same time, there were frequent attempts to have the baptized Jews exempt from the deportation measures. Burzio said as much in a telegram to the Secretariat of State on October 6, when he informed his superiors that he had intervened with the Slovak president, Monsignor Joseph Tiso, seeking his intervention on behalf of the baptized Jews.[53]

We note, therefore, that it is reasonable to assume that part of the Vatican's interest at this time was for the baptized Jews, although this is not meant to exclude a wider concern. We cannot fail to take note of the time period for these activities: the fall of 1944. It was, of course, the German decision to resume the deportations that occasioned Vatican intervention at this time. But other factors were probably involved as well. The Vatican was now much freer under the occupation of the Allies. The German war effort was facing defeat on all sides.

This may sound like a begrudging recognition of the Vatican's efforts, but it is rather an attempt to put into context statements that are gratuitously put forward as proofs or demonstrations of all that the Vatican did. There are too many complexities and nuances in situations of this sort to justify simplistic approaches.

The history of the Holocaust in Hungary is unique in that it did not begin until the spring of 1944 (up until that point, Hungary had been considered a place of refuge for Jews fleeing from other countries) and that its implementation was so swift and effective that hundreds of thousands of Jews were deported within a period of a few months. For example, between May and July 1944, well over 400,000 Hungarian Jews had been deported to Auschwitz.

Vatican involvement in Hungary is often cited as an example of what efforts were made on behalf of Jews. The nuncio, Archbishop Angelo Rotta, is given great and legitimate credit for all that he did. The pope's telegram to Milkós Horthy, the regent of Hungary, on June 25, 1944, was an extraordinary and unprecedented move on his part. His words were:

> From various sources, We are being implored to do everything possible so that in this noble and chivalrous nation [Hungary], the sufferings, already so burdensome, endured by a great number of unfortunate people because of their nationality or race, not be extended and aggravated. Since Our paternal heart cannot remain insensitive to these pressing appeals because of Our ministry of charity which embraces all people, We address Ourselves personally to Your Highness appealing to your noble sentiments with the full confidence that you will do all in Your power to spare so many unfortunate people other afflictions and other sorrows.[54]

The effectiveness of the pope's intervention cannot be denied, but it cannot be exaggerated. It would appear that the deportations were suspended as a result of the papal intervention as well as that of others.

Moreover, by the time the pope intervened, over two-thirds of Hungarian Jewry had already been deported. In addition, appeals from all over had been coming into the Vatican. The first of these appears to have come from Archbishop Amleto Cicognani, apostolic delegate in Washington, in response to a request made to him by the War Refugee Board. He cabled the Vatican on March 25 asking that ". . . urgent measures [be taken] to protect the two million Jews in Hungary and Romania who are subjected to the terror of persecution and extermination because of the German invasion."[55]

On March 31, a cable was received at the Vatican from the nuncio in Bern, forwarding an appeal from the chief rabbi of Palestine asking for the pope to intervene on behalf of Hungarian Jews who were ". . . in the greatest danger."[56]

At this same time, the British Foreign Office cabled Osborne instructing him to attempt to persuade the Vatican to use its influence to prevent Jews in Hungary from being handed over to German authorities.[57]

There were dozens of similar appeals that came to the secretariat of state over the next months, many, of course, arriving during the deportation process itself. One cannot ignore these appeals for intervention coming up to three months before the pope's cable to Horthy. Whatever good that gesture may have produced, it must be counterbalanced by the realization that hundreds of thousands of lives had already been lost.

Again, it must be said that Vatican activity in Hungary must be seen in context. There were many positive as well as negative aspects. One telegram cannot be singled out as a sign of Vatican commitment to the Jews of Hungary.[58]

The effort to understand the historical context in which Pope Pius XII exercised his role as pope is an ongoing one, developing incrementally as new historical data are released and analyzed. It is an effort in which generalizations, simplifications, and accusations have no place. Indeed, it is an effort to discover historical truth, as much as possible, in order to understand Pius XII as a man of history, not above and beyond it, but, as all of us, subject to its demands, its unpredictability, its cruelty, its rewards, its never-ending challenges.

NOTES

1. Rolf Hochhuth, *The Deputy,* trans. Richard and Clara Winston (New York: Grove Press, 1964).

2. The document issued on March 16, 1998, was introduced by a letter from Pope John Paul II, and is signed by Cardinal Edward Cassidy. See *The Pontifical Council for Promoting Christian Unity Information Service,* no. 97 (1998/I–II), pp. 18–22.

3. Hochhuth, pp. 351–352.

4. *Information Service*, p. 21. Note, too, footnote 16, p. 21, which describes ". . . the wisdom of Pope Pius XII's diplomacy" by listing a series of accolades from various Jewish leaders. The source of the statistic, "hundreds of thousands of Jewish lives," is most likely Pinchas Lapide, *Three Popes and the Jews* (New York: Hawthorne Books, 1967), p. 214.

5. See Pierre Blet, *Pie XII et la Seconde Guerre Mondiale d'apres les Archives du Vatican* (Paris: Perrin, 1997); Father Blet was the French-speaking editor of the Vatican documents (see below) and, of course, is very familiar with all aspects of Vatican activity during those years.

6. See Robert Serrou, *Pie XII: le Pape-Roi* (Paris: Serrin, 1992), p. 12. The author also quotes the pope as saying, "Je serai le dernier pape a tout maintenir."

7. *Encyclical Letter of Pope Pius XII on the Mystical Body of Christ,* trans. George P. Smith (London: Catholic Truth Society, 1943), no. 28, no. 29, pp. 18–19.

8. See Georges Passelecq and Bernard Suhecky, *The Hidden Encyclical of Pius XI,* trans. Steven Rendall (New York: Harcourt Brace and Company, 1997), pp. 248–249.

9. For an excellent summary and analysis of all of Pope John Paul II's teaching and statements on Judaism, see Eugene J. Fisher and Leon Klenicki, eds., *Pope John Paul II: Spiritual Pilgrimage: Texts on Jews and Judaism 1979–1995* (New York: Crossroad, 1995).

10. See John F. Morley, *Vatican Diplomacy and the Jews during the Holocaust, 1939–1943* (New York: KTAV, 1980), pp. 8–17.

11. Valerio Valeri, *Le Relazioni Internazionali della Santa Sede dopo il Secondo Conflitto Mondiale*, speech given in Rome on February 23, 1956, under the auspices of the Italian Study Center for International Reconciliation; see Morley, p. 276, no. 12.

12. Morley, p. 14.

13. Sherman S. Hayden, *Foreign Policy of the Vatican*, January 15, 1944, in *Foreign Policy Reports*, January 1944, XIX, no. 21; Public Record Office, London [PRO]: FO 371/4427: 1561.

14. Osborne to Eden, August 23, 1944; PRO: FO 371/44235.

15. *Annuario Pontificio per l'anno 1940* (Citta del Vaticano: Tipografia Poliglotta Vaticana, 1940), pp. 79–299.

16. See above, no. 6.

17. *Divino Afflante Spiritu*, September 30, 1943, in Claudia Carlen, IHM, *The Papal Encyclicals: 1939–1958* (Raleigh, N.C.: McGrath Publishing Company: A Consortium Book, 1981), pp. 65–79.

18. *Mediator Dei,* November 20, 1947; Carlen, pp. 119–154.

19. *Humani Generis,* August 12, 1950; Carlen, pp. 175–187.

20. *Musicae Sacrae,* December 25, 1955; Carlen, pp. 279–289.

21. Cardinal Augustine Bea is considered to have had an important role at Vatican Council II. He has said that, ". . . the Second Vatican Council would not have been possible without the long and fruitful doctrinal preparation provided by Pius XII." See Michael O'Carroll, *Pius XII: Greatness Dishonoured* (Dublin: Laetare Press, 1980), p. 174.

22. Vincent A. Yzermans, ed., *The Major Addresses of Pope Pius XII,* vol. I, *Selected Addresses* (St. Paul: North Central Publishing Company, 1961), *passim*. It is no exaggeration to say that the range of subjects and the depth of the comments made by the pope remain relevant to the contemporary Church. His address to the Italian Catholic Union of Midwives on October 29, 1951, has become one of the most celebrated and studied of these addresses because it deals with obstetrics, natural family planning, artifical insemination, etc.

23. Robert A. Graham, S.J., *The Church and Modern Anti-Semitism: Pius XII: The Problematics,* unpublished paper, 1990, no pagination; no. 23.

24. Lapide, p. 214.

25. Peter Gumpel, "Pius XII as He Really Was," *The Tablet*, February 13, 1999.

26. Hochhuth, p. 348.

27. Rev. Zygmunt Zielinski, *Pope Pius XII and World War II*, paper given at Seton Hall University, unpublished, p. 2.

28. Anni Lacroix-Riz, *Le Vatican, l'Europe et le Reich de la Premiere Guerre Mondiale à la Guerre Froide* (Paris: Armand Colin, 1996), p. 379.

29. *ADSS*, I, *SSGE, Mars 1939–Août 1940,* pp. 101–102.

30. Ibid., p. 120.

31. Ibid., p. 271.

32. Ibid., pp. 263–264; 274–275.

33. These conditions were the right to life and independence of all nations, large and small; disarmament; reorganizing international life; international equilibrium; and the supremacy of Divine law; see Yzermans, vol. II, *Christmas Messages*, pp. 29–31.

34. Zielinski, p. 4.

35. Blet, p. 51.

36. Yzermans, II, pp. 27–99.

37. For a brief treatment of Vatican involvement in the German anti-Hitler resistance movement, see John H. Dombrowski, *The Unneutral Diplomacy of the Vatican during 1939 and 1940*, in *Faith and Reason*, XIV, 4, Winter 1988, pp. 349–425.

38. *ADSS, SSGE, Juin 1940–Juin 1941*, pp. 63–65; 176–179; see also Blet, pp. 123–125.

39. It is interesting to note that there is an entire chapter in Blet's book devoted to *Le Sort de la Ville eternelle*, pp. 228–254.

40. *ADSS*, vol. 7, *Le Saint Siège et la Guerre Mondiale, Novembre 1942–Decembre 1943 [SSGM]*, pp. 500–502; see also the pope's letter to the Vicar of Rome, Cardinal Francesco Marchetti-Selvaggiani, July 20, 1943, in *The Catholic Mind,* XLI, September 1943, pp. 6–8.

41. *ADSS, SSGM, Novembre 1942–Decembre 1943*, pp. 400–401; see also Blet, p. 230.

42. Cable from Eden to Osborne, May 7, 1944; PRO: FO 380/88.

43. *The Catholic Mind,* XLI, September 1943, no. 969, p. 3; it is somewhat surprising that although excerpts of this address are published in ADSS (3, p. 801; 7, pp. 396–400), these words of Pius XII were not included. The full address may be found in *Acta Apostolicae Sedis: Commentarium Officiale,* 35:13, December 31, 1943, pp. 167–168.

44. Letter of Pius XII to the Bishop of Wurtzburg, February 20, 1941; *ADSS, 2, Lettres de Pie XII aux Eveques Allemands 1939–1944,* pp. 200–203; see also Blet, p. 301.

45. Letter of Pius XII to the archbishop of Cologne, March 3, 1944; ibid., pp. 363–367; see also Blet, 301.

46. Letter of Pius XII to the bishop of Berlin, April 30, 1943; ibid., pp. 318–327; see also Morley, pp. 123–124.

47. D. G. Osborne, *Vatican: Annual Report for 1945*, March 14, 1946, PRO: FO371/60803.

48. These specific examples are being used because they were mentioned in a recent article as arguments by Father Robert Graham that demonstrate how involved and concerned the Vatican was on behalf of the Jews. See John T. Pawlikowski, "The Vatican and the Holocaust: Putting *We Remember* in Context," in *Dimensions: A Journal of Holocaust Studies*, 12:2, pp. 11–16.

49. *ADSS, 9, Le Saint Siège et les Victimes de la Guerre Janvier-Decembre 1943 [SSVG],* pp. 505–506; for a more detailed explanation, see Morley, pp. 178–186.

50. *ADSS, SSVG,* pp. 509–510; see also Blet, p. 244.

51. *ADSS, SSVG, 1944–1945,* pp. 418–419.

52. Ibid., pp. 422–423.

53. Ibid., p. 433.

54. Ibid., p. 328.

55. Ibid., p. 191.

56. Ibid., p. 196.

57. March 30, 1944; cable from Foreign Office to Osborne; PRO: FO 371/42723.

58. I hope that the reader will permit me to mention the manuscript that I am preparing on the subject of Hungary: *Vatican Diplomacy and the Jews of Hungary during the Holocaust.*

CLOSING REMARKS

CARDINAL EDWARD IDRIS CASSIDY

The present consultation has been most helpful for me. The period since the publication of the Vatican document *We Remember: A Reflection on the Shoah* has shown the importance of the initiative taken by the Commission for the Religious Relations with the Jews, but at the same time has indicated certain questions raised by that document that require further study and reflection. A small consultation such as ours, with the participation of scholars and persons with a profound experience of Catholic-Jewish dialogue, has been able to take up some of these questions and provide new insights regarding them.

Among the questions discussed during our consultation, I found of particular importance the two papers on Christian tradition, anti-Judaism and anti-Semitism. This is a subject of prime importance for the future of Catholic-Jewish relations and for a balanced appraisal of the relationship between the anti-Judaism of the Church down through the centuries and the anti-Semitism of the modern age with its tragedy of the *Shoah*.

The evolution, accompanied by tension and bitter mutual condemnations, of the Christian Church in the first centuries from being predominantly a church of Jewish people to becoming a church of the gentiles, and from being a persecuted community of disciples of Christ to recognition as the religion of the great majority of citizens in a new Christian civil society, still requires study and much common reflection.

How often, in the course of history, and unfortunately in our own time, are ethnic or religious communities the victims of discrimination and oppression simply because they are considered as being part of "the other." The attitude of the Christian Church very early on created "the otherness" of the Jewish People, and circumstances at times forced the Jewish People themselves to take refuge in this "otherness." Now we have the opportunity, as Jews and Christians, with a common biblical understanding of the value of every human being, created in the image of God, to rid our relationship of this evil of "otherness," and to work together against every similar form of discrimination wherever it may raise its ugly head.

I am grateful for the discussion on the difficult question of the understanding of the Church as sacrament and as institution. As I mentioned in my own presentation, this is not a notion that is easily understood by those who are not members of the Catholic Church. For many, it looks as if the "official" Church may be seeking to avoid responsibility for the consequences of anti-Judaism. And yet, this distinction remains an essential element of our own Catholic identity as Church. We could perhaps try to explain the Catholic understanding of this reality with other words. But is such a distinction so alien to Jewish understanding of the relationship described in the Torah between the Jewish People as the Chosen People of God and the sinful members of that community? As I have mentioned on other occasions, both the Catholic Church and the Jewish People are communities with a profound understanding of relationships based on a divine covenant, to which God remains faithful even when the people of the Covenant are found lacking.

The essential fact is that there was no attempt on the part of our commission to excuse the teaching of anti-Judaism from its responsibility in regard to the action of those members of the Church who failed to give the Christian witness required of them at the time of the *Shoah*. Nor is any member of the Church excluded, whatever office may be involved, when reference is made to the "Sons and Daughters of the Church."

Doctor Irving Greenberg has asked the question, "How did Satan get into the Gospel?" The gospel is a gospel of love. The disciples of Christ are called to love even their enemies. The question, therefore, continues to worry us: How, then, did the Church fail to express in its relations to the Jewish People the love of Christ for all of God's children?

The short reference to Pope Pius XII in the Vatican document on the *Shoah* has brought to the fore again the whole question of the actions of the pope during the period of the Second World War in relation to Germany and to the *Shoah*. Here, too, we have had some valuable insights from scholars present at this consultation. I have particularly appreciated the historical perspectives regarding the situation of the Vatican in wartime Europe. It is often forgotten that there were members of the Catholic Church fighting on both sides in the war. The Catholic Church was present in each of the countries involved in this struggle. Some of the nations on the Allied side had a long history of having persecuted the Catholic Church and severely oppressing its members. The threat to Europe and to Christianity from the Soviet Union was a reality not to be underestimated, as history was to prove. The Vatican, moreover, was a small state completely surrounded by German and Italian fascist troops—"a tiny player in the war," as Dr. Marrus expressed in his presentation. Pope Pius XII hoped that by remaining independent in the war, he might be able to exercise a role in bringing about an end to the conflict. In all these discussions, we should not forget the attitude of the Republic of Ireland, which remained neutral throughout the conflict, even though many Irish fought on the Allied side.

As far as the suffering of the Jewish people is concerned, there remains the question: Would a papal intervention of the kind now demanded not have made matters worse? And when, in fact, did it become known with certainty that a terrible genocide of the Jewish people such as the *Shoah* was indeed taking place? It is obvious that more study is needed before an objective picture of all this reality is available, but the insights we have been given here will certainly have to be part of that future study. What we must surely avoid is anachronistic thinking that would judge the past with the insights of the present. Catholic-Jewish relations at the time of Pope Pius XII were not what they are today.

In conclusion, I think we can say without any hesitation that during these days we have found in our presentations and discussions much more convergence than divergence. This augurs well for the future of our Jewish-Catholic relations. It is important to remember that there are two *audiences,* as it were, to the Vatican document *We Remember: A Reflection on the Shoah,* namely the members of the Catholic Church to whom the document was addressed, and the Jewish community about whose tragedy we were writing.

There is, of course, much work to be done within the Catholic Church to inform the bishops, clergy, and laity of the progress that has been made in our Jewish-Catholic dialogue, and to encourage them to be part of this ongoing process. I can honestly affirm that the document *We Remember* has made an invaluable contribution to this task of information-formation within the Catholic community throughout the world. This remains, however, a sensitive task that requires also of the Jewish community understanding and sensitivity.

The Vatican Commission for Religious Relations with the Jews will continue to build on *We Remember,* and we look forward to the support and expertise of all of you who have been part of this consultation in the process.

SUMMARY AND FEEDBACK

PETER STEINFELS

Three things inspired me to welcome the invitation to this conference: my long friendships with John Pawlikowski and Judith Banki; my admiration for so many of the other participants; and my intense personal concern for the topic.

As the offspring of grandparents named Steinfels, Hollahan, Kennedy, and McDevitt—one Jewish, three Irish Catholic—I was primed for the important undergraduate history classes dealing with the *Shoah* at Loyola University, classes that I shared with John Pawlikowski. Appalled at the fate of the victims, I was also agonized by the fact that this terrible event occurred in a culture shaped by my faith.

The most personally difficult and painful story that I had to cover during my years as religion correspondent at the *New York Times* was the controversy over the Auschwitz convent. As a reporter, my obligation was simply to the truth. My hope and prayer was for reconciliation. My reality was that, on both sides of the controversy, there were a minority of actors who, out of ignorance, passion, or opportunism, were exacerbating the situation—and the media was often the instrument of that exacerbation. At that time I came to truly appreciate Rabbi Marc Tanenbaum, whose work and memory are maintained by the center co-sponsoring our gathering. I came to imagine Marc enshrined in a kind of war room with emergency hot lines linking him to Warsaw and Krakow and Rome, Geneva, Paris, London, and, thank goodness, my desk at the *Times*. No rumor could swell to dangerous proportions without Marc pouncing and lancing it. No fragment of a statement could work its way into the news media without Marc prepared to fax the complete original. And then, at the Vienna meeting which marked the resumption of the official Jewish-Catholic dialogue that had been suspended while the Auschwitz controversy remained unresolved, it was Cardinal Cassidy, whose public expression of *teshuvah* and then willingness to be interviewed by phone, at home and at an inconvenient hour, helped give that more positive conclusion some of the front-page attention given the rest of the episode.

In the course of our meeting, Reverend Pawlikowski several times has promised that my summary will bring order to our multidirectional reflections—all in twenty minutes. If I achieved all he has promised in that time frame, or in any time frame, it would not be Pius XII's canonization under discussion but mine, or at least it would be a miracle that could serve in someone's canonization. Actually, my task is made easier because it is so clearly impossible. There is no realistic possibility of adequately summarizing such rich presentations. At best, I can only recall and evoke them.

But first, as a journalist, I forced myself to think what might be the lead sentence of a story summing up our time here. Perhaps:

> CHICAGO, March 30—Thirty-eight exhausted Roman
> Catholic and Jewish scholars staggered out of a South Side
> theology school today, the survivors of a three-day consul-
> tation on strengthening Jewish-Catholic relations. . . .

Or

> CHICAGO, March 30—Thirty-eight Catholic and Jewish
> scholars, in a three-day meeting here, resolved all remain-
> ing differences between their faiths. . . .

Second, two preliminary observations might be made about the pattern of the presentations. Although each of our sessions featured a presenter and a co-presenter, one Catholic and one Jewish, it is worth noting that there was far more convergence than divergence in the co-presentations. There was significant variation throughout all the presentations, however, in the degree to which speakers addressed or cited specific passages or concepts in *We Remember*: sometimes commentary on the Vatican document was quite explicit; sometimes it was only implied or left entirely to others.

The first evening's session featured two papers, by Gerard Sloyan and Claudia Setzer, unsparing in their examination of the anti-Judaism found in the earliest Christian tradition, even, as Father Sloyan said, in "the charters." The presentations left us with questions, especially about the relationship between these early images and the sentiments and the conduct over the centuries of Christian mobs and demagogues. Father Sloyan suggested that the images and sentiments operated in a negative way, paralyzing church opposition and providing a permission or rationalization for actions that, in fact, were taken out of the whole run of base human motives. Doctor Setzer focused our attention on the gap between the original intention of this early anti-Judaism and its ultimate function, especially much later in history.

Both presentations led to our first evening's discussion of the distinction in *We Remember* between anti-Judaism and anti-Semitism. No one denied the distinction at the extreme—the Nazi-form of anti-Semitism. But there was either general dissatisfaction with the distinction or a feeling that it needed considerable elaboration. Several sub-themes in this discussion were: first, concern about a moral equivalence blurring any distinctions regarding historical attitudes toward Jews and Judaism; second, a corresponding concern about a moral equivocation in distinctions rendered altogether too sharp; and third, the continuing transmission of anti-Judaism at the grassroots level—for example in passing scriptural or liturgical references that cannot be immediately set into historical context or subject to commentary.

The anti-Judaism/anti-Semitism distinction was one of the points giving rise to much talk of need for a "new language" with which to advance the whole topic. That was also a theme of the next morning's session on the "Church as Sacrament and as Institution," where convergence again emerged.

Robert Schreiter moved us through what, over time, have been leading images: Church as "perfect society," Church as "mystical body," Church as "sacrament," Church as "People of God." He indicated the sources, motivations, strengths, and weaknesses of each of these metaphors. Irving Greenberg, after a moving personal reflection on encounters such as this meeting, the Jewish analogue of *Knesset Yisrael*—assembly of Israel—as mystical, unitive, transcendent, Israel. Both speakers also converged on what

Rabbi Greenberg called the "trade off"—an ultimate fragility of this kind of understanding in the face of *the fear* of acknowledging error and failure. This led to his elaboration of an alternative, a model not focused on perfection as the unmoved and unmoving, but on the permanence of change and on perfection as capacity for growth. At the core of this alternative was recognition of brokenness, an awareness of our limits, which he saw, I dare to say, as *providentially* enforced by pluralism. He said that after the *Shoah* "there can be no more final solutions, even theological ones." And he added, "Jacob could not have become Israel until he was wounded and broken."

There was a key moment, in my view, in the discussion that followed, which was set against the background of the attribution of historical failures in *We Remember,* not to the Church itself but to its sinful sons and daughters (including those, Cardinal Cassidy was quick to note, at even the highest levels). Catholics here were searching, like Rabbi Greenberg, for alternative images and metaphors that were more compatible with admissions of institutional failure than, say, "mystical body." "People of God" was recalled but also "light of the world" and other possibilities. Father Schreiter warned of the resistance that these images provoked in some church circles, partly because of the split, which he had sketched in his presentation, between "ego-centric" (individualist) and "socio-centric" (communal) cultures. Then Cardinal Cassidy intervened, saying about such proposals in connection with the writing of *We Remember:* "The greatest difficulty was the fear that if you say the Church has been wrong in the past, then it can be wrong today and tomorrow." This fear was strongest among representatives of "new churches," he noted, especially the African ones facing an expansivist, triumphalist, confident Islam, and reluctant to give ammunition to that rival.

This would be the place to underline that Cardinal Cassidy, in his public lecture as well as throughout the group's own sessions, insisted that the distinction between Church and members is not meant to erect a "cordon sanitaire" around church authorities or deeply embedded teachings, or to minimize their responsibilities. And further, he insisted that the history in *We Remember* was not meant to be uppermost in the document's import, and that *We Remember,* in any case, was "a document in process."

The afternoon moved us swiftly—much as did *We Remember*, itself—from early Christianity and the long stretch of centuries to modern times, the last two centuries, in fact, and the circumstances of the *Shoah* itself.

Ronald Modras, like Rabbi Greenberg, offered personal recollections and reflections that were valuable and provocative in the detail, but the overall theme of his presentation was the difficulty or even the impossibility of separating the religious from the social, economic, and political components of nineteenth- and early twentieth-century anti-Judaism and (beyond the Nazi variety) anti-Semitism. There was another convergence with Steven Katz's *tour de force* sweep over Jewish and European cultural history after Jewish emancipation, a history he summed up as the project of separating Jews from Judaism. "The Church can neither be blamed nor exonerated in a simple manner," he said, before pointing to "supersessionism" as, for him, the key issue.

The discussion that followed ranged from the topic of growing Jewish interest in studying Christianity to the persistence of the kind of religio-political anti-Judaism that the speakers had described as often infecting the highest circles of church leadership. The Enlightenment and post-Enlightenment issues prominent in this session have often had a lower profile in Catholic-Jewish discussions than, say, the understandable emphasis on the earlier centuries. My own impression is that many of the thorniest practical issues creating Catholic-Jewish tensions today stem from the two traditions' different experiences of the Enlightenment and from their consequent reactions to the Enlightenment.

This morning's presentations on "Pius XII in Historical Context," being still very fresh in our minds as well as extremely systematic, precise, and well argued, need even less summary. But again, there was much convergence—on the complexity of the wartime situation and of Vatican and papal behavior, and then on the constricted ecclesiological and ideological frameworks in which people were acting. The latter included, in Michael Marrus's account, the overlapping roles of traditional theological anti-Judaism and the very kind of modern religio-political anti-Judaism that Dr. Modras described.

This session had to ponder the question, Why is the role of the Vatican and Pius XII so central in the discussion of the Church's relationship to the

Shoah? Why does it overshadow the concern with long centuries of church teaching, with the Church's adversarial stance toward modernity and gravitation, for 150 years after the French Revolution, toward anti-Enlightenment conservatism, or with the roles of national hierarchies in Germany or other parts of Nazi-occupied Europe?

It was proposed that the discussion be conceived as a triptych, with Hochhuth's portrait of Pius XII on one panel, Pius as a candidate for canonization on the opposing panel, and some more shadowed portrait or even a collage of portraits of Pius on the middle panel.

This discussion showed that the distinction between historian and moralist is about as blurry as the one between anti-Judaism and anti-Semitism. For purposes of analysis, the historian must accept the contemporary framework—the ecclesiology, ideology, and social climate of the time under examination. Ultimately, however, can historians (never mind theologians or moralists) completely work within the framework of those givens? At the very least, they create a demand for further historical inquiry, namely, about how we reached the point of this constricting framework in the first place.

My assignment is officially listed as "Summary and Feedback." Feedback? What does that mean, other than the unfortunate noise made by improperly utilized microphones? I offer several personal observations that can be placed under that heading.

First, Rabbi Greenberg stated that Catholic-Jewish relations and dialogue were currently in much better shape than intra-Jewish relations and dialogue. I would add that perhaps something similar could be said of intra-Catholic relations and dialogue, and that these strained relations inevitably played a part in the making of *We Remember*, maybe even a decisive part, and will play a part in any further discussion.

Second, there is a common but mistaken assumption regarding the audiences for *We Remember* and the pastoral challenges posed by those audiences. The assumption is that there are two audiences. One is the Jewish audience that needs and deserves a credible demonstration that Catholicism understands its failures and is forthcoming with a sign of repentance. The second is the Catholic audience that needs further instruction about its own tradition and inoculation against the toxins of anti-Judaism and anti-Semitism. This is a task that requires persistence but also a pedagogical dexterity that avoids affronting Catholic sensitivity or loyalty.

Ignored is a third audience, also of Catholics, who are knowledgeable about the failures of the past and inoculated against anti-Judaism and anti-Semitism. It is not to those toxins that they are dangerously susceptible but to something else—a real crisis of faith provoked by the *Shoah* and by the Church's own record. They want a credible theological and historical reflection responding to those events in a manner that shuns all excuses or apologetics. They are not going to be sent into confusion by an avowal of error but by anything resembling an alibi. They know that at least in everyday senses of the word, the Church has erred in the past and probably will err again in the future. They want an understanding of that reality of brokenness that can encompass the mystical, unitive, transcendent dimension, but not rely on any papering over of painful history or glaring failures.

Third, regarding the distinction between the Church and its members—its sinful sons and daughters, if you will—I think there is a solution. Father Schreiter's distinction between ego-centric and socio-centric cultures made me think of another distinction: between unselfconscious cultures that take themselves at face value and those, like ours, that have become very conscious about their own structures and institutions. Yet the metaphors proposed in our discussion, even the "people of God," leave out the level of institution (except for intimations of governing and authority structures): the art, the lore, the practices, the hymns, the favorite tropes of preachers, and so on.

We need less to reject anything in the existing images and metaphors than to find additional language specifically to encompass this institutional reality in our ecclesiology. The French bishops have indicated the way to go; in their Drancy statement on the French Church's role regarding the *Shoah*, they speak of the Church's "basic religious culture." That term captures something institutional as well as individual that "sinful sons and daughters" does not.

Fourth, the title of our meeting is "Building on *We Remember*." Who is doing the building? Cardinal Cassidy, to be sure, as he has so strongly indicated. But what is involved is much more than that. We are talking about not only the Holy See and official efforts at that level; we are also talking about our own independent initiatives—writing, lecturing, preaching, teaching, and pursuing scholarly research. We are not putting everything on official shoulders.

Fifth, I say this about who is involved, partly because the official process remains so baffling to me, both as a Catholic and as a reporter. Incidentally, whenever I am trying to find out what is happening in Vatican circles, I turn to Jewish sources, which are apt to know more, or be more forthcoming, than most Catholic ones. There is a real problem of a lack of transparency in that process, a kind of Roman black box. We see what goes in and what comes out but not what transpires within. I think that this contributes greatly to the fact that so many Catholics do not feel any sense of "ownership" of documents like *We Remember*.

I acknowledge that there is a cultural difference at work here, between Europe and the United States. Nonetheless, when Cardinal Cassidy spoke earlier in these discussions of "our historians," I want to ask who they are and why they are "ours."

Sixth, can the analysis of Christian anti-Judaism, of its deep sources but equally of the reasons for its perpetuation and its lethal interbreeding with political, economic, and social ideologies (right through to the most recent pre-war decades), can those concerns somehow be made more central—and the conduct of Pius XII be made less central—to our reflections on the Church and the *Shoah?* Not ignored, to be sure, which would be impossible and illegitimate, but still not so enlarged as to eclipse the rest?

APPENDIX A

The Vatican and the Final Solution:
What Was Known, and When[1]

KEVIN MADIGAN

In the early months of 1942, the newly formed state of Slovakia entered negotiations with the government of Germany, and in particular with Adolf Eichmann. The negotiations centered on logistical issues surrounding the deportation to Galicia and the Lublin district of the roughly ninety thousand Jewish citizens of Slovakia. As the negotiations proceeded, Eichmann demanded that Slovakia send only Jews capable of labor. While the Slovak government, which represented a population that was almost entirely Catholic, willingly complied, it was less happy to be left with the care of the elderly and children. Accordingly, it proposed to Eichmann that, "in the spirit of Christianity," families not be separated but, instead, be deported together. Although he first complained about the "technical" problems this plan would cause for Germany, Eichmann relented. By the beginning of March 1942, he had agreed to plans for the deportation of all the Jews of Slovakia.[2]

As news of the plans for deportation spread, it naturally panicked the Jewish community in Bratislava. About to be swallowed in the maw of deportation, the Jewish leaders there turned first to the Vatican *chargé d'affaires*, Monsignor Giuseppe Burzio. Because he happened to be absent, the leaders of the community composed an anguished letter of appeal to the pope himself. This they entrusted to the nuncio in Budapest, Archbishop Angelo Rotta, through whom the letter reached the Vatican on March 13, 1942. "Most Holy Father," it stated, "No one [else] can help us." Not only had everything—businesses, houses, funds, even clothing been taken from them in a ruthlessly efficient act of Aryanization. But "as we surely know," the community declared, "we are to be shipped out to Lublin, Poland." The authors of the letter were under no illusions about what this meant: "We are," they stated simply, "condemned to annihilation" (*Wir sind zum Untergang verurteilt*). Would the Holy Father, in the name of humanity and fellow feeling, admonish the president of Slovakia, a Catholic priest, to block their expulsion and certain massacre? "We place all our hope and confidence in Your Holiness," it says, "as the safest refuge of all the persecuted" (*als die sicherste Zuflucht aller Verfolgten*).[3] Less than two weeks later, a transport of one thousand young Slovakian citizens boarded a train. The first transport sent by Eichmann's Section IV B 4, the train was bound for Auschwitz. Six weeks later, more than forty thousand of their countrymen and women had also been deported.[4]

The safest refuge of all the persecuted. Those words were loaded, then, with impossible pathos—and now with an irony its desperately sincere writers could not have intended. Surely they could not have foreseen that sixty years later the recipient of their letter would be excoriated by critics for near-criminal passivity in crisis and even, by some, for complicity in Judeocide. Nor could they possibly have imagined that, far from being celebrated as a haven for the tyrannized, the Vatican and the pope in particular, had been so severely criticized for cold and craven wartime conduct that one writer, a Catholic at that, would dare to christen him "Hitler's Pope."[5]

Actually, so harsh a judgment was unthinkable not only in 1942 but through the early 1960s. In fact, for the fifteen years after the war, Pius was almost everywhere celebrated as a courageous antagonist of Nazi racial theory and policy, a benefactor of victims of war, and a compassionate collaborator—indeed, leader—in resistance and rescue efforts on behalf of Jewish civilians threatened with deportation. On the occasion of his death, no less a figure than Golda Meir, then foreign minister of the State of Israel, eulogized him thus: "When fearful martyrdom came to our people in the decade of Nazi terror, the voice of the Pope was raised for the victims. The life of our times was enriched by a voice speaking out on the great moral truths."[6] Similar sentiments were expressed by others at this time, including President Eisenhower and Moshe Sharett, the first foreign minister of Israel, as well as Albert Einstein. If opinion among leaders of the Allied governments *during* the war was not nearly so univocal or enthusiastic, the chorus of praise *after* the war and into the early 1960s was virtually unqualified.

The chorus did not exactly stop singing in the 1960s. But its numbers were depleted and its performances unceremoniously interrupted by the loud dissenting voice of the German playwright Rolf Hochhuth. In 1963, Hochhuth staged a play entitled *Der Stellvertreter*. (Translated as *The Deputy* or *The Representative,* the title is a sarcastic twist on the papal claim to be *vicarius Christi*, i.e., representative of Christ on earth).[7] In the play, Pius appears on stage pontificating about the wickedness of the Allies, whose bombing had ruined parts of the artistic patrimony of Rome. The Germans, he observes, were friendlier than the cold malefactors whose bombs had demolished San Lorenzo, an ancient basilica in Rome. Then, while the pope is murmuring about how the Allied invasion had depreciated the value of stocks the Vatican had invested in, an emissary of Kurt Gerstein[8] bursts into the room to tell the Holy Father about the death camps in Poland. Pius waves him off and continues to execrate the Allies.

While perhaps successful literarily, this picture of the pope even Pius's critics find crude; and, in fact, the picture Hochhuth draws cannot, without considerable misrepresentation or dramatic license, be reconstructed from the documents and eyewitnesses. Be that as it may, the play was simply a smash popular success. Aside from being staged in virtually all of the countries of the West and translated into more than twenty languages, it inspired more than 450 reviews and articles in English alone, the best of which have been anthologized in a volume whose title says it all about the impact of the play: *The Storm over the Deputy*.[9] More importantly, the Pius that most people knew in the 1960s—and, I think, the one still known today—is the one that is traceable to the play or its influence: a cold, calculating pope, scandalously callous in the face of unspeakable suffering, cynical and supine in the face of crimes that, had he intervened with moral force and courage, he might have prevented. As Hochhuth put it, in an article he wrote on his own play: "Perhaps never before in history have so many people paid with their lives for the passivity of one single politician."[10] In 1958, then, Pius enjoyed a reputation as a moral seraph; five years later he had transmogrified, as one of his defenders has said, into the hero of a black legend.

In 1963, the Church had just entered a new and unprecedented phase of self-examination and doctrinal and institutional reconstruction. It was a time when the bitter criticism expressed by Hochhuth and felt by millions was allowed to sting, a time when such criticism was no longer reactively dismissed as the venom of the hostile and unchurched. For many, the Hochhuth play had raised painful questions about the role of the Catholic Church at all levels—papal, diplomatic, episcopal, clerical, religious, and lay—during the Holocaust, questions that led to even more excruciating reflections on the credibility of Christianity itself. If Christianity, or at least Catholicism, could be so passive in the moment of truth—if, indeed, two millennia of ecclesiastically sponsored anti-Judaism had paved the way for the kind of nonchalance that allowed Catholics to observe without pity the spectacle of "non-Aryan" neighbors being cruelly expropriated and deported to God knew where—well, how could it answer for itself?

In this new atmosphere of self-criticism—and also undoubtedly with the self-interested hope that the caricatures of Vatican activity during the war would be disciplined by historically verifiable data—Pope Paul VI, who had been a second-in-command in the Vatican secretariat of state during the war years, waived the usually mandatory seventy-five-year delay in granting access to the Vatican archives and appointed a team of four Jesuit scholars resident in Rome to select and publish the acts and documents of the Holy See connected to the Second World War. The result was an eleven-volume collection of documents, mostly dispatches and telegrams sent between the Vatican and its international network of nunciatures and legations; it also contains memoranda and some extremely valuable private notes written by the upper-echelon staff in the secretary of state's office.[11]

While not without its flaws—the editors regrettably chose not to publish a number of crucially informative documents, and there have been questions about their principle of selection that only the unlikely opening of the archives is now capable of quieting—the volumes are an immense contribution to scholarship and a positively indispensable foundation for any scholar or writer wishing to address the questions of what the Vatican knew about the Final Solution and when, what it did with this knowledge, and why it acted as it did.

It is thus all the more perplexing that, over the fifteen or so years during which these documents were published, and in the two decades since the last of the eleven volumes came out, they have been largely unused by those who have entered the debate, both by Pius's defenders and his critics. Many of the latter—especially those who have, not without justification, demanded that the Vatican open its archives—are, I am convinced, simply unaware that these volumes exist. It is little wonder that Judah Graubhart was moved to comment, as early as 1975, that there were "few issues in the historiography of the Holocaust that are colored by more emotion and based on less knowledge than the Vatican's response to the 'final solution to the Jewish Question.'"[12]

Among the most passionate participants in the debate have been those who, since the publication of the Hochhuth play, have indignantly risen to the defense of Pius, whom they regard as the victim of ignorant polemicists and shoddy scholarship. "In the twenty two years since Pius XII died," the Spiritan priest Michael O'Carroll could write in 1980 in a volume subtitled *Greatness Dishonoured*, "the falsehood and misrepresentation published about [Pius XII] are possibly unique in biographical literature of the same years."[13] Carroll and others have argued that Pius: did and said, if, admittedly, *sotto voce*, more on behalf of imperiled Jews than is ordinarily known or admitted; could not have done more than he did for fear of reprisal, not just against the Holy See but especially against the victims whose suffering he was attempting to relieve; and did not know the full truth about the massacres in the Soviet Union and especially the Polish death camps until after the war.[14]

To address any of the moral issues involved here, it would seem that one must first carefully address historically the truth of that last claim. After all, Pius XII cannot logically be criticized for inaction if he were ignorant of the monstrosities occurring in the East. In the wake of the publication of *The Deputy*, defenders of Pius argued emphatically that Pius and the Vatican were, in fact, largely unaware of the horrors being enacted in Russia, Poland, and elsewhere, and of their awesome and cruel dimensions—or at the least, that the Vatican was dependent upon reports that were as nebulous, tendentious, or unverifiable as they were meager.[15]

My purpose here is to ask whether Pius's defenders have the support of the documentary evidence on their side. My main sources will be those eleven volumes of Vatican documents I have mentioned, especially those containing documents from 1941 to 1943, but I will also rely on documents produced by the German and American ambassadors to the Holy See during the war years. Because of the importance of simply establishing the facts, I intend to be quite empirical, and to proceed in ruthlessly chronological and narrative fashion. My main interest is to establish what precisely the Vatican knew about the Holocaust, and when, and to provide a picture of what it was like, in late 1941 through all of 1942 especially and into early 1943, to have worked in the Vatican curia and to have absorbed, piece by piece, the news of the awesome drama unfolding in the East. And I would like to integrate this narrative with the far better established narrative of the massacres enacted in Poland and the Soviet Union from 1941 to 1943.[16]

Again, this seems to me an absolutely essential foundation for posing a second set of factual questions: *What* did the Vatican do, or not do, with this knowledge? And a third set of more interpretive, analytical questions: *Why* did it do what it did and not something else? And a fourth set of speculative, counterfactual questions: What more *might* it have done? And finally, a fifth set of moral questions: What *should* it have done? But here I'd like to prescind from the analytical, interpretive, speculative, and moral issues in the interests of establishing, as precise and meticulously constructed as possible, a narrative of what the Vatican knew, and when. On the basis of a careful and, I hope, comprehensive examination of the evidence, the answer given to this question must, like it or not, be much different than that provided by Pius's defenders.

"Einsatzgruppen" Massacres

By the autumn of 1941, the definition, expropriation, and concentration of Europe's Jewish population was well underway. The next phase of the Holocaust was, of course, the work of the *Einsatzgruppen*, the mobile killing units that followed behind German forces in Operation Barbarossa, the invasion and occupation of the Soviet Union that began in late June 1941. As is well known, on arrival, the German SS and police personnel, with the aid of the *Wehrmacht,* shot, first, Jewish prisoners and then all Jewish men, women, and children, as well as Roma, Soviet political commissars, partisans, and others the Nazis judged to be racially or politically unacceptable. By the spring of 1943, more than a million Jews and tens of thousands of others would lose their lives by being shot to death by men of these mobile killing squads. Some thirty-three thousand would perish in the infamous two-day massacre at Babi Yar, a ravine northwest of the Ukrainian capital city of Kiev.[17]

The Vatican received less information about this phase of the Holocaust than about either the preceding or succeeding sequence of events. Nonetheless, some detailed data did arrive in Rome about the shootings. In fact, at least three reports about the massacre-by-shooting reached the Vatican. These were among the very first any government in the West received about the atrocities. As early as late October 1941, the Vatican got its first report. More importantly, the report came from one of its own, Burzio, *chargé d'affaires* in Slovakia. On October 27, 1941, Burzio revealed in a letter to Secretary of State Maglione that, according to Slovak military chaplains returning from the front, Jewish prisoners of war on territories overrun by German forces were being shot at once. In addition, he said, Jewish civilians, regardless of age or gender, were being rounded up and systematically "suppressed" (*soppressi*, i.e., massacred).[18]

The Vatican response to this report was, to put it mildly, odd. Diplomats in the Secretariat of State seemed to be preoccupied with the precise identity of the perpetrators, rather than with the fate of the victims and the appalling details communicated by Burzio. In fact, the secretary of state and his assistants replied only by inquiring whether it was Slovaks or Germans doing the shooting. Monsignor Tardini, one of Maglione's two principal assistants, criticized Burzio's report for being vague: was it, he wondered, "Catholic Slovaks who are committing these crimes or the Germans?" On December 20, Burzio was asked to clarify.[19]

Burzio's reply was, mysteriously, more than three months in coming. But what it lacked in promptness it made up for in angry precision of detail: "The massacres," he replied succinctly, "have been committed by squadrons of the SS by order of authorities of the German government." And, as if to emphasize the main point, Burzio repeats, "All the Jews from a given locale were concentrated far from inhabited areas and massacred (*trucidati*) with machine-gun fire."[20]

The second report received by the Vatican came on March 19, 1942, in the form of a long and detailed memorandum from Gerhart Riegner of the World Jewish Congress in Geneva, and Richard Lichtheim of the Jewish Agency for Palestine, which was given to Archbishop Filippo Bernardini, nuncio at Berne. This is an important document for a number of reasons. First, it is not just long and detailed but, as it turns out, remarkably accurate. Second, it outlined to the nuncio "rigorous measures" taken against Jews not just in Slovakia but throughout the occupied territories. Among the miseries described by Riegner and Lichtheim was the concentration in Poland and elsewhere of masses of Jews in ghettos in "indescribable misery" and in epidemic conditions that "at this moment, are literally decimating these populations." Nine months after the start of Barbarossa, they are also able to report that, in addition to this slow and steady form of execution, "thousands of Jews in Poland and in the parts of Russia occupied by Germany have been executed by German troops." They draw attention particularly to measures being taken in Slovakia, Croatia, Hungary, and unoccupied France—i.e., Catholic or largely Catholic countries—where "measures taken or in progress can perhaps still be rescinded or at least alleviated *by the intervention of the Holy See*" (emphasis added).

Their memorandum also contains some graphic comments on the killings that had occurred in Romania. The recovery, with the help of the German army, of territories that had been taken over by the Soviet Union in 1940 was used in Romania as a pretext (as, incidentally, was their loss) for launching massacres against the Jews. It is of course always dangerous, and from the point of view of the victims, probably fruitless, to compare degrees of enormity. But we know that even the *Einsatz* squads complained about the "undisciplined" Romanian zeal for killing Jews in the wake of the recovery of Bukovina and Bessarabia.[21] In fact, the Lichtheim/Riegner memorandum revealed just how brutal the killing was:

> During the reoccupation of Bessarabia by German and Romanian troops, 92,000 Jews were executed by firing squads. A trustworthy report on this subject says that in every town or village Jews were assembled in one place—men, women, children, the aged, the sick, even hospital patients—and having been tortured and starved for several days, were shot.[22]

We know for certain that Archbishop Bernardini forwarded this memorandum to the Vatican; and since 1974 we know for certain that it was received at the Vatican Secretariat of State's office. We know because the letter from Bernardini to Maglione accompanying the memorandum has been published in the eighth of the eleven volumes of official documentation on the war published by the Vatican.[23] However, the editors made a crucial scholarly decision in omitting to publish the actual text of the memorandum sent by Riegner and Lichtheim, forwarded by the nuncio at Bern, and received by the second-in-command at the Vatican. In a footnote, the editors comment only that "it [i.e., the memo] gives a record of anti-Semitic measures taken in Germany and in the territories annexed by Germany or controlled by Germany."[24] This is, of course, a rather banal and sterilized way of describing the contents of this memorandum.

A third report on the *Einsatzgruppen* massacres, this one from Andrea Szeptyckyj, the Eastern Rite archbishop of Lvov, would reach the Vatican much later, indeed about a year after the shooting there had begun.[25] In the summer of 1941, thousands of Jews were, not without the help of Ukrainian peasants, butchered by detachments of the mobile killing squads. Between June 22 and July 16 alone, three thousand Jews were massacred in Lvov, and five thousand each in nearby Bialystok, Brest-Litovsk, and Tarnopol, as well as hundreds in each of the many small towns and villages in the diocese. One year after the massacres began (August 1942), the archbishop of Lvov wrote to the Vatican:

> For no less than a year, there has not been a day when the most horrible crimes, murders, robberies and rapes . . . have occurred...the number of Jews massacred in this our small region has certainly exceeded two hundred thousand . . . and as the army advances toward the East, the number of victims multiplies.[26]

By the time he wrote this letter, deportations from Lvov to Belzec began victimizing Jews from his episcopal city (fifteen thousand in March 1942 alone) and from surrounding cities like Lublin (ten thousand in March) in frighteningly larger numbers, and the archbishop is undoubtedly referring to these crimes as well as to the open-air executions by rifle fire.

A similarly disturbing letter arrived at the Vatican on December 12, 1942, from Anthony Springovics, archbishop of Riga in Latvia, and addressed to Pius XII:

> The barbarity of nationalist doctrine [he says] has appeared in Latvia in all its cruelty and abomination: almost all of the Jews here have now been killed (*iudaei fere omnes iam necati sunt*). Just a few thousand were left [after the massacres] in the ghetto of Riga, the greater part of these imported from exterior regions.[27]

The archbishop's information was quite accurate. In November 1941, Russian POWs had dug execution pits deep in the forest some miles away from the ghetto in Riga. To the edge of that forest, rows and rows of blue buses transported, over the course of just ten days, twenty-seven thousand Jews, who were shot there by the *Einsatz* squads.[28]

By the end of 1942, then, the Vatican had received at least four reports about the *Einsatzgruppen* massacres. The credibility of three of these was certainly not diminished by the ecclesiastical status of their sources.

Deportations and Death Camps: 1942

At about the same time he was clarifying for the Vatican exactly *who* was shooting innocent Jewish civilians in the overrun territories of the Soviet Union, the *chargé d'affaires* in Bratislava was also sending back to the Vatican secretariat of state some of the first reports it was to receive concerning deportation. On March 9, 1942, Burzio accurately reported that deportations of all Slovakian Jews, without distinction of age, sex, or religion, to Galicia and the Lublin district were "imminent." He then concluded, presciently as well as soberly, "The deportation of 80,000 people to Poland, put to the mercy of the Germans, is the equivalent of condemning the greater part of them to their deaths" (*equivale condannarne gran parte morte sicura*).[29]

Burzio's was not the last letter to arrive in the Vatican about these transports. In fact, the Vatican was to receive at least two more reports, both of them, it is important to note, from their own nuncios. One day after Burzio sent his report, Archbishop Bernardini, the nuncio in Bern, forwarded a message he had received from Agudas Israel of the International Organization of Orthodox Jews, who wished to inform the pope of the imminent deportations in Slovakia. Ten days later, on March 20, the nuncio in Budapest sent a letter to the Vatican. Rotta had received a petition from the chief rabbi of Budapest asking him to beg the pope to intercede on behalf of the menaced Slovakian Jews with the Catholic president of the country.[30]

Another very disturbing report concerning deportation came a little over a month later in a letter from the Italian priest Pirro Scavizzi. Having served as an army chaplain at the front in the Great War, the remarkable Scavizzi was almost sixty years of age when the Second World War broke out. Yet he managed to get himself assigned as a military chaplain on the hospital trains of the Sovereign Order of Malta. It was in that capacity that he traveled to Germany, Poland, and the Ukraine during the war and, as he was to put it late in his life, "to see at close quarters the appalling cruelties of the Hitlerite organizations, especially of the SS, and so to inform the Holy Father."[31] On May 12, 1942, Scavizzi wrote to the pope and specified the nature of the cruelties he had witnessed. On journeys to the Ukraine and Poland, Scavizzi was able to observe, and to report back directly to the pope, that the massacre of the Jews in the Ukraine was "complete" (*è ormai al completo*). Meanwhile, the "anti-Jewish struggle" in Poland was proceeding inexorably and "becoming worse" (*va sempre più aggravandosi).* Deportations were underway and mass executions (*esecuzioni anche in massa*) were occurring as well. It seemed that—indeed, he adds, some in Poland hoped that—the system of mass executions would bring the massacre of Jews to fulfillment.[32]

This, I think, is an extremely important document. Its author is an ecclesiastical source whom the Vatican had no reason to distrust or to suspect of exaggeration or propaganda. As Carlo Falconi has written of him, "When he died on 9 September 1964 . . . he was surrounded by the scarlet of cardinals, the violet robes of bishops, military uniforms, and uniforms of knightly orders."[33] He had easy access to the pope and a relationship of trust and length with the Pacelli family. Moreover, he was serving as chaplain to the Axis armies: not just the Italian army but also for the *Wehrmacht*. In this capacity, he acquired a close-up view of the atrocities. At the same time, he had what Ribbentrop, thinking of Catholic military chaplains in general, once nervously called "compound allegiances"—i.e., loyalties not just to the Axis armies but to the Holy See. Ribbentrop was right to be anxious, because Scavizzi was able to provide the Holy See with information of considerable accuracy and detail.

At roughly the same time Scavizzi sent his report back to the Vatican on Poland, disturbing news was also arriving from Croatia. The Holy See did not initially have diplomatic relations with the Ustase regime, although Croatia was statistically one of the "most Catholic" countries in Europe.[34]

Nonetheless, there was an "apostolic visitor"—officially an observer of the religious situation there. A Benedictine abbot, Giuseppe Marcone was the *de facto* nuncio to Croatia. At least he was treated that way by the Ustase regime and by the Croat *Poglavnik* (i.e., *führer*) Ante Pavelic, with whom the apostolic visitor enjoyed a cordial diplomatic and social relationship.[35]

Nevertheless, Marcone reported to Maglione, in a letter dated July 17, 1942, that Jewish civilians in Croatia had been prepared for deportation. This appeared to omen poorly, as—he had been told by the chief of police in Croatia—two million Jews had already been killed by the Germans. Marcone observed, "It appears as if the same fate awaits the Jews of Croatia, especially if elderly or unable to work."[36] Thousands of these would, in fact, make up a significant proportion of the more than one million Jews who would finally perish in Auschwitz.

The force of Marcone's communiqué would soon be augmented by a dispatch sent directly, on August 4, 1942, by Miroslav Freiberger, chief rabbi of Zagreb, to Pius XII. "The last remnants of our community finds itself," the letter begins, "in the most dire possible situation," a situation in which "decisions are being made about our lives." In this emergency, it went on, "our eyes are fixed upon Your Holiness." Freiberger went on to appeal to the pope in the name of abandoned children, orphans, and those widowed by the deportation of spouses to do something to help them remain in their homes. There they would be willing to stay, if it were possible, even in the most straitened circumstances.[37]

The secretary of state, having received this letter, instructed the apostolic visitor to respond to the rabbi "prudently" and tactfully, and not to neglect to remind him that the Holy See always wished to alleviate suffering. He was also asked to remind the rabbi that the Holy See had not neglected to "involve itself" (*interessarsi*) on several occasions on behalf of persons recommended to it (*in favore delle persone raccomandate*).[38] Two years later, in April 1944, the German foreign minister in Croatia, Siegfried Kasche, was able to report that the Jewish question in Croatia had been essentially solved.[39]

As these dire events were unfolding in Croatia, the nuncio to Vichy, France, Archbishop Valerio Valeri, wrote to the secretary of state on July 26, 1942, that almost thirteen thousand "stateless" Jews (actually, mostly Polish and Czech refugees then resident in France) had been concentrated in Paris for deportation to the Ukraine.[40] One week later, Valeri could announce to Maglione that deportations were now occurring in the unoccupied sector of France as well. Two transports of Jewish civilians had departed from concentration camps in Vichy, France. Their destination was unknown, but it was assumed to be the General Gouvernement or the Ukraine. Perhaps most alarming, Valeri could report that ill and elderly Jews were being conveyed eastward. This made it clear that they were not being sent for purposes of labor but for other, more sinister reasons. Valeri closes the letter by reassuring Maglione that he has defended the pope against the charge that the Holy See was "shrouded in silence" (*rinchiusa nel silenzio*) in the face of diabolical evil.[41] The danger of new, draconian rigors (*provvedimenti*) in other parts of Europe, which might be accelerated by a public protest, had induced the Holy See, Valeri concludes, to a posture of "prudent delay and enlightened reserve" (*una prudente attesa e ad una illuminata riserva*).[42]

As the Vatican pursued its policy of delay and reserve, more and more Allied frustration with papal silence was expressed. In a telegram of August 3, 1942, sent to the State Department by Harold H. Tittmann, American *chargé d'affaires* and representative at the Holy See (in the absence of Myron C. Taylor), Tittmann reported that he had attempted to rebuke the Holy See for its failure to protest publicly against Nazi atrocities. Tittmann attempted to appeal to the pope's self-interest by asserting that the Vatican silence had endangered the moral prestige of the papacy and had undermined faith in the Church and in Pius XII himself. He also reports that "certain of my colleagues" (presumably other ambassadors) had made the same sort of appeal to the pope. All these appeals, he reports, were "without result." Indeed, the responses from the Vatican had, he complains, become monotonously predictable. Tittmann and his colleagues were "invariably" reminded that the pope had already condemned wartime offenses; to be more specific, the Vatican insisted, would "only make matters worse."[43]

Just five days after Tittman sent his telegram, Gerhart Riegner, the representative of the World Jewish Congress in Geneva, sent a telegram of his own (August 10, 1942) to colleagues in London and New York. In the telegram, Riegner urgently stated that he had received an "alarming report" whose source was someone with "close connections with the highest German authorities." The informer had revealed that a plan had recently been discussed in the headquarters of the führer. Its aim, the informer said, was to deport, concentrate, and exterminate "at one blow" the millions of Jews then dwelling in territory controlled by the government of Germany. The timing and method of the extermination, he said, were not yet clearly established. However, so far as timing went, the autumn had been discussed; so far as method went, so, too, had the use of prussic acid.[44] It is not clear whether this information ever reached the Vatican. A cable from the New York Office of the World Jewish Congress to the London office states that it had been in contact with Vatican officials, but says nothing about the nature of the communication. In any case, there is no record, apparently, in the Vatican archives that such communication took place.[45]

In any case, the general point made by this famous intelligence was to be all too improbably confirmed for the German Church, and possibly the Vatican, at almost the same time by the enigmatic SS Colonel, Kurt Gerstein.[46] In early 1941, Gerstein's sister-in-law had died in a mental institution in Hadamar. Suspicious about the circumstances under which Bertha Ebeling had perished, Gerstein, an erstwhile Nazi party member who was later dismissed for criticism of the Nazis and then actually interned for a time at Welzheim concentration camp, became determined to infiltrate the apparatus of death. Incredibly, it fell to Gerstein to determine the feasibility of changing the deadly gas used in the Aktion Reinhard gas chambers from carbon monoxide to Zyklon B. It was in this capacity, and in the presence of the villainous Christian Wirth, the SS head of the death camps, that he was able to witness, on August 19, 1942, the experimental gassing of some fifty-two hundred Jews from Lvov at Belzec.

In this case, the experiment was particularly gruesome. To begin with, it took almost three hours for the diesel engine to start. Gerstein reports that, during the long wait, the prisoners could be heard loudly weeping. Finally the engine began. After more than half an hour, the gassed prisoners had all expired. The doors opened and a corps of dentists stormed in and began to pry gold teeth and crowns from the teeth of the gassed. Wirth collected a can chock full of teeth to display to Gerstein and then crowed, "See for yourself the weight of that gold! You can't imagine what we find every day—currency, diamonds, gold."[47]

Aghast, Gerstein wasted no time in attempting to get the frightful news out. On a train back to Berlin, Gerstein happened, with an improbability that seems to have marked his entire life, to encounter the Swedish diplomat Baron Göran von Otter. According to van Otter, Gerstein loudly, repeatedly and at times uncontrollably blurted out the story of what he had witnessed: "Gerstein kept on recalling what he had seen. He sobbed and hid his face in his hands."[48] Back in Berlin in later August, Gerstein attempted to reveal to Cesare Orsenigo, the papal nuncio in Berlin, what he had just witnessed. The ecclesiastics at the nunciature refused to hear him because he was a soldier (and thus presumed to be untrustworthy); he was shown the door. Undaunted, Gerstein proceeded to the offices of the archbishop of Berlin and there handed a report on what he had seen to the legal advisor of Archbishop Preysing. He also requested that the report be forwarded to the Vatican. It is not known whether it was received there, but it seems altogether likely it was.[49] Preysing had a special relationship with Pius XII, who wrote to him more than to any other German bishop.[50] Of course, this would have been a report of rare importance, coming as it did not just from a German but also from an SS officer who had personally witnessed the alarming events contained in his report.[51]

At about the same time (August 31, 1942), a letter sent to the Vatican reported that twenty thousand adults had been deported from Paris (*dans des wagons a bestiaux*), leaving behind three to five thousand of their children. The writer of the letter, part of a Swiss interconfessional rescue committee, pleads with the Vatican to influence Catholic countries to open their doors to children separated from their parents, "parents whom, without a shadow of a doubt, they will never see again."[52] The significance of this letter is that its writer knew (already in August 1942) that the deportees were not coming back. Unless the Vatican authorities had reason to distrust the letter writer, they would, one presumes, had to have feared the same.

As reports of atrocities continued to arrive not only in Rome but in Washington and London, they had the effect, it seems, of arousing the diplomatic corps of several of the Allies to ever more urgent appeals to the Vatican to condemn publicly the treatment of innocent civilians in occupied territories. On September 14, 1942, for example, Tittmann sent a note to Cardinal

Maglione, the Vatican secretary of state, in which he alerts the Holy See to the commission of "incredible horrors." And he urges the pope to take some concrete action. A condemnation of these atrocities by the pope would, he states, bring about "some check on the unbridled . . . actions of the forces of the Nazi regime."[53] Similar notes were sent to the secretariat by representatives of the governments of Belgium, Great Britain, Brazil, Poland, Uruguay, and Yugoslavia.

Ten days later, Monsignor Montini, one of Maglione's two principal assistants and the later Pope Paul VI, received a letter from an Italian source.[54] In a document containing his notes about the information provided by this source, Montini remarks (the date is September 24, 1942) that the massacres of the Jews had by then reached proportions and forms which were "horribly frightful." "Incredible killings," he specified, take place every day. Worse, he thought, was still to come. By the middle of October, he was told, the Germans would empty out whole ghettos containing "hundreds of thousands of languishing unfortunates." We know that Maglione read Montini's notes. His comment on them was: "I do not believe we have information that confirms this, in particular these most grave reports. *Non è così?*"[55]

About two weeks later (end of September 1942), Myron C. Taylor sent a note to the Cardinal Secretary of State that gave the sort of confirmation he had purported to need before acting. According to two reliable witnesses whom Taylor, not unimportantly, designates "Aryans," the liquidation of the Warsaw ghetto was underway. Mass executions, he reported, were taking place in "especially prepared camps," one of which, he thought, was in Belzec. "There is," he went on to report, "not one Jew left in the entire district east of Poland, including occupied Russia." Caravans of civilians deported in cattle cars—forty per car, he says—are "often seen." Did the cardinal, Taylor concludes, have any information that would confirm these reports? If so, did the Holy Father have any suggestions about how the continuation of these barbarities might be frustrated?[56]

At the moment Taylor put this question, the Holy See was receiving reports from other sources that generally confirmed Taylor's information. One of the most important of these arrived on October 3, 1942, from the embassy of Poland in a meeting with Maglione. In his notes on the meeting, Maglione observes that the legation from Poland informed him of a variety of measures then being enacted against the Jews by the Germans in Lithuania and Poland. The legation reported that the Vilna ghetto was almost liquidated. In addition, the Warsaw ghetto was being "methodically emptied" (*méthodiquement vidé*).[57] Each day, groups of more than one thousand Jews were sent away from the ghettos by rail (he thought to Lublin). It appeared that the Jews were concentrated in a camp, where they would be immediately put to death by asphyxiation; in any case, it was certain that none of their families ever received news of them again. It was reported that in the course of the next month, the entire remaining Jewish population of the Warsaw ghetto—three hundred thousand Jews—would be sent there. What is important about this report is, first, its general accuracy;[58] second, its early date; and third and crucially, that Maglione identified the source of the information about the death camps as "a citizen of a country of the Axis who had visited these parts" (*un citoyen des pays de l'axe qui avait visité ces parages*).[59] Even so responsible, respected and so impartially non-Catholic an historian as John Conway has stated in print that "conclusive evidence" for the Holocaust was lacking to the Holy See in 1943 and that it was not until the end of 1944 that the Vatican received "an eyewitness account" of the Holocaust in Auschwitz.[60] It is true but trivial to point out that this eyewitness was not talking about Auschwitz but about different camps. The essential point is that an eyewitness from an Axis country gave to the Vatican essentially accurate information about the existence and purpose of the death camps in October of 1942. Here, though, we have not just an eyewitness but also an eyewitness from an Axis country. These credentials had to have lent this report an extremely high level of credibility.

Yet another extremely reliable witness wrote to the Vatican in October 1942. As we recall, the military chaplain Scavizzi had written to the pope five months earlier. He writes again here, reporting that the elimination of the Jewish community in Poland is "almost total" (*quasi totalitaria*). Jewish domiciles are now being occupied by "Poles" (i.e., non-Jewish Poles), because their owners were being "systematically slaughtered." It is being said, Scavizzi reports, that more than two million Jews had already been killed in Poland.[61]

This, too, I think, is a crucially important report. Aside from being written by a reliable eyewitness, the last piece of information it includes makes weaker, if not utterly unconvincing, the argument that the pope/Vatican could not verify reports of atrocities for suspicion that they were war propaganda. Even if the magnitude of the killings had been exaggerated by an order of let us say ten or twenty or forty or fifty, the magnitude of the slaughter would have been so awesomely grand, one would have thought, as to have commanded the attention of the Vatican.

What sort of response these reports in fact created in the Vatican we know very clearly. As the American ambassador to the Holy See, Taylor got a response to both questions he posed two weeks earlier—What did the Vatican know about the reported atrocities and what might it do?—on October 10, 1942. In a letter to Taylor, Cardinal Maglione acknowledged, first of all, that the Holy See had received reports from several sources (*da altre fonti*) concerning "severe measures taken against non-Aryans" (*di severi provvedimenti presi nei confronti dei non ariani*). (This he could hardly gainsay, as myriad reports by this time were flowing in quite steadily.) Maglione went on to report, however, that, "up to the present time" it had not been possible to verify the accuracy of the reports. (*Di tali notizie, pero, non è stato finora possibile alla Santa Sede di controllare l'esatezza*). Maglione also added, somewhat defensively, that it was well known that the Holy See had taken advantage of "every opportunity" to mitigate the suffering of "non-Aryans."[62] So far as Taylor's second question went, Tittmann, in a telegram sent back to Washington, regretfully reported that the cardinal's attitude had made it all too plain that it had "no practical suggestions to make." Tittmann concludes by complaining that the Vatican seemed to believe that there was little hope of checking Nazi barbarity, save by physical force.[63]

Although Tittmann, Taylor, and the entire American and British diplomatic corps were profoundly frustrated at this point, they made one last effort to induce the Holy See to do what it could to forestall the catastrophe then underway. On Christmas Eve, Tittmann sent another telegram to Washington, reporting on a "recent" conversation with Maglione. Was there not something the Holy See could do? he asked the secretary of state. Could it not issue a statement similar to the recently released Joint Declaration of the United Nations, in which the mass extermination of the Jews in Nazi occupied territory had unequivocally been denounced? Maglione simply repeated that the Holy See was doing everything possible privately to relieve the distress of the Jews; that the Vatican could only publicly denounce atrocities in general, not any particular atrocity; and, again, that it was unable to verify Allied reports regarding the number of Jews exterminated. Tittmann closes by reporting rumors then circulating in Rome that the pope, in his Christmas Day message, would take a strong stand. But he gloomily predicts, "any deviation from the generalities of his previous messages is unlikely."[64]

Tittmann turns out, in the eyes of most interpreters, to have been quite right. In a very lengthy address delivered on Christmas 1942, the pope stated, almost *en passant*, that humanity owed a vow of solidarity and aid to (among *six* other groups specified) "those hundreds of thousands who, without any fault of their own, sometimes only by reason of their nationality or race, are marked down for death or gradual extinction."[65] The pope was later to state that he believed this to be an explicit and firm condemnation of Nazi barbarity; almost none of his listeners agreed.

In fairness to the pope, the editors of the *New York Times* praised Pius, as they had the year before, for "more than ever [being] a lonely voice crying out of the silence of a continent. The Pulpit whence he speaks is more than ever like the Rock on which the Church was founded, a tiny island lashed and surrounded by a sea of war." Perhaps more significantly, Reinhard Heydrich certainly noticed and responded to the Christmas Day 1942 address (in an internal memo dated 22 January 1943):

> In a manner never known before, the Pope has repudiated the National Socialist New European Order...It is true, the Pope does not refer to the National Socialists in Germany by name, but his speech is one long attack on everything we stand for. God, he says, regards all peoples and races

as worthy of the same consideration. Here he is clearly speaking on behalf of the Jews . . . That this speech is directed exclusively against the New Order in Europe as seen in National Socialism is clear in the Papal statement that mankind owes a debt to "all who during the war have lost their Fatherland and who, although personally blameless have, simply on account of their nationality and origin, been killed or reduced to utter destitution." Here he is virtually accusing the German people of injustice toward the Jews, and makes himself the mouthpiece of the Jewish war criminals.[66]

Despite the reaction of the editors of the *New York Times* and Heydrich, most seem not to have noticed this passage at all, nor to have regarded it as a denunciation of Nazi atrocities in particular. Mussolini contemptuously dismissed the speech for being laden with platitudes, worthy not of the Vicar of Christ but of some low parish priest.[67] At least some Allied nations were outraged at the timidity and ambiguity of the pope's language. The president of the Polish government in exile, Wladislaw Raczkiewicz, for example, drew up an impassioned letter in which, after reminding the pope that "divine law knows no compromise" and acknowledging that the chances for material or diplomatic help were slim, he insisted nevertheless that the Apostolic See must break silence so that some voice "would show clearly and distinctly where the evil lies" (*une parole qui indiquerait clairement et distinctement où est le mal*).[68]

Apparently, Pius XII was blindsided by criticism like this. Shortly after the Christmas Day message was delivered, Tittmann had an audience with the pope. In a telegram sent back to Washington to report on his meeting, Tittmann reports that the pope was apparently sincere in his conviction that he had spoken clearly enough to satisfy all those who had insisted that he condemn Nazi atrocities. Was it not, the pope had asked, plain to everyone that he was referring to the Poles, Jews, and hostages when he declared that hundreds of thousands had been innocently victimized, sometimes only because of their race or nationality? Tittmann indicated that many thought, in fact, it was not. The pope, he reports, "seemed surprised" by this. The pope went on to explain that he felt that he could not name the Nazis without also mentioning Bolshevik atrocities, although he did not, apparently, indicate precisely which Bolshevik horrors he had in mind. (The infamous massacre of eleven thousand Polish officers at the Katyn Forest was not to occur until April 1943—that is, until roughly three months *after* the meeting with Tittmann.) He added that he felt the Allied reports on the atrocities had some foundation but that they were likely to have been exaggerated for purposes of propaganda.[69] This, unfortunately, is one of those instances in which Allied atrocity propaganda from the First World War (Belgian children getting hands cut off, etc.) came back to haunt the Allies in the Second World War.

Deportations and Death Camps: 1943

With the turn of the new year, the flow of reports of Nazi atrocities continued to wash in on the Tiber. On March 12, 1943, for example, the Union of Orthodox Rabbis of North America telegrammed Maglione with an urgent request for a *démarche* on behalf of Polish Jews imperiled with imminent execution. The rabbis implored the pope ("in our anguish") to attend to information contained in an urgent cable from Warsaw that they had just received:

> January Germans started liquidation of remnants Warsaw
> Ghetto. All over Poland liquidation proceeding.
> Liquidation of remnants planned for middle of February.
> Alarm the world. Apply to Pope for official intervention.
> We suffer terribly. Remaining few hundred thousand
> threatened with immediate annihilation.[70]

This cable is important for several reasons, not least being that the Warsaw Jewish community that composed it singled out only one world leader as capable of mediation. The response came in the form of a telegram from the secretariat of state to the apostolic delegate in Washington. It instructed the delegate to inform the rabbis that "the Holy See has done its best and continues to do its best on behalf of the Jews."[71]

Exactly two weeks later, on March 26, 1942, the three rabbis who had composed the telegram to the apostolic delegate in Washington appeared in Archbishop Amleto Cicognani's office without announcement, presumably dissatisfied with his written response. Later that day, the delegate wrote back to the Vatican to describe what had happened. The rabbis arrived obviously deeply affected by the news of the systematic, rapid extermination that had apparently been recently decreed by Hitler and had now "inexorably been initiated, especially in Poland." Accordingly, they had come on this day "with tears in their eyes" and had tried to persuade him that "the Holy Father could with a public appeal and plea stop the massacre and deportation."[72] On April 3, the secretariat of state responded: "The Holy See continues to exert itself on behalf of the Jews."[73]

We sense a pattern emerging in the very months when the liquidation centers were operating at peak capacity, when prisoners were being shouldered into gas chambers around the clock, crematoria ovens blazing constantly and chimneys remorselessly belching out the ashes of innocent men, women, and children. It seems true but trivial to argue that the Vatican did not know all of the gruesome details here—if, for example, it was unaware that some of these children were being tossed alive into pits of burning human fat; that does not seem to me to mean that the Vatican was "unaware" of the horrors occurring in the East.

Five days after Maglione insisted that the Holy See was doing all it could, on April 8, 1943, Abraham Silberschein, president of the Committee for Assistance to the Jewish Population Injured by the War, passed on to Bernardini, the nuncio in Bern, a report on the adverse situation faced by the Jewish communities of Poland, Romania, and Transnistria. The report—one the Vatican editors elected not to publish—was accompanied by three snapshots that gave rare photographic confirmation of the persecution that had begun to deluge the Vatican.[74]

And *deluged* is the word. The evidence for this is supplied by the pope himself, who, in a letter to the archbishop of Berlin written in April 1943, stat-

ed that "knowledge reaches us of inhuman acts *day after day*." In the same
letter, he admits to being "relatively well informed" on the situation in the
Warthegau. In the same month, Secretary of State Maglione was able to write,
in a private memo to himself, that the "deportations *en masse* of the Jews . . .
is presently verified in the various countries of Europe."[75] A few weeks later
(May 5, 1943), Maglione again left notes to himself:

> Jews. Horrendous situation (*Ebrei. Situazione orrenda*).
> 4.5 million Jews in Poland before the war, plus many
> deported there from other occupied territories . . . There
> can be no doubt that the greater part has been already been
> suppressed (*non è dubitare che la maggior parte sia stata
> soppressa*). Special death camps at Lublin (Treblinka) and
> near Brest Litovsk . . . where they are finished off under the
> action of the gas (*Speciali campi di morte vicino a Lublino
> [Treblinka] e presso Brest Litowski. dove finirebbe sotto
> l'azione di gas*). Transported there in trucks for beasts, her-
> metically sealed A (. . . *Trasportati in carri bestiame,
> ermeticamente chiusi*).[76]

On July 7, 1943, Maglione had occasion yet again to record notes of
horrors. On that day, a woman from Warsaw—Maglione designates her
"Signora X"—had reported to him: "The ghetto of Warsaw exists no more"
(*Il ghetto di Varsavia non esiste piu*). The Jews there had either perished or
had been deported.[77] These private notes were written without any equivocation or diplomatic cant and, it seems, in a state of near despair. As they were
not intended for public consumption, they constitute very strong proof that
the Vatican had accurate and detailed knowledge of the death camps and of
the horrors for which they were constructed. But at this point, a year after pursuing a policy of equivocation and hesitation, it was perhaps too late. By then
this policy had so conditioned the patterns of behavior in the Vatican that, four
months later, on October 18, 1943, when more than one thousand Roman
Jews were shipped to Auschwitz "under the windows of the Pope" (the words

are those of Ernst von Weizsäcker, the new German ambassador to the Holy See), not a word of protest was heard. Initially anxious, Weizsäcker was able to report with satisfaction ten days later (October 28, 1943) that the pope had "not allowed himself to be drawn into any demonstrative censure" of the deportation.[78] Fifteen of the deported Roman Jews returned alive.

Conclusion

The evidence we have examined suggests the following:

First, the Vatican did have some information about the *Einsatzgruppen* massacres. But, compared to the information it would receive about the Final Solution death camps, this information was relatively scarce. Moreover, it probably came too late, and this terribly brutal phase of the Holocaust ended too swiftly for the Vatican to have taken much effective action. However, it did have the effect of preparing the Vatican for the news of the atrocities to come.

Second, we come to the question of what the Vatican knew about the creation and functioning of the death camps. Without wishing at all to get caught up in fruitless semantic controversy, it is imperative, I think, to be clear on what we mean by *know*. This is especially so since Pius's defenders sometimes assume an implicit definition of knowledge that makes it impossible for him, or for anyone else, to have known anything at all. The definition they usually assume includes the elements of perfection and absolute certainty. The definition I am working with is, on the other hand, the simple, non-technical notion of acquaintance with the essential facts and trust in their basic solidity.

If this definition seems acceptable, then one can only conclude that the Vatican "knew" about the death camps: their existence, their purpose, their location, their mode of operation, and their lethal effectiveness. To be sure, the depth of its knowledge was not the same in March 1942 as it would become over the course of the next few months. But our examination of the evidence, which for the months of May, June, July, August, and September, is quite voluminous and leads me to conclude that by October 1942, at the absolute latest, the Vatican had detailed, accurate knowledge of the existence and operation of the death camps. And by the end of spring 1943, it had horrible knowledge of the overwhelming magnitude of destruction. Moreover, such information as the Vatican received came from multiple sources, including not only trusted secular diplomats and Jews whose relatives, friends, or immediate families were threatened but also the Vatican's own network of highly trained and able diplomats. These were, for the most part, sources whose credibility could not be impugned or doubted. In addition, these sources, while not completely harmonizable, did tend to confirm one another in the details of "the essential facts."

Finally, the evidence suggests that, *at the time*, many imperiled Jews and several key Allied diplomats felt—and declared to the Vatican—that decisive intervention in deed or speech by the Holy Father could have prevented catastrophe.

Whether or not that last conclusion is, and whatever judgment we make about what the pope and the Vatican did during the war, or what they should or should not have done for potential victims of the Holocaust, I do think we can answer with a high degree of confidence the question, Was the pope inhibited from speaking out or acting more decisively for lack of knowledge? In asking this question, we by no means want to imply that the Vatican said nothing on behalf of the victims of the Holocaust, still less that the pope did nothing. That would be to lend unfortunate credence to untruths, not seldom heard, that are inevitably based on nearly comprehensive innocence of the evidence and, at best, superficial awareness of the scholarship. Nevertheless, the answer to that question—Was the pope unaware?—must be, however painful for Catholics, and for Jews, a resounding no. A more plausible conclusion is that Pius XII, like Maglione, desperately wished not to know and, despite the pile of evidence growing inexorably in the offices of the secretariat of state, pursued a psychological policy of willing disbelief. A more sobering conclusion, also highly plausible, is that the Vicar of Christ knew enough, but did not care enough, about the victims to act more courageously or to speak more forcefully.[79]

As the years of conflict wore on, Pius XII ever more forcefully insisted to the Allies, and especially the British,[80] on the sanctity of the city of Rome in an effort, surely not unjustified, to keep the Eternal City (and, not incidentally, the Vatican) preserved from the destructive impact of aerial bombardment. If, as bishop of Rome, he was not wrong, and even obliged, to do that, was it not, many have asked, a higher—indeed, his transcendental—obligation as self-proclaimed Vicar of Christ on earth, to underline at least as emphatically the sanctity of those innocent Jewish souls and bodies being conveyed to the hellholes in Silesia and the general government? Was it not his role, as the Vicar of Christ on earth, to speak more emphatically for those who looked to him as the "safest refuge of all the persecuted," in order that they be sheltered from the frightful and final solution that had been so remorselessly prepared for them? However we answer that question, it simply cannot be maintained that the Vatican maintained its policy of reserve because it did not know the facts.

Notes

*This paper was not presented at the 1999 Consultation. It was prepared afterward by Professor Madigan, who was a member of the Consultation.

1. The main documentary foundation for this paper is the *Actes et Documents du Saint Siège relatifs à la Seconde Guerre Mondiale*, 11 vols. (Vatican City: Libreria editrice Vaticana, 1965–1981), ed. by Pierre Blet, Robert A. Graham, Angelo Martini, and Burkart Schneider (hereafter *Actes et Documents*). I have also relied on documents in Saul Friedländer, *Pius XII and the Third Reich: A Documentation* (New York: Farrar, Straus and Giroux, 1980); and in *Foreign Relations of the United States: Diplomatic Papers* (hereafter *FRUS*), *1942*, 7 vols. (Washington, D.C.: U.S. Government Printing Office, 1961). For immensely helpful aid in identifying the relevant documents, I have depended on John Morley's indispensable study, *Vatican Diplomacy and the Jews during the Holocaust, 1939–1943* (New York: KTAV, 1980). I am grateful to my friend Father Morley not only for this bibliographical aid and for clear-sighted analysis but also for answering several questions I had while in the course of researching this work.

2. See Nora Levin, *The Holocaust: The Destruction of European Jewry 1937–1945* (New York: Crowell, 1968), p. 531.

3. *Actes et Documents* 8:458.

4. See Yehuda Bauer, *A History of the Holocaust* (New York: Franklin Watts), pp. 310–311; and Livia Rothkirchen, "Vatican Policy and the Jewish Problem in Independent Slovakia" (1939–1945), in *Yad Vashem Studies* 6 (1967): pp. 27–53.

5. *Hitler's Pope: The Secret History of Pius XII* (New York: Viking, 1999).

6. Michael O'Carroll, *Pius XII: Greatness Dishonoured* (Chicago: Franciscan Herald Press, 1980), p. 149, n. 76.

7. *Der Stellvertreter* (Reinbek bei Hamburg: Rowohlt, 1963); *The Deputy*, trans. by Richard and Clara Winston (Baltimore: Johns Hopkins University Press, 1997).

8. Gerstein, discussed below, p. 207, was the SS colonel who attempted to inform ecclesiastical authorities in Berlin of the death camps.

9. Edited by Eric Bentley (New York: Grove Press, 1964). See also the extremely perceptive essay of Leonidas E. Hill, "History and Rolf Hochhuth's *The Deputy,"* in *From an Ancient to a Modern Theatre*, ed. by R. G. Collins (Winnipeg: University of Manitoba Press, 1972), pp. 145–157.

10. Quoted in Anthony Rhodes, *The Vatican in the Age of Dictators* (New York: Holt, Rinehart and Winston), p. 348.

11. See footnote 1 for bibliographical information.

12. "The Vatican and the Jews: Cynicism and Indifference," *Judaism* 24 (1975): pp. 168–180.

13. Pius XII, p. 11.

14. See, besides Carroll, Pierre Blet, *Pius XII and the Second World War: According to the Archives of the Vatican* (Mahwah, N.J.: Paulist Press, 1999); Robert Graham, *Pius XII and the Holocaust: A Reader* (New Rochelle, N.Y.: Catholic League for Religious and Civil Rights, 1988); Pinchas Lapide, *The Last Three Popes and the Jews* (New York: Hawthorne Books), 1967; Rhodes, *The Vatican in the Age of the Dictators*.

15. On March 27, 1963, Robert Leiber, S.J., Pacelli's secretary for thirty-four years, in an article in *Frankfürter Allgemeine Zeitung* on Hochhuth's *The Deputy*, insisted: "Pius XII did not know what was really happening. Nor did the Allies. It was not until after the war that they were able to realize the extent of the Nazi crimes," On April 5, 1963, the Permanent Representative of the Holy See at the United Nations, in an article in *L'Osservatore Romano* entitled, *Storia, Teatroe Storie* ("History, Theatre and Gossip") observed: "The immense dimensions [of the tragedy], and the monstrous cruelties that accompanied it, appeared in all their sinister light only after the war was over . . . Information about these crimes reaching the Vatican itself was scarce and vague. For the most part it originated from one belligerent side (the Allied powers) and was based

on revelations and news whose certainty could not be guaranteed even by those who divulged them" (C. Falconi, *The Silence of Pius XII* [Boston: Little, Brown, 1965], p. 7). One year later, in June 1964, Angelo Martini, in *Civiltà Cattolica* 6/6 (1964), ["La vera storia e 'il Vicario'di R. Hochhuth,] remarked: "The decision to adopt the final solution . . . was suspected from the middle of 1942, but the details were clear only when the extermination was completed, i.e. after the defeat. The World Jewish Congress, with the help of its centres for information and checking, was able to obtain approximate figures . . . The Pope also received news, though not as often nor as accurately as could have been desired . . . Unfortunately [the] data lacked the verification needed to provide grounds for denouncing it as fact" (quoted in Falconi, *The Silence*, pp. 47–48). Listen, too, to the postwar comments of Vladimir d'Ormesson, French ambassador in Rome until October 1940. "Those who were shut up in the Vatican City during the last war . . . can testify to the total isolation of the Holy See. Fascism, followed by Hitler's armies, raised a real 'wall' between the tiny pontifical city and the rest of the world . . . Upon my soul and conscience, I am absolutely convinced that, like everyone else, Pius XII was uninformed about the monstrous refinements of cruelty of which the Jews were the secret victims" (Falconi, *Silence* 49). Finally, and more recently, Robert Graham, S.J., ed., *Pius XII and the Holocaust* (New Rochelle, New York: Catholic League for Religious and Civil Rights, 1988, p. 106), says, with maddening equivocation, "The full truth of what was known only came later." (What counts as *full truth*? When is *later*?)

16. A useful study, one which I do not intend to undertake here, would be to compare what the Vatican knew with what other neutrals knew. See M. Dworzecki, "The International Red Cross and its Policy vis-à-vis the Jews in Ghettos and Concentration Camps in Nazi-Occupied Europe," in *Rescue Attempts during the Holocaust: Proceedings of the Second Yad Vashem International Historical Conference, Jerusalem, April 8–11, 1974,* ed. by Yisrael Gutman and Efraim Zuroff (Jerusalem: Yad Vashem, 1977), pp. 71–110.

17. See Raul Hilberg, *The Destruction of the European Jews* (New York: Holmes and Meier, 1985), chap. 4, pp. 99–156.

18. ". . . gli ebrei sono senz'altro fucilati (si afferma che anche i civili di razza ebraica vengano soppressi sistematicamente, senza distinzione di sesso e di età") [*Actes et Documents* 8:328]; see summary in Morley, *Vatican Diplomacy*, pp. 78, 135.

19. *Actes et Documents* 8:328.

20. *Actes et Documents* 8:456.

21. See Levin, *The Holocaust*, p. 572, where it is noted that, without the help of the *Einsatz* squads, sixty thousand Jews were killed in Odessa alone.

22. Translation taken from Friedländer, *Pius XII*, pp. 108–109.

23. *Actes et Documents* 8 [1974]:466.

24. *Actes et Documents* 8:466, n. 1. The full text of the document, from which I have quoted, has been published in Morley, *Vatican Diplomacy*, Appendix B, pp. 212–215.

25. This was not the first letter the Vatican had received from Szeptyckyj. In fact, on December 26, 1939, Szeptyckyj had written to the Vatican to complain about the many Jews who had fled to his Eastern Galician diocese in order to escape the invading German forces in Poland. They had, he reports, made an altogether nasty impression, attempting as they had to dominate the economic life of the region; and, of course, they were "sordidly avaricious" as well as unethical in their business practices (*Actes et Documents* 3:168–173).

26. "Le nombre des Juifs tués dans notre petit pays a certainement dépassé deux cent mille. A mesure que l'armée avançait vers l'est, le nombre des victimes grandissait" *(Actes et Documents* 3:625).

27. "Atrocitas doctrinae nacionalisticae apparuit in Lettonia in tota sua duritia et abominatione: iudaei fere omnes iam necati sunt, remanserunt solummodo aliquot milia in Riga (ghetto) et horum maior pars importata est de exteris regionibus" (*Actes et Documents* 3:695–696).

28. The Jewish remnant in Riga that the archbishop refers to were "Reich Jews" who had arrived as the shooting ended.

29. *Actes et Documents* 8:453.

30. Ibid., 8:470.

31. Excerpt from *La Parrochhia* (Rome, 1964); quoted in Falconi, *The Silence of Pius XII*, p. 151.

32. *Actes et Documents* 8:534.

33. Falconi, *The Silence of Pius XII*, p. 150.

34. This is not because Croatia was a creation of Hitler and accepted both his fascist and anti-Semitic convictions. Rather, it was because of a Vatican policy of not recognizing territorial changes that had taken place during time of war, preventing acknowledgment of a new state.

35. See Morley, *Vatican Diplomacy*, pp. 148–149.

36. *Actes et Documents* 8:601–602.

37. *Actes et Documents* 8:611.

38. *Actes et Documents* 8:611–612.

39. Levin, *The Holocaust*, p. 516.

40. *Actes et Documents* 8:610.

41. "... non è vero che la Santa Sede si sia rinchiusa nel silenzio ad una persecuzione così inumana" (*Actes et Documents* 8:615). This is a very important document, as it indicates that criticism of Pius for silence was being expressed, not (as his defenders would have it) *after* the war but *during*.

42. *Actes et Documents* 8:615.

43. *FRUS, 1942,* 3:772-73; reprinted in Friedländer, *Pius XII*, p. 118–119.

44. Friedländer, *Pius XII*, p. 117.

45. See Morley, *Vatican Diplomacy*, p. 177.

46. See Saul Friedländer, *Kurt Gerstein: The Ambiguity of Good* (New York: Alfred A. Knopf, 1969); and Pierre Joffroy, *A Spy of God: The Ordeal of Kurt Gerstein* (London: Collins, 1970).

47. See Yitzhak Arad, *Belzec, Sobibor, Treblinka: The Operation Reinhard Death Camps* (Indianapolis: Indiana University Press, 1987), p. 102; and Gerstein's report as quoted in Friedländer, *Kurt Gerstein*, pp. 128–129.

48. *Kurt Gerstein*, p. 124.

49. Gerstein informed Protestant authorities as well as Catholic, including the Niemöller family and Friedrich Dibelius of the Confessing Church. He also told members of the press, diplomats of various countries, and others—"thousands," all told, according to Gerstein's testimony. See his report in Ibid., pp.128–129.

50. See *Actes et Documents* 2, which contains the letters of Pius XII to the German bishops 1939–1944. My thanks to Father John Morley for pointing out this fact to me.

51. Hochhuth was to make much of this incident in *The Deputy*.

52. *Actes et Documents*: 8:632–633.

53. *FRUS 1942* 3:773; reprinted in Friedländer, *Pius XII*, p. 120.

54. *FRUS 1942* 3:775 ff.

55. *Actes et Documents* 8: 665–666; text published in *FRUS 1942 3:775* ff.

56. *FRUS* 3:775-76; reprinted in Friedländer, *Pius XII*, pp. 121–122.

57. *Actes et Documents* 8:670.

58. I say "general accuracy" because, in fact, the Germans had begun emptying the ghetto on July 22 and, in one month alone, sent sixty-seven thousand Jews to their death not to the more distant camps south of Warsaw in the Lublin district (i.e., Sobibor and Majdanek) but only forty miles north to Treblinka, and hundreds of thousands more would soon meet the same fate.

59. Ibid. It is worth noting that news of the liquidation of the Warsaw ghetto had reached London. Initially, the British did not believe the news and dismissed it as Polish anti-German propaganda. After receiving confirmation of the information, however, the BBC broadcast it in the early fall.

60. John S. Conway, "Records and Documents of the Holy See Relating to the Second World War," *Yad Vashem Studies* 15 (1983): pp. 327–345, 341. Conway does note on that page, n. 22, that the eyewitness account of Auschwitz is "referred to but not printed." See *Actes et documents* 10:381.

61. *Actes et Documents* 8:669–670, n. 4.

62. *Actes et Documents* 8: 679.

63. *FRUS* 3:777-78; reprinted in Friedländer, *Pius XII*, pp. 123–124.

64. *FRUS*, 1942, 1:70–72.

65. "Questo voto l'humanità lo deve alle centinaia di migliaia di persone, le quali, senza veruna colpa propria, talora solo per ragione di nazionalità o di stirpe, sono destinate alla morte o ad un progressivo deperimento" *(Actes et Documents* 7:166). These words are often cited without attention to their context. It is crucial to place them in context and to recognize that such a vow, the pope said, was owed to six other categories of humans. It is understandable only in this context that many missed a specific reference to Nazis and to Jews.

66. Quoted in Anthony Rhodes, *The Vatican in the Age of Dictators*, p. 272.

67. G. Ciano, *Diaries* (London: Methuen, 1947), p. 538.

68. *Actes et documents* 7:180.

69. *FRUS, 1943*, 6 vols. (Washington, D.C.: United States Government Printing Office, 1963), 2:912.

70. *Actes et Documents* 9:182.

71. *Actes et Documents* 9:182., n. 2.

72. ". . . non dovrei osare presentare nuovamente appello, ma tre Rabbini rappresentanti varie loro associazioni dietro notizie allarmanti provenienti specialmente da Londra di sistematico rapido sterminio che si dice decretato recentemente da Hitler è inesorabilmente iniziato specialmente in Polonia, sono venuti oggi da me supplicando con lacrime che Santo Padre possa con pubblico appello e preghiera arrestare massacro e deportazione" *(Actes et Documents* 9:206–207).

73. Ibid., p. 207, n. 3.

74. *Actes et Documents* 9:243.

75. *Actes et Documents* 9:216–217. See also Conway, "Documents of the Holy See," p. 338, about the "almost daily reports" flowing into the Vatican.

76. *Actes et Documents* 9:274.

77. *Actes et Documents* 9:376.

78. The translations of the German ambassador's words to the Foreign
    Ministry I take from Guenther Lewy, *The Catholic Church and Nazi
    Germany* , repr. (Cambridge, Mass.: Da Capo Press, 2000), pp. 301–302.
79. That is certainly the conclusion of G. Lewy: "Finally, one is inclined to
    conclude that the Pope and his advisors—influenced by the long tradition
    of moderate anti-Semitism so widely accepted in Vatican circles—did not
    view the plight of the Jews with a real sense of urgency and moral outrage.
    For this assertion no documentation is possible, but it is a conclusion dif-
    ficult to avoid" (*The Catholic Church and Nazi Germany,* p. 305). See
    also H. Fein, *Accounting for Genocide* (Chicago: University of Chicago
    Press, 1979) for the precise if painful term *unfortunate expendables.* For
    a much more sympathetic view, see Michael R. Marrus, *The Holocaust
    in History* (New York: Meridian, 1987), pp. 179–183; E. C. Helmreich,
    The German Churches under Hitler (Detroit: Wayne State University
    Press, 1979), p. 365; Owen Chadwick, "Weizsäcker, the Vatican, and the
    Jews of Rome," in *Journal of Ecclesiastical History* 28 (1977), 179–199;
    and John S. Conway, "Catholicism and the Jews during the Nazi Period
    and After," in *Judaism and Christianity under the Impact of National
    Socialism*, ed. by Otto Dov Kulka and Paul R. Mendes-Flohr (Jerusalem:
    Historical Society of Israel, 1987), pp. 435–451.
80. See the angry response from Francis Osborne: "In the case of the bomb-
    ing of Rome . . . the Vatican, far from adopting an international stand-
    point, would appear to be associating themselves with the interests of the
    Italian State" (*Actes et Documents* 7:170).

Vatican II Revisited

JUDITH H. BANKI

The ambivalence of Jewish reactions to the Vatican's *We Remember: A Reflection on the Shoah* rings a distinct bell. Jewish interfaith leaders, except for very few who welcomed it unreservedly, expressed disappointment, annoyance—in the words of the *Jewish Week*, "everything from anguish to anger." It was "too little, too late"; it "dashed the hopes of Jewish leaders." Sound familiar?

When *Nostra Aetate,* the declaration on the Church's relationship to the Jewish community, was finally adopted at the Second Vatican Council and promulgated by Pope Paul VI after almost four years of equivocation and an internal struggle—during which key passages were cut, restored, emasculated, and re-worded—it was similarly greeted. Jewish reactions ranged from enthusiasm to bitter denunciation. Negative reactions focused on the absence from the documents of any sense of contrition, any expression of regret, indeed, even an acknowledgment of the Church's role in creating the anti-Semitism it was now decrying.

Twenty years after *Nostra Aetate,* in 1985, the Vatican issued one of several follow-up documents designed to translate the declaration's broad principles into specific guidelines for teaching about Jews and Judaism in Catholic education. The *Notes,* as they were called, were also roundly attacked by critics who noted the schizoid nature of the document: positive affirmations about Judaism in one section were undercut by regressive, triumphalist formulations in others, and inherently contradictory theological views of Judaism were papered over by expressions of noble intention. The *Notes* appeared to reflect a tug-of-war between two incompatible mindsets toward Jews.

From a Jewish perspective, both documents were seriously flawed. Yet, they had powerful and positive consequences. *Nostra Aetate,* despite its weaknesses and compromises, launched a new Catholic-Jewish relationship—one of growing candor, mutual understanding, and cooperation toward shared goals, although with many ups and downs along the way. The *Notes,* despite their inherent contradictions, provided the basis for more accurate, more appreciative, teaching about Jews and Judaism in Catholic education. The documents were not perfect; their defects rankled those who expected more—more self-criticism, more contrition, a more scrupulous accounting of the Church's role in specific historical circumstances. Nevertheless, they initiated a systematic dialogue, studies and scholarship, informal networks, a fragile but genuine mutual trust, some real friendships. Committed Christians and Jews used the opportunities opened by these documents to build a new relationship.

Critics of the Vatican's recent *We Remember* should bear this history in mind, even as they express their disappointments. Yes, it has weaknesses. It falls short of a full reckoning of the role of the Church in fomenting antipathy to Jews across the centuries. It attributes to individual Catholics—"sons and daughters of the Church"—errors of commission and omission, and failures of courage without relating these to the Church's policies and practices. It calls for an individual, not institutional, examination of conscience.

Its distinction between anti-Judaism (rooted in religious misconceptions) and anti-Semitism (the product of racism and exacerbated nationalism, which it sees as a pagan ideology totally opposed to Catholic values) is correct. But, if Lutheran scholar and theologian Krister Stendahl's definition is correct—that "anti-Judaism is hostility to the *tenets* of Judaism; antisemitism is hostility to the *bearers* of Judaism"—the line was frequently crossed. Nazism was indeed neopagan in concept and ideology, but many of the regime's repressive measures against the Jews—book burnings, quotas in universities, the mandated wearing of distinctive clothing, confinement to ghettos—had their precedents in church legislation and practice. The document does not explore these parallels, nor does it address the question of the willing perpetrators of genocide—murderers and torturers—who considered themselves faithful Christians.

But focusing on what the document says, rather than on what it *does not* say, says a good deal.

First it affirms as "a major fact of the history of this century" the murder of millions of Jews for the sole reason that they were Jews. It stands as a forthright rebuttal to what has become an entire industry of Holocaust denial and revision. To some eight hundred million Catholic faithful and to the world at large, the Church says: "It happened!"

It affirms the religious roots of hostility toward Jews in "erroneous and unjust interpretations of the New Testament," and spells out the consequences when Jews refused to abandon their faith and customs: discrimination, expulsions, attempts at forced conversions, scapegoating, occasional violence, looting, and even massacres. Jews, who are familiar with this history of persecution rooted in religious antagonism, should realize that it may come as a surprise to most Catholics, and that the Church has done an important service to truth and justice by calling attention to these painful realities in very concrete terms.

It adds the Church's moral authority to the need to understand what gave rise to the greatest crime of the twentieth century—and to remember it, "for there is no future without memory."

The Vatican's *We Remember* opens a rich field for further common study, and its expression of human solidarity should guide the footsteps of those who seek to develop its teaching and preaching implications—to end, in the pope's moving words, of "shaping a future in which the unspeakable iniquity of the Shoah will never again be possible."

APPENDIX C

The Vatican and the Holocaust:
Putting We Remember in Context

JOHN T. PAWLIKOWSKI

W *e Remember: A Reflection on the Shoah,* the new Vatican document on the Catholic Church and the Holocaust issued in March 1998, prompts us to take a wider look at the Catholic Church's institutional response to the challenge of Nazism. Clearly, this document establishes a measure of moral failure on the part of Catholics during the Nazi era. Otherwise there would be no need for the repentance to which it summons the Church worldwide.

But questions remain: Repentance by whom? Only by individual Catholics who strayed from the authentic teachings of the Church? Or repentance by the Church as a whole? Moreover, while there clearly were individuals, such as the recently canonized Father Bernhard Lichtenburg, and groups of people such as the members of Zegota in Poland, who risked their lives to speak out against Nazi policies and to engage in heroic rescue efforts, the issue is whether *these* individuals and groups were following church policy in their efforts or acting out of a moral concern honed by other sources and experiences. The answers that are emerging from recent scholarship are quite complex.

To come to grips with these questions we need to step back and examine the role of Catholicism during the actual period of the Holocaust. It is especially important to look at the record of the institutional Church. Since the appearance of Rolf Hochhuth's play *The Deputy* in 1963, most men and women who have studied the Catholic response to the Holocaust have concentrated on the papacy of Pius XII (1939–1958; b.1876, d.1958). To what extent did he actually attempt to assist the victims of Nazism, particularly the Jews? Should much have been expected from him, given the relatively isolated position of the Vatican in the middle of fascist Italy? In the final

analysis, do such adjectives as *indifferent, callous,* or *discreetly caring* legitimately apply to Pius's overall approach to Europe's Jews? Such questions and
other, similar ones, certainly remain relevant and in need of further discussion.

However, the thrust of any examination of institutional Catholicism
during the Shoah should not fall solely on the actions of Pius XII. There is
equal need to examine how Catholic Church bodies and Catholic leaders in
other parts of Europe were responding to Hitler's efforts to annihilate the
Jewish people and to eliminate thousands of the disabled people, gay persons,
Poles, the Gypsies, and the Sinti (a small band of Gypsies, distinct from other
Gypsies), and others. Likewise, we need to examine the sense of self-identity
prevailing within institutional Catholicism during the thirties and forties
(especially in Vatican circles) and ascertain how this self-identity (what theologians term *ecclesiology*) ultimately affected its response to Nazism.
Whatever the final verdict of scholars regarding Pius XII's tenure as pope,
and much remains to be researched about those years, the contemporary
Church must also scrutinize and confront that tenure with full honesty. It cannot rewrite history. It can, however, significantly redefine its self-understanding
of how the Church as a religious institution, and its leadership, ought to respond
in the midst of a grave social crisis.

The strongest defense of Vatican activities during the Holocaust, and
of Pius XII in particular, is found in the writings of the late Vatican
archivist, Father Robert Graham, S.J. Graham spent more than two decades
collecting and organizing relevant materials related to the era of Pius XII,
concentrating, in particular, on the final year and a half of World War II.
Graham concluded that Pius XII must be judged a "great humanitarian, truly
deserving of that forest in the Judean hills that kindly people in Israel proposed to name for him in October 1958" (cf. Robert Graham, S.J., *Pius XII's
Defense of the Jews and Others: 1944–45,* 1982, 34). Since the death of Father
Graham in 1998, others have taken up Pius XII's defense, particularly Father
Pierre Blet, S.J. (cf. "Myth vs. Historical Fact," *L'Osservatore Romano,* April
17–29, 1998, 16–17; 19.)

Graham's argument, stated succinctly, is this. Although Pius XII felt
disappointment over his inability to prevent the outbreak of World War II, he

committed himself from the outset of the war to the alleviation of human suffering to the full possible extent. While Pius's concern extended to all the victims of the Nazis, Father Graham contended that the material studied clearly
reveals an increasing attention, on the part of Pius, to the plight of the Jews.
Many Vatican ventures on behalf of the Jews were a direct result of requests
for assistance by Jewish organizations—a sign, for Graham, of genuine confidence in the pope and the Catholic Church on the part of Jewish leaders;
Graham, indeed, argued that there is evidence of widespread communication
between the Holy See and Jewish leaders during the Nazi era. Other assistance was initiated by the Vatican itself. In the early years of the war, when
emigration was still a realistic option in many places for endangered Jews, the
Vatican exerted diplomatic pressure on countries with which it had close
ties, pressure formulated to persuade such nations—Spain and Portugal, for
example—to grant entry and transit visas to Jews trying to escape from
Nazi-controlled territories. And when the emigration option ceased being
available after 1940, Catholic strategy moved in the direction of diplomatic
protests against the deportation of Jews.

Father Graham cited Slovakia, Italy, and Hungary as locales where the
Vatican intervened on behalf of Jews. With respect to Slovakia, he mentions,
among other examples, a meeting in 1944 of Vatican officials with the Slovak
minister to the Vatican, during which the minister was given a formal message that read in part as follows: "The Holy See, moved by those sentiments
of humanity and Christian charity that always inspire its work in favor of the
suffering, without distinction of parties, nationalities or races, cannot remain
indifferent to such appeals" (cf. Robert Graham, S.J., *Pius XII's Defense of
the Jews and Others,* 21.) In Italy, Cardinal Maglione, the Vatican secretary
of state, had a private meeting with the German ambassador in October 1943,
during which a strong protest was lodged by the cardinal over the special SS
raid in which more than one thousand Italian Jews were taken captive for
transfer to the Nazi death camps in occupied Poland. For Graham, Hungary
was a particularly noteworthy and successful field of Vatican activity on
behalf of Jews, both during the regime of Admiral Horthy (whom the
Germans forced out of power in 1944), as well as during the highly repressive

and anti-Semitic rule of the Arrow Cross group. The papal nuncio, Angelo Rotta, played a key role in efforts to assist Jews in Hungary.

Examining Father Graham's overall argument compels one to acknowledge that it makes some important points in support of his contention that Pius XII and the Vatican in general responded responsibly to the Nazi annihilation of Jews. Pius XII was not as "silent" (in the sense of doing nothing) as many of his critics have noted. On the other hand, definite drawbacks appear in Graham's analysis of the available materials, rendering his conclusions far less substantive than he believed. Among his notable limitations is his failure to question whether the interventions he cites were pursued in a systematic way over a long period, or were they more in the nature of sporadic efforts. Another problematic aspect of Graham's argumentation is its heavy reliance on papal and Vatican activities in the last years of World War II. Graham does make some references to Vatican attempts to help Jews prior to 1944, but their inclusion serves only to obscure the question of whether, in fact, the Vatican response to the brutalities aimed at European Jews was far too slow in developing. Another problematic aspect of Graham's perspective is his insistence that Jewish organizations and the Vatican cooperated harmoniously throughout the Nazi era. Graham's subtle message in this assertion seems to be (a message that some other Catholic defenders of Pius XII have argued as well) that criticism of the Vatican's response to the *Shoah* is essentially a postwar phenomenon that ignores the testimonies of wartime Jewish leaders. Graham's contention is a clear oversimplification. The recollections of Dr. Gerhart Riegner of the World Jewish Congress are crucial when one considers this issue, because of his deep, personal involvement in the organized effort to rescue Jews trapped in Nazi-occupied territories. Riegner has said that during the war Jewish leaders believed that the policies of the Vatican and Pius XII regarding Europe's Jews were insufficient, but their public comments were restrained because, in large measure, of their recognition of the papacy's delicate position in fascist Italy.

Generally speaking, the Church has been rather defensive in responding to critics of its World War II record. (This can be justified in part because some of the criticism, particularly in the mass media—such as James

Carroll's *New Yorker* article, April 7, 1997—is based on shallow scholarship.) But despite the Church's prevalent reluctance to confront its institutional record in this area, there *has* been a growing willingness to examine critically the question of Catholic anti-Semitism. Several post-Vatican II statements and documents have done this. The two Vatican statements (1975 and 1985) from the Pontifical Commission for Religious Relations with Jews are important contributions to the analysis of this issue. In 1989 the Holy See's Pontifical Commission on Justice and Peace pushed the Church's self-examination to a new level in its general statement on racism, where it described anti-Semitism as one of the worst examples of racism, and argued that it had a significant impact on the Nazi effort to annihilate the Jewish people. (Dr. Eugene J. Fisher, associate director of the United States Bishops' Secretariat for Ecumenical and Interreligious Affairs, and Rabbi Leon Klenicki, director of the Interfaith Affairs Department of the Anti-Defamation League, have chronicled relevant developments in a book they coedited, *In Our Time: The Flowering of Jewish-Catholic Dialogue* [Paulist Press, 1990].)

In recent years Pope John Paul II has vigorously denounced anti-Semitism, often calling it a sin, particularly in his book *Crossing the Threshold of Hope* (1994). And local conferences of Catholic bishops, such as those in Poland (1995), Germany (1995), and France (1997), have issued forceful documents condemning anti-Semitism and confessing that too many people in the Catholic Church, including church leaders, fell victim to this sin during the Nazi era. The French bishops' statement is especially straightforward on the latter point: "It has to be recognized that the French bishops did not speak out, acquiescing by their silence in these flagrant violations of human rights and leaving the way open for a deadly harvest. . . . Too many pastors of the Church by their silence offended both against the Church and its mission. Today we confess that this silence was a grievous offense." The current French bishops add that ". . . a resounding word from the Church could have set up a barrier against irreparable damage."

While some greeted the Vatican document *We Remember* with considerable enthusiasm, others in the Catholic and Jewish communities have expressed disappointment that it is not as forceful as the statement issued by the bishops' conferences just cited. The response to this disappointment from the Vatican has been that *We Remember* was intended as a global document, and addressing churches in South America, Africa, and Asia (where there was little or no direct connection to the Holocaust) imposed certain constraints that would not have existed if the document had been prepared solely for the current episcopal leaders in Europe and the United States. There is some validity to the Vatican counterargument, but, in my judgment, there could have been some direct reference to the European bishops' statements in *We Remember.*

Some of the more trenchant criticism of *We Remember* has come from Catholics. The respected lay Catholic magazine *Commonweal*, for instance, expressed strong concerns about the document in an editorial (March 1998). For many Catholics, *We Remember*, coming as it does after the many ecclesial and papal statements on anti-Semitism issued since Vatican II's *Nostra Aetate*, does not appear to advance the discussion in a significant way. (*Nostra Aetate*, issued in 1965, repudiated the notion that Jews bore any collective responsibility for the death of Jesus, and asserted that Jews remained in the covenant with God.)

My own assessment of *We Remember* is rather mixed. I do see it as a document that establishes the Holocaust as a permanent and vital issue of Catholic self-reflection. But at the same time, I believe it falls short, from a scholarly point of view, in several critical areas. It brings the issues raised by the *Shoah* to the heart of Catholic theological reflection far more directly than any previous document—and it does so with a papal endorsement. Because of this document, Catholics everywhere, not just in countries directly affected by World War II, must take seriously the challenge of the *Shoah* to classical Catholic theology. Finally, although not as pivotal a contribution as the theological challenge, the document makes it intellectually impossible for Catholics to accept the arguments of Holocaust deniers.

We Remember also clearly implicates Catholics at all levels of the Church—even at the very highest levels, as Cardinal Edward Cassidy (who led the group, the Vatican Commission for Religious Relations with the Jews, that wrote the document) has stressed—in the sin of anti-Semitism. While the distinction in the document between the "pure" mystical or sacramental Church, the Body of Christ, and the wayward "sons and daughters" of the Church, may be rooted in a theological perspective no longer acceptable to leading theologians, who regard such a perspective as not fully congruent with the vision laid out in Vatican II's document on the Church, *We Remember* does at least argue that leading Catholics were guilty, during the Nazi era, of serious moral failure in their attitudes toward the Jewish people.

While *We Remember* is certainly the most important document on Catholic-Jewish relations released by the Vatican since *Nostra Aetate* itself, it is marked by some perspectives that are incomplete and sometimes even misleading. I would like to focus on three such areas. The first has to do with the distinction between the sinful actions of the "sons and daughters" of the Church and the fundamental holiness of the Church itself. As I suggested above, and as Cardinal Cassidy has reiterated in several of his own commentaries on the document, this distinction is based on a long-standing perception of the Church in Catholicism, a perception that views the Church as a sacramental reality that remains fundamentally unaffected by the sinful realities of history. In a public discussion of *We Remember* in Chicago last June, Cardinal Francis George spoke of a conversation he had with Pope John Paul II on this matter, in which the pope strongly insisted that the Church itself, as a theological reality, cannot be blamed for anti-Semitism or for the *Shoah*. Without question, Catholics must take seriously this classical theological position, even if one feels that it can lead to serious misinterpretation or that it is overly ahistorical. Surely the authors of *We Remember* were in no position to resolve this basic theological issue; nonetheless *We Remember* could have, and should have, made it clearer that the "sons and daughters" of the Church who fell into the sin of anti-Semitism did so because of what they had learned from teachers, theologians (including the church fathers), and preachers sanctioned by the institutional Church. Reading the document in its present form leaves the impression that the sinful "sons and daughters" of the Church who espoused anti-Semitism were led to this pernicious state of affairs by teachings and teachers outside the official Church. Yet, we know from many studies of anti-Semitism, such as the late Father Edward Flannery's classic volume

The Anguish of the Jews (1965, republished 1985), as well as from more recent studies such as *The Jewish-Christian Controversy from the Earliest Times to 1789* (1995) by Samuel Krauss (revised and edited by William Horbury) and Heinz Schreckenberg's *The Jews in Christian Art* (1995), that for centuries anti-Semitism permeated Catholic catechesis and preaching and the popular culture they created. (The famous facade of the medieval cathedral in Strasbourg, France, with its depiction of the vibrant Church and the bedraggled and blindfolded Synagogue, is an apt illustration of how deeply anti-Semitism was embedded in the Church's attitudes.) *We Remember* is remiss in not connecting the sinful actions of its members relative to Jews much more directly to the anti-Semitic perspectives presented them within the tradition of Catholic worship and education. A preliminary statement from the Vatican regarding the anticipated papal document of 1999 asking forgiveness for the Church's involvement in atrocities such as the Crusades and the excommunication of people such as Jan Hus leads me to believe that this document will, at least partially, surmount the failure of *We Remember* to connect directly the sinful anti-Semitic actions of Catholic believers to the anti-Semitic legacy generated by popular church teachings.

The second problematic area of *We Remember* that I would highlight is the contention that there were no links between Christian anti-Judaism (a hostility toward the Jewish religion) and anti-Semitism (the attempt to marginalize Jews and make them miserable as a people) and the anti-Semitism of Nazi ideology, which encouraged the complete annihilation of the Jews. This has a factual basis, but is significantly overdrawn. Certainly there is a body of scholarly opinion that would draw too direct a line between classical Christian anti-Judaism and anti-Semitism and the fundamental theories of the Third Reich. Nazi ideology, however, is something, ultimately, quite beyond the most gruesome forms of traditional anti-Judaism and anti-Semitism. Important Jewish and Christian scholars have acknowledged this, and it is a view I have always argued for in my own writings on the *Shoah*. *We Remember* provides the Catholic community with a service in reminding Catholics of the significant difference between classical Christian anti-Judaism and anti-Semitism, and Nazi ideology. Christian anti-Judaism and anti-Semitism by themselves would not have generated the *Shoah*. But *We Remember* leaves the strong impression that there was no inherent connection between Nazi ideology and classical Christian anti-Judaism and anti-Semitism. This is basically inaccurate. Among Europe's Christian population, Christian anti-Judaism and anti-Semitism had everything to do with wide-spread acquiescence and even collaboration with the Nazi policy devoted to the destruction of the Jews. I like to speak of classic Christian anti-Judaism and anti-Semitism as providing an indispensable "seedbed" for Nazism. Nazi ideologues drew upon classical anti-Jewish church legislation while develop-ing the laws they would use to dispossess Europe's Jews, and exploited Catholic-based cultural entities (such as the Oberammergau passion play) to promote Nazi ideology among the masses.

In a May 1998 address to the national meeting of the American Jewish Committee in Washington, D.C. (telecast nationally on C-SPAN), Cardinal Cassidy addressed the criticism that *We Remember* does a disservice in leav-ing the impression that Christian anti-Semitism played no significant role in the spread of Nazism. He argued that the document does imply that actions of members of the Catholic Church aided the cause of Nazism. As principal author of the text Cardinal Cassidy's interpretation must be taken seriously. (The U.S. Bishops' Conference publication of *We Remember* contains Cardinal Cassidy's interpretive commentary for this very reason.) Nonetheless, there remain some troubling points in the cardinal's AJC speech. First, he couples his assertion of Catholic complicity in the Holocaust with an oblique phrase asserting that one should be careful in assessing the motives of Catholic collaborators who assisted the Nazis. I have never stated that there was only one motive impelling the Nazis and their allies to terrorize and mur-der Jews. But documentary evidence has sufficiently established that the teachings of the Church on Jews and Judaism surely were a key factor insti-gating the behavior of those who planned and carried out the anti-Semitic policies of the Third Reich.

Cardinal Cassidy's insistence on the involvement of Catholics in the *Shoah* is definitely a step forward, and should help persuade those reading *We Remember* to perceive the text as close to the perspective of Pope John Paul II, who has described anti-Semitism as a sin on more than one occasion (such as in his introductory letter to *We Remember)*. But the cardinal's Washington address does not go far enough in linking the sinful actions of Catholics in the Third Reich with the Catholic tradition as such.

The second problematic statement in Cardinal Cassidy's address involves the witness of Catholics who opposed Nazism. Cardinal Cassidy is perfectly correct to emphasize that these Catholics—in Holland, France, Poland, Italy, and elsewhere—must be honored for their outstanding moral courage. But in making this point right after discussing the collaboration of Catholics, he unfortunately leaves the impression, intended or not, that those who rescued or otherwise helped Jews somehow "balanced" the collaborators and bystanders. No such balance existed within Nazi-era Catholicism.

The final point I would raise about *We Remember* concerns its depiction of Pope Pius XII. I do believe there is definite value in *We Remember*'s insistence that a number of important Jewish leaders during the Nazi era regarded Pius XII quite highly, because we are still living with the impact of Rolf Hochhuth's very distorted presentation (in *The Deputy*) of Pius's record, and because popular journalism has also misrepresented his policies. However, we need to take a much more comprehensive look at how Pius XII's contemporaries regarded him. Moreover, there are also some indications that as Pius XII was rethinking his general outlook on the social order (something evident in his Christmas addresses of the forties), his efforts on behalf of Jewish rescue intensified. This connection has been insufficiently probed, to date.

We Remember seems to imply that Pius XII's response to the Jews menaced by the Nazis was unquestionably positive. This is simply not the case, but we need to know a lot more before a final assessment of the man can be made. In sum, new scholarly investigations of Pius XII's record should be pursued in earnest. The Church's moral integrity will not permit anything but sound scholarship in this regard.

One general conclusion has emerged so far, however, from previous scholarly studies of Pius XII. Pius appears to have been profoundly committed to what we can term a *diplomatic*, rather than a *prophetic* vision of the

Church. In such a vision diplomatic channels, rather than public pronouncements, assume primary importance in achieving results. Part of Pius's profound commitment to the diplomatic church model was the result of his desire
to preserve Catholicism as an institutional force against the onslaught, as he
saw it, of Bolshevism and liberalism. His concern about liberalism is not as
well known as his antipathy toward Bolshevism. But Pius, until the forties,
was a fervent believer and participant in the century-long struggle of the
Catholic Church against the growing power of the liberal political order in
Western Europe. The so-called Berlin Culture was seen by Pius and many of
his allies in the Church (as well as by many in the Protestant churches) as a
fundamental threat to the continuation of a European civilization in which
Christianity would set the moral, cultural, and even the political tone. In some
ways, this liberal "threat" was taken more seriously by Pius than even
Bolshevism was, because it was more subtle and because it was strongest in
Western Europe.

Pius's and the Vatican's conduct during the Nazi period will provide
Catholics with extremely valuable reference points as the Church confronts
difficult new social situations. I believe that, consciously or not, the Church
is beginning to learn from the failings of its policy of reserve during the thirties and forties. Recent challenges to unjust regimes in South Africa, Malawi,
the Philippines, and elsewhere, plus the forthright manner in which the
February 1989 Pontifical Commission for Justice and Peace condemned
apartheid, anti-Semitism, and anti-Zionism by name, attest to a decided
movement away from the public caution so evident during the papacy of Pius
XII. Certainly the framers of *We Remember* were in position to examine that
caution in great detail. But by not doing so, a great opportunity was lost to
provide Catholics—and non-Catholics—with the means to ponder how religious institutions should respond to grave social crises. While the diplomatic
model of the Church has totally disappeared in Catholic circles, there now
appear clear signs that the Church is increasingly beginning to forsake this
model to speak out publicly about social issues. Speaking out on such matters unquestionably carries some measure of risk for the Church's institutional well-being.

Some scholars believe that during the Nazi era the Vatican perceived the Jews to be "unfortunate expendables" who could be abandoned to guarantee the survival of the Catholic community. If this kind of attitude no longer underpins Vatican sensibilities, the reason, at least in part, is because of the basic theological change in understanding the church-world relationship that emerged from Vatican II's document on "The Church in the Modern World." In that document's perspective there exists a sense of a far greater integration between the events of human history and the ultimate purposes of the kingdom of God than was the case for Pius XII's fundamental vision of the Church.

We Remember has broached some very important issues to which the international Catholic and Jewish communities need to respond. The document is problematic because of its limitations regarding the responsibility of the Church as a historical institution, but it is forthright in its call for remembrance of the *Shoah* and its summons to world Catholicism to repent for Christian indifference and collaboration during the Nazi era. Monsignor George Higgins could very well be correct in his recent assertion that *We Remember,* despite its imperfections, may eventually be acknowledged as being as decisive a turning point for Catholic-Jewish relations as was *Nostra Aetate.*

LIST OF PARTICIPANTS

Consultation on the Vatican Document **We Remember**

The Joseph Cardinal Bernardin Center at Catholic Theological Union
March 28–30, 1999

Dr. M. Christine Athans, B.V.M.
Professor of Church History
The Saint Paul School of Divinity
University of St. Thomas

Rabbi Michael Balinsky
Hillel Foundation
Northwestern University

Dr. Georgette F. Bennett
President
Tanenbaum Center for Interreligious Understanding

Rev. Thomas Baima, S.T.D.
Consultant
Office for Ecumenical and Interreligious Relations
Archdiocese of Chicago

Judith H. Banki
Program Director
Tanenbaum Center for Interreligious Understanding

DR. DIANNE BERGANT
Professor of Old Testament Studies
Catholic Theological Union

DR. HERBERT BRONSTEIN
North Shore Congregation Israel

JAMES CARROLL
Research Associate
The Center for the Study of Values in Public Life
Harvard Divinity School

HIS EMINENCE EDWARD CARDINAL CASSIDY
President
Holy See's Commission for Religious Relations with the Jews

DR. EVA FLEISCHNER
Professor of Theology
Marquette University

DR. IRVING GREENBERG
President
Jewish Life Network

REV. WAYNE JENKINS, S.C.J.
Chairman
Milwaukee Archdiocesan Ecumenical and Interfaith Commission

DR. JACQUES KORNBERG
Professor of History
University of Toronto

RABBI JOSEPH H. EHRENKRANZ
Executive Director
Center for Christian Jewish Understanding
Sacred Heart University

DR. LAWRENCE FRIZZELL
Institute of Judaeo-Christian Studies
Seton Hall University

DR. CAROL FRANCES JEGEN, B.V.M.
Senior Professor of Pastoral Theology
Loyola University of Chicago

DR. STEVEN T. KATZ
Professor of Jewish Studies
Center for Judaic Studies
Boston University

DR. RUTH LANGER
Assistant Professor of Jewish Studies
Theology Department
Boston College

REV. LEO LEFEBURE
Professor of Doctrinal Theology
Mundelein Seminary

DR. MICHAEL MARRUS
Dean of Graduate Studies
Professor of History

University of Toronto
SR. JOAN M. MCGUIRE
Director
Office of Ecumenical and Interreligious Affairs
Archdiocese of Chicago

DR. RONALD MODRAS
Professor of Theology
St. Louis University

DR. JOHN T. PAWLIKOWSKI, O.S.M.
Professor of Social Ethics
Catholic Theological Union

DR. KEVIN MADIGAN
Assistant Professor of Church History
Catholic Theological Union

REV. MICHAEL MCGARRY, C.S.P.
Rector Designate
Tantur Ecumenical Institute [Jerusalem]

DR. STEVEN J. MCMICHAEL
Instructor
Aquinas Institute of Theology

DR. JOHN MORLEY
Associate Professor of Religious Studies
Seton Hall University

DR. HAYIM PERELMUTER
Professor of Jewish Studies
Catholic Theological Union

DR. MICHAEL PHAYER
Professor of History
Marquette University

DR. ROBERT SCHREITER, C.PP.S.
Professor of Systematic Theology
Catholic Theological Union

PETER STEINFELS
Religion Writer, *New York Times*
Visiting Professor of History, Georgetown University

RABBI IRA YOUDOVIN
Director
Chicago Board of Rabbis

RABBI HERMAN SCHAALMAN
Emanuel Congregation

DR. CLAUDIA SETZER
Associate Professor of Religious Studies
Manhattan College

DR. GERARD SLOYAN
Distinguished Professorial Lecturer
School of Religious Studies
Catholic University of America

BR. WAYNE TEASDALE
Instructor, DePaul University
Member, The Monastic Dialogue
Catholic Theological Union

PART II

CONFERENCE ON

ETHICS AND THE HOLOCAUST

Cosponsored by the Church Relations Committee of the
United States Holocaust Memorial Museum, Washington, D.C.,
and the Joseph Cardinal Bernardin Center for Theology and Ministry
at Catholic Theological Union, Chicago

MAY 3–4, 1999

1 0

The Impact of the Holocaust on Contemporary Ethics

MICHAEL BERENBAUM

There is a paradox related to the Holocaust: The more distant we stand from the Event, the larger the Event looms. With the exception of the period immediately following the Allied entry into the concentration camps,[1] what should most properly be called the *accidental liberation* of the camps, interest in the Holocaust was greater in the fifties than in the forties, in the sixties than in the fifties, in the seventies than in the sixties, in the eighties than in the seventies, in the nineties than in the eighties, and in the first days of the new millennia than ever before. There were more headlines relating to the Holocaust in the last year of the century than throughout the period of time when the Germans were carrying out the "Final Solution."[2] Even if there is "Holocaust fatigue" within the Jewish community, there is increasing interest in this material in the non-Jewish world, both in the United States and in Europe. While one might have expected the Holocaust to recede into the background and to join the events of distant history, it seems to be coming to the foreground. Nowhere is this more evident than in the field of ethics.

There is a second paradox relating to the Holocaust, one that has been apparent for quite some time: the innocent feel guilty and the guilty innocent.[3] There is a well-developed understanding in psychology of what has come to be known as *survival guilt* and yet seemingly the perpetrators do not feel guilty. Their grandchildren, born after the war and educated in the democratic values of a new Germany, feel guilty. Daniel Jonah Goldhagen's work, *Hitler's Willing Executioners,* became a best-seller in Germany before it was translated into German. The grandchildren of perpetrators were willing to engage Goldhagen's thesis that the German people in their entirety were willing executioners of the Jews united by a commitment to eliminationalist anti-Semitism that soon became exterminationist anti-Semitism. Young Germans flocked to attend discussions at major universities. Heated conversations went long into the night throughout Germany. Three out of four of the people who attended screenings of *Schindler's List* in Germany were under the age of thirty.

This young generation of Germans reversed the course charted by former chancellor Helmut Kohl at Bitburg, where he sought to distinguish between the evil SS and the honorable German soldiers. They created, sponsored, and attended an exhibition on the *Wehrmacht* that depicted it as the handmaiden of the destruction process.

Irving Greenberg once said that not to confront is to invite repetition.[4] Ernestine Schlant described postwar West German literature's attitude toward the Holocaust as the language of silence,[5] not a respectful silence but an unuttered silence, the silence that sweeps the issue under the rug. We have seen the younger generation seek to encounter the Holocaust: they visit the camps, they visit Israel, they engage Jews, they read books, they seek to learn. In contrast, in Switzerland, the collapse of the myth of Swiss neutrality and the discovery of dimensions of Swiss complicity led to an increase in anti-Semitism—and indeed to threats of increased anti-Semitism—precisely because the myth of innocence had collapsed and they had no positive way to deal with the responsibility that came with that collapse.

Nowhere is this phenomena of the innocent feeling guilty and the guilty feeling innocent more prevalent than in the post-*Shoah* behavior of the Roman Catholic Church. The recent *We Remember: A Reflection on the Shoah* is yet another indication that Pope John Paul II has made confronting the *Shoah* and the fight against anti-Semitism a centerpiece of his papacy. Continuing the tradition established by his predecessor Pope John XXIII, John Paul II has brought Roman Catholic-Jewish relations to a new level of respect. Like his predecessor Pope John XXIII, the current pontiff was directly touched by the Holocaust and has assumed responsibility for its memory. Both men were changed by the history they experienced, and, as leaders, both changed the institutions they headed, even an institution so conservative and seemingly so reticent to change as the Roman Catholic Church.

During the *Shoah*, Pope John XXIII, then Archbishop Roncalli, provided certificates of baptism to Jews without insisting they convert, thus offering them a measure of safety. Later, as pope, he initiated Vatican II, which significantly reversed two millennia of Roman Catholic teaching on the Jews. *Nostra Aetate* reinterpreted Christian Scripture to broaden responsibility for the crucifixion. It changed scriptural readings and modified the liturgy for Good Friday so that Jews are neither portrayed as Christ-killers, nor as accepting the responsibility for his death on themselves and their children. *Nostra Aetate* recognized the religious legitimacy of continuing Jewish life and thus reversed major anti-Judaic components of Christian teaching. After *Nostra Aetate*, the Church held the sins of all humanity responsible for the death of Jesus, and the Jews were not portrayed as cursed by God for the murder of Jesus. Perhaps most importantly it addressed Jews as Jews respectfully as the sons of Abraham, bearers of a covenantal tradition.

For centuries, there was a dark side to the Christian relationship with the Jews. Supersessionist traditions maintained that Christianity had come to take the place of Judaism, the New Testament to fulfill the Old. There was a theological difficulty for believing Christians to find a religious reason why Jews should continue to be Jews, except as a sign of obstinacy of a stiff-necked people. And if there was no reason for Jews to continue to exist as Jews, there was even more motivation to convert them, and, in difficult moments, to sanction their elimination by expulsion or to turn aside during pogroms. In his discussions with the Vatican prior to *Nostra Aetate*, the late Abraham Joshua Heschel said: "Speech has power and few men realize that words do not fade . . . What starts out as a sound, ends in a deed."[6]

Much of this tradition was ended—at least in theory—for Roman Catholics by Vatican II, and, with the changes in the catechism, less of this tradition was transmitted in post-Vatican II Roman Catholic schools, at least in the United States. The result has been a substantial decrease in Roman Catholic anti-Semitism and a new era of ecumenical respect. And while the changes may not have reached every local parish level, they still are significant.

Pope John XXIII had come to terms with 1878 years of Jewish life—the years of Jewish exile from 70 C.E. to 1948—yet neither he nor his two immediate successors accepted the renascent State of Israel, the very form of Jewish life since 1948. Enter Pope John Paul II, who, as a young man in Poland, witnessed the *Shoah*. Three million Jews of Poland were killed in the Holocaust. After the war, Polish cities, which were once the home of large and thriving Jewish communities, were bereft of Jews, and the pope's hometown was the site of a large ghetto whose Jewish population was deported to death camps.

As a young university student, the current pope had Jewish friends. As a young priest, he was asked to baptize children born of Jewish parents who had been raised by Polish Catholics, who had sheltered them during the *Shoah*, thereby saving their lives. When the Jewish parents did not return after the war, the Polish families raised these children as their own. On these occasion, the future pope insisted that these children *were first informed of their Jewish origins.*[7] It was an act of courage—political, religious, and pastoral—in postwar Poland, a deed of profound respect for memory.

As Pope John Paul II, he recognized the State of Israel. He visited a synagogue for prayer and treated the rabbi and the congregation of Rome with every religious courtesy. Instead of dividing the world between Christians and Jews, he spoke of the commonality of the religious traditions, and he spoke with reverence of the Torah. Again and again, he spoke out against anti-Semitism. He visited the sites of Jewish death and acknowledged on numerous occasions the centrality of the *Shoah*.

In March 2000, Pope John Paul II visited Israel. From the moment he arrived at Ben-Gurion Airport near Tel Aviv to the moment he departed, it was clear to Roman Catholics and Jews, and to the international media, that this was an extraordinary gesture of reconciliation in the shadow not only of two millennia of Christian anti-Semitism but in the massive shadow of the Holocaust. Even if Pope John Paul II did not say everything that could be said, his bowed head at Yad Vashem and his note of apology inserted into the Western Wall said more than could be said by words alone. In the third millennium, the pontiff was determined that Roman Catholics act differently, behave differently, and believe differently. An eyewitness to the Holocaust, he had come to make amends. He took all-important steps to make certain that the full authority of the papacy was brought to bear against anti-Semitism. His theology was quite simple: anti-Semitism is a sin against God. It is anti-Christian. These are welcome words to every Jew and one could sense their power by the manner in which the Israelis received Pope John Paul II. Even ultra-Orthodox rabbis, opposed by conviction to anything ecumenical and raised on the stories transmitted through the generations of confrontations between priests and rabbis, were deeply impressed by the papal visit to the offices of the Israel's chief rabbis.

There are at least two important ethical insights that must be derived from the impact of the guilt of the innocent. First, *no religious ethic is acceptable if it demonizes another religion and disparages their right to hold their faith and the right of another religion to worship their God as they see fit.* The innocent ones who felt guilty have led contemporary Roman Catholicism to renounce anti-Semitism and to accept the integrity of the ongoing religious life of the Jews. This behavior should serve as a model for Jews and Muslims as well as for other religious leaders as to the ethical requirements of religious doctrine. It is for this reason that I oppose those who would have Jews return to the original form of the *Aleinu,* the Adoration, and reinsert the line originally removed by church censors "that they pray to naught and emptiness and to a God who does not save" (while we bow and bend before the King of Kings, the Holy One Blessed Be He). Precisely, because we have the right to say it, we can refrain from transmitting such teachings in prayer.

In a world where religious extremism is present in diverse faiths, this important ethical insight must be emphasized again and again. Jews cannot ask Christians to renounce anti-Semitism within their own tradition without accepting, at the same time, the obligation to reformulate religious doctrine to eliminate the potential of religious demonization. The same is true for Jewish behavior regarding Islam, where political tensions can fuel such demonization. And in contemporary religious discourse, Jewish, Christian, and Muslim, we can each cite example after example of demonization, even in intradenominational discourse among people of the same faith.

Second, *the Roman Catholic Church has provided us with a marvelous example of the creative use of guilt as a spur to repentance, to transformation.* Emil Fackenheim wrote of the Holocaust as rupture, an almost total rupture[8] in the fabric of Western civilization and within Christianity itself. Yet the rupture was *almost total, but quite complete.* Fackenheim suggested that the task of this generation was to mend that rupture. In Hasidic parlance, Rabbi Nachman of Bratzlav said: "Nothing is as whole as a heart that has been broken," broken and mended. In the experience of tailors, where a garment has been mended, that is where it is strongest. The notion of Tikkun, which in Kabbalistic literature is the reunification of divine sparks scattered by creation—nothing less, than making God one again—is used modestly by Fackenheim in a more limited sense as mending. The religious communities that have undergone such mending are the strongest, and that is precisely where the strength of the religion is to be found.

Political

Almost thirty years ago my teacher, Richard L. Rubenstein, wrote a slim but important volume titled *The Cunning of History: Mass Death and the American Future.*[9] Rubenstein was wrong about several issues in the book, most especially about some horrific scenarios for the American future. Yet, he was right about so much more.

Rubenstein argued that the Holocaust was an expression in the extreme of what is common to the mainstream of Western civilization. In demographics and political bureaucracy, in economics, and with regard to the treatment of superfluous populations, the Holocaust represented not an aberration but an extreme manifestation of what is present in our society. This is not the occasion to revisit all of Rubenstein's points, so I will confine myself to the relationship of the Holocaust to slavery and to the concept of superfluous population.

William Styron's *Sophie's Choice* was deeply influenced by Rubenstein's work, in part because of the manner in which Rubenstein dealt with slavery and thus touched something deep within Styron's Southern sensibilities. In the middle of Styron's masterful novel, he recapitulates

Rubenstein's understanding of slave labor in Auschwitz, and thus links the Auschwitz experience to the history of American slavery that was so central to Styron's earlier work, *The Confessions of Nat Turner.*[10] Even in the harsh conditions of North American slavery and the mistreatment of slaves in the South, the southern slave was considered a capital investment. As with any capital investment, the slave had to be protected. Basic food and shelter were provided, at least so long as the slave was of value to the master. Procreation was encouraged to produce additional slaves—additional capital assets. Medical care, horrible and inadequate as it was, was provided *so long as the slave was useful.* When no longer useful, the slave was sold to someone less fortunate, or abandoned to die, much as we—and I apologize for the analogy—might treat an old car that is either repaired until repairs are too costly and then is traded, or, when it is beyond all utility, junked.

Auschwitz was different, at least with regard to the fate of Jewish slaves. At Auschwitz, slavery was brought to its perverse perfection. Inmates were considered a consumable raw material to be discarded in the process of manufacture and recycled into the Nazi war economy. All mineral life was drained. Living conditions, food supplies, and sanitary conditions were less than adequate for sustained labor. Shelter was minimal, food was inadequate, procreation was prohibited, Jewish slaves were literally worked to death or reduced to a condition that rendered them incapable of work, and then selected for death in the gas chamber. Even body parts were then recycled into the Nazi war economy—gold teeth, hair, and body fat. (One could only imagine the current harvest of body parts given the state of contemporary science.) "Respectable corporations" throughout the Reich, and even the Reichsbank, received this material without inquiring from whence it came or at what cost. In fact, they requested more. A distinguished university awarded a Ph.D. for a theory on the reuse of dental gold and from then on, gold teeth were extracted and used.

Rubenstein highlights the continuity of the various forms of slavery and its linkage to the ordinary economic exploitation of labor that takes factories from the unionized North to the non-unionized South, from American shores to Asia, from there to Third World countries where working conditions are harsher, the restrictions on the use of labor less specific or more lenient, and the cost of labor diminished to various slave situations. Auschwitz stands at the extreme. The dead Jewish slave was a desirable byproduct of the manufacturing process. Thus, Rubenstein at once shows both the continuity and the discontinuity—the uniqueness—of the Holocaust.

Rubenstein also highlighted the issue of superfluous populations, those who have no rightful place in the societies in which they live. By choice and by ideology, the Nazis defined the Jews as a superfluous population, those who had no right to live among them, and demonized them to the extent that ethnic cleansing, what Daniel Goldhagen termed eliminationist anti-Semitism, was insufficient. Annihilation, extermination, eradication, became the chosen means of being rid of this superfluous and "cancerous" population. Rubenstein shows that the presence of superfluous populations is manifest throughout our society.

What Rubenstein did not adequately consider was the covenant among the generations inherent in the American experience. Those who are productive are responsible for those who are no longer productive, not yet productive, or unable to be productive. Those who are no longer productive are taken care of by social security and Medicare; those who are not yet productive are offered the opportunity of an education, and, while the amount and the form of assistance to those who cannot work within our society is debatable, the responsibility to provide for them is generally accepted as shared. Contemporary debates on domestic policy have centered on the issue of superfluous populations: the aged, the young, the disabled, immigrants, those on welfare, and those caught in the spiral of multigenerational poverty. The strains of the eighties and the nineties have been eased in our time of affluence, where labor itself is at a premium, but the ethics of how to deal with superfluous populations is the central political issue of our time. Is it to be every person for himself or herself, or is there a covenant that binds the generations, that shares the burden with government, assuming the responsibility for some equitable distribution that provides for those who cannot provide for themselves?

Seen in this light, the debates such as the right to die, the Oregon suicide law, schooling, healthcare, and citizenship for children of immigrants—legal and illegal—take on a larger importance than the issue itself and have consequences that go well beyond their particular detail. The strengthening of covenant, as Rubenstein stressed in the second edition of *After Auschwitz*[11] (but not two decades earlier when he wrote *The Cunning of History*) is essential to combating the ethics that would lead to destruction. Helen Fein would also add that the expansion of the universe of common obligation, those bound within the covenant, is essential.[12]

Never Again

There is no disagreement that a major impact of the Holocaust was the drafting of *A Convention for the Prevention of Crimes of Genocide,* which was adopted by the United Nations on December 9, 1948, and ratified by the United States Senate almost forty years later. Raphael Lemkin first introduced the term *genocide* in 1933, when he submitted a draft proposal to the League of Nations for an international convention on barbaric crimes and vandalism. He had a major hand in drafting the Genocide Convention, which was designed to overcome the claims of Nuremberg defendants that they had violated no law. The convention specifically defines the various aspects of Nazi genocide as criminal. It prohibits the killing of persons belonging to a group (the Final Solution); causing grievous bodily or spiritual harm to members of a group; deliberately enforcing upon the group living conditions that could lead to complete or partial extermination (ghettoization and starvation); enforcing measures to prevent births among the group (sterilization); and forcibly removing children from the group and transferring them to another group (the "Aryanization" of Polish children).

This convention enunciated new standards of behavior on the international community, standards that more often than not have been violated without consequences, but standards that are reiterated in the aftermath of mass murder. The Nuremberg trials also indicated a standard of responsibility, and have been invoked as the model for the trials in Rwanda and Bosnia.

One of the most intense responses to the Holocaust came from the American Jewish community, which, although somewhat muted throughout the war, spurred into action for rescue and rehabilitation, and in support of the establishment and later the survival of a Jewish state in Palestine. Haskel Lookstein concluded *We Are Our Brother's Keepers,* his painful study of Jewish press coverage of the Holocaust, with the following sober observation:

> The Holocaust may have been unstoppable by American Jewry, but it should have been unbearable for them. And it wasn't. This is important, not alone for our understanding of the past but for our sense of responsibility for the future.[13]

Among the other innocents to feel guilty and to act upon that guilt was American Jewry. Many students of American history have concluded that although mistakes were made—timidity, disunity, complacency, and hesitancy among them—American Jewry lacked the essential power to transform American policy toward the war against the Jews. As Arthur Hertzberg, the astute student of Jewish history, put it, "They lacked clout." Without power and adequate access at the moment of crisis, they have vowed ever since not to be caught without adequate power in the future. American Jewry has learned that powerlessness invites victimization and, therefore, it has labored hard to achieve adequate power to defend Jewish interests and has employed this power for the protection of the State of Israel, for the rescue of Soviet Jewry and Ethiopian Jews, and to protect endangered Jews everywhere.

A different lesson of powerlessness has been learned in Israel. Ehud Barak said it most eloquently and most succinctly when he first entered Auschwitz in 1994 as chief of staff of the Israel defense forces: "We have come fifty years too late." He was not alone. Benjamin Netanyahu, his predecessor as prime minister, said:

> All that was needed was to bomb the tracks. The Allies bombed targets nearby. The pilots had only to nudge their crosshairs. You

think they didn't know? They knew. They didn't bomb because
at that time the Jews didn't have a state nor the political force to
protect themselves.[14]

In the aftermath of World War I, Jews sought their rights as a protected
minority within a majority culture. In the aftermath of World War II, such a
policy of vulnerability was rejected. Instead, the Jews sought to protect themselves by reentering political history and achieving military power. The sovereign State of Israel also assumed responsibility for the protection of Jews
and for accepting Jews seeking protection who come to their shores. The Law
of Return enjoyed near universal acceptance by the Israelis and by the world
Jewish community precisely because it was an answer to the homelessness
and unwanted status of the Jews during the Holocaust. And for many years,
as the shadow of the Holocaust loomed large over young Israelis, and as the
survival of Israel seemed endangered, service in the army and the pursuit of
military might was regarded as essential to the Jewish future as a response to
the Holocaust. *The Seventh Day: Israeli Soldiers Talk about the Six-Day War*
was but one indication of how much the Israelis saw themselves as transforming the fate of the Jewish people by resorting to the power of arms, by
exercising the capacity for self-defense.

There has been a sense of American "guilt" over inaction during the
Holocaust. Historians have recently been more aggressive in arguing that
such guilt was ahistorical, but in the decades when interest in the Holocaust
first began to intensify, critiques of America in action seemed to be preemi-
nent. From Arthur Morse's *While Six Million Died* to David Wyman's *The
Abandonment of the Jews*, from Henry Feingold's *The Politics of Genocide* to
Walter Laqueur's *The Terrible Secret: The Suppression of Truth Regarding
Hitler's Final Solution*, major historical treatments were quite critical of
Allied indifference to the plight of the Jews. There were subtle disagreements
as to the motivations of such indifference, debates over how pernicious, how
anti-Semitic, how intentional or unintentional the motivations were of those
who ignored the plight of the Jews, but the *record* of indifference was hardly
challenged, and the politics of recognizing such indifference before Jewish

audiences by American governmental and political leadership became both routine and an expected rite. Only in the past several years have historians challenged this record of inaction with works such as W. D. Rubenstein's *The Myth of Rescue* and Richard Levy's essay on "The Bombing of Auschwitz."[15]

American presidents from Ford to Clinton restated this record of indifference and made the solemn pledge of "never again." This record clearly underscored American support for Israel, the fight for freedom of Soviet Jewry, and the rescue of Ethiopian Jewry in which then Vice President George Bush played such an important role. And the Holocaust has been evoked to come to the assistance of non-Jews.

Nowhere was this record of American guilt used more directly and more clearly than in the American determination to accept the "boat people" in the aftermath of the Cambodian genocide in 1979. Addressing a conference at Evian, which had been the site of the failed conference on the "refugee problem," a euphemism for the plight of Jewish refugees in 1938, Vice President Walter Mondale invoked the memory of the first Evian Conference as he called for "a world solution to the world problem of the boat people." The vice president said:

> Forty-one years ago this very week, another international conference on Lake Geneva concluded its deliberations. . . . At stake at Evian were both human lives—and the decency and self-respect of the civilized world. If each nation at Evian had agreed on that day to take in 17,000 Jews at once, every Jew in the Reich could have been saved. . . . At Evian, they began with high hopes. But they failed the test of civilization. Let us not re-enact their error. Let us not be heirs to their shame.

The United States took the lead and other Western countries followed—and within months, new homes were found throughout the West for the boat people of Southeast Asia. There is little doubt that the shadow loomed large in the issues surrounding Bosnia, Rwanda, and Kosovo; not so large that it spurred action, but large enough to spur guilt over inaction and ultimately to trigger the bombing campaign in Kosovo, a campaign that would never have been undertaken—could never have been undertaken—without the memory of the failure to bomb Auschwitz. This is not the occasion to revisit these issues, but several points are worthy of mention.

Students of the Holocaust used to argue that if only the world "knew," they would have responded. Over the past several decades, scholars have uncovered the degree to which information about the Final Solution was available, not only to decision makers and journalists but to the general public as well. When this information was first uncovered, both scholars and the general public were shocked and chagrined to learn that such information failed to produce concrete action on behalf of the victims. But contemporary Americans—contemporary citizens of the world—have no excuse because we live in the world of CNN. The images of mass murder are broadcast into our living rooms. Thus, the issue is not information, not knowledge, but the political will to respond. And the political will to respond, in turn, generates additional information.

Twenty-one years ago, in response to then current scholarship, the President's Commission on the Holocaust recommended to the president that as part of a "living memorial to the Holocaust,

> . . . that a Committee on Conscience composed of distin-
> guished moral leaders in America be appointed. This
> Committee would receive reports of genocide (actual or
> potential) anywhere in the world. In the event of any out-
> break, it would have access to the President, the Congress,
> and the public in order to alert the national conscience,
> influence policy makers, and stimulate worldwide action
> to bring such acts to a halt.[16]

The assumption behind this recommendation was that knowledge and conscience would be sufficient. I believe that regardless of our differing polit-ical perspectives, we can stipulate that Presidents George Bush and Bill

Clinton were men of conscience who did not want innocent men, women, and children to be killed. In the abstract they would have advocated a strong response to genocide. And yet for so very long no military action was undertaken on behalf of the victims. When faced with events in Bosnia, both turned to General Colin Powell and the Joint Chiefs of Staff who, operating out of what they had learned from the unsuccessful war in Vietnam about the disproportionate use of power, insisted that it would take 100,000 troops to accomplish the goal. Secretary of State James Baker said of Bosnia: "We don't have a dog in that fight"—his inelegant way of saying that vital American interests were not at stake; or in the words of Helen Fein, that the Bosnians were outside of the circle of common obligation. Both presidents concluded that they did not have the political capital to invest in such a commitment of troops, and thus they sought to change the focus of American public attention. The State Department signaled reluctance to use the "G" word in describing the events in Bosnia; the "G" word is *genocide,* and the more pervasive the consciousness of the Holocaust, the greater the "G" word is a call to active, even armed response.[17]

President Clinton's appearance at the dedication of the United States Holocaust Memorial Museum imposed upon him an obligation to give the appearance of an intense response to events in Bosnia. I know from personal experience that his speechwriters were reluctant to repeat the familiar lines against indifference to genocide for fear that the president would be asked the obvious questions about Bosnia. The gathering of European leaders for the dedication of the museum spurred the president into round after round of diplomatic meetings that were described as grappling with the problem of Bosnia. Clearly, a consciousness of the Holocaust—intensified by the dedication of the museum—would not permit indifference to other genocides or, at least, the appearance of such indifference.

The failure to bomb Auschwitz lurked in the shadows of the decision regarding the bombing of Kosovo. Surely one cannot compare the two situations. Precision bombing today is substantially different from precision bombing more than a half century ago. And the conditions in Kosovo, however bad, did not remotely resemble Auschwitz. Bombing arose as the preferred solution because it posed no major risks for those doing the bombing, and there was no political capital available to the president that would have permitted him to introduce ground troops. The president barely avoided a defeat in Congress regarding the bombing. For a while, it looked as if the entire bombing program would be ineffective and lead to more violence. Or, to borrow a phrase from the infamous letter of Assistant Secretary of War John J. McCloy turning down a request to bomb Auschwitz: "There is considerable opinion to the effect that such an action, even if practicable, might provoke more vindictive action on the part of the Germans"—read Serbians.[18]

At stake in President Clinton's decision to bomb in Kosovo was one reading of how the Allies should have behaved during the Holocaust. In the popular imagination, Auschwitz should have been bombed, and that would have stopped the killing process. The history of the bombing of Auschwitz controversy is far more complicated. Auschwitz only came within range of Allied bombers in the spring of 1944 with American advances in Italy. In early June 1944, the Jewish Agency in Palestine refused to press for bombing Auschwitz, fearing that the Germans would use the death of Jews on the ground as a major propaganda victory. It was only after the Vr'ba-Wetzler Report that the Jewish Agency changed its tactics. Still the advocates of bombing Auschwitz had to concede that those already incarcerated in the camp were in effect dead, and that bombing the Birkenau complex would hamper the killing process. Michael J. Neufeld and I have edited a book on the debate, which is much more technically complex and morally charged than it is in the popular imagination. The failure to bomb became emblematic of Allied indifference to the plight of the Jews, and bombing itself is the preferred technical solution because so little is risked while seemingly so much is gained. I often suspect that if you asked nonspecialists what it would have taken to stop the Holocaust, they might answer, "Just a few bombs." The failure to bomb Auschwitz set the stage for responses to the bombing of Kosovo, and had that bombing campaign not succeeded—as it appeared to be failing during many weeks of bombing—the result might clearly have been not only a failed policy but a rewriting of history. Opponents might have said: "There was nothing the Allies could have done. Therefore, not doing anything was justified." It would have provided moral legitimacy for a policy of inaction.

Yet, despite easily made and hopefully sincerely felt pledges of "never again," genocide has occurred elsewhere without significant Allied response. Rwanda is but one tragic example. The killing was swift and primitive. Machetes were used more often than guns. Western governments were aware of what was taking place. Military forces ran, while nongovernmental organizations engaged in humanitarian relief efforts stayed. The leaders of the non-governmental organizations were young people, college students, and post-graduates. CARE, UNICEF, Save the Children, and Doctors Without Borders remained on the ground, doing what had to be done to rescue, to relieve, to alleviate pain and suffering; and soldiers who were trained for combat were called home by their fearful governments, afraid of the political repercussion lest some harm befall them. It seems as if there is a higher political price to be paid by national leaders for losing the life of a heavily armed volunteer, a soldier who battles against genocide, than for doing nothing while acts of genocide are indeed taking place. The United States is particularly cautious. One example may suffice: a Canadian on contract staffed the U.S. government's Agency for International Development program in the months after the genocide. Why? Because if he had been taken hostage, it would have been less politically embarrassing to the administration than if an American had been taken.

The Marines entered to rescue U.S. citizens but not to stop the killing. France and Belgium, which had forces on the ground, removed their forces prior to the killing. History will determine if the color of the victims influenced the decision not to act. Clearly, there was a sentiment within the West that Rwanda—unlike Europe—was outside the universe of common obligation. So, too, the issue was not knowledge or conscience, but political will in the aftermath of the successful but undefended policy of the U.S. government in Somalia (where the introduction of American troops stemmed the famine, but where the American people proved unwilling to pay the price in American lives for the rescue of Africans from sure death by starvation). The Clinton administration did not defend its policy. Few allies on Capitol Hill were vocal in defense of these values. Fewer still were willing to ask the question as to why U.S. troops cannot be placed in harm's way not only in defense of vital national interests but also in defense of vital humanitarian interests. More unarmed, innocent American civilians, children among them, were murdered in any of our major cities in one month than the highly armed trained American military personnel who were introduced into Somalia to save hundreds of thousands of lives. Yet the death of our soldiers, tragic as it was, captured national attention. Random murder did not. The issue again is political will.

Medical

Few nonspecialists realize the impact of the Holocaust on medical ethics. At the conclusion of the International Military Tribunal Trials at Nuremberg, involving twenty-two major Nazi leaders, a series of other trials were held by the United States. One hundred eighty-five defendants in all were divided into twelve groups. Mobile killing unit leaders, camp commandants, judges, and corporate leaders were tried. Doctors were tried for their participation in selection, murder, and medical experimentation. Response to the trial of German physicians led the judges to declare ten principles of legitimate medical experimentation, principles that will sound quite familiar even to those casually concerned with medical ethics and with but limited interest in the Holocaust. They have become standard in medical ethics today:

1. The *voluntary consent* of the human subject is absolutely essential . . .

2. The experiment should be such as to yield fruitful results for the good of society, unprocurable by other methods . . .

3. [T]he anticipated results will justify the performance of the experiment.

4. The experiment should be so conducted as to avoid all unnecessary physical and mental suffering and injury.

5. No experiment should be conducted where there is an *a priori* reason to believe that death or disabling injury will occur except,

perhaps, in those experiments where the experimental physicians also serve as subject.

6.   The degree of risk to be taken should never exceed that determined by the humanitarian importance of the problem to be solved by the experiment.

7.   Proper preparations should be made and adequate facilities provided to protect the experimental subject against even remote possibilities of injury, disability, or death.

8.   The experiment should be conducted only by scientifically qualified persons. The highest degree of skill and care should be required through all stages of the experiment of those who conduct or engage in the experiment.

9.   During the course of the experiment, the human subject should be at liberty to bring the experiment to an end if he has reached the physical or mental state where continuation of the experiment seems to him to be impossible.

10. During the course of the experiment, the scientist in charge must be prepared to terminate the experiment at any stage if he has probable cause to believe, in the exercise of the good faith, superior skill, and careful judgment required of him, that a continuation of the experiment is likely to result in injury, disability, or death to the experimental subject.

Clearly, and often unknowingly, the impact of the Holocaust looms large on medical ethics. In fact, the ethics gleaned from the violations of the Holocaust are now the accepted norms of medical practice.

Curiously, the participation of German physicians in the T-4 program of medicalized killing of mentally retarded, physically handicapped, and emotionally distraught Germans, the so-called euthanasia ordered directly by Adolf Hitler was not at issue, although that aspect of Nazi "medical practice" is coming under increased scrutiny today. Over the past decade, the increasing interest of medical ethicists in the Holocaust has little to do with the ethics of experimentation at the camps, and much more to do with a formerly little-known program of "euthanasia" known as the T-4 operation, which Henry Friedlander,[19] among others, considers the origin of the Holocaust. A word of background is in order.

Mass murder of the handicapped began slowly. Hitler signed the authorization directly backdating it to September 1, 1939, to give it the appearance of a wartime measure. At first, authorization was informal and secret. Narrow in scope, it was limited only to the most serious cases. Within months, the T-4 program involved virtually the entire German psychiatric community. Operating at the Berlin Chancellery, Tiergarten 4, a statistical survey of all psychiatric institutions, hospitals, and homes for chronic patients, was ordered.

Three medical experts reviewed these forms without examining individual patients or reading detailed records. Theirs was the power to decide life or death. Economic justifications were offered for the entire program, including the amount saved that could be put to other budgetary uses for helping those who were well and serving their country. Patients ordered killed were transported to six killing centers: Hartheim, Sonnenstein, Grafeneck, Bernburg, Hadamar, and Brandenburg. The SS donned white coats for the transports to impersonate a medical situation.

The first killings were by starvation. Starvation, after all, is passive, simple, natural. Injections were then used. Children were simply put to sleep; sedatives became overdoses. Gassing soon became the preferred method of killing, however, and false showers were constructed. Chemists were employed, and physicians administered the process. Eventually, fifteen to twenty people were killed at a time. Afterwards black smoke would billow up the chimneys as the bodies were burned.

Although the protests of a few doctors and churchmen were not decisive, the domestic opposition by parents and relatives of those who were put to death was effective—at least externally. On August 24, 1941, almost two years after it began, the operation was seemingly discontinued. In fact, it was driven underground.

Mass murder, however, was just beginning. Physicians trained in the medical killing centers graduated to bigger tasks. Irmfriend Eberl, M.D., who began his career in the T-4 program, became the commandant of Treblinka. His colleagues went on to Belzec, Sobibor, Treblinka, and Auschwitz, where killing took on massive dimensions. Elsewhere I have written that:

> The murder of the handicapped was a prefiguration of the Holocaust. Killing centers for the handicapped were the antecedent of death camps. They were often staffed by the same physicians who received their specialized training—and lost their moral inhibitions—in this early training. Psychiatrists could save some patients for a time, but only if others were sent to their deaths. Judenrat leaders were later to face similar choices. The transport of the handicapped was the forerunner of deportations. Gas chambers were first developed at these killing centers. So, too, body disposal by burning. In the death camps, thousands could be killed at one time, and their bodies burned within hours.[20]

By understanding the background of the T-4 project, we can sense its increased relevance as a negative model for contemporary physicians. There is now a third party intimately involved in deciding a patient's treatment. That third party does not examine the patient, but, rather, is a bureaucrat—and only on occasion does a physician serve as an insurance company or government watchdog. Furthermore, the successful efforts at decoding the human genes will only add to the ethical issues involved in scientific efforts to improve the human species and the fascination with eugenics. The economics of dying, including the sum expended in the last months of the lives of many patients, may dictate that certain medical procedures be withheld or limited in their availability in order to conserve on resources. We live at a time of economic expansion and virtually unprecedented prosperity with budget surpluses. It doesn't take much imagination to understand what might happen if resources became scarce, if Medicare could not handle the strain of the baby-boom generation, to understand Rubenstein's fundamental point that the Holocaust is an expression in the extreme of what is common in the mainstream of Western civilization.

In my last year at what was then called the Research Institute of the United States Holocaust Memorial Museum—currently renamed the Center for Advanced Holocaust Studies—we sponsored a series of conferences on the Impact of the Holocaust on Contemporary Medical Ethics. The conferences were well attended, and the papers were of a high quality from scholars in diverse fields. Even a nonphysician could see the degree to which the shadow of this event served as a warning to physicians concerning what could happen, and as a nightmare image of what might happen if the pursuit of the scientifically possible is not restrained by considerations of the ethically permissible.

Legal

Shortly after the genocide in Rwanda, I was invited as the representative of the United States Holocaust Memorial Museum to a conference on "Genocide Accountability: Dialogue for National and International Response," sponsored by the government of Rwanda. I was struck then by how important the model of the Nuremberg trials was to a society seeking to reestablish a sense of justice. Although historians asked for understanding, the questions of lawyers were quite different. What is to be done with the perpetrators?

One major segment of the conference was devoted to the question of how to rebuild a shattered legal system, and how to deal with the perpetrators. American human rights lawyers were invited as advisors. Also joining them were lawyers from Argentina who had reconstituted their legal system after Desperados, Ugandese lawyers who rebuilt the system after Idi Amin, and post-apartheid South African lawyers. After the transition of power from governments that massively violated human rights and human dignity, those who were left in positions of power often were part of the system—judges, lawyers, and the police.

Lawyers also asked how to get testimony and how to gather material. There is a major difference between gathering legal evidence and gathering historical evidence. Still, the trials at Nuremberg provided the first under-standing of the scope of German crimes, the first definition of what happened, as has the testimony before the Truth and Reconciliation Commission in South Africa.

The Nuremberg trials served as one model for post-genocide justice. It is a model being pursued to deal with Bosnia, where its limitations and para-doxes have been revealed clearly. It is far more difficult to remove a perpe-trator from office in a situation that falls short of total victory if what awaits the leaders is a trial before an international court of justice. He or she would prefer to hold on to office and to the relative safety that their political power can provide, than to give up that office and face life in prison. Still, there must be some insistence on accountability, and the world requires the restraint imposed by that insistence if genocide is to be prevented.

Two final points on the implications of the Holocaust for contemporary legal ethics: much to the surprise of both institutions, the Museum of Tolerance in Los Angeles and the United States Holocaust Memorial Museum are involved in police training. Each August the incoming class of naval mid-shipmen serving at the United States Naval Academy in Annapolis visit the U.S. Holocaust Memorial Museum the week after they complete basic train-ing. It is only then that they receive their first lesson in military ethics. The police view the Holocaust as a police action and learn the values of tolerance and restraint, and the American military views the Holocaust as a military action and thus as directly relevant to the code of military ethics. The Federal Bureau of Investigation subjects many of its incoming officials to a lecture on the Holocaust, which they use to underscore the importance of the rule of law. When invited, I often offer a mild dissent. The Holocaust itself was a mani-festation of the rule of law—Rubenstein, among others, have argued that the Nazis committed no crime,[21] they violated no laws, everything was done legally—but we must be concerned with the values underlying the law. We must reemphasize the notion of rights that the state cannot take away, of con-straints on the power of the state, of the idea that the Creator endows human equality and human rights. These rights are far from self-evident. They are precarious and therefore ever more precious.

The Holocaust as Absolute

As we enter the new millennium, the Holocaust has taken its place as a defining moment of twentieth-century humanity. It was the moment we learned something about what we are as individuals, about human capacity for good and evil. But we have not learned about ourselves only as individuals—we have learned the power of states and institutions to shape the world and to accomplish so much, even the annihilation of a people. In a world of relativism, it has taken its place as the Absolute. We do not know what is good. We do not know what is bad. But we do know that the Holocaust is evil, absolute evil. It is for that reason that people use the word in the plural as they attempt to call attention to their suffering—the Black Holocaust, the Holocaust of the American Indians, the Holocaust in Kosovo, Rwanda, Bosnia.

The Holocaust is the nuclear bomb of moral epithets. It is an event of such magnitude that the more we sense the relativism of values, the more we require the Holocaust as the foundation for a negative absolute—absolute evil. I suspect this is why leaders of European nations have rediscovered the importance of the Holocaust for contemporary moral education. I also suspect this is why it becomes the focal point for papal visits to Israel, for German society, and for American society. And I also suspect that this is why some continue to deny an event that all reasons, all standards of rationality, demonstrate cannot be denied. It is in this function as negative absolute that the Holocaust may loom largest in the coming years.

NOTES

1. In recent years there has been a tendency to heroize the liberators. Liberation was accidental. Soldiers happened upon the camps en route to some military target. Their actions upon entry into the camps varied. In Buchenwald, for example, the camp was self-liberated—the SS left before American units arrived. So liberation can best be termed "accidental."

2. According to Laurel Leff (who is writing a book about coverage of the Holocaust), there were more than 1100 stories on the persecution and murder of the Jews, which we now call the Holocaust, between 1939 and 1945—one approximately every other day—in the *New York Times,* but only six front-page stories during this time. By contrast, there were 2233 stories on the Holocaust published in the past two years, and more than six front-page stories in the first six months of 2000 alone.

3. Irving Greenberg, "Clouds of Fire, Pillar of Smoke," in Eva Fleischner, ed., *Auschwitz: Beginning of a New Era?* (New York: Ktav, 1977), reprinted and excerpted in John Roth and Michael Berenbaum, eds., *Holocaust: Religious and Philosophical Implications* (New York: Paragon House, 1989), pp. 305–345, see pages 312–314.

4. Ibid., p. 312.

5. Ernestine Schlant, *The Language of Silence: West German Literature and the Holocaust* (New York and London: Routledge, 1999).

6. Abraham Joshua Heschel, *To Grow in Wisdom: An Anthology of Abraham Joshua Heschel*, by Abraham Joshua Heschel, Jacob Neusner and Noam M. Neusner, eds. (New York: Madison Books, 1990), p. 162.

7. See Yaffa Eliach, *Hasidic Tales of the Holocaust* (New York: Oxford University Press, 1982) pp. 142–147.

8. Emil Fackenheim, *To Mend the World: Foundations of Future Jewish Thought* (New York: Schocken Books, 1982).

9. Richard L. Rubenstein, *The Cunning of History: Mass Death and the American Future* (New York and San Francisco: Harper and Row, 1972).

10. William Styron, *Sophie's Choice* (New York: Random House, 1976), pp. 270–275.

11. Richard L. Rubenstein, *After Auschwitz: History, Theology and Contemporary Judaism,* 2nd ed. (Baltimore and London: Johns Hopkins University Press, 1992). The subtitle of the original edition was *Radical Theology and Contemporary Judaism.* Written twenty-five years after the original, the latest release has two major chapters devoted to the concept of covenant and divinity.

12. See Helen Fein, *Accounting for Genocide: National Responses and Jewish Victimization during the Holocaust* (New York: The Free Press, 1979).

13. Haskel Lookstein, *We Are Our Brother's Keeper: The Public Response of American Jews to the Holocaust 1938–1944* (New York and Bridgeport: Hartmore House, 1985).

14. Michael Neufeld and Michael Berenbaum, eds., *The Bombing of Auschwitz: Should the Allies Have Attempted It?* (New York: St. Martin's Press, 2000).

15. See Neufeld and Berenbaum, p. 214. Benjamin Netanyahu, prime minister of Israel, at Auschwitz death camp, 23 April 1998, reported by Michael Viatteau, "Netanyahu Says Allies Knowingly Let Jews Die" (Agence France-Presse, *Washington Times,* April 24, 1998, p. A15).

16. *Report to the President, The President's Commission on the Holocaust* (Washington, D.C.: Government Printing Office, 1979), p. 13.

17. Richard Johnson, then a state department official serving at the National War College, who had written an article entitled "The Pinstripe Approach to Genocide," which was excerpted in the *Washington Post,* "Some Call It Genocide, But Not Those Who Can Make a Difference" (*Washington Post,* February 13, 1994, p. C7), made these remarks in a private meeting at the United States Holocaust Memorial Museum.

18. August 9, 1944, letter from then Assistant Secretary of War John J. McCloy to Leon Kubowitzki of the World Jewish Congress. McCloy wrote:

Dear Mr. Kubowitzki:

I refer to your letter of August 9 in which you request considerations of a proposal made by Mr. Ernest Frischer that certain installations and railroad centers be bombed.

This War Department has been approached by the War Refugee Board, which raised the question of the practicability of this suggestion. After a study it became apparent that such an operation could be executed only by the diversion of considerable air support essential to the success of our forces now engaged in decisive operations elsewhere and would in any case be of such doubtful efficacy that it would not warrant the use of our resources. There has been considerable opinion to the effect that such an effort, even if practicable, might provoke even more vindictive action by the Germans.

The War Department fully appreciated the humanitarian motives which prompted the suggested operations, but for the reasons stated above it has not been felt that it can or should be undertaken, at least at this time.

I think this letter may be read a little differently in the future.

19. Henry Friedlander, *The Origins of the Holocaust: From Euthanasia to Genocide* (Chapel Hill: University of North Carolina Press, 1995).
20. Michael Berenbaum, *Witness to the Holocaust: An Illustrated Documentary History of the Holocaust in the Words of Its Victims, Perpetrators and Bystanders* (New York: HarperCollins 1997) p. 104.
21. *The Cunning of History,* p. 33.

11

The Holocaust: Its Challenges for Understanding Human Responsibility

JOHN T. PAWLIKOWSKI

In his contribution to this volume, Dr. Michael Berenbaum rightly notes how important the study of the Holocaust has become for the development of ethical understanding today. He is quite correct in emphasizing how the study of the Holocaust helps us better understand ourselves as individual people and how states exercise power, so often in oppressive ways. If I demur from his presentation, it would be in terms of whether, in the end, the Holocaust will leave a permanent and decisive impact on how we conceive humanity's role in the future. Has all the knowledge about the Holocaust that we have acquired over the last half century of research helped us to better understand our role as human agents responsible for the survival of humanity and the rest of creation? So far I do not believe we have successfully transferred the religious and ethical implications of the Holocaust to society at large. While, as Berenbaum emphasizes, specialists in fields such as law and medicine are increasingly studying the Holocaust, I fear that its implications are still ignored by a large part of humanity.

As a scholar in ethics who is committed to the Christian religious tradition, I am obliged to probe the implications of Nazi ideology for contemporary human self-understanding. I do so conscious of the need always to remember its specific victims, for as Elie Wiesel has so aptly put it, "to forget the victims is indeed to kill them a second time." I do so conscious as well of the need to connect my reflections to the "details" of the Holocaust so well uncovered by my colleagues in historical studies. That is why, for example, this essay is indebted to the work of Holocaust historians such as Peter Hayes. But I remain convinced that acts of Holocaust memory and in-depth studies of Holocaust events, as crucial as they remain, will leave us bereft of the understanding we desperately require today if the human community and the creation with which we are intertwined are to survive the challenges that lie before us.

I was recently struck by two interconnected realities. The first was the unveiling of Sue, the most intact dinosaur remains yet discovered, at the Field Museum in Chicago. The other was a film I viewed on a recent flight to London on the total destruction of the great Mayan civilization in the Americas. Both brought to light the disappearance of powerful forces in creation. Both reminded me that brute strength and power are no guarantee of future survival. The Mayan example, in particular, impressed upon me the very real possibility of great civilizations totally vanishing.

I raise these examples because Nazi ideology as I see it was perhaps the strongest assertion of power and control that we have experienced in this history of humanity. It involved the meshing of powerful military force and ideological assertions of unlimited human power to shape the future of humanity. It claimed that religion was dead as an effective counterforce to the assertion of human power. Steven Katz is absolutely correct in his contention that Nazi ideology cannot be forced into traditional categories of evil. It represented a new phase in human self-understanding, one that carried within it the seeds of creational destruction on a global scale. In my judgment the religious community has so far failed to respond adequately to the challenge that Nazi ideology poses for human responsibility. Only a few scholars, such as Irving Greenberg and Richard Rubenstein, have addressed the challenge in its very depth. Too many have simply tried to return to "religion as usual" after the Holocaust, reasserting traditional covenantal religion. One example is David Hartman, whose work I greatly admire in many areas, but who I believe has done us a great disservice by insisting that we only mourn the victims of the Holocaust and not try to reinterpret religion today in light of its profound ideological challenge.

If religion is to produce a deep ethical counterforce to the ideology of the Holocaust, it cannot do so by merely reasserting biblical religious notions. While not ignoring biblical tradition, it must seek to build a new understanding that will refashion significantly the respective roles of human and divine agency in the exercise of this responsibility. Irving Greenberg may have gone too far in asserting an almost total role reversal in human and divine responsibility after the Holocaust, as I will discuss subsequently. But I applaud him for his boldness in raising a question that far too many have simply ignored.

Human Co-Creatorship: The New Challenge

In the early seventies two futurists introduced us to a fundamentally new reality with which religious ethics has yet adequately to grapple. Victor Ferkiss, a political scientist out of the Catholic tradition, and Hans Jonas, a social philosopher of Jewish background who escaped the Nazis, served warning that humankind had reached a new point in its evolutionary journey. Humanity was now standing on a threshold between utopia and oblivion, as Buckminster Fuller has put it. The human community now faced a situation whose potential for destruction equaled its capacity for reaching new levels of creativity and human dignity. What path humanity would follow was a decision that rested with the next several generations. Neither direct divine intervention nor the arbitrary forces of nature would determine the ultimate outcome. Human choice was now more critical than ever in the past for creational survival. And the decision would have lasting impact, well beyond the lifespan of those who are destined to make it. It would, in fact, determine what forms of life will experience continued viability.

Ferkiss's 1974 volume, *The Future of Technological Civilization,* put the late twentieth century challenge to humankind in these words: "Man has . . . achieved virtually godlike powers over himself, his society, and his physical environment. As a result of his scientific and technological achievements, he has the power to alter or destroy both the human race and its physical habitat."[1]

Hans Jonas, in a groundbreaking speech in Los Angeles in 1972 at a gathering of learned societies of religion, and subsequently in published writings, conveyed essentially the same message as Ferkiss. Ours is the very first generation to have to face the question of basic creational survival. In the past, there was no human destructive behavior from which we could not recover. But today we have reached the point through technological advancement where this principle no longer holds. Humankind now seems increasingly capable of actions that inflict terminal damage on the whole of creation and raise serious questions about the future of humanity itself.[2]

For me, the Holocaust represents perhaps the clearest twentieth century example of the fundamental challenge now facing humanity as described by Ferkiss and Jonas. I have emphasized in a number of published essays[3] that in the final analysis I view the Holocaust as inaugurating a new era in human self-awareness and human possibility, an era capable of producing unprecedented destruction or unparalleled hope. With the rise of Nazism the mass extermination of human life in a guiltless fashion became thinkable and technologically feasible. The door was now ajar for dispassionate torture and the murder of millions, not out of xenophobic fear but through a calculated effort to reshape history supported by intellectual argumentation from the best and brightest minds in the society. It was an attempt, Emil Fackenheim has argued, to wipe out the "divine image" in history. "The murder camp," Fackenheim insists, "was not an accidental by-product of the Nazi empire. It was its essence."[4]

The basic challenge of the Holocaust lies in the need to alter significantly our perception of the relationship between God and humanity. Such a change carries with it profound implications for human moral responsibility. What emerges as a central reality from the study of the Holocaust is the Nazis' sense of a new Aryan humanity freed from the moral restraints previously imposed by religious beliefs and capable of exerting virtually unlimited power in the shaping of the world and its inhabitants. In a somewhat indirect though still powerful way, the Nazis had proclaimed the death of God as a governing force in the universe. In pursuit of their objective, the Nazis became convinced that all the so-called "dregs of humanity," first and foremost the Jews, but also Poles, Gypsies, gays, and the disabled, had to be eliminated, or at least their influence on culture and human development significantly curtailed.[5]

The late Uriel Tal captured as well as anyone the basic theological challenge presented by the Holocaust. In his understanding, the so-called Final Solution had as its ultimate objective the total transformation of human values. Its stated intent was liberating humanity from all previous moral ideals and codes. When the liberating process was complete, humanity would be rescued once and for all from subjection to God-belief and its related notions of moral responsibility, redemption, sin, and revelation. Nazi ideology sought to transform theological ideas into exclusively anthropological and political concepts. In Tal's perspective, the Nazis can be said to have adopted a kind of "incarnational" ideology, but not in the New Testament sense of the term. Rather, for the Nazis, "God becomes a man in a political sense as a member of the Aryan race whose highest representative on earth is the Führer."[6]

If we accept this interpretation of the ultimate implications of Nazism, we are confronted with a major theological challenge. How does the human community properly appropriate the genuine sense of human liberation that was at the core of Nazi ideology without surrendering its soul to massive evil? However horrendous their legacy, the Nazis were correct in at least one respect: they rightly perceived that some basic changes were underway in human consciousness. The impact of the new science and technology, with its underlying assumption of freedom, was beginning to provide humankind on a mass scale with a Promethean-type experience of escape from prior moral chains. People were starting to perceive, however dimly, an enhanced sense of dignity and autonomy that went well beyond what Western Christian theology was prepared to concede.

Traditional theological concepts that had shaped much of the Christian moral perspective, notions such as divine punishment, hell, divine wrath, and providence, were losing some of the hold they had exercised over moral decision making since biblical times. Christian theology had tended to accentuate the omnipotence of God which in turn intensified the impotence of the human person and the rather inconsequential role played by the human community in maintaining the sustainability of creation. The Nazis totally rejected this previous relationship. In fact, they were trying to turn it upside down.

Numerous Jewish writers have attempted to respond to the fundamental implications of the Holocaust in terms of human and divine responsibility. Emil Fackenheim, David Hartman, Richard Rubenstein, Elie Wiesel, Arthur Cohen, David Blumenthal, and Zygmunt Bauman are authors who have made significant contributions to the post-Holocaust discussion. One of the responses I still find particularly intriguing in both its theological and practical dimensions has come from Irving Greenberg.

For Greenberg the Holocaust has destroyed all further possibility of a "commanded" dimension to our understanding of the God-human community relationship. "Covenantally speaking," he has said, "one cannot order another person to step forward to die."[7] Any meaningful understanding of a covenantal relationship between God and humanity must now be understood as voluntary. The voluntary nature of the post-Holocaust covenantal relationship unquestionably heightens human responsibility in the eyes of Greenberg: "If after the Temple's destruction, Israel moved from junior partner to true partner in the covenant, then after the Holocaust, the Jewish people is called upon to become the senior partner in action. In effect, God was saying to humans: you stop the Holocaust. You bring the redemption. You act to ensure that it will never again occur. I will be with you totally in whatever happens, but you must do it."[8] Based on this theological reversal in divine-human responsibility after the Holocaust, Greenberg strongly argues for the assumption of power on the part of the human community that is unprecedented. For Greenberg, it would be morally irresponsible to abandon the quest for power today, as some in the religious community have urged. The only option in the post-Holocaust world that will enable us to avoid repetitions of human degradation and evil akin to what surfaced during the Nazi era is for the human community to combine the assumption of new power over creation with what Greenberg terms the development of "better mechanisms of self-criticism, correction and repentance." Only in this way will humankind utilize power "without being the unwitting slave of bloodshed or an exploitative status quo."[9]

Though Greenberg wrote these words some years ago, I still find them a compelling interpretation of the new challenge to human responsibility in light of the Holocaust. I especially concur with Greenberg's insistence on the human community's assumption of power. For that reason I find myself at odds as a social ethicist with those of my colleagues who espouse an unqualified pacifist position or what is known as the "deep" ecological perspective that tends to submerge humanity within creation as such, destroying awareness of the enhanced dimensions of human responsibility in our day. But I do feel that Greenberg has carried the theological role reversal too far. Viewing God as the "junior partner" renders God overly impotent in terms of creational responsibility. I would opt for a more co-equal relationship, although with a redefined understanding of divine responsibility.

The language of co-creatorship—developed mostly in Christian theological literature, even in official Catholic documents coming from Pope John Paul II and various conferences of bishops,[10] but also present in some Jewish writing,[11]—represents the most promising paradigm after the Holocaust. While this notion of co-creatorship has roots in the biblical tradition,[12] its full magnitude has become apparent only in light of such events as the Holocaust and, as theologian Philip Hefner has emphasized, with our enhanced appreciation of the vast evolutionary process in which the role of human responsibility emerges as absolutely decisive.[13]

There have been critics of the notion of human co-creatorship among biblical scholars and within ethical circles where a scholar such as Stanley Hauerwas has strongly criticized Pope John Paul II's appropriation of "co-creatorship" in his encyclical *Laborem Exercens*[14] on the grounds that it would lead to a Nazi-like mentality within the human community. Some ecological activists also reject the notion out of hand on the grounds that it would open the door to creational destruction by intensifying the already existing hierarchical model of society. Surely any affirmation of human co-creatorship must be tempered by the notion that the Creator God retains a central role in the process of caring for and preserving creation. Hence my rejection of any "junior status" role for God along the lines suggested by Greenberg. And Hauerwas's call for "humility" in the use of human power in light of the Holocaust sounds an important cautionary note for any co-creatorship paradigm. But to enshrine "humility" as the prevailing motif for understanding the human/divine responsibility problematic would likely prevent humankind from assuming full governance of creation, a failure that might well entail economic, ecological, and even nuclear disaster on a global scale.

Unless we recognize that human responsibility has been raised to a new level in consequence of the Holocaust and through our improved understanding of the evolutionary dynamic, the human community will likely refrain from taking those decisive steps that will ensure the continuity of life at all levels of creation. To follow Hauerwas or the deep ecologists in terms of envisioning humankind's role in creational governance may well result in people of faith becoming bystanders rather than central actors in human history. To insure that the notion of co-creatorship does not wind up elevating human power to a new destructive level, we need to reaffirm the role of divine responsibility, but in a refined sense. The paradigm of an all-powerful God who will intervene to halt human and creational destruction is simply dead after the Holocaust and in light of our contemporary evolutionary consciousness. On this point, the Nazi ideologues were perceptive: where their vision was fatally flawed, and so humanly destructive, was in responding to the "death" of the interventionist God with an assertion, as Michael Ryan once put it, of all-pervasive power for themselves.[15]

If we are successfully to curb the excessive use of human power within a paradigm of co-creatorship we must reintroduce into human consciousness, especially in our now highly secularized societies parented by the Enlightenment and its revolutionary heritage, a deep sense of what I have called a "compelling" God. This compelling God, whom we must come to experience through symbolic encounter that is both personal and cultural, will result in a healing, a strengthening, an affirming, that will bury any need to assert our humanity, to try to "overpower" the Creator God, through the destructive, even deadly use of human power. This sense of a compelling parent God who has gifted humanity, whose vulnerability for the Christian has been shown in the cross (as Jürgen Moltmann has well articulated in *The Crucified God*),[16] is the indispensable foundation for any adequate paradigm of co-creatorship today.

I remain convinced that the notion of a compelling God, a God to whom we are drawn rather than a God who simply imposes upon us, must be sustained in our personal consciousness as well as in our societal consciousness. This latter point is especially challenging for those of us who subscribe to the vision of church-state separation enshrined in Western democracies and which, for Catholicism, was raised to a level of theological principle at the

Second Vatican Council in its "Declaration on Religious Liberty."[17] Nonetheless, we also need to take very seriously Vatican II's "Declaration on the Church in the Modern World," which strongly emphasized the centrality of culture in shaping morality both public and personal. Unless a sense of a compelling God is integrated into Western communal consciousness, not in a fundamentalistic or exclusivistic way but as a true moral barometer, I fear that personal consciousness of a compelling God by itself will prove ineffective in guarding against the abuse of human co-creatorship. It could easily lead, as the church historian Clyde Manschreck warned some years ago, to "naked state sovereignty."[18]

To sum up my first major point, the Holocaust and our contemporary evolutionary consciousness force upon us a major reformulation of divine and human responsibility. It will have to be a reformulation that takes into account the prophetic words uttered by Catholic philosopher Romano Guardini soon after the Holocaust: "In the coming epoch, the essential problem will no longer be that of increasing power—though power will continue to increase at an even swifter tempo—but of curbing it. The core of the new epoch's intellectual task will be to integrate power into life in such a way that man can employ power without forfeiting his humanity, or to surrender his humanity to power and perish."[19] Neither a return to religious fundamentalism nor a paradigm of "junior level" divine agency will respond adequately to this challenge. Only a vision of human co-creatorship anchored in a personal and communal sense of a "compelling" God has the possibility of meeting that challenge.

The Need for Structural Justice

If the human community is truly to confront its heightened sense of responsibility in this new millennium, we will also need to deal with several other issues beyond the fundamental perception of the divine-human relationship. These include the significance of structural justice for maintaining a sense of co-creatorship, the basic importance of a commitment to human rights, and, finally, an understanding of the role of the vitalistic in sustaining moral commitment and in what some have termed the "ritual containment" of evil in society.

In recent years two leading ethicists centrally involved in the discussion about the moral implications of the Holocaust, Peter Haas of Vanderbilt and Didier Pollefeyt of the Catholic University of Leuven (Belgium), have debated the issue of structural morality during the Nazi era. Haas launched this discussion with the publication of his volume *Morality after Auschwitz: The Radical Challenge of the Nazi Ethic* in 1988.[20] Haas asked why the Nazis failed to recognize evil as evil, and, as a consequence, why they made no effort to distance themselves from it. His response given in *Morality after Auschwitz* and in subsequent writings takes the following direction. The Nazi ideologues created what appeared to many as a scientifically valid ethic. "The problem," he says, "is that a moral system that is thought out and elaborated along 'scientific' lines, that is through the application of a strict logic, hardens such facts into universal givens." This results, according to Haas, in a loss of any sense of the difference between murder and killing. "Morality" becomes much more a matter of acting in a way that "fits" the pre-established system. For Haas, the scientific system removes from my consciousness any notion of myself as having personal moral responsibility for my actions: "I then lose sight of my own moral agency, of my own power to create not only the acts through my observation of them, but also to create the text that gives the act its moral value. I at that moment stop being a moral agent and become instead a passive actor in someone else's drama."[21] Haas goes on to say that ultimately what went awry with what Haas terms "the Nazi ethic" was that it predefined morality for people under its sway. It proclaimed not only what was right and what was wrong from a scientific perspective, and therefore unquestionable, but also what actions fell into each category: "The result was," Haas insists, "that people did atrocious things because they took them to be morally mandated. The Nazi morality predefined what was acceptable to such an extent, and in such an authoritative, scientific way, that many people, especially intellectuals, simply fell into line. The living relationship between the human as moral agent on the one hand, and the moral act on the other was lost."[22] He concludes by affirming the need to maintain a moral foundation for ethics today that is rooted in the dynamics of human relationship, cooperation, openness to the other, and compassion for the other.

Didier Pollefeyt takes issue with Haas on several points, including whether we can speak of a "Nazi ethic." He prefers to speak of Nazism as having "perverted" authentic morality. But he does in the end recognize the systematic nature of the Nazi approach to human acts. For him, it is better to view Nazism as espousing a "totalitarian ethic." But, just as Haas, Pollefeyt emphasizes that such an ethic generates "moral sameness" by removing any personal sense of responsibility from the response framework. He agrees with Haas that the Nazi ideologues created a closed ethic in which any response that did not fit into the preconceived pattern was eliminated. Such an ethic, Pollefeyt also underlines, eliminates any sense of mercy and compassion. It removes God as a moral barometer of any sort. Instead, "God" is used to legitimate the closed and murderous social order.

For Pollefeyt, Nazism became a politics without a true ethical framework. It had no room for alterity, and demanded the eradication of anything that was not in conformity with "the system." "As such," he argues, "Nazism was an idolatrous effort that radicalised itself and eliminated everything that did not conform. . . . This is for us the primary lesson of the Nazi genocide, but also of other forms of racism and discrimination, such as nationalism, sexism or religious fundamentalism."[23]

In my judgment, both Haas and Pollefeyt have uncovered a crucial dimension of Nazism that remains critical for understanding the moral challenge before us today. In highlighting the importance of the Nazi framework for human response, whether one decides to call it an ethic or not, they have shown that a central characteristic of modernity (and one might argue postmodernity as well) is the determination of morality by political and cultural structures. Nazism was the first modern political system to "program" human societal responses in a systematic fashion.

Historian Peter Hayes of Northwestern University has further illuminated this dimension of Nazism in his continuing research on business leaders in the period of the Third Reich.[24] Hayes concludes that in the end German big business was willing "to walk over corpses." There were many factors internal to Germany that contributed to this process of moral numbing. But above all, says Hayes, was the fact that "the Third Reich constructed a framework of economic policy in which the effective pursuit of corporate survival or success had to serve, at least outwardly, the goals and ideological requirements of the regime."[25] The indifference of German businessmen during the Third Reich, Hayes continues, reveals the all-too-common penchant in the modern world to hide behind so-called professional responsibilities in the face of a deep moral challenge. "The obligation to achieve the best possible return for the firm and those who own or work for it to secure their long-term prospects, which in decent contexts can be a guarantee against personal corruption or frivolous management, became an excuse for participating in cruel, eventually murderous acts, indeed a mandate to do so."[26] Most alarming about this development was not even the complicity in murder, but a sense of innocence about such complicity on the part of very many of the businessmen. They were able to subdue any moral hesitations they may have experienced with the response, "What else can I do?" losing sight of the far more important question, according to Hayes, "What must I never do?"[27]

Hayes's studies provide solid data for the position of Haas and Pollyfeyt about the erosion of a sense of personal responsibility within Nazi culture. They also serve as a warning for a similar process that is taking hold in society today in the name of globalization. "What else can I do?" has in fact increasingly become a stock phrase in the vocabulary of global capitalism. The dynamics of the market must reign supreme no matter what the cost in human terms, no matter that, as a recent European Union report has shown, some 250 million children around the world are used to support this system, living in conditions, in many instances, of virtual slavery. Pope John Paul II, in what may prove in the end to be his most prophetic concern, has warned that the global ideology of the market, which has tended to replace the competing Cold War ideologies in recent years, cannot insure the preservation of human dignity.

> The rapid advance toward the globalization of economic
> and financial systems also illustrates the urgent need to

> establish who is responsible for guaranteeing the global
> common good and the exercise of economic and social
> rights. The free market by itself cannot do this, because in
> fact there are many human needs which have no place in
> the market.[28]

In an address to a Vatican meeting of scholars and political leaders con-vened by Pope John Paul II at Castel Gandolfo in August 1998, former American national security advisor Zbigniew Brzezinski argued along much the same lines as the pope himself, calling for an increasing sensitivity to social responsibility within our global economic system. "That sensitivity," he maintained, "has to be as important a consideration as efficiency and per-formance in the determination of economic decisions and guiding economic development."[29]

The so-called Nazi ethic has opened up what unquestionably is the most decisive moral question of the last century and into this millennium. How can the human community maintain a sense of human responsibility in a global system of human organization? The Holocaust has shown us how destructive a failure to address this question head-on can be for human and creational sur-vival.

The Holocaust and Human Rights

I now speak specifically as a Catholic. It is my conviction that the absence of a human rights tradition contributed significantly to moral failures on the part of Catholics during the Third Reich.

Modernity, especially the Enlightenment with its creation of new plu-ralistic societies rooted in individual equality and human rights, posed a real dilemma for classical Catholic thought. In many instances, Catholics were not above appealing for protection under the laws of the new democratic, secular societies. But their theology had not yet freed itself from the ideal of Catholic domination of the state where that could be achieved, nor the principle that human liberties were ultimately dependent on adherence to the authentic faith tradition possessed by Catholicism.[30]

In the United States the appropriation of the liberal tradition of the Enlightenment was not predicated on hostility toward religion as it was in Europe. American revolutionary leaders never placed the goddess of reason on the high altar, and some of them, such as Jefferson and Franklin, even proposed a national seal for the United States depicting Moses crossing the Red Sea—something totally unthinkable to their French compatriots. While U.S. Catholics generally continued to hold to the classical theology of church dominance over the state despite their rather enthusiastic practical embrace of American pluralism, the American liberal ethos eventually generated new thinking on the theological level as well. The most prominent name in this regard was Father John Courtney Murray, S.J., who eventually would become a primary contributor to Vatican II's "Declaration on Religious Liberty." Clearly American Catholicism was a decisive conduit for the eventual acceptance of the liberal tradition and its core commitment to human rights by global Catholicism at Vatican II.

When we come to the question of Catholicism and the Holocaust, we still are very much in a pre-Vatican II mindset in terms of the Church's attitude toward the public order. Here it is critical to stress the profound differences between liberalism in America and liberalism in Europe, which, unlike its American counterpart, displayed profound hostility toward all forms of Christianity. A virtual state of war existed between the liberals of Europe, especially in the form of freemasonry, and the Catholic leadership in particular. Even Catholic liberals who claimed a Christian basis for democratic principles were castigated by Catholic authorities, with some leaving the Church.[31] The liberals were identified with a deliberate attempt to overthrow the prevailing social order and, in the case of Italy, to undermine Rome's sovereignty over the papal states. In 1832 Pope Gregory XVI issued the encyclical *Mirari Vos* against the "errors" and "evils" of those "shameless lovers of liberty" and those Catholic reformers who maintained the idea that "liberty of conscience must be maintained for everyone."

Pope Gregory XVI's successor, Pius IX, was first thought somewhat more sympathetic to liberal ideas because of political reforms he introduced at the outset of his pontificate. But as the challenge to Vatican sovereignty over the papal states grew strong, Pius IX became more vocal in his opposition to liberalism. In 1864 he issued the famous *Syllabus of Errors,* which condemned liberalism as an "absurd principle" which argued that the state should treat all religions alike without distinction. In Italy he forbade Catholics to serve in the government or even to vote in general elections. For the clergy trained in this era and who established the tone in the Catholic Church for the coming decades, liberalism was the political program of freemasons who oppressed Christianity and opposed its values.

The accession of Leo XIII to the papacy in 1878 brought a bit of moderation to the Catholic war against liberalism. Leo encouraged French Catholics to abandon their notion of restoring a Catholic monarchy and, instead, urged them to utilize their constitutional liberties for the good of the Church. But on the theological level he described any notion of church-state separation as a "fatal error." While he was open to a measure of toleration in the public order, he refused to recognize that unconditional rights to freedom of speech, worship, etc., could ever become part of Catholic teaching. In the Italian context, he was especially condemnatory of the freemasons and their liberal ideas. He described them as part of the "Kingdom of Satan" which was at war with God in their struggle against the Church and Christendom. He spoke of a conspiracy at work that was endangering the very fabric of Christian civilization.

The thirties were a time of great anxiety among Catholic leaders in Germany, France, and elsewhere that the Weimar Republic's liberal governmental model, which in part was now associated with the Jews, would cause the final collapse of the classical Christian notion of the social order. Many Protestant leaders shared this apprehension. Pope Pius XI, in his social encyclical *Quadragesimo Anno* (1931) hoped that the experiences of the stock market crash in 1929 and the harsh realities of the Russian Revolution would turn people away from liberalism and socialism. He proposed an organic notion of society heavily rooted in the medieval Catholic social vision. Liberalism again was soundly denounced as opposed to the Catholic social vision in this encyclical.

My point is that the two popes of the Holocaust era, Pius XI and Pius XII, worked within the framework of a century-long crusade against liberalism. They were not enamored with fascism. Pius XI, in his anti-Nazi encyclical (with which Cardinal Pacelli, the future Pius XII, was closely associated in his role as Papal Secretary of State), soundly denounced Nazism. But when the Church faced the hard choice of a coalition partner, liberalism (and socialism) were ruled out as realistic possibilities because of the priority of defending the Catholic social order. Fascism and Nazism, despite their severe limitations as ideologies, became the preferred options for protecting Catholic institutional interests. Historians such as Michael Marrus are quite correct in arguing that the primary goal of Vatican policy during the Nazi era was "the safeguarding of the institutional interests of the Church in a perilous political world."[32] Marrus does not find in Vatican documents any clear indication of pro-Nazi sympathies or the supremacy of opposition to the USSR. These documents clearly demonstrate that neither simple hostility nor indifference explains Rome's posture during this critical period. What the documents do establish with reasonable certainty is the dominance of a policy of "reserve and conciliation" under Pius XII, a policy that not only shaped his personal approach but also strongly influenced the basic tenor of the Church's diplomatic corps as well. Marrus puts it this way: "The goal was to limit the global conflict where possible, and above all to protect the influence and standing of the Church as an independent voice. . . . Fearful . . . of threats from the outside, the Pope dared not confront the Nazis or the Italian Fascists directly."[33]

Within such an ecclesiastical framework, the human rights of Jews, and even of basically Catholic victims of the Nazis such as the Poles and the Roma (Gypsies), had little or no priority. Viewed in the context of a fundamental commitment to ecclesiastical preservation for the sake of a moral public order and ultimately for the sake of human salvation, Jews, Poles, Gypsies, and other victim groups became, to use the language of Nora Levin,[34] "unfortunate expendables." Polish-American historian Richard Lukas[35] and Catholic historian John Morley[36] have both noted, for example, strong Polish criticism of Pius XII within Poland itself and from the Polish government-in-exile in London. The fact that human rights was a centerpiece of the discredited liberal tradition (expressed in part in the popular culture generated during the "liberal" Weimar Republic) associated with the masonic conspiracy against Christianity only enhanced the Catholic Church's capacity to push concern for individual victims to the periphery, or even beyond the edge, of moral concern.

The lack of a human rights perspective thus significantly curtailed the Catholic institutional response to Nazism. Now that we are coming to see that, at the level of institutional Christianity, fear of liberalism and concern for the loss of the Church's influence over the public order were in fact stronger motives for acquiescence or even collaboration with Nazism and fascism than classical Christian anti-Semitism itself, we are in a position to ask seriously whether the Church's response would have been different if those Christian voices who advocated incorporation of dimensions of the liberal vision into Christianity, including its human rights vision, had been heeded. And what if Church leaders had made a concerted effort to establish a working relationship with the liberal opposition to Nazism despite that opposition's widespread hostility to religious belief?

I recognize hindsight can never reproduce the difficulty of the actual challenge in this regard, but my suspicion is that if Catholicism had embraced aspects of the liberal vision prior to the rise of Nazism, rather than adopting the position of fierce opposition that I summarized earlier, such a coalition would have proven far more feasible. Whether it would have resulted in the survival of many more Jews, Poles, and Roma is an open question. Some prominent historians such as Michael Marrus and Gunther Lewy believe it would not have made much difference. But on the level of protecting the Church's basic moral integrity, it might have proven quite significant.

The reality is that as we move toward the latter years of the Nazi era, we see some profound changes beginning, even within the mindset of Pius XII. In his Christmas radio addresses to Europe in 1940, 1941, and 1942, Pius XII began to speak of the need for an entirely new global order. What one detects here is a decisive turn by the Vatican leadership away from its linkage with Nazism and fascism and its support of the old monarchical order. No longer is liberalism denounced in the manner of the social encyclicals of 1891 and 1931. Pius, rather, was beginning to see that World War II had rendered the classical Catholic social vision barren. Something new was needed.

Although Pius XII was not to provide this new vision himself, it is interesting to note, for example, some definite increase in activity on his part in terms of the Jewish community during this period. Can we prove cause-effect? Not exactly. But I suspect that there might have been some connection between the changing political vision and the increase in humanitarian efforts on behalf of Jews.

In bringing these observations on human rights and the Holocaust to a close, let me say that while it is important to ask what might have been during the Holocaust had the Catholic Church heeded the calls of important Catholic thinkers such as Félicité de Lamennais and Henri Lacordaire for Catholicism to integrate some of the good aspects of liberal thought (including liberalism's emphasis on human rights) into its own perspective,[37] it is even more vital to reflect on what the Church's posture should be as a Christian community today. We cannot change the record of the World War II Church, although, as the late Cardinal Joseph Bernardin insisted,[38] we should confront it as honestly as possible. But we are in a position to shape the response of the Church in this new millennium.

In the first place, we need to take very seriously the point made by Professor Donald Dietrich in his volume *God and Humanity: Jewish-Christian Relations and Sanctioned Murder.* Dietrich argues that "the Holocaust has reemphasized the need to highlight the person as *the* central factor in the social order to counterbalance state power."[39] Put another way, any authentic notion of ecclesiology after the experience of the Holocaust must make human rights a central component. The vision of the Church that must direct post-Holocaust Christian thinking is one that sees the survival of all persons as integral to the authentic survival of the Church itself. Jews, Poles, the Roma, gays, and the disabled should not have been viewed as "unfortunate expendables" during the Nazi period—and there is no place for any similar classification today. There is no way for Christianity, or for any other religious tradition, to survive meaningfully if it allows the death or suffering of other people to become a byproduct of its efforts at self-preservation. Surely for Christians a communal sense of ethics must accompany the commitment to personal human rights. But no communal ethical vision can ever remove personal human rights from the center of its concern.

There definitely appears to be some understanding of the shift in ecclesiological vision demanded by the experience of the Holocaust. I can cite several examples, such as the stance of many of the churches in South Africa in the face of apartheid, the strong support given by local church leaders to the revolution that brought down the Marcos regime in the Philippines, and the courageous stance taken by the Catholic bishops of Malawi when the late Dr. Hastings Banda threatened the human rights of many of the country's citizens. The last situation is especially relevant because the bishops were willing to risk institutional church survival when President Banda made a serious threat to murder them and their catechists if they continued in their protest on behalf of people who, in most instances, were not Catholic or even Christian.

But the picture is not all positive. In the Philippines and in South Africa, Catholic bishops had to go against the papal representatives who urged caution and even support for the incumbent regimes. The situations in countries such as Haiti and Argentina clearly show a Catholic leadership that had learned little or nothing from the experience of the Holocaust.

My second concluding observation follows upon the perspective comment of Professor Gordon Zahn, author of the first major scholarly study on Catholic attitudes toward Nazism.[40] Zahn maintained that the overriding lesson for religious communities emerging from an analysis of the Holocaust is that they can ill afford to become so enmeshed in a particular sociopolitical experiment that they lose their potential for constructive dissent and disobedience. He writes:

> The Church must recognize that it has a stake in maintaining a separation of church and state as that separation is defined from its own perspective. It is a serious mistake to see that separation . . . only in terms of protecting the purity and independence of the secular order from

> unwarranted intrusions or domination by the spiritual. The problem as it developed in Germany . . . is also one of preserving the purity and independence of the spiritual community and its teaching from domination by the national state, with its definitions of situational needs and priorities.[41]

Only with such a separation will the Church have the freedom to pursue its prophetic mission of standing up for the human rights of all.

Clearly, then, I hope that I have demonstrated that the Holocaust was and remains a major challenge for reflection on the central issue of human rights in our day. This is true for Catholicism, for religious communities in general, and for society at large. Pastor Martin Niemöller remains as prophetic as ever: If we try to preserve ourselves by denying or ignoring the human rights of others, in the end we will all perish.

Sustaining Human Responsibility through Ritual

My interest in the topic of ritual and the Holocaust has been instigated by the writings of three scholars in particular: Catholic liturgist David Power, the ethicist Reinhold Niebuhr, and the historian George Mosse. In addition, my colleague in the Hyde Park cluster of theological schools, psychologist Robert Moore, has provoked my thinking with his emphasis on what he calls "ritual containment" if society is to develop a sensitivity to justice and human rights. What all these scholars have shown is that human reason by itself cannot guarantee human responsibility because the human person is an intricate blend of reason and what Niebuhr termed the "vitalistic." Any adequate social morality must recognize that good and evil emerge from both human faculties. Yet, as I have shown in other writings,[42] there has been a strong tendency in Western thinking, including Western ethical thought, to downplay the role of the vitalistic.

The regeneration of the vitalistic side of humanity, albeit in highly destructive directions, stood at the heart of the Nazi enterprise. Historian J. L. Talmon once described Nazi ideology as the denial of any "final station of redemption in history" which gave birth to a cult of power and vitality as needs in themselves.[43] The Nazis became aware of the tremendous power of this vitalistic dimension. No scholar has made this point as clearly as George Mosse who spent considerable time examining the impact of the Nazi public liturgies during his scholarly career. While it verges on the obscene to give the Nazis credit for anything, Mosse's writings demonstrate that the Nazi leadership was extremely perceptive in recognizing the influence of symbolism in human life.[44] Contemporary Holocaust scholar Irving Greenberg also has acknowledged the significance of this aspect of Nazism. Reflecting on the failure of Enlightenment-based liberalism to provide an effective moral counterweight to the Nazi manipulation of human vitalism shows the inadequacy of any exclusively rational-based morality after the Holocaust. Greenberg makes this point quite strongly:

> How naive the nineteenth-century polemic with religion appears to be in retrospect: how simple Feuerbach, Nietzsche, and many others. The entire structure of autonomous logic and sovereign human reason now takes on a sinister character. . . . For Germany was one of the most "advanced" Western countries—at the heart of the academic, scientific, and technological enterprise. All the talk about "atavism" cannot obscure the way in which such behavior is the outgrowth of democratic and modern values, as well as pagan gods.[45]

One of the convictions that has continued to deepen within me as I have studied the Holocaust these many years under the tutelage of colleagues such as Mosse and Greenberg and within a framework of reflection provided by the likes of liturgist David Power and ethicist Reinhold Niebuhr is that moral sensitivity remains an indispensable prelude to moral reasoning. We ethicists can provide the necessary clarifications of human response mandated by such sensitivity. Such clarifications are absolutely essential if religious experience is not to degenerate into religious fanaticism. But, as an ethicist, I cannot create the sensitivity itself. Mere appeals to reason, authority, and/or natural law will prove ineffective by themselves. Such sensitivity will re-emerge only through a new awareness of God's intimate link with humankind, in suffering and joy, through symbolic experience. Nothing short of this will suffice in light of the Holocaust.

I see an urgent need to counter the growing one-dimensionality in Western society in the midst of a growing awareness of human power and freedom through the development of a new moral sensitivity. This moral sensitivity must be engendered by a symbolic encounter with the Creator God, who speaks to us in a new compelling way, along the lines I outlined in the first part of this essay. Strange as it may seem, the Holocaust provides us with some help in this regard. For if the Holocaust reveals one permanent quality of human life, it is the enduring presence of, the ongoing need for, symbolic communication. Mothers often sang to their children in the camps up till the door of the gas chambers. Camp music and camp songs were vital to survival for the inmates as well as a source of defiance to the evil all around them.[46] But we must be clear: the experience of the vitalistic in our life is no guarantee of goodness. As Didier Pollefeyt observed, "Creativity . . . does not automatically generate goodness. Sometimes aesthetics and crimes coincide. Some Nazis, for example, read poetry after their duty."[47] And clearly public ritual played a central role in the implementation of Nazi ideology. That is why the text and structure of liturgy become so significant.

Although many experiences of prayer and meditation may be vitalistically energizing, they remain neutral in terms of human responsibility in the social arena, because there are no directional texts connected with them. Regrettably, in the West, ritual has often been relegated almost exclusively to the realm of play and recreation. Yet it is the power inherent in this vitalistic side of humanity that ritual has the greatest potential for channeling into an intensification of human responsibility.

In light of the Holocaust we can no longer afford to give scant attention to the vitalistic dimension of humanity, to reduce it simply to the realm of play and recreation, if we hope to develop the sense of human responsibility to which the Holocaust summons us. The development of moral reasoning remains crucial—but it is no substitute for the healing of the destructive tendencies in humanity's vitalistic side with required symbolic encounter with a loving God. Without ritual containment of the vitalistic dimension of human life, human responsibility cannot grow.

Conclusion

My reflections have primarily focused on the more overarching moral implications of the Holocaust, implications that require continued attention as we begin a new millennium. But I would be remiss if I completely overlooked the significance of the Holocaust as a central moment in the long, generally conflictual history of the Christian-Jewish relationship. Emphasizing the more general moral implications of the Holocaust can never allow us to overlook its more specific moral dimensions. While the churches and some church leaders and members did respond to the Jewish catastrophe, far too many stood on the sidelines—and some even actively collaborated with the effort. If the churches are to press the general moral implications of the Holocaust that I have outlined, they can only do so with credibility in the world community if they first confront their pronounced failure during this critical era. While I would affirm the argument made by important scholars that the Nazi attack on the Jews represented a quantum leap beyond classical Christian anti-Semitism, there is no denying that a significant link existed between the two forms of anti-Semitism. Historically the Christian church tried to marginalize the Jews and render them perpetually miserable as a punishment for their supposed killing of Christ and as a warning of what will happen to those who stray from the Christian path. The Nazis' goal was total annihilation of the world Jewish community. We cannot lose sight of the difference. But on the popular level especially, traditional Christian anti-Semitism provided an indispensable seedbed for the considerable success achieved by the Nazis in pursuit of the goal.

The Vatican document *We Remember* goes a long way in moving Catholicism toward a confrontation with its role during the Holocaust. It may yet make a profound difference if its call for Holocaust education throughout the Catholic world is heeded. But one of its significant failures is to connect complicity in the Holocaust on the part of Catholic individuals with the tradition of Christian anti-Semitism. The "wayward brothers and sisters" in terms of anti-Semitism indicted in this document went astray not because of some marginal teachers but because degradation of the Jews was commonplace in the preaching, catechesis, and church art that was the ordinary fare of their life in the Church. This is not clearly enough recognized in *We Remember,* although Cardinal Cassidy, principal author of the document, in a subsequent commentary on the text does do better in making the direct linkage.[48]

The churches must be prepared to take direct responsibility for their role in forming the prevailing negative image of Jews and Judaism over the centuries in Western society, an image which directly contributed to popular acquiescence and even outright support for Nazism despite the fact that the roots of its ideology lay elsewhere. It is insufficient for the churches merely to point to the difference between Christian anti-Semitism and the Nazi variety. If they are to restore their moral integrity and become strong supporters of the new depth of human responsibility to which the experience of the Holocaust calls humankind in the twenty-first century, they must first come to grips with their general failure in moral responsibility toward Hitler's victims, particularly the Jews. Nothing else will suffice. Anything short of this will make appeals for enhanced general moral responsibility ring hollow.

In closing, I repeat my initial assertion: studying the details of the Holocaust and continuing to memorialize its victims remains a sacred task. But we shall ultimately fail the victims of the Nazis if we do not choose life over death, as Deuteronomy instructs us, by wrestling with the ultimate ideological implication of Nazism for our time. In the Slovak Pavilion at Expo 2000 in Hannover, Germany, there was a powerful film that is in part based on the Holocaust. The film's title asks a question that remains our question after the Holocaust: QUO VADIS HUMANITY?

NOTES

1. Victor Ferkiss, *The Future of Technological Civilization* (New York: George Braziller, 1974), p. 88.

2. Hans Jonas, *The Imperative of Responsibility* (Chicago: University of Chicago Press, 1984). Jonas has also reflected on the ethical implications of the Holocaust, but regrettably has never integrated these separate reflections. See Hans Jonas, *Mortality and Morality: A Search for the Good after Auschwitz* (Evanston, Ill.: Northwestern University Press, 1996), and Hans Jonas, "The Concept of God after Auschwitz: A Jewish Voice," *Journal of Religion* (January 1987), pp. 143–157.

3. See John T. Pawlikowski, O.S.M., *The Challenge of the Holocaust for Christian Theology* (New York: Anti-Defamation League, 1982); John T. Pawlikowski, "Christian Theological Concerns after the Holocaust," in Eugene J. Fisher, ed., *Visions of the Other: Jewish and Christian Theologians Assess the Dialogue* (New York/Mahwah: Paulist, 1994), p. 285, 1; and John T. Pawlikowski, "Christian Ethics and the Holocaust: A Dialogue with Post-Auschwitz Judaism," *Theological Studies* (December 1988), pp. 649–669.

4. Emil Fackenheim, *The Jewish Return into History* (New York: Schocken Books, 1978), p. 246.

5. See John T. Pawlikowski, "Uniqueness and Universality in the Holocaust: Some Ethical Reflections," in Linda Bennett Elder, David L. Barr, and Elizabeth Struthers Malbon, eds., *Biblical and Human: A Festschrift for John R. Priest* (Atlanta: Scholars Press, 1996), pp. 275–289.

6. Uriel Tal, "Forms of Pseudo-Religion in the German Culturbereich Prior to the Holocaust," *Imannual* 3 (1973–1974), p. 69; and Uriel Tal, *Christians and Jews in Germany: Religion, Politics, and Ideology in the Second Reich, 1870–1914* (Ithaca: Cornell University Press, 1975).

7. Irving Greenberg, "The Voluntary Covenant," *Perspectives #3* (New York: National Jewish Resource Center, 1982), p. 15.

8. Irving Greenberg, "The Voluntary Covenant," pp. 17–18.

9. Irving Greenberg, "The Third Great Cycle in Jewish History," *Perspectives #1* (New York: National Jewish Resource Center, 1981), pp. 24–25.

10. For the texts of Pope John Paul II's Encyclical *Laborem Exercens* (On Human Work) and the U.S. Catholic bishops' *Pastoral Letter on the Economy*, see David J. O'Brien and Thomas A. Shannon, eds., *Catholic Social Thought: The Documentary Heritage* (Maryknoll, N.Y.: Orbis Books, 1992), pp. 350–392; 572–680. For the text of the U.S. bishops' statement on the energy, see Hugh J. Nolan, ed., *Pastoral Letters of the United States Catholic Bishops, vol. IV, 1975–1983* (Washington, D.C.: NCCB/USCC, 1983), pp. 438–463. For the text of the Canadian bishops' statement on the Canadian economy, see David M. Byers, ed., *General Introduction and Document Introductions* by John T. Pawlikowski, O.S.M., *Justice in the Marketplace: Collected Statement of the the Vatican and the United States Catholic Bishops on Economic Policy, 1891–1984* (Washington, D.C.: USCC, 1985), pp. 480–491.

11. David Hartman, *A Living Covenant: The Innovative Spirit in Traditional Judaism* (New York: Free Press and London: Collier Macmillan Publishers, 1985).

12. John T. Pawlikowski, "Co-Creators with a Compelling God," *Ecumenism* (June 1999), pp. 8–11.

13. Philip J. Hefner, *The Human Factor: Evolution, Culture and Religion* (Minneapolis: Fortress, 1993); see also John T. Pawlikowski, O.S.M., "Theological Dimensions of an Ecological Ethic," in Richard N. Fragomeni and John T. Pawlikowski, eds., *The Ecological Challenge: Ethical, Liturgical, and Spiritual Responses* (Collegeville, Minn.: Liturgical Press, 1994), pp. 39–51.

14. Stanley Hauerwas, "Jews and Christians among the Nations," *Cross Currents* (Spring 1981), p. 34.

15. Michael Ryan, "Hitler's Challenge to the Churches: A Theological-Political Analysis of *Mein Kampf*," in Franklin Littell and Hubert G. Locke, eds., *The German Church Struggle and the Holocaust* (Detroit: Wayne State University Press, 1974), pp. 160–161.

16. Jürgen Moltmann, *The Crucified God* (New York: Harper & Row, 1974).
17. See John T. Pawlikowski, O.S.M., "Catholicism and the Public Church: Recent U.S. Developments," in D. M. Yeager, ed., *The Annual of the Society of Christian Ethics 1989*, pp. 147–165; and "Walking with and beyond John Courtney Murray," *New Theology Review* (August 1996), pp. 20–40.
18. Clyde L. Manschreck, "Church-State Relations: A Question of Sovereignty," in Clyde L. Manschreck and Barbara Brown Zikmund, eds., *The American Religoius Experiment: Piety and Practicality* (Chicago: Exploration Press, 1976), p. 121.
19. Romano Guardini, *Power and Responsibility* (Chicago: Henry Regnery, 1961), p. xiii.
20. Peter J. Haas, *Morality after Auschwitz: The Radical Challenge* (Philadelphia: Fortress, 1988); also "The Morality of Auschwitz: Moral Language and the Nazi Ethic," in Franklin Littell and others, eds., *Remembering for the Future,* vol. 2 (Oxford: Pergamon, 1989), pp. 1893–1902.
21. See Peter J. Haas, "Fare etica in un'eta di scienza," in Emilio Baccarini and Lucy Thorson, eds., *Il Bene e il Male dopo Auschwitz: Implicazioni Etico-Theologiche per l'oggi* (Milano: Paoline, 1998), p. 176. An English version of this volume will appear soon from KTAV.
22. Peter Haas, "Fare etica in un'eta di scienza," pp. 176–177.
23. Didier Pollefeyt, "Ma Moralità di Auschwitz? Confronto critico con l'interpretazione etica dell'Olocausto di Peter J. Haas," in Emilio Baccarini and Lucy Thorson, eds., *Il Bene e il Male dopo Auschwitz,* p. 204.
24. See Peter Hayes, *Industry and Ideology: I. G. Farben in the Nazi Era* (Cambridge: Cambridge University Press, 1988); and "Profits and Persecution: German Big Business and the Holocaust," (Washington, D.C.: Center for Advanced Holocaust Studies, United States Holocaust Memorial Museum, 1998).
25. Peter Hayes, "Conscience, Knowledge, and 'Secondary Ethics': German Corporate Executives from 'Aryanization' to the Holocaust." Paper presented to the 1999 Bernardin Center Catholic-Jewish Studies

Conference, Catholic Theological Union, Chicago, May 4, 1999, p. 25. Pubished as part of this volume.

26. Peter Hayes, "Conscience, Knowledge, and 'Secondary Ethics,'" p. 25.

27. Peter Hayes, "Conscience, Knowledge, and 'Secondary Ethics,'" p. 26.

28. Pope John Paul II, "Respect for Human Rights: The Secret of True Peace," 1999 World Day of Peace Message, *Origins* (December 24, 1998), p. 491.

29. Zbigniew Brzezinski, "Global Dilemmas Democracy Faces," *Origins* (September 3, 1998), p. 210.

30. For more on the Catholic human rights tradition, see my articles "Human Rights in the Roman Catholic Tradition," in Max Stackhouse, ed., *Selected Papers: The American Society of Christian Ethics 1979*, pp. 145–166, and "Liberal Democracy, Human Rights, and the Holocaust: The Political and Historical Context of Pope Pius XII," *Catholic International* (October 1998), pp. 454–458.

31. There were some individual Catholic leaders who did call for reconciliation between Catholicism and the emerging liberal tradition. They gererally were marginalized in the Catholic Church and in some cases left the Church entirely. See Thomas Bokenkotter, *Church and Revolution: Catholics in the Struggle for Democracy and Social Justice* (New York: Doubleday, An Image Book, 1998).

32. See Michael R. Marrus, "The Vatican and the Holocaust," *Congress Monthly* (January 1988), p. 6.

33. Michael R. Marrus, "The Vatican and the Holocaust," p. 7.

34. Nora Levin, *The Holocaust* (New York: Schocken, 1973), p. 693.

35. Richard Lukas, *Forgotten Holocaust: The Poles under German Occupation 1939–1944* (Lexington: University Press of Kentucky, 1986), p. 16.

36. John Morley, *Vatican Diplomacy and the Jews during the Holocaust: 1939–1943*.

37. See Thomas Bokenkotter, *Church and Revolution*, chapters 1–4.

38. Cardinal Joseph L. Bernardin, *A Blessing to Each Other* (Chicago: Liturgy Training Publications, 1996), p. 132.

39. Donald Dietrich, *God and Humanity in Auschwitz: Jewish-Christian Relations and Sanctioned Murder* (New Brunswick, N.J. and London: Transaction, 1995), p. 269.

40. See Gordon Zahn, *German Catholics and Hitler's Wars: A Study in Social Control* (New York: Sheed & Ward, 1962).

41. Gordon Zahn, "Catholic Resistance? A Yes and a No," in Franklin Littell and Hubert G. Locke, eds., *The German Church Struggle and the Holocaust* (Detroit: Wayne State University Press, 1974), pp. 234–235.

42. See my "Liturgy and the Holocaust: How Do We Worship in an age of Genocide?" Paper presented to a conference on Holocaust and Genocide, Boston College, September 17, 1999.

43. See J. L. Talmon, "European History—Seedbed of the Holocaust," *Midstream* (May 1973), pp. 22–24.

44. See George Mosse, *The Nationalization of the Masses: Political Symbolism and Mass Movements in Germany from the Napoleonic Wars through the Third Reich* (New York: New American Library, 1977).

45. Irving Greenberg, "Cloud of Smoke, Pillar of Fire: Judaism, Christianity and Modernity after the Holocaust," in Eva Fleischner, ed., *Auschwitz: Beginning of a New Era?* (New York: KATV, 1977), p. 17.

46. See David H. Hirsch, "Camp Music and Camp Songs: Szymon Laks and Aleksander Kulisiewicz," in G. Jan Colijn and Marcia Sachs Littell, eds., *Confonting the Holocaust: A Mandate for the 21st Century* (Lanham/New York/Oxford: University Press of America, 1997), pp. 157–168.

47. Didier Pollefeyt, "Auschwitz or How Good People Can Do Evil: An Ethical Interpretation of the Perpetrators and Victims of the Holocaust in Light of the French Thinker Tzvetan Todorov," in G. Jan Colijn and Marcia Sachs Littell, eds., *Confonting the Holocaust*, p. 108.

48. See my essay, "The Vatican and the Holocaust: Putting *We Remember* in Context," *Dimensions* 12:2, pp. 11–16; see also Secretariat for Ecumencial and Interreligious Relations, *Catholics Remember the Holocaust* (Washington, D.C.: USCC, 1998).

12

The Ethics of Nazi Human Experimentation: Contemporary Concerns

JOHN J. MICHALCZYK

Tuskegee syphilis tests (Oak Ridge, Tennessee), radiation experiments (Dachau hypothermia research), and radium-laced cereal experimentation at the Fernald School (Waltham, Massachusetts)—all have as a bottom line the unethical and inhuman treatment of individuals for the supposed advancement of society and the betterment of our world. At the crux of these experiments, and at the focus of this essay, is the distorted belief that a violation of an individual's personal, human, and even legal rights is acceptable when a greater good is to be attained. Our case study will be the history of the evolution of Nazi policy from racial theory to human experimentation and even to outright genocide.

Fifty years after the liberation of the concentration camps, we still face the issues of an uncompensated slave labor force, art stolen from Jews by Nazis, Swiss complicity with the Third Reich, profiteering insurance companies, and the accumulation of Nazi gold, among others. All of these raise serious moral and legal concerns. In the realm of medicine, our present focus, we are obliged to ask: Have we really put all of this behind us half a century ago, and are there still similar ethical concerns today?

In Western culture, at least from the time of Hippocrates, the doctor was viewed as the healer of society. A cautionary principle in the oath stated that "he must do no harm."[1] He held the prestigious god-like position of the one who negotiates between life and death. Yet, how could the doctors, scientists, and leading intellectuals in the Third Reich, from 1933 to 1945, not only *not* heal but be *instrumental* in the torture and death of hundreds of thousands of Jews, Gypsies, homosexuals, and political prisoners?[2] This is the paradox of a history of a German medical society that indeed represented the best and the brightest in the Weimar Republic just preceding the Reich. Its development of the most proficient medical technology and its innovative treatments and procedures put it at the pinnacle of scientific advancement in its day.

The Nuremberg Physician's Trial of 1946–1947, however, showed that the doctors and scientists especially involved with human experimentation may have had a high regard for science, but in the end had a cruel callous, disregard for human life as lived by certain groups of people, who, in the final analysis, were considered dispensable.[3] Our analysis of the historical situation may help us understand this tragic development of a mindset that morally set back medicine for centuries.

Those doctors and scientists at Nuremberg, convicted of war crimes and crimes against humanity, did not develop their rationale of human experimentation in a vacuum. Their mindset was the final stage of a gradual, almost imperceptible evolution of attitudes, beliefs, philosophies, and policies. It had its roots in the turn-of-the-century international movement of eugenics, the science, or some say a pseudoscience, of well-being. At the beginning of the century, some thirty countries, such as Germany, America, France, England, and others, were represented in the eugenics movement by their leading scholars who believed they could create a perfect society.[4] They would be proactive, for example, by adapting sterilization laws to prevent the mentally deficient from reproducing. The intention of these intellectuals was to engineer society in a neo-Darwinian social fashion so that the fittest survive.[5]

It would not be long before the Germans took the basic principles of eugenics and the essence of the sterilization laws of twenty-four American states to forge the racial policies that led to national sterilization of the unfit in German society.[6] Two Germans were crucial in this evolution from racial policy to action, as the disciplines of anthropology and biology began to contribute their findings to research in racial theory: Eugen Fischer, director of the Kaiser Wilhelm Institute of Anthropology in Berlin, helped train SS physicians in the principles of race hygiene. Fritz Lenz, a prominent German racial hygienist, praised Hitler in 1930 as "the first politician of great import who has taken racial hygiene as a serious element of state policy."[7] In a type of medical apotheosis, Hitler himself would become "the great doctor of the German people."[8]

In the United States, the American-Nazi connection came with the work of Harry Laughlin, a strong proponent of eugenics and racial theory. For his work, he was awarded an honorary doctoral degree in 1933 from the University of Heidelberg.[9]

When the Nazi government took power in 1933, it attempted to create a whole new world order—a healthy biocracy that had no place for the unfit. The doctors and scientists were mobilized to establish this order.

One of the first steps to purify the race was the "Law for the Prevention of Hereditary Disease" of July 14, 1933. In order to prevent inferior physically and mentally deficient individuals from "proliferating" and "contaminating" the Aryan race, the government called upon the medical profession to aid in the implementation of the policy. Under the guise of helping to restore health to society, doctors could now compulsorily sterilize patients who suffered from epilepsy, schizophrenia, and feeblemindedness.[10]

In 1935, the racist Nuremberg Laws, which called for the protection of German blood and German honor, added non-Aryans, specifically Jews, to the "unfit." These laws prohibited marriages between Jews and Aryans, as well as limited other civil rights of Jews. Within a short time, Jewish doctors were eliminated from the practice of medicine, often for both anti-Semitic and economic reasons.[11] The latter financial motivation was most understandable to Aryan doctors who were still not quite out of the bind of the post-Versailles Treaty's drastic recession and the Great Depression. Virulent anti-Semitic stereotypes of the "capitalist" and "international oriented" Jewish doctor abounded, especially in Julius Streicher's *Der Stürmer*.

A next step that the doctors took toward creating the perfect society was *euthanasia*. In August 1939, a month prior to World War II, an ordinance required that physicians and midwives report newborn babies with deformities. This marks the formal beginning of the euthanasia of unfit children. In order to give mercy killing a rationale, Hitler sent a letter in October 1939 (backdated to September 1, 1939) to Doctors Karl Brandt and Philip Bouhler that tied euthanasia to the war effort. With time, more and more Nazi doctors became linked to the biological cleansing system.[12] Doctors and psychiatrists distributed questionnaires and filled out diagnoses targeting those that required mercy killing. This process progressed through the ranks of the medical staff across Germany, but especially at mental hospitals. Euthanasia films at this time, especially *Erb Krank* on hereditary racial sickness, linked this task with saving Germany millions of Reichsmarks, first to put into other sectors of German society, and then, after 1939, into the war effort. Economics became more important than the rights of the handicapped.

Through law and practice, the mentally retarded and severely handicapped were gassed at six euthanasia centers such as Hadamar or Hartheim. Deformed children were starved to death in an isolated ward or given a lethal injection. Nurses and doctors worked efficiently to advance the process, writing up false death certificates to be sent to unsuspecting family members at home. Instructions for this came from the T-4 doctors and researchers at the Kaiser Wilhelm Institute in Berlin, named for their address, 4 Tiergarten Strasse.[13] In 1941, Catholic bishop Count von Galen and Father Bernard Lichtenberg protested euthanasia of mental patients, which helped stop the process nationally, while it continued regionally.

Following the Wannsee Conference of January 20, 1942, where steps were taken to provide "the final solution to the Jewish question," the experienced Nazi doctors were mobilized once again. This time, in light of their knowledge of euthanasia through lethal injection and gassing, they were instructed to carry the process eastward. Some of the doctors' expertise would be used first at Chemlno, where the gassing was done with "primitive" techniques. Jews, Romani people (Gypsies), Slavs, and homosexuals soon became targets for incarceration and many for death. The doctors and scientists were proficient in rebuilding the gassing chambers and determining the necessary quantities of Zyklon-B gas to order from German factories. The doctors at the death chambers awaited their clientele—who would soon arrive from the Polish ghettoes of Warsaw, Lodz, Krakow, and other European cities.

The doctors and engineers saw to it that the gas chambers and crematoria functioned efficiently. They regulated the correct amounts of pellets, and following the gassing, the medical staff insured clinically that the victims were indeed dead.

At the crux of our focus here is the ethical concern about the use of human experimentation in the concentration camps. The camp prisoners who were not gassed immediately were experimented upon to serve as useful subjects for the advancement of German science. Although there existed a mindset that these Jews and Roma were an inferior race that had to be exterminated like lice to create a healthier society, the doctors at the selection ramps gave certain ones a reprieve. They believed that these select prisoners would die eventually, so why not use them pragmatically to advance their medical research.

What types of research was conducted on these unfortunate victims? What were the motivating factors? How did they justify their unethical procedures? Let us look at several representative examples of human experimentation.[14]

- The most notorious was, as Dr. Jay Katz states in the PBS-TV documentary *In the Shadow of the Reich: Nazi Medicine,* Dr. Mengele's fifteen hundred sets of twins.[15] At Auschwitz, many of these twins were spared the gas chamber because of Mengele's comparison of medical data of each set of twins. Hour after hour these young children were subject to countless painful and at times lethal tests. Normally if one twin died, the other would be found useless and then eliminated. In January 1995, I visited Auschwitz, specifically the areas where experimentation was carried out, accompanied by Dr. Hans Munch, a former SS doctor, and one of the Mengele twins, Eva Mozes Kor, a survivor of the experiments. Echoes of the pain and death of the experimentees can still be heard there.
- The Dachau hypothermia experiments were designed to determine how long a person could endure frigid temperatures before expiring. These were performed to determine how much time a rescue team had to pull a downed German pilot from the freezing seawater. In the *New England Journal of Medicine* (1990), Dr. Robert Berger of Boston's Beth

Israel Hospital discussed at great length the science and morality of
using the results of these experiments today. His conclusion is that the
real issue is not the morality of using tainted data but the fact that it was
dismally poor science, as in many other situations of experimentation
where data were falsified to impress supervisors or Nazi officials.[16]

- At Neuengamme concentration camp, Dr. Kurt Heissmeyer conducted
  unethical lymph gland experiments on twenty Jewish children, ages
  five to twelve. Those who did not die in the experiment were killed on
  April 20, 1945. Robert Jay Lifton, in *The Nazi Doctors,* notes that ironically after the war, Dr. Heissmeyer returned to his hometown of
  Magdeburg "where he was highly regarded as a lung and tuberculosis
  specialist."[17]

- Dr. Karl Claussburg's experiments in sterilization at Auschwitz's
  Barrack 10 were excruciatingly painful. Hoping to make new surgical
  advances in sterilization procedures, he performed these operations on
  unsuspecting women, often without anesthesia. These unfortunate victims bore this mutilation for life. We interviewed Nazi SS doctor Hans
  Munch directly in front of this building, and he graphically discussed
  the pain of these women as they unknowingly underwent these experimental operations.

- Eye experiments were brutally painful as well. Using the racial myth of
  the blue-eyed Aryan, doctors attempted to change the color of the
  cornea from brown to blue. Temporary or permanent blindness was
  normally the result.[18]

Needless to say, the subjects of these human experimentations were not
voluntary, nor were they informed of the gravity of the procedures. As the
prosecutors at the physician's trial in 1946–1947 weighed evidence against
the unethical experimentation practiced by the Nazi doctors, they helped produce a document that serves as a foundation for human experimentation
today. These ten principles of the Nuremberg Code outline for us the ethical
concerns involved in current experimentation.[19] Central to this code is the
voluntary and *informed* consent of the patient.

The practice of medicine in Nazi Germany is a far cry from the principles of the Hippocratic oath, especially as the doctor is obliged "to do no harm." Medicine in the Third Reich was a brief hiatus in the history of the medical profession. The doctors who performed the experiments and were tried for war crimes and crimes against humanity were not just recent graduates of medical school. They were well advanced in the medical profession. They were career oriented and were trained during a period in which eugenic and racial theories provided a mindset for future medical work. It leads us to ask exactly what the basic principles of medicine were in the Weimar Republic, prior to the Third Reich, and how they could be gradually co-opted in the service of the Reich.

It is perhaps shocking for some to hear bioethicist Arthur Caplan in the documentary on Nazi medicine say that the Nazi doctors did follow their conscience in their mission to heal an ailing Germany. We see with 20/20 vision in hindsight, unfortunately, that forming and following their conscience, German doctors did travel the ill-fated path to genocide. We are obliged to ask how we as individuals and as a society situated concretely in our culture shape our personal and collective conscience. In our day-to-day judgments, we do not have the luxury to look in a critical way in hindsight at what is morally right or wrong. Rather, we are in the midst of the decision-making processes and must rely on certain guidelines so that we are not trapped by current driving forces, be they governmental or technological.

Allow me to offer a few reflections that might guide our future discussion and decision making. One of the starting points that could be used in our dialogue about present ethical guidelines comes from Albert Einstein: "Science can only ascertain what is, but not what should be, and outside of its domain value judgments of all kinds remain necessary." Our stumbling block in an age of mind-boggling technological advances centers on the issue of "what should be," which has a strong ethical resonance today.

To contrast our situation with that of the Third Reich, we can readily understand that the Nazi ideology was based on a racial philosophy of the ruling government. It promoted an elitist vision of creating a new world order from the top down. The value system of the Germany of the late thirties was established by policy and propaganda, with the government determining what was good for German society. In this way, following orders was the manner in which one shaped conscience.

As we look at today's medical landscape, we have greater latitude in policy and direction. We are not ruled by a government that links medicine with racist policies, nor one that considers certain groups dispensable or inferior.[20] Instead, we live in a society that has become more and more technologically complex, yet where policies have been only recently more sensitive to the marginalized, for example, regarding the handicapped, which are based on more *inclusion* than the exclusion witnessed in early American eugenics and Nazi racial policies. Given the complexity and potential for error or abuse of humans in experiments, the government does take precautionary measures to insure that we not deviate from well-founded ethical principles.

The American system dealing with medicine and health care is driven by self-determination on one hand, and by the market and financial status of our society on the other. In terms of experimentation, some of the issues lie in private funding and corporate investment, which in a way provide for and drive the market for greater experimentation. With more refined technologies, we have been able to do very critical experimentation, whether it be with the adult sheep Dolly at the Roslin Institute in Scotland on February 24, 1997, through somatic cell nuclear transfer or the cloning of three goats at Tufts University in Boston in the spring of 1999. We are scientifically capable of doing these experiments with substantial results, but we need to ask if we are advancing along ethical paths?

Today we have to raise some of the same concerns about the individuals' human and legal rights as in the past, but with a greater emphasis on our current societal needs. This would be true especially with respect to human experimentation, cloning, genetic engineering, and health care. To get an honest reflection of our society that will be judged critically in the future, we have to hold up a mirror to it today. We can do it, for example, with the image of health care and human experimentation in mind.

In terms of health care, all we have to do is look at the most *vulnerable* members of our society and how they are treated: the sick, the homeless, and the elderly.[21] In the past we had placed these individuals on the periphery of health care and support, while today we legislate on their behalf, for example, through organizations such as TASH (The Agency for the Severely Handicapped). Very practically speaking, the government, if it is to promote social equality, has to continue to call for the equal distribution of health care, determining what are the basic needs of a member of our society. We have to begin a deeper grassroots response to learn and then to advise those individuals and institutions that control the distribution of health care.

In terms of experimentation from abortion pills to AIDS testing, we are obligated to continue to abide by principles of the Nuremberg Code and place strong emphasis on the *informed*, voluntary consent of the patients. This is in stark contrast to the experiments detailed earlier.[22]

As we considered the evolution of medicine and science from 1933 to 1945 in Nazi Germany, from racial theory to human experimentation, we can say that the doctors allowed themselves to proceed along the dangerous slippery slope that terminated in genocide. For some, like Dr. Hans Munch, it was for economic advancement and status; for others, it was a desire to create a healthier society through the advancement of science; and for others still, it was in direct allegiance to a racist government that would help eliminate the unhealthy members of society. How will future generations judge us by way of our motivation in health policies, for example, traveling the slippery slope?

Although as a freethinking and self-determined society we are reluctant to say that the slippery slope argument is operative today, we must be realistic in noting its potential. In terms of medical experimentation or genetic engineering, we have asked "Although we can, should we?" Where the trust of the German society was placed in the hands of the bureaucracy, our trust is in technology, for example, reproductive technologies.

Given this dependence on the salvific power of technology, we have to ask about the social context of our choices. Ian Barbour, in his *Ethics in an Age of Technology*, examines the contrast between selections of desirable genes, not too far afield from some of the Nazi experimentation on blue eyes and brown eyes, and the alleviation of disabilities through germ-line therapy that would correct a defect.[23] For those who call up the ghosts of eugenics, we could make an argument for a distinction between "making an improvement" and "correcting a defect."

Our analysis of medicine in the service of the Third Reich serves well as a case study for the need to develop sound ethical norms that will help carry us through the complex issues of genetic engineering, later-term abortions, euthanasia, reproductive technology, long-term medical care, and even HMOs today.[24] In every situation that occurs, it is the health and welfare of the individual that should take precedence over the demands of a society or political system. We learn from the bitter past to make decisions for today, with an eye on a healthier future for our society.

NOTES

1. The Hippocratic oath is reproduced in John J. Michalczyk, ed. *Medicine, Ethics, and the Third Reich: Historical and Contemporary Issues* (Kansas City, Mo.: Sheed and Ward, 1994), p. 219.
2. Robert Jay Lifton, in *The Nazi Doctors: Medical Killing and the Psychology of Genocide* (New York: Basic Books, 1986), was one of the early researchers who attributed this almost schizophrenic behavior to the psychological principle of "doubling."
3. See the collected essays in Part II of George J. Annas and Michael A. Grodin, *The Nazi Doctors and the Nuremberg Code* (New York: Oxford University Press, 1992), pp. 61–144.
4. Read Ian Robert Dowbiggin, "Conclusion: Reflections on the History of Eugenics," in *Keeping America Sane* (Ithaca, N.Y.: Cornell University Press, 1997), pp. 232–240. Diane B. Paul, *Controlling Human Heredity: 1865 to the Present* (Atlantic Highlands, N.J.: Humanities Press, 1995) is a very readable, illustrated overview of eugenics and its current implications.
5. Consult Troy Duster, *Backdoor to Eugenics* (New York: Routledge, 1990), in which Duster maintains that today we have directly or indirectly inherited the eugenics concerns of the 1920s and 1930s in certain public health policy issues such as health screening at workplaces, prenatal diagnoses, and the creation of sperm banks.
6. Robert Proctor of Penn State University has thoroughly researched the area of Nazi racial theory. For his detailed findings, see *Racial Hygiene: Medicine Under the Nazis* (Cambridge, Mass.: Harvard University Press, 1988). For a succinct analysis of racial medical policies, see his "Racial Hygiene: The Collaboration of Medicine and Nazism," in Michalczyk, *Medicine, Ethics, and the Third Reich,* pp. 35–41.
7. Quoted in Proctor's article, "Nazi Doctors, Racial Medicine, and Human Experimentation," in Annas and Grodin, *The Nazi Doctors and the Nuremberg Code,* p. 19.
8. Proctor, p. 19.

9. See Stefan Kuhl, *The Nazi Connection: Eugenics, American Racism, and German National Socialism* (New York: Oxford University Press, 1994) and Benno Muller-Hill, "Eugenics: The Science and Religion of the Nazis," in Arthur L. Caplan, *When Medicine Went Mad: Bioethics and the Holocaust* (Totowa, N.J.: Humana Press, 1992), pp. 43–52.

10. Daniel Nadav shows the evolution of policies that connect racial theory with genocide in his article, "Sterilization, 'Euthanasia,' and the Holocaust—the Brutal Chain," in Michalczyk, *Medicine, Ethics, and the Third Reich,* pp. 42–49.

11. See Michael H. Kater, "An Historical and Contemporary View of Jewish Doctors in Germany," in Michalczyk, *Medicine, Ethics, and the Third Reich,* pp. 161–166. Kater offers a more detailed study of the medical situation in Germany in *Doctors under Hitler* (Chapel Hill, N.C.: University of North Carolina Press, 1989).

12. For a very detailed analysis of Nazi medicine with concerns about present health care related cases, see Götz Aly, Peter Chroust, and Christian Pross, *Cleansing the Fatherland: Nazi Medicine and Racial Hygiene* (Baltimore: Johns Hopkins University Press, 1994).

13. See Götz Aly, "Medicine Against the Useless," in Aly, Chroust, and Pross, *Cleansing the Fatherland,* pp. 22–98.

14. Dr. Jay Katz of Yale University Law School has provided a most extensive study of human experimentation in *Experimentation with Human Beings: The Authority of the Investigator, Subject, Professions, and State in the Human Experimental Process* (New York: Russell Sage Foundation, 1972).

15. First Run Features, distributor, New York, 1997. See also Eva Kor's testimony about being a subject of Mengele's experiments in "The Personal, Public, and Political Dimensions of Being a Mengele Guinea Pig," in Michalczyk, *Medicine, Ethics, and the Third Reich,* pp. 101–105, and "The Mengele Twins and Human Experimentation: A Personal Account," in Annas and Grodin, *The Nazi Doctors and the Nuremberg Code,* pp. 53–59. Robert Jay Lifton discusses the larger context of the Mengele experiments in *The Nazi Doctors,* pp. 347–356.

16. Dr. Berger's *New England Journal of Medicine* article on the Dachau experiments is reproduced in Michalczyk, *Medicine, Ethics, and the Third Reich*, pp. 87–100. See also, Robert S. Pozos, "Scientific Inquiry and Ethics: The Dachau Data," in Caplan's *When Medicine Went Mad*, pp. 95–108.

17. Lifton, p. 457.

18. These eye experiments are discussed by ophthamologist Dr. Paul Vinger in our documentary, *In the Shadow of the Reich: Nazi Medicine.*

19. The ten principles of the Nuremberg Code are reprinted in Annas and Grodin, *The Nazi Doctors and the Nuremberg Code*, p. 2.

20. For a personal and yet historical study of the handicapped, see Hugh Gallagher, *By Trust Betrayed: Patients, Physicians, and the License to Kill in the Third Reich* (New York: Holt and Co., 1990).

21. Statistics in 1999 note that forty-four million Americans are not insured, primarily the immigrants, unemployed, youths, and the elderly.

22. See G. Annas, L. Glantz, and B. F. Katz, *Informed Consent to Human Experimentation: The Subject's Dilemma* (Cambridge, Mass.: Bollinger, 1977).

23. Ian G. Barbour, *Ethics in an Age of Technology* (San Francisco: Harper Collins, 1993).

24. On the ethics of health care, see George Anders, *Health Against Wealth: HMOs and the Breakdown of Medical Trust* (Boston: Houghton Mifflin, 1996); Michael L. Millenson, *Demanding Medical Excellence: Doctors and Accountability in the Information Age* (Chicago: University of Chicago Press, 1997).

13

Medical Ethics in Light of the Holocaust: A Response

PETER J. HAAS

One of the stunning aspects of the Holocaust is the readiness of so many well-educated, professional people to buy into the Nazi myth and to go on to commit unspeakable atrocities in its name. This is especially a problem for people in professions we would expect to be the natural sources of opposition—lawyers, theologians, and physicians. In fact, physicians present a special problem because they were members of the most likely professional group to be able to offer a counterbalance to the pseudoscientific claims of the Nazis as regards racial differentiation. That physicians could condone, and even take an active part in, the waging of racial warfare against their friends, colleagues, and neighbors presents, in my mind, one of the most significant challenges for our understanding of how the Holocaust could take place. It also raises in a most pointed fashion the question of professional and medical ethics, since physicians played such a central role in designing and carrying out some of the most atrocious elements of the Holocaust: the selections and the medical experiments.

It is important to state at the outset that this is more than a problem of just *the* physicians or *the* medical profession or even *the* Nazis. The complicity of the medical profession was the aggregate result of thousands of individual decisions. It was a case of physician after individual physician making his (and almost all were male) peace with the Nazi genocide. It is not so much the failure of the profession as of its many constituents. The medical aspects of the Holocaust were the result of the aggregate of many single decisions to turn from professional healers to professional killers.

To approach the problem in medical ethics that this collapse of professional and moral collapse represents, I begin on the small scale. The issue came home to me, as it were, when by chance I came across a small book dealing with the Nazi takeover of the Moabit Hospital in Berlin. The book *Nicht Misshandeln,* by Christian Pross and Rolf Winau (published by Verlag Froelich & Kaufmann, Berlin, 1984), focuses on this particular hospital because of its special place in the history of Berlin Jewry. The hospital itself was founded in 1872 as a medical quarantine facility for cholera patients. It remained a rather average Berlin hospital until the end of World War I. Then, in 1919, the Prussian government decided to turn the Hospital into a university training hospital. Over the course of the following decade, the hospital became known for its cutting-edge medical research and innovative approaches to health care delivery, especially to the residents of the largely poor and proletarian community of Moabit. During this same period, for whatever reason, it became heavily staffed with Jewish physicians, something along the lines of seventy percent. In addition, a considerable portion of the administrative and support staffs were left-wingers. So the hospital, according to Pross and Winkau, was regarded as "rot" and "jüdisch," and, insofar as it was located in a working-class area, it was ripe for a Nazi takeover.

The takeover was quick in coming. On March 12, city elections were held in Berlin. Ten days later, on March 21, the *Völkischer Beobachter* announced that a survey of the Moabit Hospital had been completed, revealing the fact that a large number of physicians there, who were then named, were found to be Jewish or foreigners. Immediately, these "Jewish or foreigners" were banned from the building. On March 24, several more doctors were arrested on the spot while at work in the hospital and hauled off, without even a chance to refer their patients to other doctors. The process of de-Judaization well underway, the parallel process of Aryanization could begin.

There is no need at this point to go into the details of what happened; you can imagine the stories yourselves. In the end, some senior members of the staff with distinguished records of service were left without jobs or pensions; a few alumni of the Moabit Hospital managed to leave Germany and rebuild their professional lives elsewhere, but most were not so successful. In all events, the Jewish staff was steadily driven out and replaced by a coterie of Nazi doctors. The administrative and support staffs were co-opted and purged as the situation seemed to warrant.

A look at the replacement staff is itself of some interest, and I wish to focus our attention on that for a moment. The authors of *Nicht Misshandeln* were able to paint a picture of what happened next through interviews and diary entries of the nurses and other staff members who stayed behind. They are cautious in their assessments even now, maybe because of nurses' professional deference to physicians, or maybe because of female nurses' deference to male doctors. In all events, their comments are muted, but the overall message is clear: patient care declined rapidly and precipitously. The new physicians, especially those in administrative positions, took great pains to indoctrinate the staff, to insure that everyone was in proper uniform, to guarantee that lines of authority were strictly adhered to, and the like. But when it came to the detailed work of dealing with patients, these same physicians often displayed the arrogant and distracted attention we associate with the camps. Physicians would march into wards in full Nazi regalia, glance at the chart, poke this or that patient here and there, and then bark out some order before moving on. Patients with significant congenital problems were often turned over to euthanasia programs or made the subjects of medical experiments. In short, Nazi medicine was efficiently administered and, not surprisingly, mortality rates soared.

Let me remind you at this point that this kind of offhanded, even cruel care was not being administered to Jews or other racially inferior types in an SS medical ward in, say, occupied Poland. This was Nazi medicine administered in a well-known Berlin hospital to members of the German working class. That is, this is how the Nazi medical profession treated its own German subjects. It is a stunning example of the collapse of medical ethics that cut across the profession in Nazi Germany. The events in Moabit raise, in even starker terms, the question of what was going on in the minds of Nazi doctors.

There are, of course, a number of explanations out there. One is that, as a group, physicians who rode the Nazi party into power were in fact the less capable members of the profession, and so were facing dead-end careers in mediocre positions. For them, the removal of Jewish physicians in places like Moabit meant the elimination of competitors and the possibility of advancement. Physicians who would have gotten nowhere were suddenly in positions of prestige and authority. They were now free to strut around imperiously in their splendid uniforms, cause problems for their enemies in the profession, and bark orders to deferential nurses and utterly passive patients. This was, of course, not true of all "Aryan" physicians, and maybe only partially true for many others, but it certainly represents a psychology that seems to have manifested itself among the Nazi staff that came into control at Moabit.

But these personal and even petty concerns do not fully account for the moral and professional collapse of the medical profession in Germany. The Nazi doctors who took over Moabit and other hospitals, and eventually the medical schools, journals, research institutes, and the like, were consolidating their positions within the larger conceptual framework of Nazi ideology, which itself was based on a kind of social Darwinism. The point here, as social Darwinism came to be understood by the Nazi party, was that all human nations, what we might call ethnic groups, were engaged in a struggle over land and increasingly scarce resources. It was completely analogous to, and even continuous with, what was happening in the natural world. The different species of animals were engaged in a constant struggle for survival. Species that were most fit were destined to dominate, while those less fit were either banished to marginal niches or died off.

This struggle to the death among the flora and fauna of the natural world was taken by Nazi social Darwinists as the ironclad and absolute law of nature. This meant—and this is important to understand the collapse of ethics in the Holocaust—that the domination of one species at the price of the extinction of its rivals was what nature demanded. This ruthless struggle, the Nazis averred based on Darwinian science, was what was supposed to happen; it is how God put the world together. In other words, cruelty, domination, and massive death were part of the natural order of things; that is, they were part of the advancement of nature toward a greater good. Transferred over to the human sphere, it meant that the battle of one nation or race against its rivals was supposed to be brutal and unrestrained. To conduct it otherwise would be to go against the laws of nature and to risk the natural progression toward the ultimate good.

What the Nazis were ultimately able to do was to harness this scientific-sounding view of racial warfare to the task of rebuilding Germany after World War I. The decline of Germany was due, social Darwinists pointed out, to the debilitation of the German national body. This was due, in turn, to the introduction of inferior genes into the gene pool. The very spirit of the German race was being diluted by the admixture of all sorts of other traits, and the historical manifestation of that dilution was the decline and degeneration of German culture. This is why Germany lost the war and was unable to recover. The solution, the only scientifically reliable solution, lay in the reconstitution of the German nation; that is, by cleansing the national gene pool of its foreign and debilitating traits. The tools for doing this in a scientific, systematic, and rigorous way were to be found in the fields of eugenics and genetic engineering. It meant, among other initiatives, the weeding out of destructive or inferior traits, whether by sterilization, euthanasia, or regulated breeding. In short, the rebuilding of Germany was cast not as a problem of politics or economics, but of public health. And in this enterprise, the physicians stood out in front. Their position was especially important, and so especially powerful. They alone had the scientific expertise to point the way toward identifying the genetic traits underlying German greatness, and to devise methods for pruning and nursing the genetic store to recover the ancient glory.

The inverted logic of this approach made the Jews in fact especially vulnerable. German Jews had taken, and were taking, great pains during this period to point out how German they in fact were. They insistently noted that they as a community had deep roots in Germany; that they were participating fully in German culture, language, and arts; and that they clearly were to be absolutely distinguished from the obviously non-German Jews of Eastern Europe. But in the Nazi image of things, these German-looking characteristics of German Jews were precisely what made them so dangerous. German Jews could pass, in effect, as "real" Germans and so, like nefarious parasites, infiltrate themselves into the body politic and drain the élan vital of the

German people. And note that this malicious effect need not be conscious; German Jews could truly believe they were true Germans and harmless, but by their very nature they were a threat, and the more German-like, the more insidious the threat. And because this was precisely the nature of the Darwinian struggle for survival, German Jews could not be persuaded to stop their insidious attacks; they had to be eliminated, just as a virus or a cancer.

In the end, it was this combination of Germany's dire social, economic, and political problems in the decades after World War I, the overarching intellectual framework of social Darwinism, and the personal hopes and frustrations of German physicians that came together to cause the moral co-option and then collapse of the medical profession in Nazi Germany. Thrust into the position of being front-line troops in the enterprise of racial warfare, physicians, in their hundreds and thousands, bought into the Nazi program and took professional leadership of what they regarded as a public health initiative. Accordingly, they allowed themselves to make the transfer from healers to killers.

What lesson does all this hold for medical ethics in the shadow of the Holocaust? For one, it points to the importance of humility. Nazi physicians were sure they had the key to the door of German success, and were willing to sacrifice everything, even their own patients, to achieve that end. There was an arrogance to Nazi medicine, in fact to much of science in general, which allowed moral concerns to be marginalized if not ignored in the face of the imputed greater scientific good. Science was taken to supply its own answers; it was the new revelation. I think it is fair to say that in the wake of the Holocaust, we no longer can have a blind and unqualified faith in science.

An incident from my own experience at Vanderbilt is relevant here. Shortly after I arrived on campus, the medical school decided to hire a staff ethical philosopher to work with the medical students. The proposal was met with polite scorn on the medical side of campus. Medicine, after all, was a science and had no need to look to philosophers or theologians for anything. But the appointment was made and the program gradually became not only accepted but essential. Today, those notions of self-sufficiency in the medical center seem outdated and even slightly quaint. Now it is impossible to imagine a major medical education program without an ethics program. This shift in consciousness was not due merely to the quality of the staff (although there is a good staff), but also to a new humility among medical students. They no longer have the sense of assured self-sufficiency that once characterized the profession. Rather, there is a willingness to listen and to learn from "outsiders."

I think we see this same dynamic at work in the renewed interest in the dialogue between science and religion. Theologians are more and more open to the insight science can give us into the complexity of God's creation and the limits of human perception and understanding. At the same time, scientists are aware of the feebleness of their own attempts to deal with the vastness of the cosmos. They are more open to the sense of awe, wonder, and respect that has been religion's contribution to the human response to the world. We now realize more and more, unlike the Nazi doctors, that we do not, and may never have, the final and ultimate answer.

I talked earlier about the hospital at Moabit. The last photograph in *Nicht Misshandeln* is of the hospital as it looked at the end of World War II: a crumbling wreck with a few desultory ambulances parked in front and a ragtag staff of exhausted nurses gamely posing for the camera. It was hardly recognizable as the innovative hospital that so wonderfully and proudly cared for its community twenty years earlier. The final picture is a powerful witness to the destructive power of human arrogance, and to the loss of direction reflected in Nazi medicine.

14

Conscience, Knowledge, and "Secondary Ethics": German Corporate Executives from "Aryanization" to the Holocaust

PETER HAYES

That most of the great enterprises of Germany had become by the end of the Second World War deeply implicated in the assault on the European Jews which we call the Holocaust is by now well known to almost every reader of an American or European newspaper. Indeed, the revelations concerning the roles of Allianz insurance and the Deutsche Bank at Auschwitz, of Degussa in the processing of plundered gold and silver, and of Siemens and Holzmann, for instance, in the ruthless exploitation of inmate laborers—all of these have come so thick and fast as already to have produced a certain numbness in many people's minds. It is the numbness that comes with the transition from novelty to familiarity, from shock to a shrug of the shoulders; it is the feeling best expressed by the colloquial question, "So what else is new?" Now that most people have gotten over their surprise at the degree of German civilian participation in what was done to Jews under the Nazi regime—now that most of us have come to grasp, for example, that the relevant question is not which great German enterprises profiteered from enslavement and murder, but whether any major ones did not do so—several new oversimplifications have begun to replace the sorts that used to divert scholars and the public from inquiring deeply into the matters that have now become common knowledge. Instead of a widespread assumption that racist elites and organizations in Germany made the Holocaust and merely took advantage of the indifference or timidity of the rest of the nation, we now have the prevailing view, repopularized by Daniel Goldhagen, that "the" Germans joined enthusiastically in the process out of inner conviction. Alongside the long-standing notion that fear and hatred animated the Holocaust, we also find the commonplace idea that greed propelled it as well.

This transition in popular thinking about the etiology of the Holocaust is occurring, of course, in response to the continuing force of a disturbing question, indeed the disturbing question that makes the subject so present to thinkers at the end of the twentieth century, more than fifty years after the collapse of Nazi Germany: How was it possible that the pillaging and murder of the European Jews became a project carried out, not just by true-believing fanatics, but by the central and in a formal sense nonpolitical institutions of a civilized, literate society? Because we now know that disposing of the property and labor of the victims required more time and more sophisticated skills than disposing of the human beings themselves—that, in other words, ripping them from society and squeezing output from them was more complicated and energy-consuming than simply shipping them away—we grasp at the most direct and most easily condemned explanations for the willingness of so many to lend their talents and time to the effort. Lust for blood and lust for gain are the motives that serve our purposes best.

My hope today is to suggest that the process of mounting corporate complicity in viciousness did not travel such straightforward routes, that at least one group of German citizens, which is often identified with anti-Semitism and cupidity and which put its abilities to the service of evil, did so but haltingly and primarily as a result of the interaction of professionally conditioned and sanctioned responses with a politically structured environment. It is my intention to use the example of German big businessmen to explore the possibility that the Holocaust was an alarming product of the "seducibility of otherwise 'normal' individuals." I am going to argue that many of the men who increasingly took part in dispossessing, exploiting, and brutalizing Jews did so despite grave initial misgivings and reservations, which they overcame by invoking what we might call "secondary ethics." Such men came to see themselves, for the most part, as doing their duty according to moral obligations more immediate than those mandated by the Ten Commandments or natural law. The touchstones of their reasoning were not only the nation or the *Volk*, as one might expect in so idolatrous a context as Nazi Germany, nor solely fear for oneself and one's family, as one might expect in so dictatorial and arbitrary a state as Hitler's. Far more often than not, the sources of legitimation were "the interests of the firm" or of its workforce and the principle of self-sacrifice in the name of a larger cause that executives, at one point or another, ceased to reconsider. Heinrich Himmler's infamous speech at Posen in 1943, which inverted morality by telling his SS officers that the very brutality of what they had done was a sign of their decency, of their moral strength, captured a thought process that, in my view, penetrated the very warp and woof of German society in the Nazi era.

Three Misconceptions

Making this argument requires me to begin by refuting three common misconceptions. First, it is simply not true that the Holocaust was a highly profitable process for the large firms that participated in it, hence that immediate pecuniary advantage became, even at its height, the usual motive for their involvement. Consider two dramatic but telling examples involving the Degussa Corporation of Frankfurt. That firm owned 42.5 percent of the stock in and dominated the management of the company called Degesch, from which the SS obtained Zyklon-B, the granular vaporizing pesticide used to massacre some 1.5 million people at Auschwitz and Majdanek. The price of the gas sold to the former camp came to a grand total of 105,000 Reichsmarks between 1941 and 1944—that is, to somewhere between $26,000 and $42,000 over four years, depending on the exchange rate one uses. Even then, this was not the sort of market worth chasing. Degussa, whose name is an acronym for German Gold and Silver Separation Institute, also possessed a virtual monopoly on German capacity to smelt and refine precious metals. Thanks to the company's well-preserved archive and the efforts of the Eizenstat commission, we now know that the firm may have processed as much as ninety percent of the gold plundered from the Jews of Europe by the Nazi regime from 1938 to 1945, which is to say, about ten U.S. tons of gold. And what was the return on such services? A commission of about 155,000 Reichsmarks over six years. The rewards of processing Jewish silver were much greater, since there was more of it and it could be sold to other industries, but the earned fees still came to less than one percent of the firm's receipts on precious metals processing during these years. Thus, cupidity alone could not have dictated the corporation's behavior. Nor is the situation essentially different with regard to slave labor, although the sums involved are larger. Whether we are talking of these matters or of the "Aryanization" of Jewish-owned property, the point to notice is not, as is so often assumed, that German corporations grew rich through participation in the Holocaust, since in general, they did not. The point is that they took what they could get and became part of it anyway. Why?

Second, it is simply not true that one can reduce the answer to this question of anti-Semitism to the supposed fact that Germans hated Jews and had for centuries. To do so is not only to mistake a half-truth for a whole one, but to block out some of the most important implications of the Holocaust for modern society. Of course, anti-Semitism abounded in interwar Germany; indeed, it acquired a new lease on life after 1918 by grafting itself onto widespread fears of revolution from the Left. But hatred was not the exclusive or even principal element in Jewish-Gentile relations in Germany in the 1920s, and most Jewish Germans did not experience it as such. If Judaeophobia was prevalent in German society prior to 1933, it was not predominant. While a necessary condition for the horrors that followed, it was hardly a sufficient one.

The best demonstration of this point, to my mind, lies in my third dissent from a widespread assumption. It is simply not true that Germany's big business leaders hungered to drive their Jewish colleagues out of economic life prior to the Nazi takeover, or that they felt no compunction when the new regime began doing so. For one thing, they lacked the motives of envy and blame. By the outset of Nazi rule in 1933, the distinctness and prominence of Jews in the upper reaches of German corporate life—in particular, the incidence of Jewish-owned firms or Jewish chief executives in the nation's roughly one hundred largest or most economically important enterprises—had been declining for over two decades. Discrimination had something to do with this pronounced trend, but not much. Its chief causes were mortality, mergers, and mismanagement. As the Jewish population in Germany both aged and fell by about one-fifth from 1910 to 1932, so did the number of potential successors as corporate leaders. Meanwhile, adverse economic conditions took their toll, exposing many Jewish-owned firms to the process of industrial concentration and many Jewish, as well as Gentile, chief executives to the frustration of shareholders. As a result, the appetite in Germany for so-called "Aryanization"—that is, for the compulsory transfer of Jews' positions and property to other Germans—immediately before and after Hitler's takeover was not concentrated among German big businessmen.

By and large, the members of the nation's commercial elite knew better than to credit Nazi claims that the German economy was "jewified," let alone that it was becoming more so; they had still less reason to believe that the nation's woes could be traced to this supposed circumstance. The jealousy, self-pity, and greed that animated such charges found their homes to a much greater extent among the Gentile participants in those middle ranges of economic life where Jews remained conspicuous as competitors or middlemen, that is to say, mostly among self-employed shopkeepers, artisans, peasant proprietors, and professionals, especially medical doctors. Not only were very few of the approximately one hundred thousand Jewish-owned economic operations in the country of sufficient size or importance to attract the avarice of the nation's major firms but also most of the corporate barons had experienced too much personal and professional contact—often through intermarriage—to consider Jews, as racist propaganda insisted, irredeemably different or dangerous. Of course, there were bigots among the corporate elite, but they were usually of the snobbish rather than the racist type, and their voices were muted by the predominance of a countervailing snobbery, that which regarded bullying and scapegoating as vulgar and beneath the dignity of decent people.

Business Leaders

Narrow-minded by the standards of our day, the leaders of the nation's largest enterprises were generally moderate, sometimes even liberal, by the standards of their own. Moreover, many of them made this known, which is why Hitler consistently avoided the subject of anti-Semitism in his meetings with them prior to his appointment as chancellor. Even after his accession unleashed the intimidating fanaticism of his followers, the führer found himself repeatedly confronted with big businessmen's displeasure at Nazi racism. That at least some of them recognized the moral issues at stake from the very beginning of Nazi persecution is apparent from three documented interventions: those of Georg von Müller-Oerlingshausen, a textile magnate; Emil Kirdorf, at the time the "grand old man" of the German coal industry; and Robert Bosch, the leader of the famous automotive and electronics parts firm that bore his name. On April 13, 1933, Müller-Oerlingshausen wrote the leaders of the National Association of German Industry to protest the removal, at the regime's behest, of Jews from its staff. Here are his defiant, ringing words:

> Political opposition would be sheer madness for a business association, but blandly falling in behind the . . . utopia of the dominant Party would be suicide. [The Association] exist[s] to preserve freedom of opinion and to persuade the authorities of its necessity. In this connection, the first commandment is clarity, including with regard to the Jewish question. The Association can and must never be drawn into agreement with the unheard of penalizing and oppression of German Jewry, if it still wants to claim any moral standing. Should this attitude mean that the Association loses the possibility, temporarily or for a longer period, of gaining a hearing from the key political leaders, and then we will have to endure that fate, sure in the knowledge that we tried to do what was best.

Two months later, Kirdorf expressed his dissent even more publicly, in the form of a letter published in the *Rheinische-Westfälische Zeitunig*. After denouncing as "a crime" and "a stab in the back" the process by which "a large number of people who have served Germany, whose families became naturalized citizens here centuries ago, have been cruelly degraded and had the ground pulled out from under them," Kirdorf announced that "My hope and confidence of experiencing a new, unstained, and proud Germany are gone." Bosch was also forthright, although in private and indirectly. He had his aide Hans Walz tell Wilhelm Keppler, Hitler's special plenipotentiary for economic matters, that the wave of attacks on Jews during the first months of Nazi rule constituted a violation of elemental human rights.

Such arguments from principle were, however, unlikely to impress convinced Nazi racists, unless presented by a united front of the nation's corporate leaders—and that did not happen. Most big business executives chose in 1933 to take a more pragmatic approach to the so-called Jewish question, one that stressed the inadvisability of the regime's actions rather than their injustice. Over and over, figures like Albert Vögler of the United Steelworks, Paul Reusch of the Gute Hoffnungshütte, Hermann Bücher of AEG, Carl Bosch of IG Farben, Carl-Friedrich von Siemens, and even Gustav Krupp von Bohlen und Halbach, whose pusillanimity as head of the National Association of German Industry had provoked Müller-Oerlingshausen's letter, seized on whatever occasions came their way to remind the new government that neither it nor the still depressed German economy could afford the material losses that persecution and foreign reprisals to it would entail. Since their stance was to prove fatefully ineffective—indeed, it amounted to squandering the one moment when they might have exerted real leverage against the regime's racist course—it is important to examine the reasoning behind their mistaken line of argument.

Although most of the principal leaders of the nation's major enterprises entered the Third Reich personally and professionally uncomfortable with the prospect of dismissing longtime, often close and valued colleagues and employees on grounds of their descent, the reaction of the corporate world to demands of this sort was shaped by habits of mind about "responsible" behavior that were to prove radically out of place in the Nazi context. The first of these was to prioritize problems according to the degree of threat they posed. For most big businessmen in early 1933, Müller-Oerlingshausen's main concerns—self-respect, moral standing, the duty to speak truth to power—seemed self-indulgent. As unsettled as he was in many cases by the party's onslaught, they thought his response would be far more likely to aggravate than alleviate it. Besides, to their minds, the chief threats in early

1933 were Communism and chaos; the chief duty of business was to achieve the economic recovery to which these were the main obstacles. In other words, most Gentile industrialists and financiers thought their choice—at least outwardly—was between offering the new regime an embrace or a handshake, between "anticipatory obedience" and "howling with the wolves" or at least seeming to comply, as the formulaic phrase went, "for the good of the firm with the requirements of the times." Of course, in the context of widespread Nazi thuggery, of recurrent extralegal threats by Nazi employees and organizations to disrupt sales and production, this attitude amounted to taking the course of least resistance. But it also emerged out of big business's experience concerning how best to get its way in a democratic or populist context. Two tactical predilections largely predisposed corporate executives to avoid an open confrontation with the regime over racism, namely their preferences for seeking agreement through compromise and for operating behind the scenes through conversations with other "responsible" figures. This, their almost reflexive political cost-benefit analysis told them, was likely to prove the most productive means of stemming the onslaught.

Taking this line came all the easier to German big businessmen in early 1933, because most of them harbored a fateful ambivalence about Jews. Usually respectful, even affectionate toward many of their Jewish colleagues— that is, toward the Jews they knew— they also often focused their anxiety about particular cultural or political developments by fixating on Jews not associated with them—that is, on Jews they did not know in walks of life they did not trust. Like, I am obligated to say in this forum, many spokesmen of the Catholic Church, including the author of Pius XI's famous draft encyclical of the late 1930s, a substantial portion of German industrialists believed that Jews were disproportionately inclined to embrace supposedly destructive modernism in the arts and leftism in politics. As a result, most of the Gentile corporate elite was prepared only to condemn discrimination in its own sphere of action and against particular individuals, not to refute the general practice. Put the other way around, most of Germany's chief executives in the early 1930s had less trouble accepting anti-Semitism than its application to specific people with whom they had much in common. Their protestations, therefore, concentrated on defending Jews as individuals, rather than as a category, and this made those protestations ring to Nazi ears of special pleading and halfheartedness.

Dismissing Jewish Employees

The weaknesses of this approach were reinforced by business's predilections for going to the top in such matters and seeking common ground with policy makers. Seeing no point in trying to dissuade or face down party zealots, executives opted to deploy "rational" arguments with people who, like them, would pay attention to the big picture, in this case, to Germany's needs and interests. This entailed, they were sure, seeming to meet the regime halfway. Thus, many of them seized in early 1933 on the middle ground provided by the decrees governing the presence of Jews in public service or the universities, decrees that set out to limit the incidence of Jews to about 1.50 percent—that is, roughly twice their share of the national population—but which exempted from dismissal people who had held their jobs when World War I began, had served in that conflict, had a father wounded or killed in it, and had never engaged in putatively "unpatriotic" political activity. By aping these official policies within firms, such managers tried to insure themselves against reproach, yet establish a basis for retaining at least some of their Jewish personnel, including many of the most senior and valued people.

Emblematic of big business's tactics on the "racial" issue was a project devised under the auspices of Max Warburg, a Jewish banker from Hamburg, and such front-rank Gentile businessmen as Krupp von Bohlen, Siemens, Carl Bosch, and Kurt Schmitt, who was the head of the insurance firm until he became economics minister in June 1933. Between April and August of that year, they hammered out a plan that they intended "to forward to a responsible office when the participants thought the moment had arrived." At the core of the initiative lay the idea of funneling Jewish young people increasingly into preparation for manual rather than mental labor, especially in agriculture. That notion not only echoed proposals various Jewish groups had been advancing since the early 1920s as antidotes to declining urban incomes and enduring German prejudice, but also dovetailed with the NSDAP's determination to reduce the so-called over-representation of Jews in certain professions. But the plan also challenged party ideology and intentions in fundamental, although sometimes subtly phrased respects. First, it posited that the existing employment pattern was a product of culture and history, not race and conspiracy, hence changing it would lessen differences between Christian and Jewish Germans and lay the basis for long-range harmony. Second, the businessmen stipulated that in the meantime each "patriotic non-Aryan" should continue in his profession to "enjoy the same rank and the same respect as every man." Third, the group's final memorandum stressed the indivisibility of "Aryan" and "non-Aryan" economic interests, arguing that political encroachment on the latter was bound to set adverse precedents regarding the former. In other words, when it came to economic rights, the businessmen discerned that Jews and non-Jews were in the same boat. To defend their common interests in the present, Jewish and Gentile executives outlined a program of concessions to Nazi ideology in the future. They thus tried to square the circle of Nazi racism, if you will, to seem accommodating without completely agreeing.

This Warburg memorandum was never formally delivered, in part because national policy, under the influence of Schmitt and Hjalmar Schacht, the new president of the national bank, seemed in the latter half of 1933 to turn in the desired direction. The cabinet then specifically rejected various suggested means of pressuring Jewish firms out of business, such as denial of access to assorted forms of credit, to government contracts, and to the stock markets. It also banned inquiries into the religion or ancestry of managers and owners doing business with government agencies. As if on cue, the labor courts reversed their earlier willingness to sanction the dismissal of Jewish employees simply because Nazi co-workers or customers demanded it. At the end of the year, the Economics and Interior ministries jointly issued a decree exempting commercial activities from all racial regulations passed to govern other walks of life during the preceding eleven months. There seemed to be good grounds to hope that the Third Reich would henceforth follow the course recommended by the IG Farben-dominated *Frankfurter Zeitung* in June 1934: "Now that German non-Aryans have been excluded from all professions to which the state assigns particular importance in the political and ideological structure, the time must finally come to assure non-Aryans a sphere in which their activities are free and in which they are not regarded by the people as enemies."

Unfortunately, however, while the businessmen talked, lobbied, and relied on their representatives in office to change the course of events, enormous injustice and damage to German Jews was done, and the basis for still more was laid. By the time the government decrees seemed to stabilize the situation, thousands of Jews had been driven from the staffs and boardrooms of German corporations by Nazi labor organizations and customer representatives, Nazified trade associations, howling storm troopers who invaded stockholders' meetings, and party officials who refused to place orders with supposedly "Jewish" firms. Moreover, the decrees merely slowed the pace of events. While the Nazis for a time refrained from an open offensive against most of the best-known Jewish entrepreneurs or firms, party activists concentrated, more or less surreptitiously, on driving small-scale Jewish proprietors, especially merchants, out of business and continued to check into the ethnicity of corporate managers and owners and to find ways of threatening the production or sales of objectionable firms. Without a free press, there seemed little way of stopping such actions, especially after the supreme court cleared the way once more in 1935 for dismissals on supposedly "racial" grounds. Consequently, many major enterprises seem to have struggled to walk a middle line, using Nazi anti-Semitism as an excuse for buying out or letting elapse the contracts of less valued, well-liked, long-standing, or prominent Jewish employees, but clinging to those who satisfied these standards until political harassment tipped the balance of practical concerns against retention. Unevenly but inexorably, a "grassroots" process had been set in irreversible motion that steadily multiplied the number of executives who thought that their professional duty to employees, shareholders, and the prosperity of their firms required abandoning, rather than defending their Jewish associates.

In distinct ways, events at the L. Hutschenreuther Porcelain Corporation of Selb in Bavaria and the Gesfürel/Ludwig Loewe AG of Berlin illustrate how the process of attrition functioned. At Hutschenreuther, the chairman of the supervisory board, Franz Urbig of the Deutsche Bank, managed for over a year to evade Nazi demands for a purge of that group, secure in the knowledge that the composition of the boards at the main rival enterprise left the party no real alternative as a supplier. But by November 1934, Rosenthal Porcelain had completed its purge, and the party boss in Selb refocused his pressure directly on Urbig, making the issue a test of the Deutsche Bank's power and political loyalty. This had the desired effect. Late in the month, the banker carried out a reorganization that deprived all but one of the Jews of their seats. Reproached by one of the victims, Urbig defended himself in pragmatic terms no doubt echoed by many Gentile business executives at the time:

> No one aspires to do unpleasant things. One tackles them, when one has to or when one wants to avoid the charge of having been blind to events in the wider world. . . . My experiences and observations in diverse professional positions have shown me that one cannot see the matter before us as one wishes to, but only as it—despite all ministerial pronouncements—in reality is.

The gradual exclusion of Erich and Egon Loewe from the company that bore their family's name demonstrates that the party sometimes needed only to wait for events to play into its hands on the so-called racial question. In 1936, Kurt Schmitt and Hermann Bücher, both of whom had spoken out against the purges of Jews in 1933 and refused to dismiss members of the boards they chaired at the financially struggling AEG, found themselves in need of official permissions to carry out a complicated financial transaction by which the Gesfürel/Loewe Corporation would buy twenty-five million marks worth of AEG shares and that firm would elect two men of Jewish descent to its supervisory board. When the regime, however, made "Aryanization" a condition of the deal, Bucher and Schmitt found themselves confronted literally with the price of their principles—in this case, precisely twenty-five million desperately needed marks. They sacrificed the posts of four Jews, in return for permission to retain one, and set in motion a process by which they eventually assumed leadership of Gesfürel itself a year later.

There is no reason to review other such cases here; from 1934 to 1937 they hardened into a general pattern. Most corporations sooner or later abandoned directors or employees whenever organs of the party or the regime got around to insisting on their removal. Although willing to write glowing references for those forced into retirement, the firms also moved to head off criticism from shareholders and the Nazi press by playing strictly by the book in determining pensions and severance payments. Sometimes a guilty conscience got the better of one executive or another, as when Karl Kimmich tried to organize a farewell breakfast at Gesfürel for the Loewes in 1937, "in order," as he put it, "that their departure not proceed so unkindly." But these were mere gestures. Long before 1937, advancement within a major German firm had become out of the question for Jews, and those who remained did so, in effect, on sufferance. Some firms, of course, fought more determined holding actions than others. For instance, the manager of IG Farbern's factories at Wolfen apparently ingeniously deflected every party demand for the dismissal of Jewish executives or researchers until April 1938. And, in the early years of Nazi rule, one rarely finds signs in the often-copious surviving records of the initiative for removals coming from within firms, or even of rival executives engineering or exploiting party pressure. It happened, but far more seldom than one would think. In general, the dismissals were reactive and perceived internally as damaging to business, although less so than continuing trouble with the party would have been.

Acquisition of Jewish-Owned Companies

With regard to the other dimension of "Aryanization," the acquisition of Jewish-owned companies and shares, an even more ambiguous, hesitant, defensive, and self-interested pattern of corporate behavior also crystallized in the first years of Nazi rule. Only about thirty percent of the major Jewish firms in Germany changed hands or went under between 1933 and the end of 1937, compared to over sixty percent of the small businesses; and of the roughly three hundred substantial transactions, only around twenty amounted to takeovers by German big businesses. During these years, in fact, would-be sellers appear to have greatly outnumbered interested corporate buyers. Whether most large firms hung back for purely commercial reasons, because of legal worries or out of principle, is impossible to say categorically on the basis of the available records. What they seem not to have been doing was merely waiting for better terms; I have found not a single instance of a major corporation later making an acquisition that it turned down in this period.

In any case, hang back they did, and on the few occasions when one of the approximately one hundred largest German firms was involved in a takeover, the terms of sale seem to have come closer to what was commercially fair than did most other transfers at the time, let alone later. Indeed, it is reasonable to say that only one major German enterprise distinguished itself for rapacity prior to 1937, the Dresdner Bank, largely because its conversion during the bank crisis of 1931–1932 into a virtually state-owned operation, coupled with the presence of ten Jews among its fifteen principal officers in 1933, made it immediately and especially vulnerable to the penetration of Nazi policies and personnel.

In sum, by late 1937, most major German firms had reached an arrangement with Nazi anti-Semitism that ran from the resigned to the callous. If they would not push to dispossess Jews, neither would they stand up for them. Like Hjalmar Schacht, most corporate executives had come to the self-excusing conclusion that the best they could achieve with regard to "Aryanization" would be to draw it out over a period of ten to fifteen years in order to minimize its unsettling effects on longtime associates, the stock markets, and production and exports. That was, by and large, the temporizing course being pursued by German big business at the moment when the Nazi regime decided, in November 1937, to intensify the economic assault on the Jews. For Hitler, the controlling fact had become the need to ready the nation for a war that might quickly become opportune under any of several conceivable scenarios. Within days of sketching these for his principal advisors at the famous Hossbach Conference, he acted on his fantasy of the Jews as a fifth column by firing Schacht as economics minister and temporarily replacing him with

Hermann Göring, who promptly decreed a series of measures for defining, detecting, and penalizing so-called "Jewish influence" over firms. Between January and December 1938, these enactments swept aside any remaining corporate reluctance to dispense with old friends or pursue their property.

The new decrees began by cutting off government contracts and raw material allocations to firms with Jewish board members, senior managers, and owners, then required their removal; they escalated from promoting the supposedly "voluntary" sale of Jewish-owned firms to mandating their seizure and sale by the state. By the middle of 1938, virtually all Jewish directors of major firms had lost their posts. As for large companies still owned by "non-Aryans," the most that could be achieved was to get them assigned to reliable Christian associates who promised to hold them in trust or at least to block their acquisition by Nazi potentates.

But there was a good deal less of even this sort of help extended to Jewish-German entrepreneurs in this period than earlier, thanks largely to changes in the commercial world and its operating environment. By early 1938, newly ascendant enterprises in key industries and managers in many of the more established companies were opting to hitch their individual wagons to the star of Nazi policy, regardless of widespread reservations about aspects of it. This development reflected, above all, the implicit pressure exerted by growing state control over the economy. Quasi-public institutions, like the regional banks or the Reichs-Kredit-Gesellschaft and the Bank für Industrie-Obligationen, not to mention the Reichswerke Hermann Göring, now stood ready to gobble up what private firms neglected. At the same time, government regulations had become so complete that growth, profits, and market shares depended almost entirely on satisfying the regime, and increased allocations of key materials often could be obtained only by annexing another firm's quotas through acquisition. In this context, with massive "Aryanization" a given ordained from Berlin and sellers bargaining positions weakened, many large firms saw nothing to be gained and little to be lost—save honor—by refusing to scramble for the spoils. Above all, they acted to prevent either old or new rivals from coming away with more or long-standing business ties from being upset by inept new owners. In other words, "Aryanization" within

Germany in 1938, as in the occupied lands later, became an illustration of one of the key motivating methods of Nazism, "the threat in cases of recalcitrance," as another historian has put it, "to entrust the dirty work to another."

That German executives still felt the pangs of human sympathy with their Jewish colleagues as this onslaught got underway—and that the force of these deteriorated rapidly under the pressure of events—can be traced in the words and actions of Ernst Busemann, the chairman of the Degussa Corporation, who found himself compelled to act in 1937–1938 against members of two Jewish families who still had management posts and minority shareholdings in two of his subsidiaries. As the first case came to a head, Busemann replied to the managing director's request for advice on what to do in these strongly humane terms:

> Your letter touched me greatly, since I know the Messrs. Meyer and their father as skilled and thoroughly fair businessmen. They have stood by Degussa and myself and showed us loyalty [and] . . . placed their fate in our hands . . . and now . . . I must negotiate with them over a further, considerable reduction in their influence. These negotiations will be all the more difficult for me because two equal partners will not be represented; for a variety of reasons, there will be nothing that can be done about my decision. Your letter shows quite clearly that something has to be done in way of Aryanization. It is pointless to swim against the stream. Our efforts, both in the interests of the firm and the family, have to be directed at retaining Messrs. Theo and Viktor Meyer for our plant. . . . I hope that the gentlemen will trust us to arrange the matter as well as possible. I will try hard to justify the confidence that they have shown me for years.

For a few months, Busemann struggled to keep the Meyer brothers on; when he finally gave up, he purchased their stock at twice its face and 125 percent of its market value at the time. Consider the contrast, however, with his con-duct toward the Margulies family in the second case scarcely five months later, when they tried to obtain something approximating the market value of their minority stock packet. Upbraiding the sympathetic business manager negotiating on his behalf, Busemann wrote that, for that kind of money, he would prefer to tear down the old factory and build a new one, hence the fam-ily should be told that "despite all conceivable sentimental ties, we can pay only for the Margulies shares only what they are worth to us. That value is very small." He, therefore, dared the family to find another buyer, knowing that none would bid for stock in a firm over which he or she would obtain no real influence. In the end, Busemann held firm, and the family's stock fell to Degussa by public auction after the German State confiscated it for supposed non-payment of taxes by the family.

Pivotal in and typical of the feeding frenzy that resulted from the Hossbach Conference and that Busemann's hardening of heart exemplified was the behavior of Dresdner and Deutsche banks. They now competed intensely to identify "Aryanizable" firms, to collect brokerage commissions that came to one to two percent of the purchase prices, to loan the necessary capital, to speculate on blocs of shares, to hold on to the regular business of client firms that were changing hands and/or to secure that of new owners, and even to augment their balance sheets by making their own advantageous acquisitions. Meanwhile, takeover costs were driven down by the number and desperation of the sellers, the illiquidity of some of the largest firms in con-sequence of the drives for armaments and economic self-sufficiency, and the regime's oversight of the sales, which established strict parameters for the purchase prices. This is one of the reasons why restitution payments on "Aryanization" deals came to four billion Deutschmarks in the 1950s; even when purchasers paid the maximum legally allowed price in the late thirties, they vastly underpaid, and the buyers knew it. But the closest they could come to proceeding fairly, which they often did, was to pay more than the book value of a corporation's stock, sometimes even the by-now depressed market value, or to overpay, which they did less often, for goods on hand or inventory. Their only real choice, however, was whether to participate, not on what terms, and that choice came down to a matter of corporate self-interest in a particular commercial and political setting. Ironically, in joining in the pillaging, most large firms merely ended up chasing their own tails. The banks, for instance, which eagerly pursued "Aaryanization" business as a compensation for lost income on stock issues, may have thus recouped millions from the pillaging, but they then lost other millions through the liquidation of Jews' deposits, which nearly all ended up in the regime's coffers. Similarly, the big buyers perceived with annoyance what they dared articulate only indirectly: that they had been drawn into a revenue-raising program, one which maneuvered them into putting up the money for a process that turned Jews' fixed assets (plants) into liquid ones (purchase prices), which were then, in stages, taxed away by the Reich.

Indeed, the biggest profiteer from "Aryanization" was indubitably the Nazi State, which eventually raked off sixty to eighty percent of the prices paid for large-scale property transfers within the Reich and a total of some three billion of the 7.1 billion marks in wealth that native and stateless Jews possessed according to the compulsory property declarations of April 1938—not to mention increased proceeds from taxes on stock market transactions throughout 1938 and 1939. Such receipts proved essential to the German rearmament effort, contributing some five percent of the national budget in the final year prior to the Second World War, precisely at a time when laggard sales of government bonds would otherwise have forced a cutback in military expenditures. Moreover, the unleashing of competitive impulses against the Jews assured the regime of something less quantifiable but equally valuable: the fact that the transfers and confiscations occurred without appreciable damage to the German economy. The banks, for instance, found ways of insulating stock market prices from the sudden flood of Jewish-owned shares being sold in 1938–1939. Once more, the carrot-and-stick method of the Third Reich paid off. The prospect of income combined with the fear of damage to interests if one did *not* act to mobilize Nazi and non-Nazi business executives alike to make the best of the given situation. Essentially, the same considerations account for such measures as Degussa's readiness to smelt plundered precious metals and the Deutsche Bank's readiness to serve as financier not only for parts of Auschwitz, but also—through a subsidiary—for Theresienstadt. Increasingly, participation in the persecution of the Jews became either, as in the case of the banks, one of the only remaining ways to sustain or increase corporate income, or, in the case of Degussa, a way of demonstrating one's suitability for far more lucrative assignments, such as the smelting of the metals plundered from the treasuries of the occupied nations.

Crossing the Divide

All in all, by the end of the great "Aryanization" wave in 1939, which is the less-dramatic and frightful part of the history of corporate complicity in the Holocaust, a divide had been crossed. The Nazi regime had succeeded in transforming Jewish colleagues from people many of the nation's business magnates had once thought it in their interest to protect, to people it was in their interest to exploit. Having accomplished this gradually and in the face of some pangs of conscience, the interaction of the regime's racism and the corporate world's devotion to secondary ethical obligations succeeded after 1939, now rapidly and against almost no resistance, in effecting a further transformation of Jews to people it was in businessmen's interest to use up like any other factor of production. That this process reached its moral nadir so rapidly and was accompanied by so little even covert foot-dragging—in contrast to the history of "Aryanization"—has, I believe, two primary, although not exclusive explanations: first, that the pattern of abdicating in the face of immediate demands, now reinforced by the perceived emergency condition of being at war, had become reflexive; and, second, that after 1939 the Jewish victims of this reflex so decreasingly resembled the businessmen who exploited them (to a large degree, these victims were not even German-speakers any longer) that almost all lingering inhibitions fell away.

In one sense, the mounting recourse to slave labor reflected the mathematics of a situation in which eleven million workers were being called into uniform; a higher percentage of German women were already working in 1939 than was ever the case in the U.S. and Britain during the war, and the regime opposed further increases for ideological and political reasons; and seven and a half million conscripted foreigners were proving insufficient to generate the output demanded by the conflict. In this context, it was perhaps only a matter of time until the hard-pressed German labor allocation offices and their industrial clients sought to expand on two precedents: the military's practice of "leasing" prisoners of war to factories, which became routine following the Polish and French campaigns; and the forced employment of German Jews in industry, which had begun, especially in Berlin, during 1939–1940.

But the decisive moment came quickly, at the turn of 1940–1941, as the failure to defeat Britain led to the setting of expanded production targets and the siting of numerous new factories out of the reach of British bombers, which meant in regions where the German labor force was thin to begin with or already fully employed. Particularly at these locations—but soon at most existing installations—industrialists recognized that their choices had come down to not meeting their building and production targets or accepting whatever labor could be found, regardless of the source. Thus, IG Farben eagerly pursued the rumored possibility that it could secure construction workers for its new Auschwitz plant from the nearby concentration camp; and thus Volkswagen snapped up Heinrich Himmler's suggestion that a camp be built on the factory grounds.

To date, there is little proof that industrialists suggested the system of "leasing" laborers from the SS, but equally little that they hesitated to grasp it. Moreover, once this practice came into being, most firms not only eagerly and persistently demanded their share, but pursued self-interested policies that increased the need for such workers and worsened the conditions they were forced to suffer. Sure that, whatever the outcome of the war, the best placed firms would be those that secured the most resources during it, most major German corporations inflated their labor needs and struggled to avoid any cutbacks in production, both by exaggerating the military value of their output and by blocking the transfer of civilian manufacturing to underutilized competitors in the occupied countries.

Worst of all, German industry generally agreed to a price per worker per day from the SS that exceeded the value of the work they could perform, since inmates were usually unsuited to the brutish work assigned and often arrived at the factories already weakened by malnourishment and exposure. The firms then frequently sought to drive down the cost per worker by economizing on food, clothing, and barracks and to raise productivity by extending working hours and wielding physical violence. The alternative strategy of trying to improve performance by bettering conditions was possible, but it was handicapped by the existence of tight specifications regarding rations, housing, discipline, and, in particular, the treatment of Jews. For the most part, German managers did not want to bother themselves with the conditions of such laborers, a matter they largely delegated to the German Labor Front or SS officials who ran the barracks' compounds, or to subcontractors on the building sites, so long as replacements could be found for those workers who were being, quite literally, used up. Pragmatic, patriotic, and preoccupied, the responsible executives appear seldom to have asked themselves any questions about what they were doing and to have lost little or no sleep over it. They were driven, instead, by ambition, duty, and what Hans Mommsen has termed an almost "neurotic compulsion . . . to do their best in 'the national defensive struggle.'"

Neither patriotism nor the deference and fear that promoted strict adherence to regulations quite suffices, however, to explain the increasingly barbaric conditions to which some one half million inmate laborers were subjected at hundreds of German factories in the final nine months of the war. To be sure, the coarsening effects of the conflict, the breakdown of the German supply system, and the mounting shortages of almost everything aggravated the situation. So did, it must be said, the inroads that racism had made on German executives' thinking during the twelve years of Nazi rule. Allowing for all of that, the role of individual and corporate self-interest, even in this most murderously irrational phase of industrial involvement in the Holocaust, strikes me as, once again, overriding. As the newest study of Mercedes documents indicates, once most of that firm's managers knew the war was lost, their appetite for labor from concentration camps grew even more insistent and vicious, not less. Desperate to transfer machinery valuable to postwar survival to underground locations and to keep plants operating as long as possible so as to avoid being called up for military duty, these men demanded ever more inmate workers, who they had ever less capacity to feed and house, then drove them with ever-mounting ferocity. It was a pattern of behavior characteristic of many plants in the waning months of the conflict, and it amounted to—as is often the case in war—buying one's chances in the future with others' lives in the present.

The complicity of German big business in the Holocaust culminated during the war years in a readiness, in the German phrase, "to walk over corpses." The leaders of firms simply came to accept the use and death of slave laborers as a condition of business in Nazi Germany. Of course, the dreadful indifference that permitted such behavior had many sources. It reflected historical circumstances, above all, the excessive, bitter, self-pitying, and finally aggressive German reaction to the outcome of the First World War and the economic crises that followed, which allowed many Germans to see themselves as victims after 1918, hence entitled to fight back with all necessary means. The prevalent indifference also testified to the strength of certain cultural patterns, such as deference to authority, the overvaluation of doing one's duty, the glorification of the nation, and the associated racism that routinely and powerfully characterized Germany prior to 1945. Moreover, behind this indifference, as I have taken pains to make vivid, stood hard realities: the Third Reich constructed a framework of economic policy in which the effective pursuit of corporate survival or success had to serve, at least outwardly, the goals and ideological requirements of the regime.

Yet, when all due allowance is made for time and place, the indifference exhibited by German businessmen also expressed all-too-human weaknesses that, in the modern world, are often allowed to masquerade behind professional responsibilities. The obligation to achieve the best possible return for the firm and those who own or work for it or to secure their long-term prospects, which in decent contexts can be a guarantee against personal corruption or frivolous management, became an excuse for participating in cruel, eventually murderous acts, indeed a mandate to do so. The result was not only complicity, but also—and this may be more alarming—a sense of innocence on the part of those who engaged in these acts. Foregrounding their professional obligations, most German industrialists increasingly succeeded over time in strangling the voice of their consciences with the question, "What else can I do?" instead of remembering to ask themselves the far more difficult and appropriate question, as Avraham Barkai has formulated it, "What must I never do?"

Not all of the leaders of German big business had consciences when it came to the so-called Jewish question, but showing that many did, at least initially and partially, is why most of these remarks focus on the first phase of Nazi rule. Not all of them had perfect knowledge of what was happening to forced laborers at their factories or on the sites that they financed, but those who lacked it almost certainly had to make an effort to do so. It was not absence of conscience or absence of knowledge that enabled German big businessmen, in the end, to help make the Holocaust, but a professionally sanctioned readiness to maneuver within the given circumstances, a readiness that privileged the perceived obligations of one's occupational role over those of one's humanity. For a time, a sense of identification with or personal and professional proximity to some of the victims, namely Jewish German businessmen like themselves, served as a partial brake on the transformation of a morally slippery slope on which German executives stood in 1933 into the avalanche they sought to ride after 1938. Indeed, the very gradualness of the initial slippage and the slow narrowing of the possibility of alleviating the harm being done discouraged the search for a moment or the will for concerted countermeasures until the landslide had broken loose. Once it had, the executives of Germany's greatest enterprises behaved in a manner that terribly underlines the instructive force of the German proverb *Wehret den Anfängen*: fight the beginnings.

15

Conscience, Knowledge, and "Secondary Ethics": German Corporate Executives from "Aryanization" to the Holocaust: A Response to Peter Hayes

DONALD J. DIETRICH

Individuals and groups embody values, i.e., they possess a moral ethos gained through learning and experience. The fact that every society has a moral code implies that a concern with good and evil is a biologically rooted and a culturally reinforced characteristic. The specific content of that code is influenced by historical, religious, and economic factors. In essence, what we see happening in the Third Reich is that harming and killing Jews became possible when a feeling for their welfare was lost as a result of the profound devaluation by their society, which was shaped by the anti-Semitic ideology embedded in European culture. Other scholars[1] have explored the legal and medical professions, but the presentation of Professor Hayes is one of the most recent attempts to explore the world of big business and the mutation of the corporate ethos from one of earning profits into one that helped perpetrate the barbarity of the *Shoah*. To understand what he has described, the psychosocial dynamics that seem in part to undergird the formation of values and attitudes should first be explored. The formation of the corporate ethos in Nazi Germany is a historical task that Professor Hayes has only just begun today. The social learning components, necessary to understand the behavior of the corporate executives, have yet to be included into such a historical analysis.

The exclusivistic characteristics of German culture and the authoritarian structure of even democratic Weimar society, joined to such stresses as the 1923 inflation along with the social tensions that typified interwar Germany, helped nurture an environment that was rooted in anomie, and in turn, helped lead to genocide and mass killing.[2] The socially generated psychological needs helped direct gentile German society against the Jewish subgroup within the

Weimar Republic. Gradually the increasing mistreatment of this subgroup ended in genocide. German society, like most Christian organizations in Europe, had long devalued Jews[3] and discriminated against them, had strong respect for authority, and had an overly superior as well as vulnerable self-concept. It is not surprising that Nazi Germany could easily, even if slowly, turn against the Jews, who had long been marginalized within it. There has been enough research, for example, to indicate that Christianity has been vigorously anti-Semitic, since at least the middle of the second century.

Germany emerged in the twentieth century as a nation rooted in an authoritarian culture, one open to nondemocratic solutions to its political and economic problems. Weimar Germany itself experienced frightening economic cycles, and, politically, was classified impotent by its own citizens. Such an environment encouraged ethnocentrism, and so anti-Semitism became increasingly a politically volatile issue. Along with others, Hitler insisted that the Jewish conspiracy had promoted Bolshevism, capitalism, democracy, miscegenation, and even modern abstract art. For some Germans, unfortunately too many, all evil—i.e., defeat in World War I, the Weimar Republic, inflation, depression, and the fragmented and seemingly sterile political system—could be located in the Jewish presence in Germany. Most Germans were at least latently and culturally, even if not blatantly anti-Semitic. Germans could support Hitler's platform of national renewal, anti-Bolshevism, anti-liberalism and, anti-democracy, despite his anti-Semitism.[4]

Genocide does not easily become a political policy. There is usually a progression of actions, i.e., a continuum of destruction.[5] The *Shoah* was an end product of hate, fear, and discrimination. Small steps led to Auschwitz. Bias, boycotts, discriminatory laws, ghettoization, sterilization, euthanasia, and, finally, extermination were landmarks on this twisted road. Acts growing gradually more harmful ultimately helped cause ethical changes in individual perpetrators and bystanders. In essence, people learned to hate and to do harm.

Moral configurations among persons emerge through social interactions within the parameters of a culture. Men and women learn their morality from parents, friends, and peers. Additionally, given the normative belief in a *just world,* victims being harmed are usually viewed as deserving their punishment. In this context, merely defining people as *them* can cause immediate devaluation and marginalization. Such distinguishing characteristics as race, religion, status, wealth, power, and political views have generally helped reinforce the primary in-group differentiation. How a culture reinforces its members' evaluation, categorization, and labeling is significant because devaluation makes mistreatment likely and can remove a group from the community's universe of obligation.

Necessary to genocide is also an incremental progression along a continuum of destruction, on which people both learn and change by doing. Gradually more intrusive acts seem ultimately to introduce psychological changes that can virtually eliminate inhibitions, which in turn can help reinforce the devaluation of the outgroup and make possible increasingly more serious victimology. People learn to increase levels of brutalization. The *Shoah* was itself the end product of a continuum of fear and discrimination, which helped soften the consciences of the participants. Psychological socialization processes, along with the institutional ethos of corporate profit making, helped to deaden moral restraints among businessmen. In brief, the values of the corporate executives cited by Hayes inspired behavior that could then be organized into rational, technological processes.

Three social and institutional processes helped diminish their moral responsibilities.[6]

1. Authorization absolves the individual from moral responsibility for doing harm.
2. Routinization breaks the process into component parts so that no opportunity for moral reflection ever fully emerges.
3. Dehumanization, i.e., creating nonpersonhood, historically helped shape cultural attitudes toward the target so that it became neither necessary nor likely that the perpetrator would view an officially ordered action in moral terms. If moral responsibilities are not carefully delineated and concretely assigned, guilt-free massacres can and, in fact, did occur. The perpetrators, then, did not see themselves as doing evil, but only viewed their activities as the extensions of

legitimate authority. In modern society, people tend to obey the authority of their superiors and to adapt to the culture, with all of its biases, in which they have been.

Clearly in the realm of ethics, virtually all persons have to deal with sustaining moral equilibrium, making choices, and accepting responsibility. In the Third Reich, Germans started with varying degrees of anti-Semitic and nationalistic predispositions, and then were channeled or induced into increasingly destructive acts toward the enemy out-group. They morally changed as they coped with Nazism, and they created a destructive system that assumed a life of its own and restricted the possibility of personal moral decisions. In the final analysis, this development reduced moral responsibility. Along the way for every person, of course, there were many opportunities for choice. Unfortunately, because of the group, professional, or corporate ethos, choosing often took place without conscious deliberation as individuals sublimated their ethical norms in favor of those of the group. The art of moral decision making is very complex, but some observations for reflection are helpful before analyzing the contribution of Professor Hayes.

To make a valid, i.e., nondissonant provoking, choice when facing a conflict between an economic motive and a moral value that would usually prohibit actions politically required to fulfill, for example, a corporate goal, a person would have to be aware of the conflict between act and value. And some of the corporate executives, as Hayes has shown, apparently had to confront some degree of cognitive dissonance to manipulate values to agree with the needed economic behavior. Ultimately, the person psychologically distressed while making values consonant with behavior must bring in additional considerations, i.e., further values and norms that can conclusively tilt the balance in favor of stressful moral restraint, or a moral action that can be accommodated. Rationalizations, i.e., reasons that might not seem valid to impartial outside observers, and justifications that tilt the balance against long-lived moral values were required to function in the Third Reich without suffering cognitive dissonance. This "work of choosing" places demands on cognitive processing and usually is accompanied by intense feelings that can help a person resolve the cognitive and moral dissonance states that have arisen. From the presentation of Professor Hayes, I presume that we have very little evidence of the mental and moral gymnastics needed from our corporate executives in Nazi Germany, since we do not have access to their candid memoirs or personal correspondence. Even without such materials, however, we know what usually occurs in most attempts consciously to navigate moral conundrums—and we have to assume that our experience replicates that of the businessmen in the Third Reich. They had to work to reduce cognitive dissonance.

But in the process of living, many choices are made without explicit awareness. We frequently do what our identity in a group requires with very little thought. All of us have a wide range of moral values at our disposal. Some have been superseded, but remain in our repertoire and can be called forth when needed. Some coexist with others, even though they are potentially contradictory. Facing a conflict between an immoral behavior and a moral value, a person may reduce the conflict by equilibration, i.e., by shifting among different moral values or principles. For example, the moral principles that prohibit killing or harming other human beings can be replaced, as they were in the Nazi case, by the principle of social, national, ethnic, or racial good, which was defined as the protection of the German *Volk* from internal subversion and genetic contamination by the Jews. A case could be made, then, that Germany was actually at war from 1933 to 1945, and, in a state of war, many actions can become permissible. Peter Haas[7] has made a very significant contribution in this area by suggesting that in this context the German perpetrators may well have thought that they were acting morally in a state of self-defense. Coming at this issue from another direction, loyalty and obedience to authority could also become the relevant "moral" principles that could help explain a developing corporate moral ethos directed to conform with Nazi ideology.

Such Nazi leaders as Eichmann and Himmler, for example, were sickened by the sight of mounds of bodies. Our records indicate that Nazi doctors were initially shocked by Auschwitz. Such emotionally and bodily reactions should serve as signals to the self, but they can be forcibly muted. By 1942

and thereafter, Himmler's and the Nazi doctors' commitment to the Final
Solution as part of Hitler's plan for national and racial renewal and their personal identity with the Nazi movement, in which they had rooted their professional destiny, made a renewal of moral dissonance or change in modes of
resolution and action unlikely.

In the progress toward genocide, there were many "choice points" for
each perpetrator or bystander, but they could be ignored by men and women
firmly attached to the culture's dominant ethos. The responsibility of individuals is in part functionally derived from their culture and social group. Groups
socialize the behavior of their members. To the extent that a group completely socializes its members into specific forms of conduct, a person would
lose some autonomous decision-making capacity or the ability to question
independently his or her conduct in relation to personally held values. Is there
an ideology that can support the critique of moral values?

Especially since the Enlightenment, democracy as an ideology has
attempted to foster individual responsibility. To the extent that democratic
socialization teaches such conscious decision making, it is reasonable to hold
people responsible for their moral decisions and actions. However, there can
be ambiguous and conflicting signals that emanate from nondemocratic societies. Loyalty and obedience to the group, for example in Nazi Germany, were
frequently taught as the primary moral values in the society. Part of the
tragedy of Nazi Germany was that loyalty and obedience to the *Volk* and its
servant, the corporation, were exalted over individual moral responsibility.

Another foundational support for individual responsibility has been the
self-awareness of one's needs, motives, desires, and psychological processes.
That is, individuals form their identities according to their needs. Devaluation
leading to depersonalization and scapegoating seem often to be nonreflective
psychological processes that spontaneously seem to emerge out of our attachment to a specific culture. Such psychological processes make negative moral
equilibration easier. In essence, it is easier to blame "the other" than to highlight one's own responsibilities. Absorbing an ideology that helps me com-
prehend a chaotic world may emerge gradually on a day-to-day basis and may
be largely nonreflective. The ideology or value system is learned slowly as a

person engages his or her culture. Some cultures and modes of socialization enlarge the capacity to bring such nonreflective processes into awareness so that values and attitudes can be critiqued. German culture did not, and it tended to inhibit the "processing mechanisms" that a more open society would allow.

Citizens in a democracy develop "processing strategies" that enable them critically to test their psychological reactions and consciously to evaluate them in light of their goals, moral values, and beliefs. Such persons are less likely to be pushed and pulled by external forces. Who they are and what they believe and value will define both their initial reaction and how they process their decisions, but their greater internal flexibility provides them with the opportunity for a more personal moral choice based on independently established principles. If a culture mandates an organic or communitarian ethos, a sense of individual responsibility can lose its potency—and we can see that dynamic operant in Weimar and Nazi Germany, where community had a primacy over the individual.

Even in a society that fosters individual moral responsibility, there is no guarantee that individuals can or even will oppose the group to which they belong. Resisting a group ethos on an issue of national ideology is extremely difficult. It requires courage and strong motivation arising from deeply rooted moral values or from empathic caring. The capacity to choose and exercise moral responsibility requires an independent identity, which makes differentiation from the group possible, which facilitates the awareness of psychological processes, and which helps construct moral values that are inclusive, i.e., values that can be applied to a broad range or preferably all of humanity. Thus, a moral responsibility for others is an ideal that society has to foster for all of its members. Nazi culture, among others, did not foster this sense of obligation.[8] That said, let us look more concretely at the excellent paper offered to us by Peter Hayes

I would like to reflect on his contribution to our colloquium, to raise some issues, and to urge some clarification of the points that he has so eloquently made. His paper should challenge us to look at the corporate ethos in Nazi Germany as well as at that in corporate North America at the end of this

DONALD J. DIETRICH

century. How can a corporate ethos be grounded in moral ideals? No one is immune from the "softening of conscience" that occurred with horrific consequences in the Third Reich. In cultures that are being incrementally undermined, how do we establish powerful moral guidelines? Both churches and corporations failed in Nazi Germany.

From the example of the Third Reich, it would seem clear that any group, corporate or otherwise, has a duty to establish a mechanism to critique its goals and ideals.[9] While corporations may want to think that they are nonpolitical, even in a democracy they are political in the sense that they economically maintain the dominant political culture. It is, therefore, not surprising that the corporations in Nazi Germany became part of the system, since no one really seemed to evaluate the regime and its ideology with respect to its inclusivism and respect for human dignity. Anti-Semitism was only one part of the moral corruption.

I fully agree with Professor Hayes that we cannot reduce the reactions of Germans to anti-Semitism, and we certainly cannot accept the exterminationist or eliminationist theme of the Goldhagen thesis.[10] Anti-Semitism played a mobilization function and nurtured the internal Nazi terror, but we have to be equally interested in the cognitive and moral non-anti-Semitic manipulations, i.e., careerism or the desire for financial gain, which led businessmen into the Nazi web. Reflection on these developments stands us in good stead even today. Through their professions, occupations, and churches, Germans experienced a "softening of conscience," with which we can all identify. But human greed and normal petty jealousies were at work as well.

I found Hayes's nuanced discussion of the business elites and organizations very refreshing, since I am convinced that when it comes to Holocaust issues, we cannot be reductionistic. German-Jewish relations then and today are as complex as are individual persons. Such corporate leaders as Kirdorf and Vogler have all of our own faults, failings, and discomfort in confronting political authority, which is why the history of the Third Reich speaks to all of us. When we hear Hayes's comments, the question that emerges with respect to Hitler and even Milosevich is "How do normal people deal with leaders who are for all intents and purposes evil?"

Hayes's comments on the Catholic Church and Pius XI's unpublished encyclical reminds us that anti-Semitism has for centuries been part of our culture, and that even a papal document opposing racism could still, according to a Christian conscience, defend cultural and economic ant-Semitism. The fact that many could defend Jewish friends while still accepting ideological anti-Semitism also needs further exploration by all of us. After all, even Hitler saved Dr. Bloch, who attended the führer's dying mother, from the results of the Anschluss.

I found the initiatives of funneling Jewish young men and women into manual labor particularly disturbing, since it suggests that at a very early point in our story "resettlement" initiatives were being discussed even outside the SS. If such strategies were widely discussed in the 1930s, it may help explain why Germans might not have been disturbed by the 1941 Himmler/Heydrich approaches to "The Final Solution." And to see that even Jews advocated such a strategy may help suggest why some Jews could travel East with no protest. I think that more research is required in this area.

To return to the ethics issues, I think that even today we need more discussion on "rights." To stress business rights over human rights, which is even done today, e.g., in Asian sweatshops, would seem to mean that the issue is not dead. Professor Hayes illustrates the technique of softening a conscience. The Nazis used such "salami tactics," i.e., incrementalism, gradually to drive Jews from firms and to take over trade associations. From the perspective of our century, the incremental approach seems to work best when trying to establish totalitarianism without any protest.[11] Such a study of incrementalism could help us understand the dynamics operating in Rwanda and Serbia over the last few years. We can all, apparently, surrender one commitment at a time. We all find it difficult to resist what appear to be incursions that occur gradually. Most of us think that "this is the last time we will be impacted," and we surrender our positions one by one.

This paper by Professor Hayes nicely highlights what happens when secondary ethical obligations gradually become primary. Corporate executives moved along the continuum of destruction just like other Germans. They engaged in dehumanization tactics, obeyed orders, and became part of the routinized process. We can also empathize with how human weaknesses were allowed to masquerade behind professional responsibilities and protective bureaucratic walls. Today, we see it in HMOs, the IRS, and universities. I fully agree with Peter that the most horrifying conclusion is that the businessmen became willingly complicit, and felt that they were innocent of the human degradations that they perpetrated in the name of profits, company survival, and the *Volk*.

Just as there seems to be a continuum of destruction, we might also want to reflect on how we might try to institutionalize human dignity. Let me mention some points for a future discussion.

1.   At the societal and group level, we should actively establish norms that can help amplify a universe of obligation that can be developed and then strengthened to guard against any routine acceptance of dehumanizing cruelty based on exclusivism.[12] Community and group obligations to protect those who can be marginalized have to be developed to help maintain constructive social interaction.

2.   Policies and laws, which even potentially can threaten human dignity, have to be challenged, even if initially specific governmental statutes and corporate policies seem neutral and have been seemingly designed for an efficient socioeconomic functioning that is supportive of state and culture. I am thinking here of medical and social security issues.

3.   Seeing sanctioned violence can desensitize participants. Hence, we cannot permit sanctioned or governmental violence without protest. Simultaneously, a staunch defense of human rights has to be maintained and asserted.

4.   The elimination of everyday discrimination by laws or customs, etc., has to be sought. Such discrimination frequently has occurred on standardized academic tests and through other mechanisms of "categorizing" our fellow citizens with respect to social welfare issues.

5.   The attempt to ensure that potential victims have faces is crucial. We can see examples of this helpful stance in *Schindler's List*.

6. Nurturing a realistic empathy toward all the inhabitants within the community can serve to integrate diverse persons into the community and unite us all.
7. Ethnocentric/racial categorizations have to be targeted for elimination through law and education.

Diverse accounts of altruistic behavior all seem to verify that some consciousness of human dignity motivated those who rescued or assisted Jews. Therefore, a vision of the future controlled by ideals that are rooted in the welfare of the person, who has a unique dignity, rather than in either a religious or secular vision for "improving humanity" seems basic. There has to be nurtured a beneficial and mutual interaction between the person and the community. Both are necessary and neither can be stressed without a danger to the other. Pure, unabashed individual freedom is as dangerous as a type of communitarianism that stresses the benefit of the group and so the subservience of the individual.

NOTES

1. See Michael Kater, *The Nazi Party: A Social Profile of Members and Leaders, 1919–1945* (Oxford: Blackwell, 1983), for a review of the literature and his own analysis.

2. Fred Weinstein, *The Dynamics of Nazism: Leadership, Ideology, and the Holocaust* (New York: Academic Press, 1980).

3. Edward Flannery, *The Anguish of the Jews: Twenty-Three Centuries of Anti-Semitism* (New York: Paulist Press, 1985).

4. Donald J. Dietrich, *Catholic Citizens in the Third Reich: Psycho-Social Principles and Moral Reasoning* (New Brunswick: Transaction Books, 1988), esp. chapter 3.

5. Erwin Staub, *The Roots of Evil: The Origins of Genocide and Other Group Violence* (New York: Cambridge University Press, 1989).

6. Herbert Kelman and V. Lee Hamilton, *Crimes of Obedience: Toward a Social Psychology of Authority and Responsibility* (New Haven: Yale University Press, 1989).

7. Peter Haas, *Morality after Auschwitz: The Radical Challenge of the Nazi Ethic* (Philadelphia: Fortress Press, 1988).

8. Ian Kershaw, *Popular Opinion and Political Dissent in the Third Reich: Bavaria, 1933–1945* (Oxford: Oxford University Press, 1983).

9. Donald J. Dietrich, *God and Humanity in Auschwitz: Jewish-Christian Relations and Sanctioned Murder* (New Brunswick: Transaction Publishers, 1995).

10. Daniel Jonah Goldhagen, *Hitler's Willing Executioners: Ordinary Germans and the Holocaust* (New York: Alfred A. Knopf, 1996.

11. Leo Kuper, *The Prevention of Genocide* (New Haven: Yale University Press, 1985).

12. Philip Hallie, *Lest Innocent Blood Be Shed: The Story of the Village of La Chambon and How Goodness Happened There* (New York: Harper and Row, 1994).

CONTRIBUTORS

JUDITH H. BANKI is program director for the Tanenbaum Center for Interreligious Understanding in New York. She has been deeply involved in Christian-Jewish relations for many years, and is co-editing a new collection of the writings of Rabbi Marc Tanenbaum. She recently was awarded an honorary doctorate by Seton Hall University for her work in promoting Jewish-Christian understanding.

MICHAEL BERENBAUM has taught at Georgetown University, at the United States Holocaust Memorial Museum (where he was deeply involved with the creation of its permanent exhibition and its research unit), and at the Survivors of the Shoah Foundation. He has authored and contributed to many books on the Holocaust, including *The World Must Know*, the official guide to the Holocaust Museum in Washington, D.C.

CARDINAL EDWARD LDRIS CASSIDY, a native of Australia, served in the Vatican diplomatic corps for many years. Most recently he served as President of the Holy See's Commission for Religious Relations with the Jews, where he was instrumental in building constructive Catholic-Jewish relations throughout the world. He is the principal author of the Vatican statement on the Holocaust, *We Remember*.

DONALD J. DIETRICH teaches in the theology department at Boston College, where he has also served as chair of the department. He has written on numerous aspects on the history of the Holocaust and also explored its social ramifications in his book *God and Humanity in Auschwitz*.

RABBI IRVING GREENBERG, a noted writer on the Holocaust, has taught at the City University of New York, and worked with several national Jewish organizations including the Jewish Life Network. He has been closely associated with the United States Holocaust Memorial Museum, and presently chairs the museum's national council.

PETER HAAS has had a long interest in the ethical dimensions of the Holocaust, particularly its implications for medical ethics. He has taught at Vanderbilt University and currently is a faculty member in Jewish studies at Case Western Reserve University.

PETER HAYES has been one of the leading historians in studies on the Holocaust. He has undertaken detailed research on the role played by German corporate executives in the development of Nazism. He has been a resident fellow at the United States Holocaust Memorial Museum and currently is a member of the history department at Northwestern University.

STEVEN T. KATZ teaches in the Center for Judaic Studies at Boston University, and is currently at work on a three-volume study of the Holocaust. The first volume of this study has been published under the title *The Holocaust in Historical Context*. He currently chairs the Academic Committee at the United States Holocaust Memorial Museum.

KEVIN MADIGAN has taught church history at the Catholic Theological Union in Chicago, and now teaches at Harvard Divinity School. At both institutions he has offered courses on the Holocaust with a special interest in the role of the Christian churches during the Nazi era.

MICHAEL R. MARRUS, a distinguished scholar on the Holocaust, serves as Dean of Humanities at the University of Toronto. He has published widely on the Holocaust, including *The Holocaust in History*. He recently served as part of the joint Jewish-Catholic team of scholars that examined the Nazi-era archival materials released by the Vatican.

JOHN J. MICHALCZYK teaches in the fine arts department at Boston College. He has had a long-standing interest in the implications of Nazism for medical ethics. He has written and produced a video on this topic as well as the volume *Medicine, Ethics, and the Third Reich.*

RONALD MODRAS is a member of the theology faculty at St. Louis University. He has had a special interest in anti-Semitism, especially in Poland. His major work on the topic is *The Catholic Church and Anti-Semitism: Poland, 1933–1939.*

JOHN F. MORLEY teaches at Seton Hall University and is an acknowledged specialist on the Vatican and Pope Pius XII during the Holocaust. His major work on the subject is *Vatican Diplomacy and the Holocaust.* He is a priest of the Archdiocese of Newark and recently served on the joint Catholic-Jewish scholarly commission investigating the Vatican archives.

JOHN T. PAWLIKOWSKI is a Servite Priest and professor of Social Ethics at the Catholic Theological Union, where he also directs the Catholic-Jewish Studies program in CTU's Cardinal Bernardin Center. He has written extensively on the Holocaust and on Christian-Jewish relations, including *Jesus and the Theology of Israel.* He has served on the United States Holocaust Memorial Council by presidential appointment since 1980.

ROBERT SCHREITER, a priest of the Congregation of the Precious Blood, is Vatican II Professor of Theology at Catholic Theological Union. He has written widely on the subject of reconciliation. His major work in the field is *The Ministry of Reconciliation: Spiritualities and Strategies.* He recently completed a term as president of the Catholic Theological Society of America.

CLAUDIA SETZER teaches biblical studies at Manhattan College in New York City. She has a special interest in the relationship between Jews and Christians in the early centuries of the common era.

GERARD S. SLOYAN, a Catholic priest, is a noted expert in the fields of biblical studies and ecumenism. He taught for many years at Temple University and currently is an adjunct professor at the Catholic University of America. He has written extensively on Christian-Jewish relations and has served as president of the Catholic Theological Society of America.

PETER STEINFELS teaches at Georgetown University and contributes regular columns on religion to the *New York Times,* where he served as religion editor for several years. He is also a regular correspondent for the PBS program *Religion & Ethics Weekly.*

INDEX

O

Oberammergau passion play, 223
O'Carroll, Michael, 179
Odrodzenie, 91
Operation Barbarossa, 181, 182
Oral Torah, the, 37
Origen, 29
Orsenigo, Cesare, 190
Osborne, Francis d'Arcy, 127, 139, 148, 149-50, 157

P

Paul, 26, 36, 39, 44, 45, 46, 55, 67
and his letters, 26-27
and his mission to the Jews, 44
Paul VI (Giovanni Montini), 122-23, 178, 191, 211
Pavelic, Ante, 128, 186
Petain, Philippe, 125
Peter, 27, 28
Pharisees, the, 23
Philippines, the, 279
Philo's "special laws," 26
Pilate, Pontius, 24, 25, 27
Pilsudski, Marshall Joseph, 86
Pines, Professor Shlomo, 24
Pius, 128
Pius IX, 89, 274-75
Pius XI, 93, 121, 122, 136, 139, 275, 276
Pius XII (Eugenio Pacelli), 14, 15, 56, 119, 120-21, 122, 124, 126, 133, 134, 136, 137, 139, 140, 142, 143, 144, 147, 149, 150, 151, 164, 165, 171, 172, 174, 179, 180, 184, 187, 190, 197-98, 199, 201, 215-16, 225, 276, 277-78
and accusations of fencesitting, 133-34
and biography, 134
and canonization of, 143, 168
and Christmas Day 1942 address, 194-95, 224

and College of Cardinals, 148
and complicity in Judeocide, 176
and *The Deputy*, 177
and efforts to save Jews during World War II, 14, 15, 134, 142, 217-18
and influence on the contemporary Church, 140
and Nazis, 63
and peace initiatives, 121, 144-46
and personal intervention in Hungary, 156
and reaction of contemporaries toward, 224
and regal status, 135
and supersessionism, 136
as "Hitler's Pope," 176
as moral authority, 144
historical context, 134-35, 151, 157
Plato, 46
Poland
and anti-Semitism, 96
and boycott of Jewish merchants, 90, 91
and casualties of Holocaust in, 93, 197, 198
and genocide, 94
and guilt, 95
and identity as Catholic country, 85, 86
and Jewish-Catholic relations in, 9
and life under the czars. 85
and the Middle Ages, 85
and National Democrats, 86
and nationhood, 85, 86, 87
and response to Nazism, 95
and secularization of Polish culture, 90
and violence against Jews in, 91
and World War I, 85
Polish-American Jewish American Council, 84
Polish-Jewish relations, 84

and converted Jews, 125
and the Final Solution, 178-79
and foreign policy of, 138-39
and German atrocities, 127, 180-85,
    186-88, 190, 191-93, 196-98, 200
and intervention in Hungary, 156-57,
    217-18
and Jewish emigration, 217
and Jewish persecutions in Europe,
    125, 128
and knowledge of death camps, 199-200
and neutrality, 122, 141, 146, 147
and papal policy, 141-42
and rejection of modern secular state, 89
and Slovak Jews, 155, 175, 217
and vulnerability to attacks, 123
Vatican Commission for Religious Relations
    with the Jews, 7, 166, 220
Vögler, Albert, 319, 344
Volksgeist, the, 111
von Bergen, Diego, 121
von Bohlen und Halbach, Gustav Krupp,
    319, 321
von Galen, Count, 284
von Müller-Oerlingshaursen, Georg, 318,
    319
von Siemens, Carl-Friedrich, 319, 321
von Weizsäcker, Ernst, 151, 153, 154, 199
Vr'ba-Wetzler Report, 249

W

Wagner, Richard, 89, 111
    and "Jewification," 111
Walz, Hans, 319
Wannsee Conference, 294
    and the "Final Solution," 294
Warburg, Max, 321
    and Warburg memorandum, 321
Warsaw, Max, 321
We Are Our Brother's Keepers, 244

Weimar Republic, 275, 277, 297, 337-38,
    343
We Remember: A Reflection on the Shoah, 5,
    8, 10, 13, 14, 15, 35, 57, 58, 62, 63,
    64, 68, 69, 73, 74, 76, 78, 117-18, 119,
    120, 133, 142, 163, 165-66, 168, 169,
    171, 172, 173, 174, 211, 215, 219-20,
    221, 224-25, 236, 283, 284
    and anti-Judaism and anti-Semi-
        tism, 63, 212, 222-23
    and criticism of from the Catholic
        press, 220
    and euphemisms in text, 63
    and negative reception toward, 13
    and Pope Pius XII, 63
    as rebuttal of Holocaust denial,
        213
    and weaknesses of, 212
While Six Million Died, 245
Why Did the Heavens Not Darken?, 109
Wiesel, Elie, 261, 265
Kaiser Wilhelm Institute of Anthropology, 292
    and T-4 (4 Tiergarten Strasse), 294
Willebrands, Johannes, 11
Wirth, Christian, 189
World Jewish Congress, 127, 182, 188, 189,
    218
Wyman, David, 245

Y
Yad Vashem (Jerusalem), 94, 238

Z
Zahn, Gordon, 279-80
Zegota, 215
Zimmerman, Moshe, 89
Zionism, 107